CW01081794

Tracking the Texas Ranger Historians

Edited by Bruce A. Glasrud
and Harold J. Weiss Jr.

University of North Texas Press
Denton, Texas

10 9 8 7 6 5 4 3 2 1

Permissions:
University of North Texas Press
1155 Union Circle #311336
Denton, TX 76203-5017

The paper used in this book meets the minimum requirements of the
American National Standard for Permanence of Paper for Printed Library
Materials, z39.48.1984. Binding materials have been chosen for durability.

Library of Congress Cataloging-in-Publication Data

Names: Glasrud, Bruce A., editor. | Weiss, Harold J., Jr., 1932- editor. |
   McCaslin, Richard B., writer of foreword.
Title: Tracking the Texas Ranger historians / edited by Bruce A. Glasrud
   and Harold J. Weiss Jr.
Description: Denton, Texas : University of North Texas Press, [2024] |
   Includes bibliographical references and index.
Identifiers: LCCN 2024017559 (print) | LCCN 2024017560 (ebook) | ISBN
   9781574419306 (cloth) | ISBN 9781574419399 (ebook)
Subjects: LCSH: Texas Rangers--Historiography. | Law
   enforcement--Texas--Historiography. | Historians--Texas--Biography. |
   Texas--Historiography. | BISAC: HISTORY / United States / State & Local
   / Southwest (AZ, NM, OK, TX) | HISTORY / Historiography
Classification: LCC F385.2 .T73 2024 (print) | LCC F385.2 (ebook) | DDC
   363.209764072/2--dc23/eng/20240705
LC record available at https://lccn.loc.gov/2024017559
LC ebook record available at https://lccn.loc.gov/2024017560

The electronic edition of this book was made possible by the support of the
Vick Family Foundation. Typeset by vPrompt eServices.

Contents

Acknowledgments

This book, *Tracking the Texas Ranger Historians*, is the third in our *Tracking* studies of the Texas Rangers published by the University of North Texas Press. We initially approached Ron Chrisman, the director of that press, and ever since he has been supportive and encouraging. Thanks once more, Ron. The initial two works—*Tracking the Texas Rangers: The Nineteenth Century* and *Tracking the Texas Rangers: The Twentieth Century*—were vetted by members of the historical community, and we thank them for the encouragement and suggestions that helped make these works even better. That list included Donaly Brice, Paul H. Carlson, Michael L. Collins, Mike Cox, Tom Crum, Arnoldo De Leon, Andrew Graybill, Stephen L. Hardin, Chuck Parsons, Louis L. Sadler, Paul N. Spellman, Charles Spurlin, and Robert M. Utley. The concept for *Tracking the Texas Ranger Historians* additionally was reviewed and aided by Director Chrisman as well as by Jimmy L. Bryan of Lamar University and Richard B. McCaslin at the University of North Texas. Each made encouraging comments and gave invaluable and helpful suggestions. Many, many thanks, gentlemen.

Tracking the Texas Ranger Historians would not have been acceptable or complete without the support of our authors. Each readily agreed to prepare previously unpublished articles for this book. Thanks to every one of those astute and supportive historians. Coeditor Bruce A. Glasrud also wants to thank coeditor Harold J. Weiss Jr. Weiss developed the idea for the books in the *Tracking* series and aided in gathering authors; he also wrote the informative and helpful introduction as well as one of the chapters for this book.

We cannot overlook other support that we received. At the University of North Texas Press, as we have already noted, Ron Chrisman encouraged and worked with us on this book. The staff at the

Texas Ranger Museum in Waco has been especially helpful. Bonnie Tompkins, Harold Weiss's daughter, assisted with the preparation of the computer copy. We really appreciated your skills, Bonnie. As usual for any of Bruce's writings, Pearlene Vestal Glasrud supported and made suggestions. Any errors or omissions we realize are our own, for which we remain responsible.

Bruce A. Glasrud, San Antonio, Texas

Harold J. Weiss Jr., Leander, Texas

Foreword

Few law enforcement agencies around the world are as well-known as the Texas Rangers, and arguably none are more popular. Founded in 1823, they have endured, and changed, for two centuries. There have never been more than a few hundred in the field at once, and often only a small fraction of that or even none, and yet they have become the focus of a voluminous literature that includes historical books of all descriptions and perspectives. To some who write these works, the Rangers embody the highest ideals as frontier defenders, as they were until late in the nineteenth century, and as law enforcement officers, which they have been for many more decades. Other writers blame them for all the ills that have attended the settlement of Texas and the development of its legal system since 1823. Perhaps such scholarly polarization is almost inevitable for a human agency charged with promoting order and security in a borderland where multiple cultures have clashed violently and continue to do so in many ways. Certainly, the Rangers have encountered extreme situations, and it cannot be denied that they have responded in ways that exceeded ethical and legal boundaries. But most historians, both lay and academic, scatter along the dialectic spectrum between the two opposing archetypes of the Rangers—hero and villain—continuing to debate and, of course, write in pursuit of whatever truth they embrace. This book is for all of them, and for the public they hope to teach about the Rangers.

There have been many kinds of Rangers in Texas. Those who write about them, or pursue other popular avenues of communication, are no less diverse. This work makes that clear, but it also tells about their influences and impacts. Based on their personal perspectives and experiences, everyone interested in the Rangers has their favorite sources. Hopefully most of those are found here, but readers should take some time to read about the "other side." If the authors achieve their purpose, the material found here about Ranger historians will lead to more debate in a more informed manner. In keeping with a popular quip, they hope the discussion will continue on a higher level.

Richard B. McCaslin, PhD
University of North Texas (retired)

Introduction

Historical Vistas

Texas Rangers and Their Interpreters

Harold J. Weiss Jr.

One of the integral elements of studying what has become known as "Texas exceptionalism" is the analysis of the Texas Rangers—today the investigative and enforcement arm of the Department of Public Safety (DPS). After Stephen F. Austin in a message in 1823 used the word *ranger*, armed parties ranging the land in Texas went through a threefold transformation: (1) a military period before the Civil War in which Rangers battled Indians, Mexicans, and outlaws of all races; (2) an era of law enforcement under the adjutant general and governor with the Frontier Battalion after 1874 and the Ranger Force after 1901; and (3) the modern age of the Rangers as detectives after the creation of the DPS in 1935. Two centuries of evolution has produced not only a story that is complex and sometimes controversial but also a growing host of writers, lay and academic, with differing perspectives on the Rangers. It has been said that controversy is the lifeblood of historical writing. It leads to debates, encourages research, and creates new approaches. In that spirit this book is intended to contribute to the discussion, not complicate it. It can thus appeal to an audience of both scholars and general readers.

History, Historians, Terminology, and the Rangers

Not coincidentally, the objectives involved in putting this book together were also threefold:

1. Someone has said that the meaning of history is clear, but the writing is not. In numerous ways, the term *history* has been defined as happenings in time and space recorded orally or in the written record. To some *history* means everything said or done. To others *history* must be based on written facts about how, when, and where events take place. This pioneer book attempts to clarify this belief. It includes biographical facts about Ranger authors and how they created their narratives. This volume also summarizes these works in literary categories of general histories, biographies, periodical literature, and autobiographies. Such patterns can be useful. The emphasis is on historical writing, not how Ranger authors contributed to or challenged preexisting scholarship or how their writings were influenced or challenged by later scholars, though some contributors do grapple with these issues.

2. Historical writers are not all of one kind. A basic division has been between academic and nonacademic. The following pages and essays attempt to show how professional historians arose in higher education in Texas and the nation. At the same time, nonacademic historical writers, sometimes through novels and folkloric stories, influenced popular culture. This totality of Ranger historical writings—those who carry out a critical examination of sources as well as the ones who write in a more popular mode—becomes crucial in understanding Rangers as regional icons and international celebrities. In this duality historians are both technicians and storytellers. History becomes high adventure.

3. Three approaches in Texas historical writings have impacted the narrative on the Rangers. First, traditionalist writers stress

the revered happenings in the nineteenth century that brought about the Lone Star State and its empire-building Ranger force. To these historical writers, the Rangers were heroic figures who participated in violent actions and territorial expansion. This older methodology has variations, like updated knowledge and changes in language, but the point remains the same. Second, revisionist historians pull back from adulation, emphasize the importance of overlooked ethnic and racial groups, and point out Ranger misbehavior. Initially, revisionists intended to give balance to the traditional story, but another revisionist outlook has arisen. It means to replace the incomplete and uncritical Ranger history written by others. Several essays in the book appear within this category. Finally, cultural constructionists focus on an interconnected past that includes theoretical approaches and the study of memory and regional identities. This approach is covered in the essays on reframing Indian-Anglo-Ranger relations and those on Hispanic-Ranger relations.

Two criteria have been used in the selection of authors and subject matter: (1) their body of work, mainly books, and (2) being a torch-bearer in any generation, which goes beyond publishing to include activities useful to the historical profession, from presenting research findings to colleagues to speaking to the public. Some criteria can be quantified, but subjective analysis is also an important part of the process.

A special problem arose in the handling of Walter Prescott Webb, the dean of Ranger historians. After a lot of debate, the decision was made to not have an entire essay on him. His life and works permeate the entire book, especially the introduction, essays on general histories and periodical literature, and the lengthy analysis of the way his work entered popular culture. This combination of academic history and pop culture is one of the keys to understanding the Ranger mystique in the modern world.

Ranger Themes in a Changing Texas

The most striking feature of the Rangers has been their ability to adapt
to the different modes of life in Texas for several centuries. They fought
for the flag when called upon to do their duty. They put felons into
prisons in order to combat crime and disorder. They changed their
methods of transportation from horses and wagons to railroad cars,
motorized vehicles, and airplanes. And their weaponry became more
automatic and deadly in shootouts. During these time periods, Texas
became a meeting ground for people with different cultures. Texans
first built an agricultural society with cotton fields and cattle ranches.
In time an industrial-urban age emerged: farm machinery, oil derricks,
railroads, telegraph and telephone lines, paved roadways, and finally
high-tech production and communication. But at the same time, Texans
combined Southern lifestyles with Western knowhow. The former
stressed honor, vengeance, and familial solidarity. The latter rein-
forced ideals such as independence and self-reliance.[1]

Texas historians have noted a number of themes in the operations
of the Rangers. The first is how they changed from unorganized
mounted militia to organized cavalry forces with six-shooter
firepower who served as a military arm of the state. The second is
how dichotomous views of the Rangers—as patriot warriors or
bloody avengers—left an imprint on Anglo and Hispanic society.
This divergent examination especially derived from incidents in the
US-Mexican War, the period from 1910 to 1920, and the Lower Rio
Grande Valley in the 1960s. Third is how the Rangers sometimes
resisted, yet ultimately absorbed, many creeds and colors into their
ranks: Anglo Rangers, African American Rangers, Hispanic Rangers,
Indian Rangers, and Women Rangers. It should be pointed out that
this limited integration began in the early nineteenth century, but it
became more prominent in the latter twentieth century.

Through the centuries the violent interplay between Rangers,
Indians, and Mexicans has resulted in controversy. The story of such
conflict usually has been framed in opposing archetypes. For some

the Rangers became heroic figures who had vital attributes of being strong, brave, and honorable; who excelled in horseback charges and the use of revolvers, rifles, and Bowie knives; and who served as an empire-building arm of the state and nation as they helped to save Texas from foreign invasion and rampant crime. For others, though, the image of the Rangers changed to that of wanton killers who pillaged and shot noncombatants in wartime and who carried out acts outside the scope of the law as police officers in peacetime. One historian describes this dichotomy like this: "In some quarters the Texas Rangers have been lionized as fearless, incorruptible demigods; in others, vilified as murderous tools of an oppressive and racially discriminatory establishment."[2] Understanding these opposite poles is the first step on the road to a better understanding of the Texas Rangers and their authors. Efforts to tell the story of the Rangers have been complicated by the context in which they began.

They emerged at a time when adventurous individuals narrated their wandering lives as trappers, traders, fortune seekers, and explorers in the American West. Their widely printed, circulated, and romanticized stories helped to influence the popular mind to view the western frontier as a land of hope, attainability, and a satisfying life. In their scouting expeditions as military or law officers, the Rangers explored hills and valleys and plains, traversed the waterways, and hunted wild game. Around campfires they spun yarns about Indian fights, gun battles, and their own exploits. One study noted: "As expert storytellers, adventurers positioned themselves as the vanguard of US territorial expansion."[3]

The Rangers, and many of their chroniclers, did the same.

To further understand the modern Ranger, one must also come to grips with the ins and outs of detective work in fact and in fiction. In dictionary terms a detective is an individual who tries to solve a crime by gathering information that is not readily accessible. Detectives in the modern world must possess several traits. First and foremost, they need inquiring minds. Detectives must ask questions and develop the know-how to examine crime scenes and to collect physical evidence. Equally important, they must have the desire to converse with witnesses and protect them from retaliation by the criminal element. Detectives as sleuthhounds in modern police work also take part in undercover work, as they conceal their identities in carrying out their duties.

Both real-life detectives and those in the world of fiction appeared in Europe and the United States in the nineteenth and early twentieth centuries. The 1800s can be seen as the age of the detective, with the emergence of centralized command systems and the use of technical analysis in crime detection. The 1900s were characterized by a professionalizing movement for detectives and the police in general. Education, training, and the use of crime labs and computers became bywords in law enforcement. The movement from one century to the other in criminal investigation can be seen in the careers of Texas Ranger Captains William J. "Bill" McDonald and Manuel T. "Lone Wolf" Gonzaullas.[4]

Key Ranger Captains in Their Historical Setting

The expression *ranging the land* has become a well-known aspect of European and American culture. During modern times in the North American backcountry, a bloody struggle took place between Indians and colonizers of European descent. This war on the run, *petite guerre* or *kleiner krieg* (small war), can be called by different names: guerrilla, irregular, partisan, unconventional, special oper- ations, or even asymmetric and low intensity. When Anglo-Ameri- can settlers moved into the region called "Texas" in the 1820s, their names for the ranging parties stressed different operating styles. They might be called minutemen, scouts, spies, volunteers, or some other apt designation. Moreover, during the nineteenth century the words *Texas Rangers* appeared more in the popular mind than in official records of the state and nation. Over time Texans learned to fight *petite guerre*, as had their predecessors.

The theory and practice of irregular warfare has three fundamental and defining characteristics. Most important would be the necessity of putting together a small military unit. In ranging tactics this meant a company of foot or horse soldiers (or a combination of companies) who could engage in hit-and-run warfare. This stood in contrast, for example, with the importance of the regiment in the British regular army. The English company was basically an administrative unit used to issue supplies and pay for the men on the rolls. A second pillar in unconventional warfare was the use of guerrilla operations. This included carrying out a well-conceived plan of bushfighting with skirmishes and surprise attacks, as happened in the terrain of North America. The irregular war strategist made sure that the blueprint for a campaign included the three *s* words: stealth, surprise, and speed. The third leg in partisan struggles involved the use of terror. Here inhabitants learned to obey commands through the use of force, or noncombatants died in the burning and sacking of villages.[5]

In two tumultuous decades, beginning in 1823, the Texas Rangers as military figures came of age. They came from all walks of life, had many creeds and colors, and possessed different physical attributes. The 1830s brought the first transforming events. Ad hoc ranging parties who took the field in fits and starts became more organized and experienced light-horse cavalry who could compete with Indian raiders on horseback and Mexican flying companies. In this the names of two Ranger officers stood out: Robert M. Coleman and Robert M. "Three-Legged-Willie" Williamson (who had a deformed leg bent backward with an attached peg leg). The former not only led a ranging party in an attack on Indians in North Texas in 1835 but also had his riflemen paid for "ranging service." In the same year, Major Williamson took charge of a "Corps of Rangers." The provisional government during the turmoil of the Texas Revolution created this tactical unit. It was an early statutory mention of the force.[6]

The crucial decade for change in the Rangers was the 1840s. They became known as fierce, bearded fighters who made horse charges while firing Colt revolvers. Two events of note contributed to a Ranger mystique. First, in 1840 in the Great Comanche Raid to the Gulf of Mexico, the Texans clashed with the returning Indians. At the Battle of Plum Creek in Central Texas, a horseback charge by Texans, some of whom had ranging experience, scattered the Comanche over the endless countryside. Second, in 1844 at Walker's Creek a band of Rangers on horseback, led by John C. "Jack" Hays, used five-shot Paterson Colt revolvers, changing the nature of warfare in the American West.[7] By the end of the decade, others replaced Hays in leadership roles, including John S. "Rip" Ford and Benjamin "Ben" McCulloch.

Ford and McCulloch were among the new Ranger officers who rose to prominence in the US-Mexican War (1846–1848). In this bloody struggle, the Rangers showed their mettle on the battlefield and gained a national reputation. At the same time, their desire to kill Mexicans—any Mexican—resulted in wanton destruction. McCulloch and his cohorts acted as scouts and spies for General Zachary Taylor, and Hays led several ranging columns, now taken into federal service, across the border into Mexico. Initially Hays and his troops joined Taylor's army and played a key role in storming Monterrey. Another regiment led by Hays, with Ford as his adjutant, accompanied General Winfield Scott's army and protected supply lines by fighting Mexican guerrillas in the push to take Mexico City. Yet the actions of others showed the dark side of human nature. This included both the notorious John Glanton, a scalp-hunter, and Mabry B. "Mustang" Gray and his company, who executed the men of a Mexican village in retaliation for the killing and mutilation of American teamsters by other Mexicans. Such doings tarnished the flags of Mexico, Texas, and the United States.[8]

In the 1850s the Rangers continued their violent interaction with Indians and Mexicans, adding new stories to their chronicles. In 1855 James H. Callahan led a company into Mexico in search of Indian raiders, engaged regular Mexican troops, and burned a village as he moved back across the river.[9] In 1858 Ford took charge of a large

force of Rangers, Indian allies, and federal troops and attacked a
Comanche village near the Canadian River. Then came the violent
activities of Juan N. Cortina on both sides of the Mexican border,
after he attacked the town of Brownsville in 1859. In the view of
some writers, this became a personal duel between Cortina and Ford.
Their conflict made Cortina a robber and murderer to Anglo-Texans
and an avenger of social injustice to the Hispanic populace.[10]

The American Civil War divided Texan loyalties. The majority
displayed martial fervor, supported slavery, and joined the Confederate
States of America. Fewer supported the Union cause. As expected,
Texans surpassed other states in its zeal for mobilizing cavalry troops.
Horse soldiers led by former Ranger captains such as Ford, McCulloch,
and Lawrence S. "Sul" Ross fought in the western theater and the
Trans-Mississippi West. In reality and folklore, the 8th Texas Cavalry,
popularly known as Terry's Texas Rangers, combined mobility and
firepower to distinguish themselves in the war. Defeated, Texas
and other Southern states went through a period of Reconstruction
before being readmitted to the federal union of states. During this
time Texas officials organized the Frontier Forces (1870–1871) to
stop Indian depredations and go after cattle thieves. The mounted
Ranger companies, some with Hispanic captains, "played a brief but
creditable role."[11]

As Texas passed from frontier conditions to a regional culture in
the nineteenth century, its inhabitants had ambivalent feelings about
law and order. They might look to marshals, Rangers, sheriffs, and even
private detective agencies for protection. But they also had no difficulty
in taking the law into their own hands through lynching, vigilantism,
and other mob actions. They feared killers and outlaws, but they
sometimes protected Robin-Hood-style bandits. Above all, Texans took
sides in the power struggle between capital and labor in the industrial
age. Some might stand with the bankers, owners of large ranches, and
railroad magnates. Others stood with the cowboys, miners, and small
farmers, tangled in what a prominent historian of American violence
called the "Western Civil War of Incorporation."[12]

For a few years in the early 1870s, the Texas State Police tried to reduce levels of crime, but Black/white discord and political rivalries brought about their demise.[13] To maintain law and order, the legislature in 1874 created a special force of mounted militia under Captain Leander H. McNelly to combat outlaws along the Mexican border and organized the Frontier Battalion under the command of Major John B. Jones to protect against Indian depredations and white desperadoes. The law that created the Frontier Battalion had one section that laid the groundwork for future law enforcement operations. Each Ranger officer had "all the powers of a peace officer" and had the "duty to execute all criminal process directed to him, and make arrests under *capias* [writ] properly issued, of any and all parties charged with offense against the laws of this State."[14] The inevitable happened as the frontier became settled and conflict with Indians faded: the military role of the Rangers gave way to new policing and courtroom duties. Due to a legal dispute about arrest powers, the law was changed in 1901 to assure that all Rangers could make arrests, and the name of the Frontier Battalion was changed to the Ranger Force.

The members of the Frontier Battalion and the Ranger Force (1874–1935) had ample means to carry out criminal investigations. First, as peace officers they could make arrests for crimes, with or without warrants, and use deadly force whenever needed.[15] Second, a command structure existed in Ranger operations. Power flowed downward in the organization from the governor's office to the adjutant general and his staff, including the battalion quartermaster, to the field captains and those in charge of subcompanies stationed here and there. One historical writer called these substations or outposts "an early day effort at community policing."[16] Third, although Rangers followed procedures issued by central command, the officers had leeway in investigations. "In classic Ranger tradition," a noted historian wrote, a captain "made his own rules based on the immediate situation, educated guesses, and simple instinct."[17] By the turn of the twentieth century, however, the Ranger service in Texas joined in the movement to organize centralized police agencies in the American states.[18]

In fact and fiction, the public at large have been very interested in the gun battles between the Rangers and outlaws in the Old West. The outlaw era in western America can be divided into two halves. The first occurred in the period after the Civil War; the second ended with the Great Depression and the demise of the gangster era. Desperadoes moved around differently in these two time periods, either on horseback or riding in cars, while firing six-shooters or tommy guns. In song and story, the doings of Sam Bass, the Texas Robin Hood, took place in the early era. Rangers gunned down Sam and others of his gang as they attempted to rob a bank in Round Rock, Texas, in 1878.[19] In the last stage came the robbery and killing spree of Bonnie Parker and Clyde Barrow, sometimes called latter-day Robin Hoods. In 1934 on a road in Louisiana, a small group of lawmen, including Francis A. "Frank" Hamer of Ranger fame, put numerous bullet holes into a car and those inside—Bonnie and Clyde. Hamer said, "We just shot the devil out of them, that's all."[20]

By the turn of the twentieth century, several names kept reappearing in Ranger records. First came the Four Great Captains: hard-drinking James A. Brooks, well-rounded John R. Hughes, flamboyant William J. "Bill" McDonald, and religious-oriented John H. Rogers, who carried his Bible with his guns. These men survived gun battles and played important roles in advancing criminal investigative work. Both Brooks and Rogers received gunshot wounds when the Conner gang ambushed a Ranger company in the Piney Woods of East Texas in 1887. In the next decade McDonald had several bullet holes after a street fight with Sheriff John P. Matthews. By the turn of the new century, both Hughes and McDonald excelled in investigations, questioning witnesses and examining dental records, hoofprints, and hand impressions. McDonald worked with other law officers to send lynchers to prison and killers to the gallows. Yet he failed to identify the shooters in the Brownsville Raid of 1906.[21]

As the twentieth century continued, a new generation of Rangers handled burning societal issues. First came the Mexican Revolution from 1910 to 1920, followed by two world wars and the Great Depression. During the civil war in Mexico, the Rangers and others guarded the border. Plots, raids, and murderous actions occurred in this frightful scenario of disorder. The Rangers received both praise for defending the border against bandit gangs and criticism for carrying out acts of brutality and unlawful executions of Mexican citizens at Porvenir and other places. At the top of the list of rogues in Ranger annals were two names: Captains J. Monroe Fox and Henry L. Ransom.[22]

During the years between the world wars, the Ranger service went through up and downs depending on the governor in office. The low point came with the administrations of Governor Miriam A. "Ma" Ferguson, whose husband, James E. Ferguson, had appointed Fox and Ransom as captains while he was governor. In two separate terms, Ma Ferguson appointed political hacks and hindered Ranger operations. The effort of Governor Daniel J. Moody, who hired capable Rangers and restored respectability to the law enforcement agency, provided only a brief respite. Politicized interference and the need to modernize the force made the state legislature create the DPS in 1935 during the administration of Governor James V. Allred. The DPS housed the Rangers and the Highway Patrol, with organized administrative bureaus and a crime lab. Throughout this turbulent era, new Ranger leaders emerged, including the Big Four: Hamer, Gonzaullas, Thomas R. Hickman, and William L. Wright.[23]

In the DPS the Rangers remained relevant as frontline police officers for the state. The most prominent early figure was soft-spoken Homer T. Garrison, who became chief of the Rangers and director of the DPS for decades. He installed esprit de corps in the Rangers through better selection and training, a more effective communications and transportation system, and posting Rangers in a geographical network. The new breed of Ranger detectives idolized Garrison, and he returned the feeling.[24] In the last half of the twentieth century, high-profile cases revealed new Ranger leaders. Violent encounters with prison rioters, robbers, and killers involved Captains E. J. "Jay" Banks, Robert A. "Bob" Crowder, and Clint Peoples. Other Rangers built a reputation with new technologies. This included Jack O. Dean, Glenn Elliott, and H. Joaquin Jackson. At the same time, Captain A. Y. Allee and his Rangers were accused of brutality in the struggle between Hispanic workers and farm owners in the Rio Grande Valley during the 1960s. The Rangers responded by becoming more inclusive. Christine Nix, Arturo Rodriguez, and Lee Roy Young, one of several African Americans, joined the organization. By the end of the century, two high-profile cases reaffirmed the Rangers' stature. Rangers investigated the violent encounter between federal agents and the Branch Davidians, and they became involved, especially Captain Barry Caver, with stopping the Republic of Texas movement from spreading in the state.[25]

Historical Writings before 1900

In the nineteenth century, American historical writing passed through two phases: the first was a branch of literature, with picturesque and poetic storytelling; the second tried to write more detached history by emphasizing factual material in less expressive and more clear and simple language. The history of Texas was no exception. Historical writers, newspaper reporters, and novelists had their say. In their eyes events were colored with a romantic hue. As state histories became more popular in the 1800s, they brought a new vista. Texas historians had to look at source materials and make judgments about the facts presented.[26]

Prior to the twentieth century, the historical record of the Rangers fit into these two categories. The first came from outside observers and American journalists. Adventurous travelers recorded their impressions of Texas and Texans, including those who ranged the land. At the same time, other writers popularized the Ranger mystique in publications like the *American Review*, while newspaper reporters covered the US-Mexican War and turned the Rangers into national figures.[27] Next came state histories, which added a new approach to Ranger historical writing. Amateur authors wrote accounts of the Lone Star State that were part history, part memoir. These volumes combined both storytelling and the use of evidential facts.

Among the travelers to the Southwest during the early nineteenth century was Washington Irving. He gave a vivid story of the existence of rangers on the frontier. They were not Texas Rangers, but they lived at the same time and their lifestyles resembled those who ranged the Texan countryside. Irving noted many of the mores associated with ranger lore. After returning from a trip to Europe, Irving joined a federal Indian commissioner and others and traveled to Fort Gibson in present-day Oklahoma in 1832. During his travels Irving kept notes and filled his book, as one author explained, with "enthusiastic passages of the grasslands, chasing wild horses and buffalo, riding with Captain Jesse Bean's rangers, and savoring prairie solitude."[28] Bean had fought with Andrew Jackson in the War of 1812 and led a ranging company in the federal service. Irving described the captain as a "thorough woodsman, and a first-rate hunter," who dressed in "leathern" garments. Bean and his rangers had a disorderly camp, lived mainly in the open on wild game, and encountered various Indian tribes. Before the trip ended, Irving shot a buffalo (which did not always excite him) and had a dangerous time crossing a river. His account of his travels, published in 1835, has become a minor classic on the virtues of living the primitive life.[29]

More than two decades later, another noted author actually toured Texas. Late in 1853 Frederick Law Olmsted and his tubercular brother left a farm in New York and traveled by rail and steamboat to the border of Texas. Here they bought two horses and a mule and entered the new state in the depths of winter. Poor housing, bad food, and dirty conditions plagued their trip until they reached the German settlements in Central Texas. As they moved around the state for months, Olmsted especially tried to show that slavery was not in keeping with sound agricultural methods. For Texas, though, he noticed something else.

Troops stationed in forts were of little use in protecting settlements. Texas Rangers were much more effective. On horseback; armed with rifles, pistols, and knives; and dressed "generally in flannel shirts and felt hats, sometimes in buckskin suits," the Rangers gained respect in their encounters with Indians and Mexicans. Olmsted also noted that the German Texans in the Ranger ranks "were not required to understand English, beyond the words of the general orders."[30] In time both brothers wrote the manuscript for the book. It has been described as the "most readable," "most dependable," and "most interesting" of the travel volumes on Texas and the American scene.[31]

In the first half of the nineteenth century, the adventurous tales of moral and physical regeneration in the American western lands reached its zenith. The climax came with the US-Mexican War. Wartime correspondents like James Freaner, Christopher M. Haile, and George W. Kendall wrote melodramatic but factual dispatches for American newspapers that stirred the public's imagination. The best-known of them was Kendall. He founded the New Orleans *Picayune* (named after a Louisiana coin) and covered the war at first by joining the ranging company in federal service led by McCulloch. Kendall's dispatches featured more melodramatic verse than battlefield minutiae. Furthermore, his compelling narratives were rushed into print by a system of horseback couriers, steamers, and other means. This delivery system has been called "Mr. Kendall's express."[32] In his wartime reporting, Kendall acted as a trumpeter for the Texas Rangers.

Equally inspiring and beguiling, Louisiana lawyer Samuel C. Reid Jr. also joined McCulloch during the war. Reid wrote a personal and detailed book on wartime activities from his journal notes entitled *The Scouting Expeditions of McCulloch's Texas Rangers*, published in 1847. This in-depth volume covered the movements and actions of the Rangers in the northern campaign under Taylor, as well as the attitudes and camp life of McCulloch's men. His work has been described as the "best contemporary account" and the "best at the anecdotal level." As one study concluded, "Reid understood and sympathized with the attitude of the rangers. He does not hide their violence but neither does he condemn it. His chief complaints are against the restraints imposed by higher command; they had come, in his and the rangers' opinion, to kill Mexicans. In every contest they did just that, until none were left or until commanded to stop."[33]

An examination of the early romantic era in Ranger historical writing would not be complete without mentioning Charles Webber. He stood out among his peers. Born in the Midwest, Webber came to Texas in the late 1830s and allied himself for a year or two with Hays and the Rangers. Then he studied journalism and became a key author with his storytelling about adventurous males in journals and novels (sometimes writing under a pen name). Webber had two central convictions. First, he believed that the Rangers were a close-knit body of men who combined brutality and gentleness. His description of Hays showed his picturesque ability with words: "His figure, though scarce the average height, was stout, and molded with remarkable symmetry—his hands and feet were womanishly delicate, while his Grecian features were almost severely beautiful in their classic chiseling."[34]

Webber also wrote about his philosophy of the savage life. In all ways, he argued, primitive existence and understanding of nature was far superior to the learned tomes of civilized mankind. The Anglo-American frontiersmen had encountered and accepted to a great extent the Indian way of life with its righteous brutality. "The character and creed of the border ranger," in the author's words, "when not entirely corrupted by the civilization he has left behind him, resembles that of his natural foe in very many respects."[35] To Webber the image of the Indian as a noble-fierce-uncivilized human being was all-important, especially in defining the Rangers.

In the second half of the nineteenth century, histories of the state of Texas became prevalent. This time period was defined by two historical writers: Henderson K. Yoakum and John Henry Brown. Both were amateur historians who did not have any formal training in historical research. Both personally knew Rangers and their operations in the field. Both wrote massive two-volume works often cited in historical literature. And both received criticism and praise for their efforts to publish comprehensive histories of the Lone Star State.

Born in Tennessee, Yoakum pursued a military and political career before he came to Texas in the 1840s. He practiced law in the Lone Star State, joined the Rangers under Hays in the US-Mexican War, then composed his *History of Texas*, which he completed in 1855. Yoakum has been called "the first Texas historian to take his task seriously." And the result from his pen was described as the "first scholarly history of Texas written after annexation."[36] In one volume Yoakum particularly used source materials, which showed in his ample notes and dialogue.[37] His limited success as a historical writer—even with factual mistakes, a prejudicial outlook, and a romantic tone—resulted from his belief in the Jefferson-Jackson heritage of democratic agrarianism and his support of American expansion into the lands of the Indians and Mexicans. One final analysis of Yoakum read, "His history was a turning point. It marked the beginning of the institutionalization of Texas' mythistory."[38]

Yoakum's coverage of the Rangers was basically episodic. He did provide, however, an extended look at the interaction between Rangers, Indians, and Mexicans in the 1840s. Yoakum described the Great Comanche Raid at the start of that decade and the Mexican invasion by General Adrian Woll two years later. In the former the author showed how hundreds of Comanches attacked Victoria in Central Texas and the town of Linnville situated on the Gulf Coast. They killed several individuals, plundered livestock, and destroyed buildings. Yoakum stressed the names of the leaders of the ranging parties who battled the returning Indians, including McCulloch, Edward Burleson Sr., Felix Huston, and John H. Moore.

Yoakum believed the continuing bloody struggle between Texans and Mexicans deserved a lengthy narrative. Woll's Mexican army occupied San Antonio in 1842. When these soldiers ventured outside the town, Texans and their ranging forces—led by Hays, Mathew Caldwell, and others—engaged them. Finally, Woll decided to leave

San Antonio and return to Mexico. A large Texas force under Alexander Somervell followed. Ultimately, part of Somervell's men returned to their homes, but the others carried out the ill-fated Mier Expedition inside of Mexico. To Yoakum, Texas lacked the preparation needed to invade that country. The Mier Expedition, the author wrote, proved that "Texans, though never wanting in prowess, were not in 1842 under the same discipline, and as obedient to orders, as the men of 1836."[39]

Surprisingly, Yoakum ended his two-volume history of Texas with the negotiations that allowed the Lone Star State to join the American Union. The Texas flag came down; the Stars and Stripes went up. The author, therefore, did not cover the ranging columns under Hays and his cohorts in the US-Mexican War. Yoakum missed an opportunity to show how this war played a role in the development of Texas and the West, as well as the Rangers.

Brown was a more prolific historical writer than Yoakum. Born in Missouri, he had little formal schooling but worked in a printing shop at an early age. He migrated to Texas in the late 1830s and took part in frontier warfare as an Indian fighter. In the decades to come, Brown became a commissioned officer in various ranging forces. During his lifetime he edited newspapers, held political offices, and knew the foremost Ranger leaders of his day, including Hays, McCulloch, and Ford.[40] Brown spent years collecting historical materials and writing his books. A key one was *History of Texas*, which he published in the early 1890s. This two-volume work has been described as the "earliest comprehensive history of Texas written by an active participant."[41] Basically, it was part history, part memoir. The text had an upside and a downside. For those enthralled with Texas history, Brown covered Anglo Texas in glorified depth and portrayed Ranger events and leaders in a favorable light. Equally significant, the author's inclusion of documents, reports, and correspondence with ample explanatory notes made this set a valuable research tool on early Texas. The naysayers will point out that Brown gave short shrift to the Spanish era and skimpy coverage to the governors of the state in the late 1800s. "Despite his claims of impartiality, one study pointed out, 'Brown was utterly biased and selective in his presentation of facts and devoted to romantic assumptions about liberty, progress, and Providence.'"[42] In the author's mind, though, this study, which he said avoided fiction, was one of his more ambitious projects.[43] Brown covered Ranger lore in his estimable way. Like Yoakum, he especially emphasized events that involved ranging parties in the 1840s.[44] In doing so Brown used the phrases that Texians liked to apply to their horse soldiers—"Hays' Texas Rangers" and "Texas rangers."[45] In addition, the author's brief look at Indian fighters included the words "Texas rangers" and "State rangers."[46]

By the end of the nineteenth century, a third noteworthy writer tried his hand at doing a comprehensive history of the Lone Star State. Dudley G. Wooten came to Texas from the Midwest in the 1860s as a child. In many ways he differed from his fellow Texas historians. For one thing, Wooten graduated from universities in the northeastern United States, obtained a law degree, and served in both Texan judicial and state and national political offices. For another thing, Wooten criticized fellow authors in his writings. He believed that they put too much emphasis on the French and not enough on the Spanish footprints in early Texas. Too, their storytelling had become inaccurate and misleading, and their narratives had become "manifestly imaginative and romantic fictions."[47]

Wooten's approach to a comprehensive history of the state differed from the plans used by Yoakum and Brown. He edited a work of essays done by other knowledgeable writers on pertinent topics related to the development of Texas culture. In nearly 1,800 pages, the monographs covered Texas geography, the revolutionary era and early statehood, and the Civil War and its aftermath to the 1890s. Wooten composed an essay on the Texas land system and reprinted Yoakum's comprehensive history with modifications.[48] Wooten's collaborative effort contained the two methods used to organize historical writings in general and the Rangers in particular. One essay by Kate S. Terrell dealt with Terry's Texas Rangers in the Civil War. This monographic approach can produce a learned treatise on a particular subject at a given time and place. A more complex and provocative way—the overview—has been used to create an understanding of a field of study from its beginning to its end. Here Wooten made his most important contribution to Ranger historiography with an essay by Wilburn H. King entitled "The Texas Ranger Service and History of the Rangers, with Observations on Their Value as a Police Protection." This massive work has remained a "cornerstone of any Texana library."[49]

King had a distinguished career in Texas that shaped his perspective. Born and educated in Georgia, he came to Texas during the Civil War. King became a colonel and was wounded in battle. After the war he served in the Texas Legislature and was appointed adjutant general at the start of the 1880s. In the latter role, he supervised the Rangers. "The King decade," in the words of a Ranger historian, "completed the transformation of the Texas Rangers from a mounted battalion of Indian fighters into a compact force of lawmen."[50] King wrote his overview of the Rangers after serving as adjutant general. As editor Wooten inserted a good sketch of early Ranger operations before King's essay. Then King provided a framework with his composition that foreshadowed the way future Ranger historians would cover the field. He first placed the Rangers in their historical setting, noting the interaction between the Spanish, Mexicans, and Anglo-Americans. In vivid and biased language, King wrote that the "Anglo-Saxon stock were frank and fearless in giving expression to their views and characteristically reckless and forward in conduct, while the Mexicans were silent, secretive, and treacherous." The author also noted that in border warfare the Mexicans and the Indians were "always on horseback—a sort of Western Arab."[51]

In tracing the shift from the military era to the age of law enforcement, King stressed the identification of Ranger personnel more than the bloody happenings in the field. He covered the soldiery Hays and his cohorts, but he also mentioned lessor known figures such as Coleman, Sam Highsmith, and Shapley P. Ross. Effusive in his praise, the author wrote that Hays and his men "were not only the eyes and ears of General Taylor's army, but its right and left arms as well." He ended his historical account with a long discussion of the Frontier Battalion. He showed the importance of Major Jones and the early battalion quartermasters, Neal Coldwell and Lamartine P. "Lam" Sieker, in shaping the initial organization of this constabulary. The author then covered in detail the command structure of the Ranger companies. Many well-known names appeared, such as the Four Great Captains—Brooks, Hughes, McDonald, and Rogers. King's Rangers pushed far into West Texas in search of cattle and horse thieves, outlaw gangs, and killers. By the end of the 1800s, they rode horses and the rails, as Texas acquired a railroad system. Captains like George W. Arrington, known as the iron-fisted Panhandle Ranger, received high praise for trying to maintain law and order. King even covered the ranging force of militia led by McNelly, Lee Hall, and others. King ended his narrative by writing that Texans were "indebted to the Rangers and their valuable and long-continued services."[52]

A survey of the historical literature on the Rangers in the nineteenth century would not be complete without examining a popular way of recording individuals and their livelihoods. Several noted authors compiled hundreds of names and incidents of pioneers, settlers, Rangers, and Indian fighters on the early Texas frontier. The authors of these encyclopedic works have earned a place in Texas historical records: Brown, James T. DeShields, Andrew J. Sowell, and John W. Wilbarger. None of them were born in Texas. They came to the state with their parents or to be with other relatives. Their volumes showed that clashes between settlers and Indians took many forms, from major events involving large numbers to lesser incidents of hand-to-hand combat. The writers' perspective is that the pioneers and ranging companies built a civilized society while the savage Indians tried to block their advance. One preface put it bluntly: frontiersmen "cut the brush and blazed the way for immigration, and drove the wild beast and wilder men from the path of civilization."[53]

The authors of these volumes collected historical materials for years. The writings of three of the four—Brown, Sowell, and Wilbarger—are considered essential for Texas research. Each volume, moreover, had its own unique features and message. One analyst said that Brown's massive volume for "interest, information, and reliability" was more important than his comprehensive history. Early Rangers in Brown's estimation, like Hays and McCulloch, were mentioned on page after page. Brown, though, talked about his own writings more than his experiences in the Ranger service.[54] In comparison, the volumes by Sowell and Wilbarger have been judged equivalent to the one written by Brown. Sowell collected evidence from participants, while Wilbarger, a preacher, sometimes used the writings of other informed authors. Compared to the works by these three noted authors, the volume by DeShields has been considered an inferior piece of writing.

In his two different volumes on early Texas pioneers, Sowell wrote more about the Rangers than other authors of his generation. These works were partly history, partly memoir. In one account he especially sketched the lives of prominent Rangers from the military and law enforcement eras. This included Hays, H. J. Richarz (a Hispanic captain of the Frontier Forces), and Rogers. Sowell also provided a brief account of his family. His father served with Hays and other Rangers. He himself joined the Rangers in the Wichita campaign of 1870–1871 and fought Indians in freezing weather and close-in fighting.[55] His other volume on Texan pioneers and Rangers, published before those of Brown and Wilbarger, has been called "one of the most important and authentic accounts of the Indian Wars in Texas."[56] The first half of the book was a tour de force that dealt with Texan settlers, Rangers, and Indians. The second half of the work was entitled "Campaign of the Texas Rangers in the Wichita Mountains in 1871." Sowell himself took part in the events of this essay, camping in cold, sleet, and snow, and battling Comanche, Kiowa, and other Indians. For more detail about Sowell and the Ranger service, this work contained numerous quotations from newspapers and remembrances.[57]

The historical record of the Rangers in the nineteenth century laid the groundwork for those who followed. This included the dichotomy between virtuous Anglo-Texans and their villainous enemies. Historical writers like Webber, Brown, King, and Sowell covered events with a mix of reality and fiction or with unadorned factual information. In the popular mindset, several Ranger officers became fixtures: Hays, McCulloch, McNelly, and McDonald. They became Übermensch in reality and myth.

Transitional Mode: Nineteenth to Twentieth Centuries

In the historical record of the Texas Rangers, the twentieth century did not open at a certain time and place. The decades at the turn of the centuries acted as a bridge between the old and the new. This happened in a number of different ways. Research centers continued to increase in number and kind at universities and other depositories. They collected vast amounts of primary and secondary materials for future generations of historians. The developing fields of the social sciences also left their imprint on historical writings. Some Rangers, moreover, had their careers in one century and their influential firsthand accounts of their lives published and distributed in the next. In this mix the general public looked upon certain people and events in the ever-changing culture as the beginning of the twentieth century.

At some point in this historical flux, a split took place in the writings about history in general and Rangers in particular. One approach stressed action-oriented stories that appealed to common people. The plots were quickly put together and printed on cheap paper in magazines and dime novels. The other avenue for historical literature went through the colleges and universities. Learned treatises came from faculty members. This scholarly output made for a better understanding of Texans and their Ranger force.

Before authors write pages of history, documentary evidence must be assembled and kept in public and private libraries. By the time of his death in the early 1900s, Hubert Howe Bancroft had collected books, manuscripts, and other materials on western America. This vast accumulation, which contained records of the US-Mexican War and the life of Hays, has been housed in a library named in his honor. Bancroft, and numerous assistants, also wrote a multi-history of the American West. It included a two-volume narrative of the northern Mexican states and Texas printed in the late 1800s. Bancroft noted that the Rangers arose from the policies of Mirabeau B. Lamar during the republic years. In addition he pointed out the intrepid efforts by Hays and his cohorts on horses and on foot during the US-Mexican War. By the twentieth century, Texana specialists and researchers of the West thought highly of the Bancroft Library and the published historical works for their extensive coverage and ample notations.[58]

In the passage from one century to the next, the study of social forces played a major role in the historiography of the United States. James Harvey Robinson in his *The New History* (1912) advocated using the tools of the social sciences, from anthropology to economics and psychology, to understand humanity and guide future generations.[59] An American historian and philosopher who studied at home and abroad, Robinson wanted to broaden the scope of historical studies beyond merely looking at war, diplomacy, and politics. At the same time, Texas historian George P. Garrison published a volume on the American West in the American Nation series and another on Texas civilization. In his contributions to historical knowledge, Garrison stressed causation, economic enterprises, and social evolution. By the turn of the twentieth century, historical writers, and the Rangers themselves, also sought the reasons for the Texas Ranger bloodlust in the US-Mexican War.[60]

The generational shifts at the turn of the twentieth century also pushed ex-Rangers to write firsthand accounts of their ranging days. Their careers took place in the 1800s, but their reminiscences appeared and were disseminated in the 1900s. These chronicles showed that memoirs can be self-serving and do not always record what happened in the past. Yet historians can take such disparate primary sources and put them into a framework that gives them shape and meaning.

Several noted Rangers who used their pens fitted this mold. First, Noah Smithwick's vivid memoir appeared in the first year of the new century. He served as a Ranger during the era of the Texas Revolution. His reminiscence, often quoted in Texan histories, became a classic anecdotal pioneer memoir and was seen as part of the case for Texas exceptionalism. Second, Napoleon A. Jennings joined the ranging force headed by McNelly in southern Texas. Published in 1899 and reprinted several times with commentaries added by well-known historians, the reminiscence by Jennings dealt with gunmen, feudists, and outlaws. It has been praised for its readability and vivid coverage and vilified for factual mistakes and doubtful reliability. Third, a more respected historical writer, James B. Gillett, rose to the rank of Ranger sergeant in the early days of the Frontier Battalion. His memoir covered clashes with Indians and outlaws. It has been described as one of the better Ranger narratives, although the text is faulty at times in details.[61]

Ford was a more influential Texan whose lifetime and dissemination of writings in Ranger historiography spanned many decades. Besides being a doctor, lawyer, politician, newspaperman, and Confederate officer, Ford was a key Ranger leader in the middle of the 1800s. Before passing away at the end of that century, Ford took on another role: historian. He wrote and collected materials for a memoir containing hundreds of pages on the life and times of his generation. Although excerpts appeared in newspapers and a magazine, the memoir by Ford remained unpublished well into the 1900s because of problems with arrangement, chronology, repetition, and a lack of focus. In the 1960s Stephen B. Oates edited the memoir, and this publication has been used ever since. Oates did a workmanlike job, but his omissions helped to obscure Ford's role in shaping Texas history.[62]

During the first decades of the twentieth century, popular culture acquired new formats: films and radio programs. In both, a formulaic Western story emerged from popular literature, which called for action and a struggle between good and evil in gunfights and horse chases over endless prairies. The Rangers in Texas became a favorite topic in these Wild West dramas, just as they were in dime novels, especially those by Prentiss Ingraham, who created the fictional cowboy-Ranger Buck Taylor. Rangers also covered the pages in the wild and woolly pulp magazines—like the one called the *Texas Rangers*—that became popular between the world wars. In addition, the Ranger story became the basis for leading novels in the modern era such as *The Lone Star Ranger* (1915) by Zane Grey and those written by Louis L'Amour, Elmer Kelton, and Larry McMurtry. Most important, Rangers rode across silent film screens in movies starring Broncho Billy Anderson, Tom Mix, and others. The Texas story also came over the radio waves. In 1933 a Detroit radio station aired a new program—*The Lone Ranger*. Put together by Fran Striker and George Trendle, this iconic fictional masked man and Tonto, his faithful Indian pal, fought for justice in the Old West.[63] This storyline with its stirring musical score captured the public's imagination, creating a new market for more substantive Ranger history.

By the early twentieth century, a striking feature of the historical record of Texas and its Ranger force was the rise of the professional historian at the universities. During the late 1800s, the historical method began to be taught in collegiate classrooms in Europe and America. A prime mover was Leopold von Ranke of Germany, who lectured about a factual-objective approach in his seminars. This move-ment at the University of Texas at Austin included several faculty in the History Department who took historical writing about Texas in a different direction.

George P. Garrison chaired the department, established the Texas State Historical Association (TSHA), secured documentary collections, and labored to improve the state library. Among his publications was a volume on Texas. Here he noted the main events between Anglo-Americans, Indians, and Mexicans. At one point he mentioned the Rangers as Indian fighters.[64] Garrison saw the development of Texas as part of the westward movement and Manifest Destiny, and he believed in Anglo superiority and a southern heritage.

In his endeavors to encourage the study of Texas history, Garrison was assisted by Lester G. Bugbee, who died at a young age. Together these two historians made Texas history more professional and less romantic, with a regional narrative that was both southern and southwestern.[65]

Garrison died in 1910, leaving Eugene C. Barker in charge of the department and the TSHA. Friendly yet stern looking, Barker presided over both for years and with faculty like Walter Prescott Webb enhanced their reputations. Barker collected and published the papers of Stephen F. Austin and Sam Houston. He also penned an influential biography of Austin. He even made comments about the memorable use of the word *ranger* by Austin in 1823.[66] J. Frank Dobie was a colleague and friend of the members of the History Department. He became a noted folklorist who published works on legends like lost mines and gold, but he also taught an influential course on the life and literature of the Southwest at the University of Texas. He and Webb became especially close and talked about Texan affairs. When Webb published his history of the Rangers, Dobie penned a glowing summation: "the beginning, middle, and end of the subject."[67]

Walter Prescott Webb's Journey through the Historical Profession

Among those who have practiced the historians' craft in Texas, Webb holds an honored place. Although his writings on the Texas Rangers do not have the scope and erudition of his works on the Great Plains or world frontier societies, nevertheless he has left a deep imprint on the Ranger record. Throughout his career Webb faced trials and tribulations but persevered. How did this happen?

Webb was born in Panola County, Texas, on April 3, 1888, the son of Casner P. and Mary Elizabeth (Kyle) Webb. His parents then moved the family west to Eastland and Stephens Counties. This passage from the woodlands to the prairies became a major stepping-stone in Webb's understanding of the westward trek. Casner Webb was a part-time farmer who taught school. His son's education was intermittent, but he read a lot. Furthermore, he did not like farm life. In time he graduated from Ranger High School with a teaching certificate, which he used at several small schools. Webb wanted to be a writer and received all his collegiate degrees from the University of Texas. After more than four decades of teaching and scholarship, Webb died in an automobile accident in 1963 and was buried in the Texas State Cemetery.

Webb faced two unexpected happenings that changed the course of events in his life. First, as a boy he wrote a letter to the editor of a magazine asking how he could become a writer. William E. Hinds, a New York businessman, answered and encouraged him to keep his goal, sent books and magazines, and gave him financial support to enroll in the University of Texas. Second, Webb initially sought a doctorate at the University of Chicago. He enrolled in courses (although he liked to just read rather than follow a course of study). Webb accepted the suggestion to set an early date to take the preliminary examination for the degree, which he failed due to his lack of preparation. He finished his coursework, returned to Texas and the study of the American West, and ultimately received his doctoral degree from his original alma mater in 1932 after he published *The Great Plains* one year earlier. In time that book won several prestigious awards, and the University of Chicago gave Webb an honorary doctorate of history in the 1950s. In that same decade, in his presidential address for the American Historical Association, Webb put into words the moral of his failure at Chicago: "Don't take an original idea into a graduate school."[68]

Webb taught numerous undergraduate and graduate students at the University of Texas, published many numerous books, essays, and edited works, and wrote for magazines and newspapers. And he revived and reorganized the TSHA and launched the landmark *Handbook of Texas* to complement the *Southwestern Historical Quarterly*, begun by Garrison as an association publication in 1897. Webb saw history as an art form rather than as conforming to the principles of an exact science. He wanted to give his audience an understanding of the past in memorable language. He had the ability to search through archival materials, collect factual information, and put the results into a meaningful narrative.

Webb was better with small groups of students in historical seminars than as a lecturer since he had poor speaking ability with large groups. His two most important books resulted from such moments of inspiration. He and his students in seminars developed theses about the Great Plains. Webb saw that pioneers in the woodlands differed from the settlers in the Great Plains, as timber and water became scarce beyond the ninety-eighth meridian. To overcome this institutional fault line, new technological inventions were needed: six-shooters, barbed wire, and windmills, to name a few. Webb's study of the Great Plains was more than geographical determinism. It carried out the ideas of Lindley M. Keasbey. Webb studied with him and learned to look at an environment by beginning with geology and then moving to flora, fauna, anthropology, and modern civilization. This was the methodology that Webb used in *The Great Plains*.[69] In another seminar Webb and his students examined world frontier societies that came about after the voyages by Christopher Columbus. The result was the Boom Hypothesis of Modern Times. Webb saw Europe as a metropolis that received a windfall from the newly discovered areas: land, minerals, animals, gold, and silver, to name a few. This gave a dynamic quality to Western civilization that contributed to the growth of capitalism and progress. By the opening of the twentieth century the boom had ended, and Western culture faced new challenges. Webb regarded his book on this, *The Great Frontier* (1952), as his most intellectual and thought-provoking work.[70]

Webb took years to research and write his study of the Texas Rangers. His work emerged in many forms: a master's thesis on Rangers in the US-Mexican War, which showed solid research and a fluid writing style; a series of articles on Ranger operations in the 1920s for the *Michigan State Trooper*; and stories for various popular newspapers and magazines. For a time Webb even put his Ranger efforts on a back burner in order to study how a plains pioneer differed from a woods pioneer. He published an article on the adaptation and use of the revolver in a plains environment in Texas and the West. In the interplay between Anglo-Americans, Indians, and Mexicans, the six-shooter, popular among Rangers, arose in Webb's words, "in response to a genuine need for a horseman's weapon."[71]

A commercial press published Webb's *The Texas Rangers: A Century of Frontier Defense* (1935). This classic study of the Rangers from records and field trips contained a number of striking features. It became the focal point for understanding the key roles played by company captains in Ranger affairs. It magnified the heroic Ranger tradition of Hays and his fellow officers. And it mapped the fundamental changes in Ranger operations, from battling enemies as horse soldiers to pinning on badges as peace officers. From the pages of history Webb told the story of Rangers like Hays, McCulloch, Ford, McNelly, Arrington, Brooks, McDonald, Hughes, Rogers, and Hamer, to name a few.

Webb saw his history of the Rangers as just a workmanlike study. He knew that he needed to address the book's shortcomings and intended to revise the volume before he died. He wanted to downplay the chauvinistic world of his generation in which Anglo Rangers appeared more noble and heroic in peace and war than Indians or Mexicans. He also needed to revise his helter-skelter cover-age of events that impacted Ranger actions in the early twentieth century. In addition, Webb did not clearly understand the evolution of Ranger historical writings before him (although he mentioned a few names like Brown). He did not see any other ties between Ranger eras except the roles of captains and other officers. Once thought to be the last word on the subject, the writings by Webb on the Rangers must be seen as one marker, albeit an important one, on the long road to record their history in the Lone Star State.

Webb enjoyed writing and talking about the Ranger aura. Once he wrote in his distinctive style about the captains as leaders:

If the Rangers became champions because they were able to win out over all opponents in the contest of battle, the officers became officers because they proved to be the best leaders among their men. In this way the Rangers differed from a regular military establishment, where men are taught to respect rank and to obey an officer whether he is any good or not. The Rangers had no military discipline, were independent by nature, and did not accept a man as leader unless he was the best in the outfit. He must have courage equal to any, judgment better than most, and physical strength to outlast his men on the longest march or the hardest ride. In time of danger, the captain never said to his men "go," but he said to them "come," and it became part of the tradition that the officer goes first into any place of danger.[72]

Frontier studies came of age with the writings of Webb on the Great Plains and the Rangers, adding to the insights of Frederick Jackson Turner on the pioneers in the Middle West. As a professor and scholar Webb gained fame and honors. Most importantly, he saw history and his tracking of the Rangers as high adventure. Historians have to try to fathom the interconnections between past events, and they need to be skillful in using words. Webb did both, but his habit in his Ranger book of quoting letters verbatim detracted from its readability. While this kept him from being a novelist, he became a noted historian.

From Webb to Ben H. Procter: Keeping the Faith

Webb was arguably a great writer and an alright teacher; other historians who have advanced the study of the Rangers were the opposite—great teachers and passable writers. Born in Temple, Texas, in 1927, Ben Hamill Procter moved with his parents to Austin at the end of the next decade. Imposing in stature, he became a student athlete in high school and college. At the University of Texas, he earned BA and MA degrees in history and starred on the football field. In the early 1950s, Procter took his professional football earnings and entered Harvard University to pursue a doctorate in history, which he received with a dissertation on John H. Reagan. His major professor was Frederick Merk, whose course of study on the American West was in turn directed by Turner.

Procter spent his entire forty-three-year career as a teacher and scholar at Texas Christian University (TCU), where he worked from 1957 until his retirement in 2000. His lectures on US history, Texas, and the American West were informative and dramatic, as Procter enthralled students with animated presentations. He took an interest in the well-being of his students, and they responded. They fondly remembered the meetings with "Uncle Ben" and being taught to critically think and write, although one student used the word *quirky* for his examinations. Inside and outside of the classroom, Procter made his mark as a great teacher.

Procter also took an active role in spreading the word about the life and times of the Texas Rangers. He wrote articles, book chapters and reviews, introductions, and a monograph; gave conference papers; mentored history students; and spoke to the news media and the public. More than other historians of his generation, Procter personified a goodwill ambassador with his talkative style about the modern Rangers. To the surprise of some, Procter published only one book on the Rangers entitled *Just One Riot: Episodes of Texas Rangers in the 20th Century* (1991). Here he gave in one chapter an overview of the modern Rangers—his forte. Other chapters covered heroic Ranger leaders and events in an episodic way. This volume and his other Ranger writings were more traditional than revisionist. Like Webb, Procter had a profound liking for Ranger captains, such as McCulloch, who performed heroic actions. More than once in his various historical writings, however, Procter presented the face of the ugly Ranger. In one well-written piece (often cited), he told the story about the interrelationships between agricultural growers, field hands, and union organizers in the Rio Grande Valley in the 1960s. The local police and the Rangers under Captain Allee tried to maintain order. But the Rangers fell back upon old tactics in confronting modern civil and criminal matters. Charges of intimidation, brutality, and strikebreaking brought adverse publicity and involvement by public groups, politicians, and judicial officials.

For a long time, one test for the standing of a Ranger scholar in the historical profession was to be compared to Webb. Procter followed in the footsteps of Webb and emphasized heroic men in arms with an emphasis on Ranger captains. Unlike Webb, Procter gave a more balanced interpretation by covering in pointed language the numerous misdeeds by Rangers in peace and war. In addition, more than Webb, Procter became an authority on the Rangers in the twentieth century. Although he complemented and expanded upon Webb's perspective, Procter failed to write his own definitive history of the Rangers before he passed away in 2012 of Parkinson's disease.[73]

Prelude to the Ranger Historians Found in This Book

A salient feature of historical works on Texas and its Rangers since the turn of the twenty-first century has been the increase in the output of books, both in number and kind. They have appeared in all types of formats: general histories, biographies, essays, gun battle accounts, novels, periodical literature, topical works, and documentaries. Commercial and university presses have solicited, edited, and published a flood of appropriate manuscripts. Kudos go the university presses at North Texas, Oklahoma, and Texas A&M for their efforts to satisfy those who want to read Ranger history.

But a problem still exists in Ranger historical writings: How do writers handle the story of the two images—hero and villain? Each generation adds new dimensions to the war of words. Research and writing on twentieth-century topics has uncovered new names to be included in the Ranger Hall of Fame. Some present-day historians have argued that the dastardly actions by the Rangers can be viewed as ethnic cleansing in the removal of the Indian tribes and as continuous extralegal violence by the state against Mexicans living in the borderlands. Ultimately, the clash for centuries on the southern border of Texas has endured as a cultural conflict between Anglos and Mexicans in which Rangers play their part.[74]

In 2020 Viking Press published Doug Swanson's *Cult of Glory: The Bold and Brutal History of the Texas Rangers*. This readable general history with ample notes has an upside and a downside. In the positive vein, it aptly covers the conflicting views of the Rangers as heroic patriot fighters and bloody avengers in their roles as an empire-building military force and law enforcement body in the Lone Star State. The author's account of the thoughts and actions of Hays is especially well-written and memorable. Swanson also showed the importance of oral, written, and visual works in the making of the Ranger mystique that endures in popular culture. The downside comes when the author emphasizes some dastardly events in Ranger lore. Swanson denounces actions by Callahan, Ford, McNelly, and Ross. However, he misses an opportunity to give a more balanced treatment of the early Rangers by not including, for example, the Frontier Forces with its Hispanic members and captains and the patrols by the Frontier Battalion against the criminal element in Kimble County. Most important, Swanson fails to include the criminal investigative work, arrests, and convictions of felons by numerous Rangers. This was especially true for the Four Great Captains, Gonzaullas, and those who served at the beginning of the twenty-first century. The rise and spread of detective work are keys to understanding the Rangers. At its best Swanson's book is one of the better revisionist histories for pointing out the misdeeds of captains such as Gray, Fox, and Ransom. At its worst the volume was put together in a selective and pointed way, even making some Rangers into caricatures.

While Swanson's book drew much attention, it is far from the only prominent work on the Rangers published since the demise of Webb. The Ranger annals have also been interpreted by many historians whose work is discussed in these pages. Being a historian calls for, in simple terms, knowing one's stuff. "Anybody who is industrious enough to read books," Webb wrote, "turn over the original documents and intelligent enough to see cause and effect can write history. I must add, however, that talent and imagination do not hurt the historian if he [or she] has them."[75] Historians must not confuse gaining knowledge with acquiring information, which can be readily accessed in the computer age. Knowledge is a deeper understanding of people and events, as Webb noted. And hopefully this book, through the information it provides, can spark that understanding among the many intelligent, talented, and even imaginative scholars who continue to explore Ranger lore.[76]

Notes

1. For an up-to-date historical work about Texans and their culture, see Randolph B. Campbell, *Gone to Texas: A History of the Lone Star State* (New York: Oxford University Press, 2003). Interesting perspectives on Texan ideals will be found in Ty Cashion, *Lone Star Mind: Reimagining Texas History* (Norman: University of Oklahoma Press, 2018).
2. Jody E. Ginn, "The Texas Rangers in Myth and Memory," in *Texan Identities: Moving beyond Myth, Memory, and Fallacy in Texas History*, ed. Light Townsend Cummins and Mary L. Scheer (Denton: University of North Texas Press, 2016), 89.
3. Jimmy L. Bryan Jr., *The American Elsewhere: Adventure and Manliness in the Age of Expansion* (Lawrence: University Press of Kansas, 2017), 12.
4. For a look at detective work at the beginning of the 1900s, see Harold J. Weiss Jr., *Yours to Command: The Life and Legend of Texas Ranger Captain Bill McDonald* (Denton: University of North Texas Press, 2009). The link between Gonzaullas and modern Ranger detectives is aptly covered in Robert M. Utley, *Lone Star Lawmen: The Second Century of the Texas Rangers* (New York: Oxford University Press, 2007). See also Brownson Malsch, *"Lone Wolf" Gonzaullas, Texas Ranger* (1980; repr., Norman: University of Oklahoma Press, 1998).
5. John Arquilla, *Insurgents, Raiders, and Bandits: How Masters of Irregular Warfare Have Shaped Our World* (Chicago: Ivan R. Dee, 2011), 3–13. The early ranging parties in Texas are covered in detail in Nathan A. Jennings, *Riding for the Lone Star: Frontier Cavalry and the Texas Way of War, 1822–1865* (Denton: University of North Texas Press, 2016).
6. Robert M. Utley, *Lone Star Justice: The First Century of the Texas Rangers* (New York: Oxford University Press, 2002), 18–21, with quotations on pp. 19 and 20.

7. Donaly E. Brice, "The Great Comanche Raid of 1840," in *Tracking the Texas Rangers: The Nineteenth Century*, ed. Bruce A. Glasrud and Harold J. Weiss Jr. (Denton: University of North Texas Press, 2012), 62–86. See also Donaly E. Brice, *The Great Comanche Raid: Boldest Indian Attack of the Texas Republic* (Austin: Eakin Press, 1987). For more on Hays, see Stephen L. Moore, *Savage Frontier: Rangers, Riflemen, and Indian Wars of Texas*, vol. 4, *1842–1845* (Denton: University of North Texas Press, 2010), 139–54.

8. For an up-to-date look at the Rangers in the war, see Utley, *Lone Star Justice*, 57–86. See also Frederick Wilkins, *The Highly Irregular Irregulars: Texas Rangers in the Mexican War* (Austin: Eakin Press, 1990), and Charles D. Spurlin, *Texas Volunteers in the Mexican War* (Austin: Eakin Press, 1998).

9. Michael L. Collins, *Texas Devils: Rangers and Regulars on the Lower Rio Grande, 1846–1861* (Norman: University of Oklahoma Press, 2008), 79–88. For a more detailed analysis, see Thomas O. McDonald, *Texas Rangers, Ranchers, and Realtors: James Hughes Callahan and the Day Family in the Guadalupe River Basin* (Norman: University of Oklahoma Press, 2021).

10. Richard B. McCaslin, *Fighting Stock: John S. "Rip" Ford of Texas* (Fort Worth: TCU Press, 2011), 67–76, 82–100; Jerry Thompson, *Cortina: Defending the Mexican Name in Texas* (College Station: Texas A&M University Press, 2007).

11. Jennings, *Riding for the Lone Star*, chap. 8; Utley, *Lone Star Justice*, 137–42, quotation on p. 142.

12. Richard Maxwell Brown, *No Duty to Retreat: Violence and Values in American History and Society* (New York: Oxford University Press, 1991).

13. Barry A. Crouch and Donaly E. Brice, *The Governor's Hounds: The Texas State Police, 1870–1873* (Austin: University of Texas Press, 2011).

14. H. P. N. Gammel, comp., *The Laws of Texas: 1822–1897* (Austin: Gammel Book Company, 1898), 8:89–91, quotation on p. 91. One of the better accounts of the formation of the Frontier Battalion is Utley, *Lone Star Justice*, 143–59. For biographies see Rick Miller, *Texas Ranger John B. Jones and the Frontier Battalion, 1874–1881* (Denton: University of North Texas Press, 2012); and Chuck Parsons and Marianne E. Hall Little, *Captain L. H. McNelly, Texas Ranger: The Life and Times of a Fighting Man* (Austin: State House Press, 2001).

15. For an elaboration of legal authority and sources, see Weiss, *Yours to Command*, 7–9, 512n.
16. Bob Alexander, *Winchester Warriors: Texas Rangers of Company D, 1874–1901* (Denton: University of North Texas Press, 2009), 179.
17. Charles M. Robinson III, *The Men Who Wear the Star: The Story of the Texas Rangers* (New York: Random House, 2000), xvii.
18. H. Kenneth Bechtel, *State Police in the United States: A Socio-Historical Analysis* (Westport, CT: Greenwood Press, 1995).
19. For an up-to-date account, see Rick Miller, *Sam Bass and Gang* (Austin: State House Press, 1999).
20. John Boessenecker, *Texas Ranger: The Epic Life of Frank Hamer, the Man Who Killed Bonnie and Clyde* (New York: Thomas Dunne Books, 2016), 437. For a look at the different outlaw eras, see Mitchel Roth, "Bonnie and Clyde in Texas: The End of the Texas Outlaw Tradition," *East Texas Historical Journal* 35, no. 2 (October 1997): 30–38.
21. Chuck Parsons, *Captain John R. Hughes, Lone Star Ranger* (Denton: University of North Texas Press, 2011); Paul N. Spellman, *Captain J. A. Brooks, Texas Ranger* (Denton: University of North Texas Press, 2007); Spellman, *Captain John H. Rogers, Texas Ranger* (Denton: University of North Texas Press, 2008); Weiss, *Yours to Command*.
22. In the vast literature on the Mexican Revolution and the Rangers on the border, among the best are the writings of Charles H. Harris III and Louis R. Sadler, especially *The Texas Rangers and the Mexican Revolution: The Bloodiest Decade, 1910-1920* (Albuquerque: University of New Mexico Press, 2004).
23. The relations between the Rangers and the various Texas governors are covered in detail in Utley, *Lone Star Lawmen*. See also Malsch, *"Lone Wolf" Gonzaullas*; Richard B. McCaslin, *Texas Ranger Captain William L. Wright* (Denton: University of North Texas Press, 2021); and Jody E. Ginn, *East Texas Troubles: The Allred Rangers' Cleanup of San Augustine* (Norman: University of Oklahoma Press, 2019).
24. An excellent introduction to Garrison can be found in Utley, *Lone Star Lawmen*, chap. 12.
25. Ranger events and personnel by the opening of the twenty-first century are covered in detail in Utley, *Lone Star Lawmen*. See also Bob Alexander, *Old Riot, New Ranger: Captain Jack Dean, Texas Ranger and US Marshal* (Denton: University of North Texas Press, 2018); H. Joaquin Jackson and David M. Wilkinson, *One Ranger:*

A Memoir (Austin: University of Texas Press, 2005); Ben Procter, "The Modern Texas Rangers: A Law-Enforcement Dilemma in the Rio Grande Valley," in *Reflections of Western Historians*, ed. John Carroll (Tucson: University of Arizona Press, 1969), 215–31; and Julian Samora, Joe Bernal, and Albert Peña, *Gunpowder Justice: A Reassessment of the Texas Rangers* (Notre Dame: University of Notre Dame Press, 1979).

26. For the beginning phases of writing about Texas history, see Laura L. McLemore, *Inventing Texas: Early Historians of the Lone Star State* (College Station: Texas A&M University Press, 2004).

27. Mention of such happenings and their chroniclers will be found in Bryan, *American Elsewhere*, 239–42.

28. Bryan, *American Elsewhere*, 95.

29. Washington Irving, *A Tour of the Prairies* (London: John Murray, 1835), 59 (quotations); Brian Jay Jones, *Washington Irving: An American Original* (New York: Arcade, 2008), 300–315.

30. Frederick L. Olmsted, *A Journey through Texas; Or, a Saddle-Trip on the Southwestern Frontier* (1857; repr., Austin: University of Texas Press, 1978), 298–303, first quotation p. 301, second quotation p. 302.

31. John H. Jenkins, *Basic Texas Books: An Annotated Bibliography of Selected Works for a Research Library* (1983; rev. ed., Austin: Texas State Historical Association, 1988), 421.

32. Mitchel Roth, "Journalism and the US-Mexican War," in *Dueling Eagles: Reinterpreting the US-Mexican War, 1846–1848*, ed. Richard Fancaviglia and Douglas Richmond (Fort Worth: TCU Press, 2000), 108. For his wartime reports, see George Kendall, *Dispatches from the Mexican War*, ed. Lawrence Cress (Norman: University of Oklahoma Press, 1999). The best study of wartime correspondents will be found in Tom Reilly, *War with Mexico! America's Reporters Cover the Battlefront*, ed. Manley Witten (Lawrence: University Press of Kansas, 2010).

33. Samuel C. Reid Jr., *The Scouting Expeditions of McCulloch's Texas Rangers* [. . .] (1847; reprint, Austin: Steck, 1935); Jenkins, *Basic Texas Books*, 456 (first quotation), 458 (second quotation). For a stimulating presentation of the impact of the war on the American mind, see Robert Johannsen, *To the Halls of the Montezumas: The Mexican War in the American Imagination* (New York: Oxford University Press, 1985).

34. Charles W. Webber, *Tales of the Southern Border* (Philadelphia: Lippincott, 1856), 54–55.

35. Charles W. Webber, *Old Hicks the Guide* (1848; repr., Upper Saddle River, NJ: Literature House/Gregg Press, 1970), 304–18, quotation p. 310.
36. Jenkins, *Basic Texas Books*, 590.
37. Henderson K. Yoakum, *History of Texas: From Its First Settlement in 1685 to Its Annexation to the United States in 1846*, 2 vols. (1855; repr., Austin: Steck, 1935).
38. For a discussion of Yoakum's place in historical literature, see Cashion, *Lone Star Mind*, 42–43; McLemore, *Inventing Texas*, 67–70, quotation on p. 70.
39. Yoakum, *History of Texas*, 2:298–306, 363–78, quotation on p. 378.
40. Erma Baker, "Brown, John Henry," in *The New Handbook of Texas*, ed. Ron Tyler, 6 vols. (Austin: Texas State Historical Association, 1996), 1:765.
41. Jenkins, *Basic Texas Books*, 54.
42. McLemore, *Inventing Texas*, 88.
43. John Henry Brown, *History of Texas, from 1685 to 1892*, 2 vols. (St. Louis: L. E. Daniell, 1892–93). Both Brown and his wife published textbooks to be used in the Texas school system. McLemore, *Inventing Texas*, 88.
44. Brown, *History of Texas*, 2:178–85, 222–53, 318–43.
45. Brown, *History of Texas*, 2:340 (first quotation), 343 (second quotation).
46. Brown, *History of Texas*, 2:359 (first quotation), 361 (second quotation).
47. Mary Beth Fleischer, ed., "Dudley G. Wooten's Comment on Texas Histories and Historians of the Nineteenth Century," *Southwestern Historical Quarterly* 73, no. 2 (October 1969): 237–38.
48. Dudley G. Wooten, ed., *A Comprehensive History of Texas, 1685–1897*, 2 vols. (Dallas: William G. Scarff, 1898).
49. Jenkins, *Basic Texas Books*, 582.
50. Utley, *Lone Star Justice*, 251. For King's service in the Civil War, see Ralph A. Wooster, *Lone Star Generals in Gray* (Austin: Eakin Press, 2000), 139–42.
51. Wilburn H. King, "The Texas Ranger Service and History of the Rangers, with Observations on Their Value as a Police Protection," in Wooten, *Comprehensive History of Texas*, 2:333, 335.
52. King, "Texas Ranger Service," in Wooten, *Comprehensive History of Texas*, 2:338, 367.
53. Andrew J. Sowell, *Early Settlers and Indian Fighters of Southwest Texas* (1900; repr., Austin: State House Press, 1986), preface. See also John

Henry Brown, *Indian Wars and Pioneers of Texas* (Austin: L. E. Daniell, 1896); James T. DeShields, *Border Wars of Texas* [. . .] (1912; rev. ed., Austin: State House Press, 1993); Sowell, *Rangers and Pioneers of Texas* [. . .] (San Antonio: Shepard Brothers, 1884); John W. Wilbarger, *Indian Depredations in Texas* [. . .] (1889; reprint, Austin: Eakin Press and Statehouse Books, 1985).

54. Jenkins, *Basic Texas Books*, 57–59 (quotation on p. 57), 509–13, 575–77; Brown, *Indian Wars and Pioneers of Texas*. A four-page sketch of the life of Brown as a Ranger, politician, newspaperman, and Civil War veteran appeared in Wilbarger, *Indian Depredations in Texas*, 375–78.

55. Sowell, *Early Settlers and Indian Fighters*, 202–05, 331–36, 624–33, 794–97.

56. Jenkins, *Basic Texas Books*, 509.

57. Sowell, *Rangers and Pioneers of Texas*.

58. Hubert Howe Bancroft, *History of the North Mexican States and Texas*, vol. 2 (San Francisco: History Company, 1889), 317, 394–97.

59. James Harvey Robinson, *The New History: Essays Illustrating the Modern Historical Outlook* (New York: Macmillan, 1912).

60. For historical context see Stephen L. Hardin, "'Valor, Wisdom, and Experience': Early Texas Rangers and the Nature of Frontier Leadership," in Glasrud and Weiss, *Tracking: Nineteenth Century*, 50–61.

61. Noah Smithwick, *The Evolution of a State; Or, Recollections of Old Texas Days* (1900; repr., Austin: University of Texas Press, 1983); Napoleon A. Jennings, *A Texas Ranger* (1899; repr., Norman: University of Oklahoma Press, 1997); James B. Gillett, *Six Years with the Texas Rangers, 1875 to 1881* (Austin: n.p. 1921; new ed., ed. M. M. Quaife, New Haven: Yale University Press, 1925). This has become the standard edition of Gillett's work.

62. John S. Ford, *Rip Ford's Texas: Personal Narratives of the West*, ed. Stephen B. Oates (Austin: University of Texas Press, 1963); McCaslin, *Fighting Stock*, chap. 8. DeShields was a historian who worked at times with Ford. Prolific but largely forgotten, DeShields lived and wrote at the turn of the twentieth century. His often-cited account of Indians and pioneers in frontier Texas has been judged inferior to the works of other historians. See McCaslin, *Fighting Stock*, 264, 269, 331n25.

63. Daryl Jones, *The Dime Novel Western* (Bowling Green, OH: Bowling Green University Popular Press, 1978); Bill O'Neal, *Reel Rangers:*

Texas Rangers in Movies, TV, Radio, and Other Forms of Popular Culture (Waco: Eakin Press, 2008).

64. George P. Garrison, *Texas: A Contest of Civilizations* (Boston: Houghton Mifflin, 1903), 232–233 (Rangers as Indian fighters).

65. McLemore, *Inventing Texas*, 10, 89–93.

66. Eugene C. Barker, *The Life of Stephen F. Austin: Founder of Texas, 1793–1836* (1925; repr., New York: Da Capo Press, 1968), 102–3. For Barker's life and times, see William C. Pool, *Eugene C. Barker: Historian* (Austin: Texas State Historical Association, 1971).

67. Llerena Friend, "W. P. Webb's Texas Rangers," *Southwestern Historical Quarterly* 74 (Jan. 1971): 315; Lon Tinkle, *An American Original: The Life of J. Frank Dobie* (Boston: Little, Brown, 1978).

68. Walter Prescott Webb, "History as High Adventure," *American Historical Review* 64, no. 2 (Jan. 1959): 271 (quotation). See also Michael L. Collins, ed., *A Texan's Story: The Autobiography of Walter Prescott Webb* (Norman: University of Oklahoma Press, 2020); Necah Stewart Furman, *Walter Prescott Webb: His Life and Impact* (Albuquerque: University of New Mexico Press, 1976).

69. Gregory M. Tobin, *The Making of a History: Walter Prescott Webb and the Great Plains* (Austin: University of Texas Press, 1976); Walter Prescott Webb, *The Great Plains* (Boston: Ginn, 1931).

70. Archibald R. Lewis and Thomas F. McGann, eds., *The New World Looks at Its History* (Austin: University of Texas Press, 1963); Walter Prescott Webb, *The Great Frontier* (Boston: Houghton Mifflin, 1952).

71. Walter Prescott Webb, "The American Revolver and the West," *Scribner's Magazine* 81 (January-June 1927): 171-178, quotation on p. 178. For the master's thesis, see Webb, *The Texas Rangers in the Mexican War* (Austin: Jenkins Garrett Press, 1975).

72. Walter Prescott Webb, *The Texas Rangers: A Century of Frontier Defense* (Boston: Houghton Mifflin, 1935). Webb preferred his other volume without the "deadening facts": *The Story of the Texas Rangers* (1957; 2nd ed. Austin: Encino Press, 1971), 8–9 (quotation). For the ups and downs of his Ranger writings, see Friend, "W. P. Webb's Texas Rangers."

73. For key historical writings by Procter, see Ben Procter, *Just One Riot: Episodes of Texas Rangers in the 20th Century* (Austin: Eakin Press, 1991); Procter, "Modern Texas Rangers"; Procter, "Texas Rangers," in Tyler, *New Handbook of Texas*, 6:393–95; Procter, "The Texas Rangers: An Overview," in *The Texas Heritage*, ed. Ben Procter and

Archie P. McDonald (St. Louis, MO: Forum Press, 1980), 119–31. Procter's obituary is found on the internet at https://www.legacy.com/us/obituaries/dfw/name/ben-procter-obituary?id=9063480.

74. See, for example, Gary Clayton Anderson, *The Conquest of Texas: Ethnic Cleansing in the Promised Land, 1820–1875* (Norman: University of Oklahoma Press, 2005); Anderson, *Ethnic Cleansing and the Indian: The Crime That Should Haunt America* (Norman: University of Oklahoma Press, 2014); Monica M. Martinez, *The Injustice Never Leaves You: Anti-Mexican Violence in Texas* (Cambridge: Harvard University Press, 2018). See also Richard Ribb, *"La Rinchada*: Revolution, Revenge, and the Rangers, 1910–1920," in *War along the Border: The Mexican Revolution and Tejano Communities*, ed. Arnoldo De Leon, 56–106 (College Station: Texas A&M University Press, 2012).

75. Walter Prescott Webb, "The Art of Historical Writing," in *History as High Adventure*, ed. E. C. Barksdale (Austin: Pemberton Press, 1969), 133.

76. For a recent historiographical essay, see Nathan A. Jennings, "Riding into Controversy: A Study in Contrasting Views of the Texas Rangers," *Journal of the West* 52, no. 2 (Spring 2013): 42–52. Each generation modifies, even rewrites, the history of Texas and its Ranger service. Along the way a few popular historical writers in past decades will be de-emphasized. This has already happened to James Michener.

PART 1

Understanding Ranger History
Two Cardinal Points

Chapter 1

Primary Sources of Ranger History in Public Depositories

Donaly E. Brice

A thoughtless person might suppose that the writing of history is a simple matter, a mere gathering of facts and putting them together in a connected way. But neither the gathering of facts nor the putting them together is a very easy process. It is true that even a child of normal capacity may be taught to collect simple data from a number of sources and to combine them to an original form; but in their advanced aspects both collection and presentation require superior mentality and special training.

—Homer Cary Hockett, *Introduction to Research in American History*

After working for thirty-seven years in the Archives and Information Services Division of the Texas State Library and Archives Commission, where many original Texas Ranger records are housed, two questions were commonly asked of me by archive patrons. The first was, "Do you have a comprehensive list of names of all the men who served in the Texas Rangers?" The answer was, "No, there is no complete list of names of Texas Rangers." The second question was, "Is there any one library, archive, or depository where all the official Texas Ranger records have been deposited?" The answer to that question was, "There is no one central location for all official records of the Texas Rangers." A historian who has done research on the Texas Rangers or has written any scholarly books on the subject of the Rangers will not be surprised by the answers to these two questions. However, a historian or any individual who has not done previous research into the subject of the Rangers might be astonished at these answers. The truth is that primary records relating to the Texas Rangers can be found in hundreds of places. Most archives, university libraries, and a myriad of depositories of official county and state records in Texas are likely to hold numerous primary-source records that may relate to the Texas Rangers.

Since there are literally hundreds of locations for finding primary-source Texas Ranger records, it is necessary to focus attention to only several of the institutions where the bulk of these records can be found. And even then the total extent of records found in several of these sources cannot be examined thoroughly in the scope of this work. Hopefully, the information provided will enlighten Ranger historians to some of the more heavily used Ranger records in these selected locations. The knowledgeable librarians, archivists, and staff personnel at these places should be able to lead the researcher to other records not discussed in this chapter.

Arguably, the largest collection of primary materials relating to the Texas Rangers can be found in the Archives and Information Services Division of the Texas State Library and Archives Commission in Austin.[1] Their records begin with the early Ranger activities during the Republic of Texas and extend into the twentieth century. The Texas Office of the Adjutant General records consist, in part, of muster rolls, correspondence, service records, quartermaster records, monthly returns / records of scouts, and statements of arrest. Comprehensive finding aids can assist a researcher in navigating through these extensive records. Paper copy finding aids are located in the State Archives reading room. These finding aids can also be accessed online.[2] Among the secretary of state records in the archives can be found records of rewards, extradition papers, executive clemency records, and executive record books. Many of the fugitives apprehended by the Rangers were eventually sent to the Texas State Penitentiary. Records for them can also be found in Convict Record Books (1849–1954) and Conduct Registers (1875–1945) in the records of the Texas Department of Criminal Justice, housed in the State Archives. Other records for those who were arrested and convicted for various offenses can be found in the governors' Executive Clemency records and Executive Record Books.

Adjutant general service records are among the basic primary-source materials to check when researching a Texas Ranger. These records have been scanned and put online for the convenience of the researcher and are helpful in determining dates of enlistment and discharge from the Ranger service and sometimes give additional descriptive information on the individual Ranger.[3]

Another basic primary-source material in the State Archives consists of the vast collection of muster rolls and payrolls for the various companies of Rangers. These records show the names of the numerous men who served in a particular Ranger unit. Other information found on these muster/payrolls may include dates of enlistment and discharge, amount of pay, brief comments regarding an individual Ranger, and physical descriptive information about the individual. Most Ranger historians have utilized these records in their histories and biographies of Texas Rangers, including Charles H. Harris III and Louis R. Sadler in their book *The Texas Rangers and the Mexican Revolution: The Bloodiest Decade, 1910–1920*; Chuck Parsons in *Captain John R. Hughes, Lone Star Ranger*; and Stephen L. Moore in his four-volume set of books *Savage Frontier: Rangers, Riflemen, and Indian Wars in Texas*. One volume in particular, *Texas Rangers: Lives, Legend, and Legacy* by Bob Alexander and Donaly E. Brice, heavily used the muster rolls of the newly formed companies of the Frontier Battalion, beginning at their inception in 1874 through the year of 1875, to depict what type of men came together to create these Ranger units on the Texas frontier. By studying these muster rolls of the Frontier Battalion, a better image of the type of person who desired to live the life of a Ranger came into focus by learning more about the men's ages, nativity, and trade or occupation.[4]

Probably the most heavily used primary-source records for Texas Rangers at the Texas State Archives are the adjutant general and Ranger correspondence files, which cover the period from 1846 to 1943. The bulk of the material covers the years of 1861 to 1933 and fills 107.63 cubic feet of space on the shelves in the archive's stacks. These correspondence files include thousands of letters and telegrams sent to the adjutant general's office and correspondence between various Ranger units. These records are the "meat" of any in-depth research for a book on the Texas Rangers. It is in these records that one can find accounts of Indian fights on the frontier, shootouts with desperadoes, or accounts of the deaths of Rangers or other individuals. The correspondence also paints a picture of the everyday Ranger life, showing its exciting moments as well as the dull monotony that also wore on these early Rangers. No well-researched or scholarly book written about the Texas Rangers should fail to utilize these correspondence files. Almost all Ranger historians have used these records in their numerous works. However, a number of these historians have relied more on the correspondence files than others. Some of these include Rick Miller in his book *Texas Ranger John B. Jones and the Frontier Battalion, 1874–1881*; Harold J. Weiss Jr. in his *Yours to Command*; Bob Alexander in a number of his books, including *Whiskey River Ranger: The Old West Life of Baz Outlaw*; and Robert M. Utley in his book *Lone Star Justice: The First Century of the Texas Rangers*.[5]

Almost as important in Texas Ranger research as the adjutant general and Ranger correspondence files are the adjutant general letter books and letterpress books containing outgoing correspondence from the adjutant general's office. Most of this correspondence contains directives and responses to various Rangers and others who had corresponded with the adjutant general. Because of the difficulty in using these records, many Ranger historians have not utilized the records as much as they should. These letterpress books are very fragile and are copies of original letters pressed onto very thin onionskin paper. The writing can be blurry and faded and presents problems in reading the letters. This process of creating copies of correspondence could be considered the forerunners of the mimeograph, carbon paper, and the photocopies of today. Regardless, these copies of letters sent out by the adjutant general contain vitally important information and are sometimes overlooked when historians are researching in the State Archives. There are a number of Ranger historians who have devoted their time to go through these valuable papers. Some of these writers include Paul Spellman in *Captain John H. Rogers, Texas Ranger*; Robert W. Stephens in *Captain George H. Schmitt: Texas Ranger*; and Weiss in *Yours to Command*.[6]

When researching Ranger correspondence files in the Texas State Archives, one will find that there is a sparse amount of correspondence dealing with Ranger activities prior to 1861. Fortunately, if the researcher will search the governors' records for that period, it is possible to find a wealth of correspondence and material relating to the Rangers' activities during the decade before the Civil War. The governors' records for J. Pinckney Henderson, George T. Wood, Peter H. Bell, J. W. Henderson, Elisha M. Pease, Hardin R. Runnels, and Sam Houston provide much information regarding Ranger activity between 1846 and 1861. The records of Governors Edward Clark, Francis R. Lubbock, and Pendleton Murrah also provide information relating to Ranger activities during the Civil War years.

After the Civil War and Reconstruction, Texas reorganized their Ranger forces into the Frontier Battalion in 1874. During the period of the Frontier Battalion (1874–1901) the adjutant general and Ranger correspondence files provide a wealth of material relating to Ranger activities. However, after 1901 the Frontier Battalion was disbanded, and these law enforcement units were reorganized into the Ranger Force. Again, there seems to be a sparse amount of material in the adjutant general correspondence files. Historians are again forced to turn to the governors' papers for some of the information regarding the activities of the Rangers. Examples of some of those historians who have utilized the governors' papers include Robert M. Utley in his book *Lone Star Lawmen: The Second Century of the Texas Rangers*; Michael Collins's *Texas Devils: Rangers and Regulators on the Lower Rio Grande, 1846–1861* and *A Crooked River: Rustlers, Rangers, and Regulators on the Lower Rio Grande, 1861–1877*; Frederick Wilkins in *The Law Comes to Texas* and *Defending the Borders*; Charles H. Harris III and Louis R. Sadler in *The Texas Rangers in Transition: From Gunfighters to Criminal Investigators, 1921–1935*; and Weiss in *Yours To Command*.[7] Finding aids to the governors' records can be found online, along with all the other processed finding aids for various state agency records housed at the State Archives.[8]

Among the more important files found in the adjutant general records at the Texas State Archives are the monthly returns and records of scouts of the various companies of the Frontier Battalion. These records provide monthly reports on the various Ranger units and explain what activities the units were involved in on a daily basis. The returns provide a duty station where the unit was located; the names of officers and men who were present or absent; the number of horses, mules, and other equipment that could be found in the Ranger camps; and a list of any public property that was recovered by the Rangers and the disposition of that property. Even more important than these bits of information are the daily records of the activities of the men of the various units, which provide a record of their many scouts. Many of these monthly returns also give a list of persons who were arrested or names of those who the Rangers were attempting to arrest for the month. Many Ranger historians have made good use of this particular group of records. Some of these historians include Bob Alexander in *Winchester Warriors: Texas Rangers of Company D, 1874–1901*; David Johnson in *The Mason County "Hoo Doo" War, 1874–1902*; Darren L. Ivey in *The Ranger Ideal: The Rangers in the Hall of Fame*, volumes 1–3; and Paul Spellman in his book *Captain J. A. Brooks, Texas Ranger*.[9]

One group of Texas Ranger records at the Texas State Archives that is not used by as many Ranger historians is that of the quartermaster's department. These records can provside vital information in writing about the Texas Ranger. The quartermaster records are split up into various periods of time: Republic of Texas, pre–Civil War, Frontier Forces (1870–1874), Special State Troops (1874–1880), Frontier Battalion (1874–1901), and the Ranger Force (1901–1939), with the bulk of these records for 1901–1915. These records document activities of the office of the quartermaster, who is responsible for the supplies (including provisions, forage, medicines, and ordnance) and the services (payrolls, transportation, and other items) required for maintaining a force of Rangers. These records vary according to the different periods of time that a historian is researching. Some Ranger historians have made good use of the quartermaster records in their works. One historian, Frederick Wilkins, has utilized these records in a number of his books, including *The Legend Begins: The Texas Rangers, 1823–1845; Defending the Borders: The Texas Rangers, 1848–1861*; and *The Law Comes to Texas: The Texas Rangers 1870–1901.* Another historian who has made good use of the quartermaster records is Weiss, in his book *Yours to Command.*[10]

When a historian is researching the activities of a Texas Ranger during the period of the Republic of Texas, there are a number of additional sources of information to examine at the Texas State Archives. Of course, one should first check the service record files to see if the individual they are researching can be found there. Unfortunately, there are not as many names in the adjutant general service record files for Republic of Texas Rangers. Earlier in this chapter service records were discussed briefly, and it was noted that these records have been scanned and are online for researchers. Note 2 explains how to access these service records. A Republic-era service record or enlistment record would normally contain such information as city and date, name of enlistee, place of birth, age, height, complexion, color of eyes and hair, profession, and term of enlistment. These Republic service records usually contain more personal information on the enlistee than later service records after statehood.

Republic of Texas military rolls at the State Archives consist of muster rolls, payrolls, receipt rolls, and lists of officers and/or men for the various military and paramilitary organizations of the republic period (1835–1846). Information contained on these rolls vary considerably. However, historians who research the Republic of Texas period have utilized these muster rolls to their advantage. Some of these historians include Frederick Wilkins in *The Legend Begins*; Moore in his four-volume set, *Savage Frontier*; and Darren L. Ivey in *The Ranger Ideal: Texas Rangers in the Hall of Fame*, volume 1.[11]

The most important primary source of records at the Texas State Library for researching Rangers or anyone who served in the military during the period of the republic (1836–1845) are the republic claims. The archive finding aid said: "The Republic Claims series of Comptroller's records include claims for payment, reimbursement, or restitution submitted by citizens to the Republic of Texas government from 1835 through 1846. It also includes records relating to Republic pensions and claims against the republic submitted as public debt claims after 1846. The files include supporting documents such as vouchers, financial accounts, military records, receipts, notes, or letters."[12] These republic claims are divided into four categories: audited claims (civil and military), republic pensions, public debt claims, and unpaid claims. The audited claims (1835–1846) include claims that were submitted to the comptroller or treasurer of the republic and were audited and approved prior to 1846; the public debt claims (1848–1860) were papers filed for services or goods provided between 1835–1846; the republic pensions (1870–ca. 1900) relate to claims filed for pensions for service during the Texas Revolution and for serving as a Mier prisoner (later state legislation allowed others who served during the republic period to file for pensions); and unpaid and miscellaneous claims. This last group of republic claims included those submitted to the government that were not audited or allowed. However, the claims are still in these files. A more in-depth discussion of the various types of information that can be found in these republic claims can be found online.[13]

In addition to the important state agency records available at the Texas State Archives regarding Texas Rangers, there are several important manuscript collections in their holdings that contain useful materials for doing Ranger research. One of these manuscript collections is the Andrew Jackson Houston Papers. This collection contains approximately 4,800 items inherited by Andrew Jackson Houston from his father, Sam Houston. This collection includes "correspondence, reports, resolutions, proclamations, affidavits, depositions and a wealth of other material dated, primarily, between 1835 and 1859." An introduction to this collection can be found online and will lead the researcher to a database that can be searched by name, date, or subject. A number of historians have benefited by using this manuscript collection. They include Mike Cox in *The Texas Rangers: Wearing the Cinco Peso, 1821–1900*; Darren L. Ivey in *The Ranger Ideal*, volume 1; Wilkins in *The Legend Begins*; and Utley in *Lone Star Justice*.[14]

Another manuscript collection that may be helpful to researchers who are focusing on the period of the 1840s and the Mexican War would be the Samuel Hamilton Walker Papers. This manuscript collection covers the period of 1836–1905, with the bulk of the material from 1842 to 1847. The collection includes correspondence, military orders, quartermaster records, and numerous other items. Most of these papers cover a period when he served in the Mexican War (1846–1847). The records have been digitized and can be seen online. A number of Ranger historians have been able to utilize the collection, including Utley, Ivey, and Collins.[15]

One more group of official state agency records that exists at the Texas State Archives that can be very beneficial to Ranger historians, but are not actual Ranger records, are penitentiary records consisting of Convict Record Ledgers (1849–1954) and Conduct Registers (1855–1945). These records provide much information regarding individuals who were convicted and sentenced to the Texas State Penitentiary. Some of the information in these records include the convict's name, age, physical description, reason for conviction, where they were convicted, time of incarceration, and other comments. The Conduct Registers usually provide a record of the conduct of each prisoner and punishments meted out for any misconduct. They can also provide a date of release from prison or a date of death if the prisoner died while incarcerated. These records have been microfilmed and also have been digitized and indexed. The digitized records and index are currently available through Ancestry.com and Ancestry Library Edition. If researchers or their local libraries have access to one of these resources, the records can be accessed and printed. More information can be found online on how to access the records and what types of information can be found on the actual records.[16] Numerous Ranger historians have used these records to help give a more complete record of many of the individuals who were arrested by Texas Rangers and were convicted and sentenced to the State Penitentiary. Some of these historians include Ivey, Weiss, Alexander, and Brice.[17]

Among the books and official publications housed at the Archives and Information Services Division of the Texas State Library and Archives Commission (TSLAC) are many of the Texas adjutant general annual and biennial reports. These published reports provide vital information regarding statistics and activities of the Office of the Adjutant General. Names and dates of death of Rangers are often given when a Ranger dies in the line of duty. Since the Texas Rangers were a part of the adjutant general's department until they merged, along with the Texas Highway Patrol, into the newly formed Texas Department of Public Safety in 1935, many historians have utilized these published reports in learning more about the Rangers' activities over the years. Some of these historians include Utley, Wilkins, and Spellman.[18]

When reviewing the bibliographies in books by many Ranger historians, one will notice a considerable number of specific titles and references listed under "public and official documents" or "government documents." Most of these refer to official documents in Texas State Legislative Journals or in Congressional Journals, sometimes referred to as "Serial Sets." The TSLAC is designated as a regional depository library (RDL). Therefore, the library acquires and retains copies of all the state and congressional documents that are made available to the RDLs. A few of these documents that are most often cited include: *Troubles on the Texas Frontier*, H.R. Exec. Doc. 81, 36th Cong., 1st sess., Washington: 1860; *Depredations on the Frontiers of Texas*, H.R. Exec. Doc. 39, 42nd Cong., 3rd sess., Washington: 1872; *Texas Border Troubles*, H.R. Exec. Doc. 343, 44th Cong., 1st sess., Washington: 1876; *El Paso Troubles in Texas*, H.R. Exec. Doc. 93, 45th Cong., 2nd sess., Washington: 1878; and *Texas Border Troubles*, H.R. Misc. Doc. 64, 45th Cong., 2nd sess., Washington: 1878. These government documents can all be found in the holdings at the TSLAC.

One state government document that has received much usage by Texas Ranger historians is the *Proceedings of the Joint Committee of the Senate and House in the Investigation of the Texas Ranger Force*, Texas Legislature, 1919. Usually referred to as the Canales Investigation, this in-depth and extensive document was generated in 1919 when the Texas Legislature investigated the many allegations of Ranger brutality and misconduct along the Texas-Mexican border during the period between 1915 and 1919. "As a result of the investigation, the Loyalty Rangers were abolished, and the Texas Rangers were reduced in force. Higher recruiting standards were put in place, and the pay of Rangers was increased to attract and retain higher-quality officers. Finally, procedures were implemented to better hear complaints from citizens about misconduct. These reforms helped the Rangers return to a position of respect during the 1920s and 1930s."[19] Because of the importance of this piece of legislation, the entire joint committee investigation by the Texas Senate and House has been digitized and can be accessed online. Many historians who have researched the early twentieth-century Rangers have found these records very important to their work. Several of these Ranger works include Utley in *Lone Star Lawmen*; Harris and Sadler in *Texas Rangers and the Mexican Revolution*; Spellman in *Captain John H. Rogers*; Benjamin Heber Johnson in *Revolution in Texas: How a Forgotten Rebellion and Its Bloody Suppression Turned Mexicans into Americans*; Monica Muñoz Martinez in *The Injustice Never Leaves You: Anti-Mexican Violence in Texas*; and Doug J. Swanson in *Cult of Glory: The Bold and Brutal History of the Texas Rangers*.[20]

Although much information has been provided regarding the
holdings in the TSLAC, there are a number of other institutions
and libraries that should be discussed in this chapter. One of these
institutions is the Texas Ranger Hall of Fame and Museum (TRHF&M)
in Waco, Texas. Their mission statement, in part, is "To collect,
preserve, study and exhibit artifacts, artwork and archives relating to
the Texas Ranger service; To permanently document the service of
Texas Rangers past and present."[21] Today, these collections are housed
in the Tobin and Anne Armstrong Texas Ranger Research Center,
located on the grounds of the TRHF&M. This would be the place one
would find research materials when writing about the Texas Rangers.[22]
In 1997 the Texas Legislature passed a resolution "designating the
Texas Ranger Hall of Fame and Museum as the official repository
for memorabilia, archives, and other materials relating to the Texas
Rangers." To research on-site at the TRHF&M it is strongly suggested
that the researcher make an appointment with the staff before arriving.
If the researcher is planning to do research by mail, it is important to
acquire a research request form and mail it to the research center.[23]

Collections at the TRHF&M have continued to grow over the years,
and today researchers may find service records of Rangers, personal
papers, criminal case files, photographs, correspondence, books, and
documents dating back to the 1830s. Among the individual collections
of records and materials for Rangers (many from the twentieth century)
are those for Frank Hamer, M. T. "Lone Wolf" Gonzaullas, Lee
Trimble, Bob Mitchell, M. D. "Kelly" Rogers, Marvin "Red" Burton,
Jack Dean, Glenn Elliott, Ed Gooding, Bob Goss, and Jim Greer.
These are only a few of the names that are available.[24] Some Ranger
historians have heavily utilized the collections of Ranger papers at the
TRHF&M. Utley cited records for at least fifteen different Rangers in
his book *Lone Star Lawmen*. Spellman used records for J. A. Brooks
and John H. Rogers in his books *Captain J. A. Brooks* and *Captain
John H. Rogers*. Harris and Sadler used files on Francis "Frank"
Johnson, Henry Lee Ransom, Lee Trimble, and William M. Hanson in
their book *Texas Rangers and the Mexican Revolution*.

Some of these files are personal papers and others are vertical files. However, there are primary-source materials in many of the vertical files. One example of such a case is that of William M. Alsobrook. Will Alsobrook was accidentally shot and died from his wounds in 1919. In Bob Alexander's *Riding Lucifer's Line: Ranger Deaths along the Texas-Mexico Border*, there is a fine chapter devoted to the Ranger career of William Alsobrook. The author covered the final hours of Alsobrook's life as thoroughly as any researcher could have done. Still, there were questions regarding the actual shooting of Alsobrook. It was not until years later, after Alexander's book was published in 2013, that a letter written by an eyewitness to the shooting episode was discovered by a descendent of the eyewitness and donated to the TRHF&M. The important document, which answered many questions, was finally added to the vertical file of William Alsobrook.[25]

Among the many collections at the TRHF&M are over sixty oral histories of Texas Rangers. These oral histories have been digitized as a joint educational and preservation program of the TRHF&M and the Texas Ranger Association Foundation. The oral histories are indexed by the name of the person being interviewed, the date of the interview, and the number of pages included in the interview. A few of the names of the Rangers who were interview include Barry Caver, Joe Davis, Jack Dean, Glenn Elliott, Bob Favor, Manuel T. "Lone Wolf" Gonzaullas, Bob Goss, Joaquin Jackson, the family of Frank Hamer, and Ray Martinez. These oral histories have been transcribed and can be accessed online.[26] Various Ranger historians have cited some of these interviews. They include Harris and Sadler in their book *Texas Rangers in Transition*; Utley in *Lone Star Lawmen*; and Bob Alexander in *Old Riot, New Ranger*.[27]

The holdings of the TRHF&M also contain personal papers of some nineteenth-century Rangers, including George Washington Arrington, W. J. L. Sullivan, Ira Aten, and W. T. Smith (ca. 1879). Most of the personal papers are for retired Rangers from the twentieth century. The contents of these files vary according to the particular Ranger. Some of the files contain little information while others hold a treasure trove of materials. One excellent example of a wealth of material in a Ranger's personal file is that of Captain Jack Dean. In Alexander's biography *Old Riot, New Ranger: Captain Jack Dean, Texas Ranger and US Marshal*, researchers will be astonished at the tremendous number of official records that were saved in Captain Dean's personal file. It is true that not all retired Rangers who donate their files to the TRHF&M will have saved as many of their papers as Jack Dean. However, by looking through the endnotes of Bob Alexander's book, one can get an idea of the types of personal records that might be found in other Rangers' files.

The TRHF&M also has a large collection of individual Ranger case files for the time period of 1960–1990. These files contain important information regarding the individual Ranger who was involved with a particular case when the Ranger was still on active service. Some of these case files still have great importance when cold case investigations are revived. They have helped to provide information for recent investigations, although the case had been closed for many years.

For researchers who may be looking for the various general and special orders for the Texas Rangers, the research center has these records for the period from 1910 up into the 1930s. Earlier general and special orders from the nineteenth century are primarily found in the various correspondence files in the Texas State Archives in Austin.

According to the TRHF&M staff, several additional collections of materials have been acquired recently. One collection contains the papers of Charles H. Harris III and Louis R. Sadler, who have published a number of well-researched and successful books relating to the Texas Rangers during the first several decades of the twentieth century. This collection includes photographs, artifacts, photocopies of original documents relating to the Rangers, and correspondence. Another collection is the Sutton family collection (of Sutton-Taylor Feud fame). Items in this collection include photographs, family Bibles, and various artifacts.[28]

Another important Texas institution where one can find primary records for Texas Rangers is the Dolph Briscoe Center for American History (BCAH), located next to the Lyndon B. Johnson Presidential Library on the campus of the University of Texas at Austin.[29] Two of their most important groups of primary source materials are found in their newspaper collection and their manuscript collections. The BCAH is the home to the largest Texas newspaper collection in the world, which consists of over 4,500 different newspaper titles for Texas, southern US, and non-US papers. A large portion of the collection consists of Texas titles. These papers can provide a wealth of primary information concerning the Texas Rangers and their activities. However, it is always wise to be cautious when using material found in newspapers. One should try to verify any information found there with other possible sources. A large number of their newspapers are on microfilm, but many are found only in hard copy originals. An extensive index to the Texas newspapers helps the researcher in locating specific papers.[30] Many of the Texas titles have been digitized and can be found online at the Portal to Texas History, hosted by the University of North Texas Libraries.[31]

The manuscript collections at the BCAH are extensive and contain much information for the researcher. The vastness of these collections precludes going into detail about the various information that can be found. In this chapter only a handful of specific collections will be mentioned. Some of these were archival collections that appear in a number of previously published books relating to the Texas Rangers. One of the most utilized manuscript collections is that of the Walter Prescott Webb Papers. Webb's *The Texas Rangers: A Century of Frontier Defense*, published in 1935, was considered by most historians for decades as the definitive work on the Texas Rangers. Webb's papers consist of both primary and secondary materials. Some of the information contained in Webb's papers include research materials, articles, lectures, correspondence, business records, maps, typescripts, and photographs of many Texas Rangers. Many present-day Ranger historians have researched Webb's papers and have cited them in their works. Several of these historians include Collins in *A Crooked River*, Harris and Sadler in *Texas Rangers and the Mexican Revolution*, Utley's *Lone Star Lawmen*, Miller in *Texas Ranger John B. Jones*, and Weiss in *Yours to Command*. A finding aid to the Webb Papers can be found online.[32]

Another manuscript collection at the BCAH is the John S. "Rip" Ford Papers. The bulk of this collection consists of Ford's personal memoirs (1815–1892). In addition to the memoirs there is also a typescript copy of *John C. Hays in Texas* by Colonel John S. Ford. There are only several original documents of correspondence in this collection. Several Ranger historians who have used this collection at the BCAH include Moore in several of his volumes of *Savage Frontier*, Ivey in *The Ranger Ideal*, Cox in *Wearing the Cinco Peso*, Richard B. McCaslin in *Fighting Stock*, and Collins in his *Texas Devils*.[33] If the researcher cannot access this collection at the BCAH, printed copies of Ford's personal memoirs can be found in a number of places, including the Texas State Archives and the Haley Memorial Library and History Center in Midland.

Several other manuscript collections at the BCAH include the Edward Burleson Jr. Papers, the Ben and Henry Eustace McCulloch Family Papers, and the John Coffee Hays Collection. In these collections the researcher may find such records as original correspondence relating to family matters, military and Ranger service, journals, muster rolls, newspaper clippings, and reports.[34]

One final manuscript collection at the BCAH that will be mentioned in this chapter is the Roy Wilkinson Aldrich Papers. This collection contains a wealth of material relating to the early twentieth-century Texas Rangers. About one-quarter of the Aldrich Papers relate to the Texas Rangers and Aldrich's thirty-two-year career with that organization. The collection includes correspondence, scrapbooks, literary productions, printed materials, newspaper clippings, and a large person photograph collection. The guide to the Roy Wilkinson Aldrich Papers, 1858–1956, provides a much more detailed description of the collection of papers.[35] Several historians who have found important information in these records include Harris and Sadler in their book *Texas Rangers and the Mexican Revolution* and Utley in his volume two on the Texas Rangers, *Lone Star Lawmen*.

In addition to the Roy W. Aldrich Papers at the BCAH, there is also another collection of Aldrich's papers housed in the Archives of the Big Bend, located in the Bryan Wildenthal Memorial Library on the campus of Sul Ross State University in Alpine. The Aldrich Papers are extensive and contain, among other family and personal records, Ranger correspondence, appointments, rosters, case notes, newspaper clippings, and information on other Rangers. A number of Ranger historians have used these records to great advantage. Several of them include Harris and Sadler in *The Texas Rangers in Transition* and Mike Cox in *Time of the Rangers: Texas Rangers from 1900 to the Present.* A finding aid at the Archives of the Big Bend can provide more detailed information regarding the collection's holdings.[36] Another important manuscript collection found in the Archives of the Big Bend is that of E. E. Townsend. Townsend had served in Company E, Frontier Battalion, from 1891 until 1893, when he briefly held the title of deputy US marshal. From 1894 until 1899 he served as a US customs agent. He served again briefly with the Texas Rangers before becoming a ranch manager in 1900. He later served as sheriff of Brewster County from 1918 to 1924 and then was elected to the Texas Legislature in 1932, where he was instrumental in helping to create Big Bend National Park (BBNP). He served as commissioner of BBNP from 1947 until his death in 1948. For much of his life, Townsend had served in some capacity of law enforcement and continued to have contact with many other Rangers. His papers contain Ranger correspondence (1918–1941), newspaper clippings, scrapbooks, and memorabilia. This collection has been used by a number of Ranger historians, including Alexander in *Winchester Warriors* and Parsons in *Captain John R. Hughes*.[37]

Additional information regarding E. E. Townsend can be found among the various interviews housed at the Nita Stewart Haley Memorial Library and the J. Evetts Haley History Center in Midland.[38]

This institution contains a wealth of materials in the form of hundreds of interviews, photographs, and biographical files, many of which relate to Texas Rangers. One of the interviews collected by J. Evetts Haley was that of E. E. Townsend. Portions of this interview were used in Alexander's book *Winchester Warriors*. Alexander also used several interviews with Ira Aten and a number of others in writing his biography of Aten, *Rawhide Ranger*. The Haley Library also provided interviews and records on Robert G. "Bob" Goss for Cox's *Wearing the Cinco Peso* and Harris and Sadler in their book *Texas Rangers in Transition*. The interviews and papers on Jeff Milton are a part of the records at the Haley Library and were of great importance in J. Evetts Haley's biography *Jeff Milton: A Good Man with a Gun*.[39] Ira Aten was one of the early Rangers who was inducted into the Texas Ranger Hall of Fame. These records and interviews were also important to Ivey in his second volume of *The Ranger Ideal*. A few other names appearing in the index to interviews include B. P. Abbott, Dee Harkey, Bob Beverly, and Mrs. G. W. Arrington.[40]

One final source of primary Ranger records that will be discussed in this chapter is that of the West Texas Collection, housed in the Porter Henderson Library on the campus of Angelo State University in San Angelo.[41] Most modern-day historians who have written on twentieth-century Rangers have one thing in common: there is a noticeable lack of original Ranger reports and correspondence to be found in the endnotes of their works. In place of such records, the historians have relied upon one particular doctoral dissertation entitled "The Texas Rangers, 1919–1935: A Study in Law Enforcement," by James Randolph Ward.[42] In this dissertation are citations of hundreds of reports and correspondence for the Texas Rangers during the period of 1919–1935. When one searches for the original records, they do not seem to be found. One historian, Robert Utley, in the preface of his book *Lone Star Lawmen*, states that "as late as the 1960s, doctoral students used these records in the basement of the Department of Public Safety headquarters in Austin. They are no longer there, nor in the state archives, and all attempts to learn what happened to them have met with failure."[43] James Ward, even before his dissertation was finally approved, began teaching in the History Department at Angelo State and remained there until his death in 2006. In about 2013, at a historical conference, Dr. Harold Weiss and this writer were visiting with Suzanne Campbell, then the head of Special Collections and Programs with the West Texas Collection. We were discussing James Ward's dissertation and she mentioned that his papers were in their collections. At that time we were interested in the possibility of getting the Ward dissertation published. We decided on a trip to the library at Angelo State to check what materials might be found in his papers. Upon further inspection of the Ward Papers it was learned that all the reports and correspondence found cited in his dissertation, as well as many more records, were not totally lost. When Ward was working on his dissertation, it was a period before the advent of photocopiers and cell phones with photographic capabilities. Jim Ward had actually spent hours sitting in the basement of the Department of Public Safety's headquarters dictating all these records on reel-to-reel tapes. These tapes, among many other records that he had collected over his years of teaching, were deposited in the Special Collections at Angelo State. Most of these tapes have been transferred to compact discs because of the fragile condition of the old tapes. In addition to the correspondence that was on the tapes, Ward, along with Dr. Ben Procter and others at TCU, had conducted interviews with almost twenty Rangers and had these on tape as well. Some of the interviews were with such Rangers as Tom Hickman, Leo Bishop, J. Monroe Fox, Marvin "Red" Burton, E. A. "Dogie" Wright, W. W. Sterling, Martin Koonsman, and Alonzo Y. Allee.[44] One example of the tremendous importance of these records can be seen in the Harris and Sadler book *Texas Rangers in Transition.*

It is disappointing that more libraries, institutions, and repositories cannot be covered within the restrictions of the space constraints in this chapter. There are literally hundreds of places where primary sources for Texas Ranger research can be found. It seems that locating one source of materials will often lead to other sources. This is the thrill of the hunt.

Notes

1. The Texas State Library and Archives Commission is located in the Lorenzo de Zavala State Library and Archives Building at 1201 Brazos Street, Austin, TX 78701. The mailing address is Texas State Library and Archives Commission, PO Box 12927, Austin, TX 78711-2927. The telephone number is (512) 463-5455 and their website is https://www.tsl.texas.gov.
2. Online finding aids to the Processed State and Local Records can be found at https://tsl.texas.gov/arc/findingaids/recordsfindingaids.html.
3. An index to the Texas Adjutant General Department's Service Records (1836–1935) can be found at https://www.tsl.texas.gov/apps/arc/service/. It must be noted that not all men who served have service records on file.
4. Charles H. Harris III and Louis R. Sadler, *The Texas Rangers and the Mexican Revolution: The Bloodiest Decade, 1910–1920* (Albuquerque: University of New Mexico Press, 2004); Chuck Parsons, *Captain John R. Hughes, Lone Star Ranger* (Denton: University of North Texas Press, 2011); Stephen L. Moore, *Savage Frontier: Rangers, Riflemen, and Indian Wars in Texas*, 4 vols. (Denton: University of North Texas Press, 2002–2010); Bob Alexander and Donaly E. Brice, *Texas Rangers: Lives, Legend, and Legacy* (Denton: University of North Texas Press, 2017. The finding aid discussing an introduction to the military rolls in the Texas State Library can be found at https://txarchives.org/tslac/finding_aids/30075.xml. The finding aid for Reconstruction-Era military rolls (1865–1866 and 1870–1877) can be found online at https://txarchives.org/tslac/finding_aids/30074.xml.
5. Rick Miller, *Texas Ranger John B. Jones and the Frontier Battalion, 1874–1881* (Denton: University of North Texas Press, 2012); Harold J. Weiss Jr., *Yours to Command: The Life and Legend of Texas Ranger Captain Bill McDonald* (Denton: University of North Texas Press, 2009); Bob Alexander, *Whiskey River Ranger: The Old West Life of Baz Outlaw* (Denton: University of North Texas Press, 2016); Robert M. Utley, *Lone Star Justice: The First Century of the Texas Rangers* (New York: Oxford University Press, 2002).
6. Paul N. Spellman, *Captain John H. Rogers, Texas Ranger* (Denton: University of North Texas Press, 2008); Robert W. Stephens, *Captain George H. Schmitt: Texas Ranger* (Dallas: Robert W. Stephens, 2006).
7. For Allred, Colquitt, James and Miriam Ferguson, Moody, Neff, and Sterling, see Robert M. Utley, *Lone Star Lawmen: The Second Century of*

the Texas Rangers (New York: Oxford University Press, 2007); for Bell, Clark, Houston, Murrah, Pease, and Runnels, see Michael L. Collins, *Texas Devils: Rangers and Regulators on the Lower Rio Grande, 1846–1861* (Norman: University of Oklahoma Press, 2008); for Coke, Davis, Hamilton, Murrah, and Throckmorton, see Collins, *A Crooked River: Rustlers, Rangers, and Regulators on the Lower Rio Grande, 1861–1877* (Norman: University of Oklahoma Press, 2018); for Coke, Hubbard, and Ireland, see Frederick Wilkins, *The Law Comes to Texas: The Texas Rangers 1870-1901* (Austin: State House Press, 1999); for Bell, Houston, Pease, and Runnels, see Wilkins, *Defending the Borders: The Texas Rangers, 1848–1861* (Austin: State House Press, 2001); for Allred, James Ferguson, Miriam Ferguson, Moody, and Sterling, see Charles H. Harris III and Louis R. Sadler, *The Texas Rangers in Transition: From Gunfighters to Criminal Investigators, 1921–1935* (Norman: University of Oklahoma Press, 2019); for Hogg, Culberson, Sayers, Lanham and Campbell, see Weiss, *Yours To Command.*

8. Many of the finding aids to the Processed State and Local Records housed at the Texas State Archives can be found online at https://www.tsl.texas.gov/arc/findingaids/recordsfindingaids.html.

9. Bob Alexander, *Winchester Warriors: Texas Rangers of Company D, 1874–1901* (Denton: University of North Texas Press, 2009); David Johnson, *The Mason County "Hoo Doo" War, 1874–1902* (Denton: University of North Texas Press, 2006); Darren L. Ivey, *The Ranger Ideal: Texas Rangers in the Hall of Fame*, 3 vols. (Denton: University of North Texas, 2017–21); Paul N. Spellman, *Captain J. A. Brooks, Texas Ranger* (Denton: University of North Texas, 2007). These monthly returns and records of scouts were of particular importance to Bob Alexander in writing *Winchester Warriors* since he was compiling a complete history of one specific Frontier Battalion company (Company D).

10. Frederick Wilkins, *The Legend Begins: The Texas Rangers, 1823–1845* (Austin: State House Press, 1996); Wilkins, *The Law Comes to Texas: The Texas Rangers, 1870–1901* (Austin: State House Press, 1999). The finding aid for the Texas Ranger records at the State Archives that include quartermaster records can be found online at https://txarchives.org/tslac/finding_aids/30027.xml.

11. The online finding aid to the Republic of Texas military rolls can be found at https://txarchives.org/tslac/finding_aids/30072.xml.

12. Republic Claims index is found at https://www.tsl.texas.gov/arc/repclaims/repintro.html.

13. These claims have all been digitized and the researcher can access the records with a name search on keyword search at https://www.tsl.texas.gov/apps/arc/repclaims/.
14. An introduction to the Andrew Jackson Houston Collection can be found online at https://www.tsl.texas.gov/arc/ajhouston/introhelp.html. Mike Cox, *The Texas Rangers: Wearing the Cinco Peso, 1821–1900* (New York: Forge Books, 2008).
15. Access the Samuel Hamilton Walker Papers on the Texas Digital Archive at https://tsl.access.preservica.com/tda/manuscripts-collections/#walker. From here one may enter the actual records or access the online finding aid to the Walker Papers.
16. For accessing or learning more about the Convict Records Ledgers and Conduct Registers, go to https://www.tsl.texas.gov/arc/convict.html.
17. Ivey, *Ranger Ideal*, vol. 2; Weiss, *Yours to Command*; Alexander, *Whiskey River Ranger*; Alexander and Brice, *Texas Rangers*.
18. Utley, *Lone Star Justice*; Utley, *Lone Star Lawmen*; Wilkins, *Law Comes to Texas*; Spellman, *Captain John H. Rogers*.
19. The Canales Investigation of 1919 can be accessed online at https://www.tsl.texas.gov/treasures/law/index.html.
20. Benjamin Heber Johnson, *Revolution in Texas: How a Forgotten Rebellion and Its Bloody Suppression Turned Mexicans into Americans* (New Haven: Yale University Press, 2003); Monica Muñoz Martinez, *The Injustice Never Leaves You: Anti-Mexican Violence in Texas* (Cambridge, MA: Harvard University Press, 2018); and Doug J. Swanson, *Cult of Glory: The Bold and Brutal History of the Texas Rangers* (New York: Viking, 2020).
21. "Mission," *Texas Ranger Hall of Fame & Museum*, accessed March 29, 2024, https://www.texasranger.org/texas-ranger-museum/visit/our-mission/.
22. "Tobin & Anne Armstrong Texas Ranger Research Center," *Texas Ranger Hall of Fame & Museum*, accessed March 29, 2024, https://www.texasranger.org/Pages/Research-Center.
23. For on-site research the researcher needs to contact the staff at (254) 750-8631 between the hours of 9:00 a.m. to 3:00 p.m. on Mondays–Fridays (CST) or email the staff at info.texasranger.org. For services by mail, a Research Request Form may be obtained at https://www.texasranger.org/texas-ranger-museum/researching-rangers/research-a-ranger/.
24. Correspondence between Rusty Bloxom, research librarian, TRHF&M, to Donaly E. Brice, September 2, 2020.

25. Bloxom to Brice, September 2, 2020.

26. The oral histories can be accessed and read online at https://www. texasranger.org/texas-ranger-museum/history/oral-histories/.

27. M. T. Gonzaullas, Hamer family, and Tom Hickman in Harris and Sadler, *Texas Rangers in Transition*; Marvin "Red" Burton, Barry Caver, and Bob Prince in Utley, *Lone Star Lawmen*; Bob Alexander, *Old Riot, New Ranger: Captain Jack Dean, Texas Ranger and US Marshal* (Denton: University of North Texas Press, 2018).

28. Telephone conversation with Rusty Bloxom, research librarian, TRHF&M, September 1, 2020.

29. The Dolph Briscoe Center for American History is physically located at 2300 Red River Street, Austin, TX 78712. For questions, hours of operation, or location call (512) 495-4515. Their reference number is (512) 495-4166 (leave a voicemail). Reference request forms can be acquired at https://www.cah.utexas.edu/research/reference_help.php.

30. The Texas newspaper index can be found online at https:// briscoecenter.org/research/online-reference-tools/newspapers/ texas-newspapers-texas-county-town-index/.

31. Access the digitized newspapers at https://texashistory.unt.edu/search.

32. The Guide to the Walter Prescott Webb Papers can be found at https:// collections.briscoecenter.org/repositories/2/resources/382.

33. The guide to the John S. "Rip" Ford Papers is found online at https://txar-chives.org/utcah/finding_aids//01239.xml. Richard B. McCaslin, *Fighting Stock: John S. "Rip" Ford of Texas* (Fort Worth: TCU Press, 2011).

34. A guide to the Edward Burleson Jr. Papers can be found at https:// txarchives.org/utcah/finding_aids//01616.xml. The guide to the Ben and Henry Eustace McCulloch Family Papers can be found online at https://txarchives.org/utcah/finding_aids//00126.xml. The guide to the John Coffee Hays Collection can be accessed at https://txarchives.org/ utcah/finding_aids//01769.xml.

35. The guide to the Roy Wilkinson Aldrich Papers can be accessed at https://txarchives.org/utcah/finding_aids/00048.xml.

36. The Archives of the Big Bend is located in the Bryan Wildenthal Memorial Library on the campus of Sul Ross State University. They can be reached at (432) 837-8123 and their USPS shipping address is PO Box C-109, Alpine, TX 79832. Their USP address is 400 N. Harrison Street, Alpine, TX 79832. A guide to the Roy W. Aldrich Papers at Sul Ross can be found online at http://libit.sulross. edu/archives/NewWebSite/findingaids/A365_Roy%20Aldrich%20 Collection_updated.pdf.

37. For more information on E. E. Townsend and a guide to his papers, see libit.sulross.edu/archives/NewWebSite/findingaids/T747_EE%20 Townsend%20Papers_updated.pdf. Bob Alexander, *Winchester Warriors: Texas Rangers of Company D, 1874–1901* (Denton: University of North Texas Press, 2009); and Chuck Parsons, *Captain John R. Hughes, Lone Star Ranger* (Denton: University of North Texas Press, 2011).

38. The Nita Stewart Haley Memorial Library and the J. Evetts Haley History Center is located at 1805 W. Indiana Avenue, Midland, TX 78701. An archivist is available by appointment and can be contacted by phone at (432) 682-5785 or by e-mail at archives@haleylibrary.com. To find a listing of other interviews online, go to https//haleylibrary.com/j-evetts-haley-collection/ and scroll down to Series II—Research files and click on "JEH Interviews II, IX Rev. 9-08."

39. Bob Alexander, *Rawhide Ranger, Ira Aten: Enforcing Law on the Texas Frontier* (Denton: University of North Texas Press, 2011); J. Evetts Haley, *Jeff Milton: A Good Man with a Gun* (Norman: University of Oklahoma Press, 1949).

40. In addition to the interviews of Ira Aten and Mrs. G. W. Arrington, other records for Aten and George W. Arrington can be found (1) in the Research Center of the Panhandle Plains Historical Museum in Canyon; a telephone number for reference assistance is (806) 651-2254; (2) at the Texas Ranger Hall of Fame and Museum in Waco; to discuss your needs or make an appointment, call (254) 750-8631; (3) throughout the Adjutant General records at the Archives and Information Services Division of the Texas State Library and Archives Commission; to contact the Archives go to https://www.tsl.texas.gov/contact or call (512) 463-5455.

41. For information concerning the West Texas Collection, contact West Texas Collection, Porter Henderson Library, ASU Station #11013, San Angelo, TX 76909. Their telephone number is (325) 942-2222 and their e-mail address is library@angelo.edu.

42. James Randolph Ward, "The Texas Rangers, 1919-1935: A Study of Law Enforcement" (PhD diss., Texas Christian University, 1972).

43. Utley, *Lone Star Lawmen*, xi.

44. Information provided by Suzanne Campbell, a colleague and personal friend of James Ward. Suzanne Campbell to Harold Weiss, April 10, April 11, and April 16, 2013.

Chapter 2

From Austin to Hollywood

Walter Prescott Webb, King Vidor, and *The Texas Rangers*

Light Townsend Cummins

T wo individuals did much during the mid-1930s to bring the story of the Texas Rangers to the American people and especially to those in Texas: Walter Prescott Webb (1888–1963) and King Vidor (1894–1982). They set in stone a congratulatory and praise-filled characterization of the Rangers that has become indelibly etched into the popular culture of Texas. They both approached the Rangers as examples of unquestioned frontier heroism, a viewpoint that can still be seen today across the state in the minds of some Texans. Webb was a historian at the University of Texas in Austin while Vidor was one of Hollywood's most respected motion picture directors. Webb and Vidor worked in tandem during the decade of the Great Depression to disseminate an extremely positive myth and mystique about the Texas Rangers, one that gave the organization a place in the historical pantheon of American nobility.

Walter Prescott Webb's contribution to Ranger history began several decades before that of King Vidor. Webb enjoys a special place in the roster of Texas historians as one of the legendary figures of the historical profession in the Lone Star State. Affiliated with the University of Texas at Austin for most of his adult life, first as a student and then as a long-time faculty member, Webb served the cause of Texas history in a variety of important ways. He edited the *Southwestern Historical Quarterly*, served as director of the Texas State Historical Association, wrote a shelfful of books and scholarly articles, and supervised a considerable number of master's theses and doctoral dissertations. He also conceptualized and created the *Handbook of Texas*. As president of the American Historical Association, he significantly legitimized the study of Texas and Western frontier history in the eyes of historians across the rest of the nation. By the time of his passing in 1963, his accomplishments had become synonymous with Texas history itself, a reality recognized today by the fact that an important lecture series, a historical association for young people, and a building on the University of Texas campus all bear his name. Some of his books remain in print today, sixty years after his passing.[1]

Webb became the great historical champion—perhaps the greatest ever—of the Texas Rangers as a frontier law enforcement organization. He can in that regard accurately be called the original dean of Texas Ranger historians. He saw them as a virtuous and beneficial group that helped to eradicate lawlessness from the state while providing it with a commendable uniqueness. Researching and writing about the Rangers became for a Webb a continuing interest during his lifetime. He always viewed them within an extremely favorable framework of analysis. This was markedly the case regarding his 1935 landmark book dealing with their history, *The Texas Rangers: A Century of Frontier Defense*. In it he explicitly manifested an idealized view of the Rangers as the force that civilized the state for Anglo frontiersmen, therein evoking a romanticism first seen in the book's opening pages. "In order to win, or even to survive, they combined the fighting qualities of three races," he wrote. "In the words of an observer a Texas Ranger could ride like a Mexican, trail like an Indian, shoot like a Tennessean, and fight like a devil."[2] Webb's very favorable interpretive orientation accurately reflected the historical viewpoint of the Texas Rangers held by most, if not all, Anglo-Texans in the state at the time of its 1935 publication, a viewpoint that retained validity in many quarters well into the closing decades of the twentieth century. The book's stature was such that President Lyndon B. Johnson wrote the forward for the 1965 reissue of the volume two years after Webb's death.

Webb's interest the Rangers began when he researched and wrote his 1920 MA thesis at the University of Texas on the history of their participation in the Mexican War. He employed historical sources available to him in Austin library and archival repositories, especially official records in the state archives.[3] Webb's marked ability to conduct solid research, along with his fluid writing style, placed the quality of his master's thesis well above similar undertakings by less talented neophyte authors. The narrative of his thesis follows a straightforward chronological organization that gives survey-level attention to the main exploits of those Texans who served in the Ranger Corps of General Zachary Taylor's army during its invasion of Mexico. Like much of the historical writing of that era, Webb's thesis presents a very factual exposition of historical events and occurrences with little overt interpretation or conceptual analysis. Nevertheless, two viewpoints permeate the thesis, and these can be seen by modern readers as examples of Webb's approach to writing about the Rangers during all of his subsequent historical career. First, Webb saw Texas Rangers as true heroes. Heroism thus became a lens through which he viewed their history. This can be seen, for example, in his treatment of Samuel Walker's activities in Mexico. "Captain Walker," he wrote, "in the first engagement of the war, had set an example of heroic service for all Texas Rangers to emulate, and had gained a reputation for the organization which every member felt constrained to uphold."[4] Second, Webb's general presentation of Mexico and the Mexican people had a subtle jingoistic, if not condemnatory, cast to it. He wrote in the opening pages of his thesis, "From long experience with Mexico, the Texans had come to distrust every word and deed of the race." He continued this orientation by explaining that "the affair at the Alamo had taught them to expect no mercy; the Massacre of Fannin's men in violation of all law had taught them distrust of Mexican honor; the fate of the Mier prisoners in Perote prison had taught them never to surrender; and the victory of San Jacinto taught them contempt for Mexican valor."[5] Webb did not offer counterbalances to these viewpoints in his thesis.

Throughout the 1920s Webb wrote several dozen popular articles dealing with the Rangers for magazines and newspapers. He published the first of these in April of 1921, a piece about the Texas Rangers for the magazine supplement of the *Dallas Morning News* and for which he received a check in payment. This feature article in the *Morning News* continued the praiseworthy view of the Rangers with which Webb had approached them in his thesis. "They were, in a sense," he told his newspaper readers "indigenous to Texas, having sprung from the soil made fertile by the blood of their kinsmen, and they soon became the frontier fighting force par excellence of the world." Webb styled the Texas Rangers as "the Anglo-American solution to the problem of the frontier."[6] The sale of this article to the Dallas newspaper determined him to continue researching and writing short pieces on various aspects of Ranger history, which he did regularly over the decade of the 1920s as time permitted. Webb preferred newspapers and magazines oriented toward the general public as the outlets for these articles, all of which were nonetheless based on diligent historical research.[7] As he later related, "I went back to the dusty archives in the state capitol and grubbed deeper into the records; I began to run the files of the newspapers and never ceased until I covered almost a century."[8] Webb approached his gathering of information about the Rangers in a methodical manner. Not only did he continue to read archival materials about them but he also sought out active and retired Rangers, engaging them in correspondence about their experiences and knowledge of the force. He collected various materials relating to the Rangers, including old photographs from some of its retired members. Webb contacted representatives of other law enforcement organizations, such as the Canadian Northwest Mounted Police, in order to draw comparisons between them and the Rangers.[9] He also conducted what might be called "field observations" of the Rangers in action across Texas while performing their law enforcement duties. He bought a new automobile for the purpose of making these trips away from Austin, noting years later, "One purpose I had in mind in buying the Ford was to make a trip along the Mexican border to visit the Ranger camps and see how the Rangers operated under about all that was left of frontier conditions." Webb visited a number Ranger encampments over the ensuing years, accompanied by various members of the organization, including R. W. Aldrich and E. E. Townsend. In that regard the historian took special interest in observing Ranger activities in the Big Bend area along the Rio Grande border—then, as now, one of the most unsettled areas of Texas.[10]

Publication of Webb's magazine articles dealing with the Texas Rangers during the 1920s had to compete with his time-consuming academic duties at the university, which involved both his teaching activities and his efforts to gain tenure on the faculty. During the late 1920s, he also turned his attention to writing another book, *The Great Plains*, which was published in 1931 by Ginn and Company. Finishing that title gave Webb the opportunity to turn his scholarly efforts back to his interest in writing a book-length history of the Texas Rangers. He thus began work on that manuscript about 1930. Webb's knowledge that Texas would be celebrating the centennial of its independence from Mexico six years later during 1936 also served as a motivation for this project. He believed the centennial celebration would be a propitious time for publication of his book on the Rangers. Webb did not see this as a difficult deadline to meet. He had already amassed over the years a considerable number of notes, copies of documents, and other historical sources, while also having corresponded and talked with many people knowledgeable about Ranger history. Webb accordingly embarked on a plan of action that would enable him to continue his travel to places he would mention in the book, meet with members of the Rangers, and observe their law enforcement activities firsthand. In the early 1930s, he attended meetings of the Former Texas Rangers Association, again toured the Mexican border and the Big Bend with active Rangers, and closely observed their activities. "By riding with the Rangers," one of Webb's biographers later noted, "sharing their campfires, and drinking their camp coffee, he received a special understanding of the contemporary Ranger force." Webb wrote with focus and dedication during 1932 and 1933. He was a person who worked best during the late nighttime; those who knew him regularly saw him into the early hours of the morning at the twenty-four-hour Night Hawk Restaurant on Austin's Guadalupe Street, sitting in a back booth drinking coffee and writing.[11]

Webb had finished the manuscript by mid-1934 and sought a publisher. Always oriented toward the general reader, he preferred placing it with a commercial publishing firm instead of seeking an academic press. A trip to New York City brought him to the editorial offices of Houghton Mifflin, where he found that publishing house had much interest in bringing his book into print. Liking what they read, the New York editorial staff directed Webb to Boston, where he met with Ferris Greenslet at his home. Greenslet was the chief literary advisor for Houghton Mifflin and only he could grant final approval for any book the firm published. Webb and Greenslet negotiated a contract on the spot, and Webb turned the manuscript over to Houghton Mifflin for publication. The book arrived in bookstores across the country during September of 1935 to great popular and scholarly acclaim.[12] Newspaper reviews raved about the book's readability and its significant examination of Ranger history. Noted historian William C. Binkley of Vanderbilt University gushed about the volume. "From the point of view of the historian," he wrote in the *Journal of Southern History*, "the study is important not only for the light which it throws on a particular institution, but also for new clues on various phases of American history in general." The Texas historian Rupert Richardson expressed his absolutely favorable opinion: "Wisely conceived, well organized, profusely illustrated, and beautifully written, the book is a fitting monument to a great institution."[13]

By the scholarly standards of the 1930s, *The Texas Rangers* constituted a tour de force in the world of academic history when it appeared. It contained 585 pages and offered a comprehensive discussion about the history of the Texas Rangers, beginning with the arrival of Anglo-American settlers during the 1820s and concluding with Ranger Captain Frank Hamer's 1934 ambush of Bonnie and Clyde. Its final chapter (entitled "Adventures with a Ranger Historian") was autobiographical, recounting Webb's experiences traveling with the Rangers and relating some of his personal encounters with them. All of the chapters, especially those dealing with the nineteenth century, contain factual discussions of Ranger history in a straightforward manner that presents a very readable narrative, although some of Webb's language might be considered somewhat archaic and stilted by today's standards. In general, the cast of the book might best be described as storytelling instead of academic analysis. That is because Webb constructed his narrative by lacing together anecdotes to form his presentation of Ranger history. There are few places in the book— hardly any, in fact—where he engages in an interpretive discussion that sets the Rangers into a larger philosophical or historiographical context. In that regard he consistently avoids offering any negative judgments about their activities or the events he discusses. Indeed, the fundamental assumptions in the book probably differed very little from those held by the Rangers whom he researched or knew personally.[14]

Given this approach, Webb's book might best be understood by the modern reader as the Anglo-American–based history of the Texas Rangers. This interpretive orientation is today most deficient regarding Webb's prejudiced treatment of Mexican people, although in places Native Americans were accorded no greater approbation. It is therefore not surprising that present-day scholars and historians have found much to criticize in this book. As Webb biographer Michael L. Collins has noted, he "admittedly constructed a narrative woven around a single fabric—the heroic deeds of Anglo-Texan heroes. In so doing, he failed to acknowledge a more diverse and multicultural weave of Texas history." "The book's most significant shortcoming by far is its racist rhetoric," the late Don Graham has recently written about its context. Graham further notes, "In the process of lionizing the Rangers, it whitewashes their excesses, offering excuses and justifications for illegal actions such as torture and murder." Gregory Curtis, writing in a 1999 *Texas Monthly* article, offered what might be the most biting criticism of the book made to date. "He was so awed by the Rangers," Curtis observed about Webb, "that he treated even their plunder, torture, and murder along the Mexican border with such equanimity and even admiration that the book becomes unreadable."[15] Webb and a majority of white Texans alive during the 1930s, as a matter of course, would have been oblivious to these modern, harsh commentaries about the book, all of which would have fallen outside their concepts of the world and how they perceived the realities of their life. Theirs was a time period of history when legal segregation and rampant white racial discrimination against ethnic minorities proved the order of the day. Accordingly, the book today must be approached by modern readers as an artifact of that era now reflecting obsolete values regarding race and race relations.

These present-day criticisms, of course, lay decades in the future at the time Webb's book was published in 1935. Following Webb's desire Houghton Mifflin marketed *The Texas Rangers* as a trade book instead of an academic volume. Such would prove significant for him, because during the early era of sound motion pictures, the California movie studios routinely purchased screen rights to a continuing stream of commercial trade books upon which to potentially base their scripts. The film companies employed special acquisition agents in New York City for this purpose, and they regularly purchased the options to more books than could ever be brought to the screen. Under these circumstances Houghton Mifflin sold the film rights to the Paramount Pictures Corporation, which at that time had a preference for making Westerns. Adolph Zukor, president of Paramount Pictures, accordingly acquired the film rights for *The Texas Rangers* in late 1935 for $11,000, 80 percent of which went to Webb as the author. Zukor hoped the film would be especially profitable for the studio because he planned to release it the following year, coinciding with the Texas Centennial Celebration of 1936. It would therefore be filmed as an A-level first-run picture, and, as such, it would enjoy much greater status than the majority of B-level Western pictures being made at the time. Studio executives provided a shooting budget of $600,000, an extravagant sum during the Depression, and approved on-location shooting away from Southern California for the out-of-doors segments, a rare occurrence reserved only for important pictures. William LeBaron, head of production at Paramount, assigned the picture to one of its staff directors, King Vidor, who had already established himself as an important figure in the film community.[16]

King Wallis Vidor was a native Texan, a fact that qualified him in the minds of Paramount executives to direct the picture. He had already shot films on location in Texas, most notably the critically and commercially successful *The Big Parade*, filmed in 1927 at Kelly Field in San Antonio. Born in Galveston on February 8, 1894, Vidor was the grandson of Hungarian immigrants who had settled there to build a fortune in the lumber business and had become wealthy in the process. The Texas town of Vidor bears his family name. He was for a while a boarding student at Peacock Military Academy in San Antonio, later followed by schools in Galveston. Vidor developed an interest in motion pictures from an early age, including making an amateur film about the then-recent Galveston hurricane of 1900. Forsaking the family lumber business, he worked as a projectionist at Galveston's Globe Theater during his teenage years. After high school he started making movies commercially, eventually going to Houston, where he organized a nascent film company called Hotex Pictures, named after the city and the state, and enjoyed some financial success with several small films. Then, at the age of 19, Vidor decided to resettle in Hollywood and make his career there. Interested in production rather than acting, he first worked as a cameraman and screenwriter, in the process meeting and befriending many pioneers of the motion picture industry, including D. W. Griffith and Charlie Chaplin, the latter of whom became a lifelong friend. Vidor felt he had a special calling for his work. "I see the hand of Fate calling me to reform the world," he wrote in his diary as a young man at age 20, and "I will start with the movies." Vidor directed his first film in 1919 and quickly rose to become one of the most respected directors in Hollywood.[17]

The possibility exists that no Paramount executive had read Walter Webb's book about the Texas Rangers when the company purchased the film options in 1935, especially since such acquisitions often came as part of relatively automatic, routine transactions with publishing houses. King Vidor, of course, read the book closely once he became the film's director, learning in the process that it was a traditional history monograph without a storyline suited in any way to the screen as audience entertainment. That would have to change. Starting during the holiday season of 1935 and into the New Year, Vidor began brainstorming a narrative structure that could hold the film together. This would involve creating fictional characters around which the entire script could be oriented. Then, once those connecting threads had been established, Vidor planned to blend vignettes and historical occurrences from Webb's book into the action sequences of the film. He turned for assistance to his wife, Elizabeth "Betsy" Hill, who had years of experience working in studio script departments. They immediately decided to limit the time frame of the movie to the two decades after the Civil War while Webb's book began earlier and covered into the twentieth century. Thereafter, Vidor and Hill spent over a month considering various strategies and, by early February of 1936, they had a story line ready for script writing. There would be five main fictional characters. The central protagonists would be Jim Hawkins and his comedic sidekick, Wahoo Jones, who begin the film as outlaws in league with Sam, the "Polka Dot" bandit, along with a Major Bailey as the commander of Texas Ranger Frontier Battalion D. The fictionalized Hawkins, Jones, Sam, and Bailey became the main characters appearing throughout the film, with the addition of Bailey's daughter, Amanda, who would be the picture's love interest for Hawkins. Bandits Jim Hawkins and Wahoo Jones would join the Rangers while resting from their criminal activities in order to get inside information useful for the future robberies to be undertaken in concert with their partner, Sam. However, as they move from adventure to adventure while feigning as Texas Rangers, Hawkins and Jones become imbued with the high-minded noble goals of the organization, motivated along the way by preachy dialogue offered by Major Bailey. In the end, after a series of complicated plot turnings, the two leave their outlaw past behind and become committed, true Texas Rangers, abandoning their association with Sam the bandit. They instead become determined to bring their former outlaw partner to justice. Jim and Wahoo begin the movie as outlaws and end it as Ranger heroes.[18]

Once this general story line had been established, Vidor enlisted the services of Louis Stevens, an accomplished screenwriter, who would produce the dialogue and stage directions for the final shooting script. As a young man, Stevens had been a protégé of the famed adventure author Jack London. He enjoyed a Hollywood reputation as an accomplished "script doctor" who could render almost any story idea into what was needed for a shootable film. A native of Lithuania, he had come to the United States as a young man, anglicized his name, and been working as a screenwriter for almost twenty years. Stevens later told *New York Times* reporter Idwal Jones he had signed on to the project because of his special fondness for Western pictures, observing "the old west is gone forever but, on the screen, it will never die out."[19] He collaborated with Vidor and Hill in producing the screen-ready script. Vidor began casting even before the script was finished. He secured Gary Cooper to play the role of Ranger Jim Hawkins. A modern reading of the script gives rise to the suspicion that some of the laconic, low-key dialogue given to Hawkins in the film came from Vidor's assumption Cooper would play that part. Film comedian and musical comedy star Jack Oakie signed on as Wahoo Jones, while Lloyd Nolan, then at the start of a lengthy acting career in motion pictures, took the role of Sam, the "Polka Dot" bandit. Veteran character actor Edward Ellis assumed the part of Major Bailey, while Jean Parker played his daughter, Amanda.[20]

The Vidor/Hill/Stevens script raises an interesting question: Was the motion picture faithful and accurate to Walter P. Webb's book?

Critics at the time, and those who have written on this question over the last seventy-five years, have generally taken the position that the film and the book were not much alike.[21] Both were indeed very different in one respect—namely, the film's overarching narrative involving fictional characters created by Vidor and Hill, none of whom appear in Webb's book. Much of the movie's plot revolves around these dramatic characters. The picture focuses on their changing relationships as they interact with each other, all the while evoking emotional responses from the audience as part of film's drama. There are, however, two different, intertwined narratives embodied in the film. The first, on an overt level, involves these fictional characters. The second narrative, however, takes place in those parts of the movie that ignore the main actors, instead centering on the activities and exploits of the Texas Rangers themselves. Each of these two narrative themes constitute approximately 50 percent of the picture's total running time. The film segments given to the parts of the movie relating to the activities of the Texas Ranger force, which sometimes include Vidor's fictional characters for dramatic effect, has content that bears remarkable similarity to the book and constitutes a mirror image of its organizational structure. The finished film has four major segments that deal explicitly with events involving the Rangers: an attempt to stop cattle rustling along the Rio Grande, the Rangers fighting in an Indian War, Rangers implementing lawful public order in Kimble County, Texas, and, finally, the Rangers' efforts to bring Sam "the Polka Dot" bandit to justice. Webb's book—starting with the chapter on McNelly's command of the Rangers, followed by the one on the Las Cuevas War, then the Mason County War, and, finally, the chapter detailing with the outlaw Sam Bass—corresponds exactly to the same topics developed in the film and unfolds in exactly the same order. Moreover, the script appropriated specific occurrences and anecdotes dealing with Ranger exploits directly from the book, although doing so in a general way without providing the actual names, the real locations, or any exact historical identifications. It can therefore be said the fictional characters Vidor invented for the film served as narrative devices that strung together a series of screen adaptations about Ranger historical activities taken directly from Webb's book.

Vidor also began selecting on-location sites away from Southern California for the outdoor, Western-themed segments. He had a special problem in that regard. In his opinion Texas did not have a place well-suited for filming for a variety of reasons except for the existence of suitable background scenery of an authentic nature. Outdoor location filming in the 1930s involved significant logistical and technical considerations, which few places in Texas could easily meet. These included ready access to railroad lines for transportation of people, cumbersome movie equipment, and unwieldy electrical generators. The on-location crew and actors also needed suitable hotels and food services in an urbanized area still conveniently close to rural landscapes for filming, along with the local availability of extras for background parts, which for this picture included large numbers of Native Americans. Prior to the use of Panchromatic cameras and portable sound equipment, out-of-doors filming demanded using unwieldly equipment in bright sunlight, with some clouds, but not too many, needed for cinematographic effect, along with predictably good weather free from rain or storms, but with the temperature being not too hot or too cold for the comfort of the film crew and actors. The prevalence of spring thunderstorms in many parts of Texas constituted a special problem of some significance for location filming in that state. Santa Fe and Gallup, New Mexico, however, had all of the attributes that Vidor sought. Gallup, once sound pictures had arrived, had by 1936 already become a favorite location for shooting a number of Western films, with its popularity continuing into the 1960s. Vidor, in fact, had already filmed on location at Gallup, shooting the film *Billy the Kid* there in 1930.[22] These New Mexico filming locations would give *The Texas Rangers* a decidedly New Mexican look, with craggy mountains, lots of juniper and piñon trees, and expansive vistas of scrub land not evocative of Texas in the least. However, this proved of little concern to Vidor, who showed his appreciation for filming sites in the state by giving New Mexico governor Clyde Tingley a small part in the picture.[23]

By April 1936 Vidor was ready to move the picture into production. Over one hundred actors and crew members arrived in Gallup on the twenty-first of that month ready to begin work. They traveled on a special eight-car train that also carried all of their equipment. He brought along with him noted cinematographer Edward Cronjager, one of the most respected such specialists in Hollywood. Belonging to a famous family of cinematographers—including a father, a brother, and an uncle—he specialized in out-of-doors filming involving complicated camera setups to seamlessly shoot large groups of people in rapid motion.[24] Cronjager's participation gave the completed film an artistic backdrop and polished visual sophistication not often seen in Western pictures. Second Unit Director Otho Lovering had already been on hand in Gallup for several weeks to organize several hundred Zuni from their pueblo south of Gallup for segments of the picture involving battles between the Rangers and their Native American adversaries. Gary Cooper, however, was no longer participating in the picture because a commitment to another film prevented him from being in *The Texas Rangers*. At the last minute, Paramount provided one of its contract players, Fred MacMurray, to take Cooper's place as the main protagonist, Jim Hawkins. MacMurray was at the start of what would be a long career as an actor, having already played the lead in several successful movies. Vidor began filming the day after arriving in Gallup by participating in an unusual publicity stunt. Texas governor James V. Allred would then be speaking at a noon banquet being held at a Dallas hotel. A dedicated telephone connection was established between the Dallas hotel and the on-location site near Gallup so Allred could converse with those on the set. The governor would "direct" the actors in the first filmed scene of the movie while standing at the podium of the banquet room dais. While the audience in the Dallas hotel ballroom watched, Allred discussed the scene with those on the set in Gallup as they traded dramatic impressions. At the appropriate time, Allred proclaimed "action" and the scene began as the cameras in New Mexico rolled for the first time, setting the picture in motion.[25]

Vidor and his crew remained in Gallup for several weeks and then moved to Santa Fe for additional exterior shooting at nearby Fort Burgwin. The filming activities in New Mexico became the subject of a tremendous publicity campaign, generated both by Paramount Pictures and the management of the Texas Centennial Celebration. Trans World Airlines, with great fanfare since long distance passenger air travel was still in its infancy, flew one of its DC-3 flagships filled with reporters, movie critics, and columnists to Gallup to spend several days on location. Dozens of magazine articles and newspaper stories about *The Texas Rangers* movie blanketed the nation during the weeks that followed. The National Broadcasting Company arranged for a program to be relayed simultaneously from several filming sites around Gallup to its central transmitter in New York City for a nationwide broadcast live over its entire radio network, a technical feat involving battery-powered shortwave transmissions from remote locations, which had never before been attempted. [26] This broadcast proved so successful that NBC decided to invest in additional shortwave radio relay equipment, a decision it would soon thereafter turn to advantage when it shifted these sets to Europe for reporting on the growing war crisis there. Although he never visited Gallup during the filming, Governor Allred followed up his directorial debut by awarding commissions as honorary Texas Rangers to Vidor and all of the main cast members while McKinley County, New Mexico, made them deputy sheriffs.[27]

Much of the publicity for the film focused on young people across Texas, a target audience Paramount Pictures had identified as a lucrative one already attuned to Western films as a favorite genre. In cooperation with the General Mills Company, once the film was debuted, some theaters across the state gave free matinee admission to any child who presented a box top from Kellogg's Corn Flakes. The Paramount Theater in Abilene would hold special "box top" screenings for young people who wanted to take advantage of this offer.[28] While the picture was filming in Gallup, William A. Webb, the director of the Central Texas Centennial Celebration in Dallas, sponsored an essay competition directed to some thirty thousand Boy Scouts across the state. Participants would write an essay about the historical importance of the Rangers and submit it to a committee of judges. Any scout who submitted an entry would receive an autographed picture of Fred MacMurray, while the winner would be awarded a free trip to Fair Park in Dallas to attend the centennial celebration along with a deluxe, autographed copy of Webb's book and twenty-five dollars contributed by King Vidor. Louis Stall, a Big Spring Boy Scout, won the contest with a five-hundred-word essay glorifying the history of the Texas Rangers. He and his family became special guests of Vidor at the premier of the movie when it was held in Dallas.[29]

Location filming in New Mexico ended in May 1936. The entire cast and crew returned to Hollywood, where they worked into July shooting interior scenes of the picture on specially constructed sets at the Paramount Studios. Thereafter, Vidor supervised the editing department in assembling the final screen version of the picture, adding background music and sound effects to the finished product. It was at this point he appended two segments to the beginning and ending of the picture, respectively. These additions would provide many audience members, especially in Texas, with their most emotional moments while they viewed the movie: an introductory dedication and an epilogue. Both of these emotive, spoken narratives appeared over the visual backdrop of a troop of Rangers riding horseback along a mountain trail, accompanied by the rousing music of a marching song with lively lyrics especially composed for the film. Sam Coslow, one of Paramount's in-house composers, wrote "The Texas Ranger Song" which provided the musical theme for the movie. It quickly became identified with the Texas Rangers, used later in other Paramount films while it also proved a staple of marching bands across the Lone Star State for years afterward.[30]

Vidor engaged noted voice actor and radio announcer Gayne Whitman to read the film's stirring introduction and epilogue. These remain of interest to historians today because they provided a concise exposition of absolute clarity regarding the main theme of both Webb's book and Vidor's motion picture. As the opening credits ended and the martial music rose to crescendo, Whitman dramatically proclaimed in the most stentorian of tones: "Throughout their history, the Rangers have been men of exceptional character, unyielding courage, rare physical endurance, hard riding, fast shooting, their service was to a state they loved, for an ideal they were willing to give up their lives, and gladly." Just before the rolling of the final credits at the end of the film, as the images of the Rangers riding along in synchronization to the marching music again reappeared on the screen, Whitman intoned elegantly to the audience, "Unsung though their names may be in future years, it shall be known that in the turbulent years of a state's transformation, it was their deeds of individual sacrifice, their acts of dauntless courage, that made possible the changing of a lawless frontier into a civilized land. These are the men called Texas Rangers—molded in the crucible of heroic struggle, guardians of the frontier, makers of the peace."[31]

Vidor finished his editing work in early August and sent a print to the studio's corporate office in New York City for final review. Paramount Pictures invited Webb to New York to attend a special advanced screening prior to the film's general release. The historian liked what he saw, holding the opinion that it had both strengths and weaknesses, which he later shared with a reporter from Austin's *Daily Texan*. All in all he felt it was "a very excellent production." "It is not a great one" Webb related, "but is far above the average Western picture." In particular, he found the scenery "grand" and felt the producers had put "art into the picture." He admitted much of the storyline relating to the principal actors had little relationship to his book. "The different episodes," he observed about the treatment accorded the Rangers, "are based on incidents in the book, but are all changed to an extent." This apparently did not bother him, as he felt "nobody but the author and a few others will see the difference." He did congratulate King Vidor for keeping Jean Parker's role as female love interest to a bare minimum since the historian apparently did not see screen romance as vital for understanding the Texas Rangers. All in all Webb had a rather magnanimous attitude about the translation of his book into a motion picture, explaining "the producers had to satisfy the public in all parts of the country and other countries." Two aspects of the picture, however, did not prove to his liking. First, Webb took mild umbrage that the two main characters played by Fred MacMurray and Jack Oakie began the picture as outlaws and stagecoach robbers before turning to the good side and becoming Texas Rangers. Second, and perhaps more illustrative about Webb, was his concern that the picture had dropped all mention of Ranger law enforcement activities dealing with Mexican people, a part of the history highlighted in the book and that he believed to have been historically significant. Vidor, in attempting to mollify Webb about this, enlisted the Paramount Pictures legal department for the purpose of explaining to him "that border scenes of the Rangers fighting Mexicans could not be produced because of the likelihood of arousing national displeasure in Mexico and other places," an explanation that the historian accepted.[32]

Paramount Pictures held the official world premiere of the film at the Majestic Theater in Dallas on August 21, 1936, several days before its general release across the nation. This gala premier included appearances by King Vidor, Jean Parker, and Lloyd Nolan. Governor Allred was on hand as well at the theater, having proclaimed Texas Ranger week in honor of the premier. The two United States senators from Texas, Morris Sheppard and Tom Connally, could also be found among the special guests along with officials from the Texas Centennial celebration. A band played "The Eyes of Texas" while Texas Ranger Captain Leonard Pack rode his horse into the lobby after leading a formal parade down the street to the doors of the theater. "The front of the theater," the *Dallas Morning News* reported, "was a blaze of floodlights" while "photographers darted back and forth snapping pictures and a battery of Paramount newsreel cameras recorded the

events on celluloid." Several radio networks broadcast the festivities
to dozens of stations across Texas over statewide hookups. Once all
of the dignitaries and special invitees had found their seats in the
theater, Dallas mayor George Sergeant introduced King Vidor who,
by all accounts, gave a stirring speech in praise of both Texas and of
the Rangers. "I have made many pictures, for various reasons," he
told the admiring audience, "but this is one I wanted to make, simply
because as a native Texan I wished to produce a film I could be proud
of." Vidor and the other Hollywood personalities spent the next day
touring the Texas Centennial celebration at Fair Park.[33]

For reasons unknown to him, Webb did not receive an invitation to
attend the gala premier in Dallas, a slight that bothered him for many
years thereafter, as he believed that he should have been invited.[34]
From Webb's perspective, therefore, the Austin premiere of *The Texas
Rangers* on November 20, 1936, constituted the major public debut of
the film for him, although he had already attended the advance private
screening in New York City. This Austin film event coincided with the
grand opening of a new theater on Guadalupe Street at Twenty-Fourth
Street: the Varsity. This art-deco style, state-of-the-art film venue had
resulted from the efforts of Karl Hoblitzelle, head of the Interstate
Theater Circuit based in Dallas, who had long been a supporter of the
University of Texas and would eventually serve on its board of regents.
Hoblitzelle built his new theater across the street from the campus and
chose to open it with King Vidor's picture. Newspapers heralded the
Varsity as one of the finest suburban move theaters in the nation.[35]
The Austin premier no doubt captured the attention of every person in
the city and at the university because it involved much civic celebration
coupled to a Hollywood-style publicity campaign. The opening night
saw Guadalupe Street teeming with people who watched the dignitaries
arrive and give live radio interviews before entering the theater.
Governor Allred was once again in the audience, along with Walter
Webb, most high-ranking administrators of the university, leaders
of the town's business community, and an impressive roster of state
officials and agency heads. Officers of the University of Texas Student

Association attended as special representatives of their colleagues, including its president, Jimmie Brinkley, and its vice president, Light T. Cummins Jr. The audience greeted the introductory narrative of the film with thunderous applause and ribald cheering, a phenomenon that also occurred several times later during particularly stirring parts of the story and at the end of the movie.[36]

As the decades have passed since that long-ago night at Austin's Varsity Theater, Webb's book and Vidor's film have become increasingly less credible over time in telling the history of the Texas Rangers, especially for our own era today. Over the last eighty years or so, there have been a considerable number of nonfiction history books written about the Texas Rangers in both a popular and a scholarly vein. The number of fictional works touching on the Rangers, especially novels and magazine articles, is probably beyond anyone's calculation. The Texas Ranger Hall of Fame in Waco has identified well over one hundred Hollywood films, radio programs, and television series that explicitly deal with the Rangers. Yet of all these books and films, it is doubtful if any of them have had the overwhelming impact on popular culture in Texas at the time of their debut than did Walter P. Webb's book and King Vidor's film. Both Webb and Vidor stand alone in the cultural history of Texas for that reason, especially because their book and film touched deep currents of approval among the mostly white Americans who constituted their intended audience in the racially segregated mid-1930s.

Nonetheless, in taking a longer historiographical viewpoint, both the book and the film have not aged gracefully. Decades of academic historical writing have increasingly called into question the explicit one-dimensionality of Webb's book, with some of these later historical works having provided unabashed and harsh criticism. By the same token, Vidor's film also might appear today almost cartoonish in its unsophisticated simplicity as an example of Depression-era Hollywood movie factory cliché, likely seen by modern viewers as little more than a typical Saturday matinee Western. Whatever the case, however, it must be noted that the book and the film accurately reflected how a considerable number of white Texans felt about the Texas Rangers at the time when both appeared before the public. As well, the interpretations presented in the book and the motion picture continue to linger in the popular culture of Texas. It would likely be an easy task to find some people who still today agree with Webb and Vidor. Most importantly, it remains impossible to understand the evolving role that the Texas Rangers have played in defining the history of the Lone Star State without considering what Walter Prescott Webb and King Vidor accomplished in print and on celluloid during 1935 and 1936.

Notes

1. The author thanks Michael L. Collins for reading and commenting on this chapter while in manuscript. The standard book-length academic biography of Webb is Necah Furman, *Walter Prescott Webb: His Life and Impact* (Albuquerque: University of New Mexico Press, 1976). See also Michael L. Collins, "Walter Prescott Webb," in *Writing the Story of Texas*, edited by Patrick L. Cox and Kenneth E. Hendrickson Jr. (Austin: University of Texas Press, 2013), 43–66; Joe B. Frantz, "Remembering Walter Prescott Webb," *Southwestern Historical Quarterly* 92, no. 1 (1988): 16–30; Walter Rundell Jr., "Walter Prescott Webb: Product of Environment," *Arizona and the West* 5, no. (1963): 4–28; "A Guide to the Walter Prescott Webb Papers," *Briscoe Center for American History, the University of Texas at Austin*, accessed February 2020, https://collections.briscoecenter.org/repositories/2/resources/382.
2. Walter Prescott Webb, *The Texas Rangers: A Century of Frontier Defense*, edited and reprinted from the original edition, with a foreword by Lyndon B. Johnson (Austin: University of Texas Press, 1965), 15.
3. Walter Prescott Webb, "The Texas Rangers in the Mexican War" (MA thesis, University of Texas, 1920).
4. Webb, "Texas Rangers in the Mexican War," 14. The concept of heroism in United States history had historiographical validity from the 1920s to the 1940s. A considerable number of academic historians wrote about heroism in the history of the United States as an identifiable attribute of national development, especially during wartime and as part of the advancing frontier. The best example of this interpretive orientation

is Dixon Wecter, *The Hero in America: A Chronical of Hero Worship* (New York: Charles Scribner's Sons, 1941). A 1942 scholarly review of Wecter's book noted that "heroes are very significant figures in the history of American ideas because we not only enjoy their biographies but by using them as patterns we make them continuing influences in national life." Roy F. Nichols, review of *The Hero in America: A Chronical of Hero Worship*, by Dixon Wecter, *American Historical Review* 47, no. 2 (January 1942): 341.

5. Webb, "Texas Rangers in the Mexican War," 8. For a more balanced historical update to Webb's thesis, see Ian B. Lyles, "Mixed Blessing: The Role of the Texas Rangers in the Mexican War, 1846–1848" (thesis, Military Command and General Staff College, Fort Leavenworth, KS, 2003). Lyles also employs this quotation from Webb, p. 5.

6. Webb, "Unique Character of Original Texas Ranger Force," *Dallas Morning News*, Magazine Section, April 19, 1921, p. 5.

7. Webb had an entrepreneurial talent that be brought to these activities. He sent a customizable form letter of inquiry to a number of popular outlets in an attempt to sell them articles about the Rangers. These included, in addition to the *Dallas Morning News*, publications such as the *Owenwood Magazine, Sunset, Outdoor Life, Recreation, Redbook, National Geographic, Scribner's, Harper's*, and others. Llerena B. Friend, "W. P. Webb's Texas Rangers," *Southwestern Historical Quarterly* 74, no. 3 (January 1971): 299.

8. Webb, "Autobiography," Walter Prescott Webb Papers, 1857–1966, box 2M245, Dolph Briscoe Center for American History, University of Texas at Austin (hereafter cited as Webb "Autobiography"). It was my good fortune to review in manuscript form Michael L. Collins's transcribed and edited version of this autobiography. It contains much specific information about Webb's ongoing, lifelong interest in the Texas Rangers, which, in its rich detail, goes far beyond the ability of this essay to develop, given its space limitations. Michael L. Collins, ed., *A Texan's Story: The Autobiography of Walter Prescott Webb* (Norman: University of Oklahoma Press, 2020).

9. Friend, "Webb's Texas Rangers," 298.

10. Furman, *Walter Prescott Webb*, 115. Webb noted in his autobiography about a 1924 trip: "We spent more than two weeks on the trip, and I saw the Big Bend country for the first time. . . . I have returned to the Big Bend time and again and expect to do so on every possible occasion"; Webb "Autobiography." Later, after publication of the

Texas Rangers book, Webb became a special consultant in establishing the Big Bend National Park, working closely with former Texas Ranger E. E. Townsend of Alpine, whom he had met during his early Ranger research trips in the 1920s. Michael Welsh, *Landscape of Ghosts, River of Dreams: An Administrative History of Big Bend National Park* (Washington, DC: Department of the Interior, National Park Service, 2002); Clifford B. Casey and Lewis H. Saxton, *The Life of Everett Ewing Townsend* (Alpine: West Texas Historical and Scientific Society, 1958).

11. I have been unable to locate explicit, written historical documentation regarding Webb writing much of *The Texas Rangers* late at night in Austin's Night Hawk Restaurant, which had opened several years earlier near the campus. During my own graduate school days, I was often in the company of then senior historians William C. Pool and Joe B. Frantz, both of whom knew Webb well because they were history graduate students during the 1930s. They spoke of Webb on occasion to me and told me about his preference for writing into the small hours of the morning at the Night Hawk. Additionally, my late father, Light Townsend Cummins Jr., was an undergraduate student at the university in those same years and also knew Webb as one of his professors. My father delighted in telling stories of his college years and recounted to me his having seen and talked to Webb writing under such circumstances at the restaurant. In addition, my father also had stories from his college years about Webb and our family relation, Texas Ranger Everett Ewing Townsend, especially regarding the historian's research trips to West Texas.

12. "Books to Be Published During the Autumn Months," *New York Times*, September 22, 1935.

13. William C. Binkley, review of *The Texas Rangers: A Century of Frontier Defense*, by Walter Prescott Webb, *Journal of Southern History* 2, no. 3 (August 1936): 419–21; Rupert N. Richardson, review of *The Texas Rangers: A Century of Frontier Defense*, by Walter Prescott Webb, *Southwestern Historical Quarterly* 39, no. 4 (April 1936): 333–35.

14. Webb, "Autobiography."

15. Collins, "Walter Prescott Webb," 53; Don Graham, "Fallen Heroes," *Texas Monthly*, February 2005, https://www.texasmonthly.com/articles/fallen-heroes/; Gregory Curtis, "West Is West," *Texas Monthly*, July 1999, https://www.texasmonthly.com/articles/west-is-west/.

16. The Texas Centennial motivated the release of several other Hollywood films during 1936 in addition to *The Texas Rangers*. These included *Pigskin Parade, The Big Show,* and *Hats Off.* Light T. Cummins, "History, Memory, and Rebranding Texas as Western for the Texas Centennial of 1936," in *This Corner of Canaan: Essays on Texas in Honor of Randolph B. Campbell,* ed. Richard B. McCaslin, Donald E. Chipman, and Andrew J. Torget (Denton: University of North Texas Press, 2013), 37; Kenneth Baxter Ragsdale, *The Year America Discovered Texas: Centennial '36* (College Station: Texas A&M University Press), 28; Light Townsend Cummins, "From the Midway to the Hall of State at Fair Park: Two Competing Views of Women at the Dallas Celebration of 1936," *Southwestern Historical Quarterly* 114, no. 3 (January 2011): 225–51; Raymond Durgnat and Scott Simmon, *King Vidor: American* (Berkeley: University of California Press, 1988), 19–42.

17. Durgnat and Simmon, *King Vidor,* 23; "Long Live King Vidor: A Hollywood King," *New York Times,* September 3, 1972. Vidor remained active until his retirement from directing in 1960, thereafter teaching film courses at UCLA. Among his best-known films are *The Crowd* (1928), *Hallelujah* (1929), *Our Daily Bread* (1934), *Stella Dallas* (1937), *Northwest Passage* (1940), *Duel in the Sun* (1946), *War and Peace* (1956), and *Solomon and Sheba* (1959). He received an honorary Oscar for his lifetime of achievement at the 1978 Academy Awards ceremony. King Vidor passed away in Los Angeles on November 1, 1982. M. Scott Sosebee, "The 'King' of Texas Filmmakers: King Wallis Vidor," *Nacogdoches (Texas) Daily Sentinel,* June 25, 2021.

18. At this writing the entire shooting script of *The Texas Rangers* can be found online at Scripts.com, accessed September 19, 2019, https://www.scripts.com/script/the_texas_rangers_21456. The original is in the Script Collection, Archives Building, Paramount Pictures Corporation, 5555 Melrose Avenue, Los Angeles, CA.

19. "New Mexico Spring Winds Worry King Vidor," *Gallup Independent,* April 4, 1936; Idwall Jones, "Where Rabbits and Cameramen Roam," *New York Times,* August 2, 1936.

20. "Odds and Ends from Hollywood," *New York Times,* March 22, 1936; at this writing it is possible to see the entire film *The Texas Rangers* online at YouTube.com, accessed September 19, 2019, https://www.youtube.com/watch?v=-dPILLtJyEA.

21. For example, the *Daily Texan*, the University of Texas newspaper, observed little similarity between Webb's book and Vidor's film when the movie premiered. It noted, "King Vidor revamped history to suit the needs of the motion picture." See "Addenda on the Lively Arts," *Daily Texan*, September 27, 1936.

22. The Gallup Chamber of Commerce notes that over seventy-five motion pictures were filmed on location there from the 1930s to the 1960s. It is today possible to view a series of these movies and recognize specific backgrounds, which appear from picture to picture; Jeff Berg, *New Mexico Film Making* (Charleston, SC: History Press, 2015), 27. By the late 1930s, in part because of *The Texas Rangers*, Gallup had become such a popular on-location destination for Hollywood directors that the brother of Vidor's close friend, film pioneer D. W. Griffith, built an opulent hotel, the El Rancho, on the main street to meet their needs. Today the El Rancho is a still-operating hotel. It is an official New Mexico landmark filled with photographs and memorabilia related to the dozens of film crews and famous actors who have stayed there. One of its suites is named for Fred MacMurray. *Hotel El Rancho*, accessed October 12, 2020, https://elranchohotelgallup.com/western-movies/.

23. Even so, Gallup presented Vidor with problems once filming began. He often had to stop his activities because of high winds, which he felt plagued the production. On one occasion crew members used dynamite to blast away rock formations to create wide vistas for the camera angles Vidor wanted to shoot. "New Mexico Spring Winds Worry King Vidor," *Gallup Independent*, April 4, 1936.

24. Cronjager would be nominated during his career for seven Academy Awards. By the time of his work on *The Texas Rangers*, he was already famous for shooting the land rush scene in the 1931 film *Cimarron*. The American Film Institute has recognized this as one of the most iconic examples of early cinematography. It noted of this 1931 film, "The justly celebrated land rush sequence took a week to film, using 5,000 extras, 28 cameramen, six still photographers, and 27 camera assistants. The scene is so iconic that, three decades later, when MGM remade the film, the camera angles for the land rush sequence remained almost identical to the original"; "*Cimarron* Trivia," *IMDb*, accessed April 23, 2021, https://m.imdb.com/title/tt0021746/trivia/?item=tr0619712&ref_=ext_shr_lnk.

25. "Texas Governor 'Directs' Stars: Allred Says Action and the Picture Starts," *Gallup Independent*, April 28, 1936. This involved the

Mountain States Telephone company rigging a special temporary line from its Gallup switching center to a remote location where the film crew was shooting, something that had never done before. "Movie Gossip for Brick Walk Fans," *Albuquerque Journal*, May 3, 1936.

26. "Picture Company in Gallup for Two Weeks Work," *Gallup Independent*, April 21, 1936; "Movie Gossip for Brick Walk Fans, Weekly Column," *Albuquerque Journal*, June 26, July 12, 1936.

27. "Movie Stars and Producers Soon Buzz around Ancient Santa Fe," *Santa Fe New Mexican*, April 11, 1936; "All the King's Horses and All the King's Men—King Vidor's Here for the 'Texas Rangers' Film," *Santa Fe New Mexican*, May 18, 1936; "Film Stars, Director Named Texas Rangers," *Wilmet Life*, September 17, 1936.

28. "Cereal Admission Good Sunday Afternoon," *Big Spring Daily Herald*, September 20, 1936; "Picture Based on History of State Rangers," *Abilene Morning Reporter-News*, September 6, 1936.

29. "Boy Scouts Offered Trip to Centennial," *Robstown Record*, June 18, 1936; "Big Spring Boy Is Contest Winner," *Abilene Morning Reporter-News*, July 23, 1936. Likely because MacMurray signed a relatively large number of his Paramount Publicity photos as part of this competition, exemplars still appear today for sale on various internet movie memorabilia websites. For an example, see "Fred MacMurray Signed 8" x 10" Photo, Paramount Pictures, 1935," ebay.com, accessed April 23, 2021, https://www.ebay.com/itm/Fred-MacMurray-Signed-8x10-Photo-/333622144264.

30. "Sheet Music for The Texas Ranger Song," Famous Music Corporation, 1610 Broadway, New York City, 1936; copy in possession of the author. Coslow began his career as a New York composer and became the first songwriter hired by Paramount Pictures once sound pictures arrived. He gained fame as the person who wrote most of Bing Crosby's song hits during the early 1930s. Coslow would win an Academy Award in 1943. "Sam Coslow," Songwriter's Hall of Fame, accessed September 29, 2019, https://www.songhall.org/profile/Sam_Coslow.

31. Shooting Script, *The Texas Rangers*, Archives, Paramount Pictures Corporation.

32. "Author of 'The Texas Rangers' Is Satisfied with Screen Play," *Daily Texan*, September 25, 1936.

33. "Gay Premier of the Texas Rangers at the Majestic," *Dallas Morning News*, August 22, 1936.

34. Webb later wrote in his autobiography, "I did not receive an invitation to the premiere, though I lived within four blocks of the state official who was most prominent [Governor Allred at the Governor's Mansion in Austin]. I always thought he would have been a better politician had he said to the Hollywood people, 'The man that wrote this book lives here. Suppose we let him know about all this. Of course, he is only the author, but we probably ought to extend him a slight courtesy." Webb did later admit somewhat prosaically, "The film undeservedly increased my reputation in Texas and the contract I signed increased my bank account for a short time." Collins, *Texan's Story*, 182–83.

35. "The Texas Rangers,' Epic of Lone Star State to Show at Capitol," *Brownsville Herald*, September 27, 1936. At the time of this writing, the Varsity Theater has been long closed, supplanted by modern, suburban Austin movie venues. Its neon marquee remains, as does the general appearance of the building's exterior. However, retail shops and fast-food outlets fill most of remodeled interior of the theater.

36. "Varsity, Neighborhood Theater, to Open Tonight," *Austin Daily Texan*, November 20, 1936.

PART 2

Patterns of Ranger Historical Writings

Chapter 3

General Histories
Themes and Issues
Michael L. Collins

I n their earliest days they were known by many names. Variously
called minute companies, volunteer militia, mounted rifles,
irregulars, state troops, and, by 1874, the Frontier Battalion, they
all grew out of the same legend. The Comanche people of the plains
may not have had a name for them, but if they did it must have been
something akin to "terrifying enemy." On horseback, armed with
six-shooters and repeating rifles, riding onto the field of battle they
appeared to their Native American foes to have bullets flying from
both fists, seemingly a deadly round for every finger on both hands.
To Texans of Mexican heritage and the people of Mexico, they were
los diablos Tejanos—"Texas Devils." But to Anglo frontiersman who
relied on them to defend their border settlements, they had but one
reputation for bravery and fearlessness, and one name—Rangers.

Few topics on the literary landscape of the Lone Star State have
held a more enduring appeal than the Texas Rangers. A recent search
of one popular online website revealed over four thousand book titles
under the subject heading of the Texas Rangers. And that figure does
not even include the beloved professional baseball team in Arlington

that is their namesake. The image of the hard-riding, straight-shooting Ranger remains an integral part of the romance and attraction of Texas legends. Passed down through the generations, their story is a familiar one, but despite that they seem as elusive as the outlaws they hunted. Even today the Rangers still ride somewhere on the borderlands between Texas history and American myth.

When Anglo-Texans tell stories about their native state, they are talking not only about themselves but also about their own collective identity as Texans. After all, storytelling is a favorite sport of folks from the Lone Star State, and few people relish regaling others with their past more than Texans. Quick to remember the fallen defenders of the Alamo and the victims of the Goliad Massacre, they proudly recount how Texas was born in a violent struggle with Mexico and how their forefathers, and thus they themselves, were baptized in the blood of martyrs. Such legends are central to the Texan's sense of place.[1]

Riding alongside the heroes of the Texas Revolution are two other mythic figures who complete what might be termed a holy trinity of Anglo-Texan traditions: the American cowboy, fiercely independent and longhorn tough, and a third horseman of legendary proportions— the intrepid Texas Ranger. Never mind that most Texans cannot even name a single Ranger, except maybe Chuck Norris or Clayton Moore. The Ranger's legendary stature still casts a long shadow over the life and lore of Texas. Through the decades the Ranger remains a constant of the Texas mystique, celebrated in song, cinema, pulp fiction, and popular culture as the quintessential heroic Texan.

Anglo-Texans consider their history hallowed ground. You just don't mess with Texas history, and certainly not with the Rangers. In the words of novelist John Steinbeck, "I have said that Texas is a state of mind, but I think it is more than that. It is a mystique closely approximating a religion. And it is true to the extent that people either passionately love Texas or passionately hate it and, as in other religions, few people dare to inspect it for fear of losing their bearings in mystery or paradox."[2]

From the beginning myth has played a central part in the very conception of Texas. For Anglo-Texans at least, the figure of the invincible mounted Ranger remains a critical component of the story of the Lone Star State. So has the long-held belief that Texans hold a distinct identity that is unique from that of their fellow Americans. "Texceptionalism," some term it. Only a few would dare to call it a Texan Creation Myth.[3]

As scholars sift through the historical record, they should recognize that the past should not be so easily branded. To begin with, any general account of the Texas Rangers must acknowledge that their saga is not one story but a mosaic of many stories. The first historian to understand that fact was Walter Prescott Webb, a young scholar at the University of Texas who undertook the lofty task of weaving together an entire century's worth of episodes, incidents, and events into the fabric of the fabled frontier institution—and doing so within the covers of a single volume.

But first Webb gained national attention with his groundbreaking study *The Great Plains* (1931), which garnered him recognition and respect across the American historical community. Only when that task was completed did he take aim at finishing his history of the Texas Rangers, which had already been a decade in the making. What began as an MA thesis under the direction of his mentor, Dr. Eugene C. Barker, and a string of newspaper and magazine articles about the early Rangers and their exploits (as well as the significance of Samuel Colt's revolver) at last evolved into a sweeping account titled *The Texas Rangers: A Century of Frontier Defense* (1935).[4] Released in time to coincide with the Texas Centennial celebration, the study was timely for another important reason. The book hit the shelves when the Rangers as an institution were under siege and the Texas State Legislature was embroiled in yet another divisive debate over whether to disband the force or reform and reorganize it.[5]

Against the backdrop of such a highly politicized environment, Webb's narrative takes on the appearance of an apologist's defense of the Texas Rangers. In each chapter Webb paints a heroic portrait of the archetypal Texas Ranger as a product of his harsh and unforgiving environment. As the story goes, the Ranger was hewn by the primitive conditions of the Texas frontier, a land as spread out as it is sparse, and defined by his interaction with the crude forces and unpredictable elements of nature and the Native American inhabitants. In what might be termed a Genesis account, Webb sets the stage for ongoing racial and cultural conflict during border wars with Mexico, which the author argues also shaped the Rangers' basic character. Tracing the origins of Ranger traditions, Webb describes how the early Texans were tempered by the stern lessons of revolution and nation building. "The affair of the Alamo had taught them to expect no mercy; the massacre of Fannin's men [at Goliad] . . . had taught them distrust for Mexican honor; the fate of the Mier prisoners in Perote prison had taught them never to surrender; and the victory of San Jacinto had taught them contempt for Mexican valor."[6]

In writing his history of the iconic Texas Rangers, Walter Prescott Webb reflected his generation's deeply ingrained racial biases. But he also led the way in identifying and exploring a number of themes that have run through most every general history written to date. The Rangers' extraordinary horsemanship, including their understanding of the importance of a good mount; their exceptional marksmanship; their excellent tracking skills and uncanny ability to read hoofprints like handwriting; their unconventional military tactics, which in many ways mirrored those of the Plains Indians; their legendary ferocity in battle; their resourcefulness and aptitude for survival under the most difficult of circumstances: these traits, along with a growing reputation for toughness and courage, all contributed to an aura of invincibility. So did their Colt revolvers and Winchester repeating rifles. With a gift for brevity, Webb paraphrased John S. "Rip" Ford, who once characterized the quintessential Ranger as one who "could ride like a Mexican, trail like an Indian, shoot like a Tennessean, and fight like a devil."[7]

Webb acknowledged that the frontier Ranger units that made the legend, and some more recent law enforcement companies that lived it, were only as good as their leaders. He likewise traced their transition in the early twentieth century from horseback to motorized vehicles. From predatory cattle rustlers and horse thieves to gunsling-ing shootists, from brazen bank robbers and dynamite-slinging train robbers to vicious roughnecks and rowdies in the oil fields of the Roaring Twenties and the desperate years of the Great Depression, the modern-day Rangers suppressed riots, tracked down bootleggers, apprehended or killed machine gun–toting gangsters, and through it all managed as an institution to adapt to changing times and shift-ing political tides. When necessary, they and their leaders even rein-vented themselves.

Webb later admitted his struggles in writing the history of the storied frontier institution, and he recalled his greatest challenge with the project. "The Rangers had a glorious past and had performed enough exploits to fill many volumes." But "the history was episodical [sic]," he explained, "so it became a question of finding some thread of unity on which to hang the incidents, and the only one available seemed to be the great leaders, the captains." Tracing the origins and development of the fabled Texas Rangers from their primitive beginnings to the emergence of a modern law enforcement agency renowned the world over, he offered a historian's defense of an agency that again had come under increasing fire by politicians critical of the Rangers' harsh methods, particularly in South Texas and along the Mexican border.[8]

With each chapter and with every subheading, Webb wove his narrative around the exploits of a courageous leader who performed extraordinary feats in the service of Texas and, in so doing, contrib-uted to the growth of a genuine Lone Star legend. John Coffee "Jack" Hays, El Diablo to his enemies on the border, who led Texan Rangers into the storms of the War with Mexico; the gallant Samuel H. Walker, the quintessential warrior who designed the .44 Colt revolver that revolutionized plains warfare; Ben McCulloch, famed scout, adven-turer, and soldier of fortune; the irrepressible John S. "Rip" Ford, frontiersman and Indian fighter; Leander H. McNelly, the fearless

lawman who swept the most notorious of bad men from the Nueces
Strip; and many more: together these leaders and those who followed
in their tradition—such legends as Bill McDonald, Frank Hamer, and
Manuel T. "Lone Wolf" Gonzaullas—provided Webb with a fabric of
stories that could be stitched together into a continuous, lively narrative of heroic deeds and dramatic events.[9]

In following the trail of the Texas Rangers, Webb confessed
that he wove a narrative around a single loose fabric—the heroism
of Anglo-Texan leaders. But in so doing he viewed the institution of
the Rangers from the top down, and thus he neglected a more critical
view of the rank-and-file of the force. At the same time, he failed to
acknowledge a more diverse, multicolored, and multilayered weave of
Texas history. Texans of Mexican heritage and their kinsmen south of
the Rio Grande justly recounted a much different story of los Rinches,
as Tejanos termed the Rangers. To them the Rangers rode across the
pages of their history as mounted demons on horseback, terrorizing
the Spanish-speaking people of the border.[10]

With the publication of Webb's groundbreaking study, the apoth-
eosis of the Texas Rangers seemed complete—at least for the time
being. As folklorist and friend J. Frank Dobie summarized Webb's
work in his *Guide to Life and Literature of the Southwest*, the book
would take its place as "the beginning, middle, and end of the subject."
Characteristically more modest in his own assessment, Webb admitted
that the book was merely a "competent journeyman's job." Anyone
could have written it, he humbly suggested.[11]

Trailing a half century behind Walter Prescott Webb, retired United
States Army colonel turned historian Frederick Wilkins of San Antonio
took aim at the enduring myths of the Ranger story. He launched his
studies with a survey of Texans in the war with Mexico, *The Highly
Irregular Irregulars: Texas Rangers in the Mexican War* (1990). Like
Webb Wilkins also reintroduced readers to all of the Ranger immortals. Then he stretched the story into three more volumes that spanned
the turbulent last half of the nineteenth century: *The Legend Begins:
The Texas Rangers, 1823–1845* (1996); *The Law Comes to Texas:*

The Texas Rangers, 1870–1901 (1999); and, finally, a survey of the much-neglected period in Ranger history, *Defending the Borders: The Texas Rangers, 1848–1861* (2001). In chronicling the latter period, he contributed considerably to our collective understanding of the Rangers' operations during the largely unexplored decade of the 1850s.[12]

Although his narratives of the Rangers appealed mostly to the general public, Wilkins's achievement was most notable in another respect. With an appropriate degree of skepticism, he applied a military history authority's scrutiny to the origins of some of the earliest legends in Ranger lore, among them the contemporary accounts of Captain Jack Hays' legendary fight with Comanches atop a granite hill known as Enchanted Rock, and his much-cited skirmish with another Comanche party at Walker Creek in 1844. In dissecting the legends and questioning how Hays and others became heroes of Homeric proportions, Wilkins ventured where Webb had not fully explored, reexamining time-honored stories of the Rangers' primitive beginnings, some of which had probably been lost forever in the mists of history.[13]

Not far behind Fred Wilkins, historian Charles M. Robinson III, also a native of Texas, weighed in with his own survey, *The Men Who Wear the Star: The Story of the Texas Rangers* (2000). This lean volume of vignettes demonstrated once again the difficulty in trying to chase down and corral the Texas Rangers in a single volume. While Robinson's crowded, fast-paced, and mostly anecdotal narrative of 288 pages leaves the reader with some answers, most readers would be left wanting to know more. With Robinson, as with Webb, the Rangers' trail abruptly goes cold in 1935 with a brief conclusion titled "The End and the Myth."[14]

By the turn of the new century and new millennium, the field of Ranger historians was fast becoming more crowded. At the head of the herd stood one of the most celebrated national authorities on the American West, longtime chief historian of the National Park Service Robert M. Utley. The sage historian contributed what is arguably the most comprehensive general study yet of the storied frontier fighting force. Appropriately, Utley chose to break the narrative into two volumes, the first being *Lone Star Justice: The First Century of the Texas Rangers* (2002), the second following the epic story through the modern era, *Lone Star Lawmen: The Second Century of the Texas Rangers* (2007).[15]

Utley had several advantages over Webb. Most notably, he had access to public records that Webb was unaware of and some documents not yet available to the researcher in the 1920s and early 1930s. Some might even argue that Utley searched out and used sources that Webb had neglected or had even chosen to ignore. As with Webb, Utley's stature as a writer allowed him an audience with numerous living Rangers who were willing to open up and tell their stories. In seeking to extend and correct Webb's work, Utley also had the vantage point of several decades of experience and perspective.

Utley's history also has the feeling of being unfettered from politics and free of any sense of obligation to serve as an apologist for a revered and time-honored institution in the crosshairs of public criticism. More than Webb, Utley also confronts the trail of patronage and corruption, as well as atrocities along the border, in the early twentieth century that stained the reputation of the Ranger force. Notably, too, he offers an illuminating survey and analysis of the watershed reorganization of 1935 and subsequent restructuring under the leadership of the legendary Homer Garrison, who from 1938 to 1968 served as director of the Texas Department of Public Safety. The "Garrison Rangers . . . inherited the traditions of their predecessors," Utley observed, and "the stamp of the Old West lawmen remained conspicuous." But "they bore only superficial resemblance" to the horseback Rangers of earlier days. Their uniforms and badges offered a hint of the discipline and professionalism that Garrison instilled in the organization.[16]

In the fall of 2002 Robert Utley sat down for an interview with Stacy Hollister of *Texas Monthly*. With characteristic candor and clarity, the venerable historian explained the layers of complexity, contradiction, and controversy that confronted him during the course of his research and writing. He admitted that he had set out to do more than simply update Webb's account. He fully intended to dispel both the myths about the Rangers' past and what he called the "blanketing defamations posed by revisionists." After chasing numerous real-life heroes and a few villains along the way, he discovered that, as far as the Rangers' reputation is concerned, the "historical reality lies somewhere between the two extremes."[17]

When asked if his purpose had been to revise Webb's general history, Utley responded, "My intent was, indeed, to replace Webb, not just update him. He is no longer universally regarded as definitive, if such a term can be applied to any work of history." Utley criticized Webb for offering a study that was "entirely hagiographic," where Texas Rangers were "all courteous, heroic, fearless, indomitable men of high competence and sterling integrity." At the same time, he conceded that Webb was a "product of his time and place," just like the Rangers he wrote about. "Webb shared the values and attitudes of his peers," Utley offered, "and his book especially reflects the . . . superiority his generation of Anglos felt toward Mexicans and Mexican-Americans."[18]

"Each generation writes its own history, and [they] should," Utley affirmed. At the same time, he cautioned that historians must resist presentism, the interpretation of the past solely in terms of their current perspective and values. Echoing both Webb and Wilkins, he insisted, "The old time Rangers should be judged according to their time and place, not ours." Historians should thus avoid the temptation to project and overlay their own ethos onto those who came before them.[19]

Fast on the heels of Robert Utley's sweeping two-volume survey came Mike Cox, former chief spokesman for the Texas Department of Public Safety. Arguably the most gifted storyteller yet to undertake a general history of the Texas Rangers, Cox—also a longtime newspaperman and freelance writer—produced a highly readable two-volume study, the first being *The Texas Rangers: Wearing the Cinco Peso, 1821–1900* (2008) aimed at the general reading public more than the academic community. To begin with, Cox, a self-described "writer-historian" (as opposed to a "historian-writer" like

Utley), admitted that the famed Texas Rangers were as controversial
as they were heroic. Following the frontier force, from their origins
as Indian fighters and border defenders to their transition as fabled
lawmen, he offers a rousing account of not just the "good" but also
"the bad and the ugly" who stained the Rangers' reputation along the
way. In the words of famed Western novelist Elmer Kelton, "Though
he gives us the flashes of glory, he does not flinch from the dark side
of the Rangers' past." Most notably, Cox also relied more heavily on
old newspaper accounts than his predecessors to add both color and
authenticity to the story.[20]

The ink was hardly dry on the first volume when Cox trotted out the
sequel, *Time of the Rangers: From 1900 to the Present* (2009). As in the
case with Utley, Cox outdistanced Webb in tracking the Rangers across
modern Texas. Not only updating Webb, he also extended his coverage
throughout the twentieth century to include such incidents as the Fred
Gomez Carrasco–led Huntsville Prison riot and hostage drama of 1974,
the Branch Davidian siege at Mount Carmel outside Waco in 1993, and
the Brewster County standoff with a few crackpots of the self-proclaimed
"Republic of Texas" in 1998.[21]

Author Eddie Michel, a native of Pretoria, South Africa, offers a
unique perspective from one who grew up in the shadow of apartheid
in *A Breed Apart: The History of the Texas Rangers* (2012). Balanced
in his coverage of the subject, and with a sensitivity to issues of race
and class, he blends both traditionalist and revisionist scholarship as
he examines both the Rangers' heroic exploits and the more unsettling
parts of their story. Many of the devoted and a few of the disgraced—
just about all of the familiar faces are there.[22]

Independent scholar Darren L. Ivey, well respected in both
academic and popular circles, is no stranger to Texas Rangers history.
He has spent years chasing down the Ranger immortals. Although
he may be better known for his artfully crafted three volumes of
biographical essays, the first titled *The Ranger Ideal: Texas Rangers
in the Hall of Fame, 1823–1861*, and its companion volumes by the
same brand covering the years 1874 to 1930 and 1898 to 1987, these

notable contributions do not qualify as "general histories." Of particular value to scholars, however, is Ivey's overview and sweeping compendium of entries detailing the history and operations of every known Ranger company since their inception in *The Texas Rangers: A Registry and History* (2010). In this volume Ivey even fills a notable gap by offering both scholars and laymen a brief history of the fabled Ranger badge.[23]

Joining in pursuit of the legend are prominent Ranger historians and educators Bruce Glasrud and Harold J. Weiss Jr., who have partnered to provide yet another approach to the subject. In *Tracking the Texas Rangers: The Nineteenth Century* (2012) and *Tracking the Texas Rangers: The Twentieth Century* (2013), Glasrud and Weiss have pulled together companion anthologies of previously published essays contributed by the most respected authorities in the field. Tracing the topic across two centuries, through times of change and continuity, controversy and commendation, their skillfully arranged volumes provide an overview and reassessment of the major themes and issues as seen through the lens of many.[24]

Among the most recent to round up the scattered history of the Rangers are Donaly Brice, dean of Texas archivists, and Bob Alexander, a highly acclaimed and respected Western writer known for his skill in telling a good tale. The two historians team up to produce what might be arguably the most comprehensive and balanced single volume history of the Rangers yet written. In *Texas Rangers: Lives, Legend, and Legacy* (2017), the authors craft a narrative that is both colorful and casual in style and complete in documentation. Presenting an objective appraisal of the nineteenth-century frontier force that evolved into one of the most respected modern law enforcement agencies in the world, they bring a breadth and depth of research that few have matched. Most notably, their format includes six chapters that summarize each of the six companies that formed the famed Frontier Battalion. Paying particular attention to the rank-and-file members of the service, not just their leaders, and documenting biographical details of some

450 Rangers, the authors thus avoid the temptation to paint just another top-down portrait of the Rangers.[25]

The latest addition to the growing list of legend makers and myth breakers is award-winning investigative journalist Doug J. Swanson, a feature writer and editor for the *Dallas Morning News*. Perhaps no general history of the subject has caused a greater ruckus than Swanson's *Cult of Glory: The Bold and Brutal History of the Texas Rangers* (2020). In what might be best termed an unauthorized biography of the famed force, Swanson presents a strikingly different interpretation, a darker and sometimes more sinister collective portrait that depicts the Rangers first as advanced shock troops of Anglo conquest, then as instruments of racial repression and agents of an established monied elite and entrenched political hierarchy. Sometimes men of extraordinary courage, but more often actors of less honor than previously advertised, the "real Rangers" of Swanson's narrative are mostly characters of diminished virtue and exaggerated valor. Jack Hays, Rip Ford, Leander McNelly, Bill McDonald, Frank Hamer, and all the rest, including the likes of lesser-known notables such as J. Monroe Fox and Henry Lee Ransom: as Swanson reveals the uncomfortable realities, they are not your grandfather's Rangers or Webb's untarnished heroes. In sum, Swanson's controversial contribution should convince any reader with an open mind—regardless of their previous perspective—that the sweeping history of the world-famous Texas Rangers is, to say the least, complicated.[26]

And so the muster roll of Ranger histories continues. After several generations of tracking the Rangers, historians still grapple with another central question, that being how their story fits into a larger national narrative. The recent trend seems to support—or at least fails to challenge—the notion that the Rangers' historical development provides yet more evidence that the Texan identity is unique to the Lone Star State. Perhaps too easily fenced in by this argument, some writers merely echo Webb by deploying the same cast of colorful characters (Webb called them "transplanted Americans") against the backdrop of their unconventional tactics in the field during the war with

Mexico, in the wilds of Comanche country, and along the borderlands of the Rio Grande.

As historians continue the hunt, maybe they should pay even more attention to the early Texas Rangers as an important chapter in the greater American frontier experience and, more specifically, the citizen-soldier tradition so central to American beginnings. Perhaps, rather than debating endlessly whether Texas is more Southern or Western in character, future writers should consider whether Texas is a mirror image of America, albeit an exaggerated one.

Beyond those questions lies another long-neglected issue: the relationship and interaction of Texas State troops with United States regular forces on the Indian frontier and on the border with Mexico. To date too many writers have treated the storied Texas Rangers as if they existed in a historical vacuum, or at least as though their institution and traditions evolved in an environment peculiar to the Lone Star State (there we go again, "Texceptionalism"). Such questions remain to be addressed, and much work is yet be done.

Another word of caution should be shared with those historians who follow the trail of the Texas Rangers in future years. More challenges await, perhaps chief among them the reality that we now live in a fact-free world dominated by websites and social (and antisocial) media that appeal to those "users" who are looking for information (or misinformation) that merely confirms and reinforces what they already believe to be "the truth." Writing and publishing in this rapidly changing technological and social environment should neither intimidate nor discourage scholars from taking up the topic. Too many traditionalists will always reject anything that contests or even questions their time-honored narrative. That is a given.

Despite the criticism of traditionalists, contemporary historians who uncover discomforting truths that challenge past interpretations are not simply engaged in "Ranger bashing," as one Texas historian recently complained. Rewriting any aspect of the Rangers' history, no matter the evidence or conclusions, will surely rankle some who insist that revisionists are simply guilty of rewriting the past for the sake of political correctness. Rather than simply debunking the Texas Rangers, serious scholars in our own time should be driven by no agenda other than to follow the trail of evidence to discover the truth about the past—no matter where that trail might lead. Not presenting "history as it should have been," in the words of filmmaker Cecil B. De Mille, but history as it actually happened.

That said, current and future historians should find encouragement from an unlikely source—Walter Prescott Webb. Near the end of his life, Webb reminded us that no subject is the exclusive territory or domain of any small circle of writers or gaggle of scholars, and that each generation will rewrite the past in light of its own experiences. "We shouldn't hang a 'Men at Work' detour sign" on our own field of study, he confided to a colleague. There must be no stop signs, no caution signs, no red lights, no barricades blocking the road of discovery that leads to historical truth. No controversies are off limits, and the only guardrails should be the evidence collected along the way.

Perhaps, then, it is appropriate to come full circle, from the most recent reexaminations of the Rangers back to the once venerable, though now justly criticized, founding father of Ranger historians. At the least, Walter Prescott Webb deserves to be revisited, if for nothing more than as a point of departure. As Robert Utley conceded, it was Webb who first "gave scholarly respectability to the popular image" of the Texas Ranger and who blazed a trail for others to follow.[27]

To paraphrase Texas's most famed frontier philosopher, if everyone were to agree with what we write, then we have added nothing to the larger conversation. In his day Webb saw the Rangers as an endangered relic from the past. Little did he know that his study, though largely discredited now for its blatant racial bias, remained an unfinished story in other respects. In closing his account, Webb bid a nostalgic farewell to the Texas Rangers. Quoting a report in the *New York Herald Tribune* of August 4, 1935, he lamented the apparent imminent demise of the Rangers. "Famous in tradition as the Southwest's most fearless law-enforcement group, the Texas Rangers as now constituted will pass out of existence," the article declared. "It is safe to say that as time goes on the functions of the . . . Texas Rangers will gradually slip away."[28]

But Webb and the editorialist were wrong. Of course, while Webb's history of the Texas Rangers ends in 1935, the institution and their traditions did not. For the next nine decades the Rangers have continued as a division in the Texas Department of Public Safety. With a current authorized strength of more than 160 officers, still serving in six companies across the state, they perform various vital law enforcement functions. Their ranks include women, Latinos, and African Americans. A wide range of field operations fall within their purview: from a Special Weapons and Tactics (SWAT) Team and an Explosive Ordnance Team (or bomb squad) to a Border Security Operations division, a Crisis Negotiations unit, and even an elite Reconnaissance Team trained to operate in some of the most treacherous terrain and difficult environments across the state. "Under the radar," a few remain out of view in the Public Corruption office, while others serve in an Unsolved Crimes Investigation unit that takes up so-called "cold case" files left open for years.[29]

On a daily basis most of today's Rangers are engaged in a multitude of other major criminal investigations (including cybercrimes). Simply put, they are detectives, modern-day sleuths who oftentimes assist local law enforcement or, when called upon, federal investigators. Equipped with the most modern crime-fighting tools and techniques, they are armed with state-of-the-art assault weapons, but they also carry GPS tracking devices and laptop computers linked to national criminal databases, as well as the most up-to-date tactical gear for night operations. The vehicles that transport them across the vast reaches of the state, including armored cars, helicopters, and airplanes, resemble mobile crime labs. Even so, just like in the days of the horseback Rangers, their job is to bring to justice some of the worst criminals ever to stalk across Texas—whether murderers, rapists, robbers, radical separatists, racist hatemongers, or sophisticated con artists who defraud the most vulnerable among us.

And make no mistake, these predators are still out there threatening the public safety. That much will never change.[30]

According to the Texas Department of Public Safety website, in 2018 alone the Texas Rangers in their line of duty made over 1,070 felony arrests, recorded more than 7,600 victim statements (a few with the aid of hypnosis), obtained some 750 confessions, and secured 524 felony convictions. In sum, while times have changed, the Rangers' fearless reputation and their role in protecting their fellow Texans has not.[31]

Perhaps no chapter in the Texas saga contains a greater contradiction, a more troubling paradox, than that of the Rangers. But it is a theme as old as the scriptures and as familiar as the greatest of Shakespearean dramas—man's capacity to be both noble and cruel. This dichotomy, the dualistic nature of humankind, not at all unique to Texas, will face future historians, folklorists, filmmakers, and novelists alike as they track the Rangers across emerging frontiers of law enforcement and crime investigation.

Without the diligent work of serious historians, the Texas Rangers' often-told story might have remained little more than a romance that defies reality, even a fable that belies fact. The recent proliferation and pace of publications on the subject confirms a continuing fascination with the Rangers' legend. Contemporary historians and their readers may disagree on some parts of the story, and how to interpret the evidence and separate the facts from fiction, but they seem to agree on at least one thing. To paraphrase Colonel Homer Garrison, as long as there is a Texas there will always be the Rangers. And, it should be added, there will always be a posse of historians hard on their trail looking to have the latest, if not the last, word on the subject.

Notes

1. For recent discussions of Texans' search for a unifying "Texan identity," see Glen Sample Ely, *Where the West Begins: Debating Texas Identity* (Lubbock: Texas Tech University Press, 2011); Ty Cashion, *Lone Star Mind: Reimagining Texas History* (Norman: University of Oklahoma

Press, 2018); Light Townsend Cummins and Mary L. Scheer, eds., *Texan Identities: Moving beyond Myth, Memory, and Fallacy in Texas History* (Denton: University of North Texas Press, 2016).

2. Don Graham, *Texas: A Literary Portrait* (San Antonio: Corona Publishing Company, 1985), 25; the Steinbeck quote is from *Travels with Charley*.

3. Cashion, *Lone Star Mind*, 1–4, 133.

4. Walter Prescott Webb, *The Texas Rangers: A Century of Frontier Defense* (Boston: Houghton Mifflin, 1935). Following Webb's death, the University of Texas Press brought his seminal study back into print. Hereafter all citations are drawn from Webb, *The Texas Rangers: A Century of Frontier Defense*, edited and reprinted from the original edition, with a foreword by Lyndon B. Johnson (Austin: University of Texas Press, 1965); Llerena Friend, "W. P. Webb's Texas Rangers," *Southwestern Historical Quarterly* 74, no. 3 (January 1971), 293–323.

5. Robert Utley, *Lone Star Lawmen: The Second Century of the Texas Rangers* (New York: Oxford University Press, 2007), 331–33.

6. Walter Prescott Webb, *The Texas Rangers in the Mexican War*. (Austin: Jenkins Garrett Press, 1975), 8.

7. Friend, "Webb's Texas Rangers," 316; Webb, *Century of Frontier Defense*, 15.

8. Walter Prescott Webb, "The Texan's Story," 184–88, typescript, Walter Prescott Webb Papers, 1857–1966, box 2M245, Dolph Briscoe Center for American History, University of Texas at Austin; Webb, *Century of Frontier Defense*, 78–83.

9. Webb, "Texan's Story," 184–88.

10. Webb, "Texan's Story," 184–88; Don Graham, "Fallen Heroes," *Texas Monthly*, February 2005, www.texasmonthly.com/articles/fallen-heroes/.

11. Webb, "Texan's Story," 184–88; Friend, "Webb's Texas Rangers," 294, 315.

12. Frederick Wilkins, *The Highly Irregular Irregulars: Texas Rangers in the Mexican War* (Austin: Eakin Press, 1990); Wilkins, *The Legend Begins: The Texas Rangers, 1823–1845* (Austin: State House Press, 1996); Wilkins, *The Law Comes to Texas: The Texas Rangers, 1870–1901* (Austin: State House Press, 1999); Wilkins, *Defending the Borders: The Texas Rangers, 1848–1861* (Austin: State House Press, 2001).

13. Wilkins, *Legend Begins*, xi–xii, 83–85, 178–81, 201–8; for additional insight into Fred Wilkins' views on the origins of the Rangers' early

legends, see Frederick Wilkins Papers, MS 283, UTSA Libraries, Special Collections, University of Texas at San Antonio.

14. Charles M. Robinson III, *The Men Who Wear the Star: The Story of the Texas Rangers* (New York: Random House, 2000), 1–6, 281–88. For an abbreviated popularized survey aimed at a general audience, see Dan E. Kilgore, *A Ranger Legacy: 150 Years of Service to Texas* (Austin: Madrona Press, 1973). Through three generations other leading scholars have offered brief but authoritative general essays. See Ben H. Procter, "The Texas Rangers: An Overview," chap. 9 in *The Texas Heritage*, ed. Ben H. Procter and Archie P. McDonald, 4th ed. (Wheeling, IL: Harlan Davidson, 2003); the richly illustrated survey by Stephen Hardin, *The Texas Rangers* (London: Osprey, 1991); and Jody Edward Ginn, "The Texas Rangers in Myth and Memory," in Cummins and Scheer, *Texan Identities, 87–120.*

15. Robert Utley, *Lone Star Justice: The First Century of the Texas Rangers* (New York: Oxford University Press, 2002); Utley, *Lone Star Lawmen.*

16. Utley, *Lone Star Lawmen,* 333.

17. Stacy Hollister, "A Q&A with Robert Utley," *Texas Monthly,* November 2002, https://www.texasmonthly.com/articles/a-qa-with-robert-utley/.

18. Hollister, "Q&A with Utley."

19. Hollister, "Q&A with Utley."

20. Mike Cox, *The Texas Rangers: Wearing the Cinco Peso, 1821–1900* (New York: Forge Books, 2008); Mike Cox, *Time of the Rangers: Texas Rangers, from 1900 to the Present* (New York: Forge Books, 2009). The Elmer Kelton quote appears on the back dust jacket of *Wearing the Cinco Peso.*

21. Cox, *Time of the Rangers,* 295–300, 341–44, 356–58.

22. Eddie Michel, *A Breed Apart: The History of the Texas Rangers* (Denver: Outskirts Press, 2012).

23. Darren L. Ivey, *The Texas Rangers: A Registry and History* (Jefferson, NC: McFarland, 2010).

24. Bruce Glasrud and Harold J. Weiss Jr., eds., *Tracking the Texas Rangers: The Nineteenth Century* (Denton: University of North Texas Press, 2012), 1–19; Bruce Glasrud and Harold J. Weiss, Jr., *Tracking the Texas Rangers: the Twentieth Century* (Denton: University of North Texas Press, 2013), 1–21.

25. Bob Alexander and Donaly Brice, *Texas Rangers: Lives, Legend, and Legacy* (Denton: University of North Texas Press, 2017; Kemp Dixon, review of *Texas Rangers: Lives, Legend, and Legacy,* by Bob Alexander

and Donaly Brice, *Southwestern Historical Quarterly* 122, no. 1 (June 2018): 121–22.

26. Doug J. Swanson, *Cult of Glory: The Bold and Brutal History of the Texas Rangers* (New York: Viking, 2020), 4–5; see also John Philip Santos, "The Secret History of the Texas Rangers: 'Cult of Glory' Upends Decades of Mythmaking," *Texas Monthly*, June 2020, https://www.texasmonthly.com/arts-entertainment/secret-history-texas-rangers/.

27. Hollister, "Q&A with Utley."

28. *New York Herald Tribune*, August 4, 1935; Webb, *Century of Frontier Defense*, 567.

29. "Texas Rangers," *Texas Department of Public Safety*, accessed April 4, 2021, https://www.dps.texas.gov/section/texas-rangers.

30. "Texas Rangers," *Texas DPS*.

31. "Texas Rangers," *Texas DPS*.

Chapter 4

Biographical Schools
From Popular to Scholarly

William C. Yancey

T exans are devoted to their long and storied history with an intensity that few other states can match. Even in the twenty-first century, many young Texans are raised on tales of heroic deeds past, and even recent arrivals to the state are often able to recount details of episodes such as The Alamo, Goliad, and numerous tales of cattle drives and Indian battles. In the pantheon of Texas heroes, Texas Rangers occupy a lofty position. The Rangers have been a favorite subject of historically minded Texans from the mid-nineteenth century to the present. It is therefore no surprise that biographies of these men, many of them larger-than-life figures, exist as early as the 1870s. Biographers have been particularly busy during the last thirty years and have produced some valuable work.

In his essay "Three Truths in Texas," historian Walter Buenger identified three interpretive streams in Texas History: traditionalism, revisionism, and more recently, cultural constructionism. Traditionalists tended to focus on a top-down approach to history and emphasized the contributions of Anglo males. Revisionists became a force in the 1950s and 1960s and began to challenge the traditional interpretation of history.

They began to highlight the contributions of other ethnic groups and social classes, particularly Black, Mexican, and female Texans. During the 1990s a third approach developed that Buenger referred to as cultural constructionism. This approach was more theoretical and more concerned with the influence of different cultures upon each other, rather than viewing each one in isolation.[1]

Buenger's interpretive framework is useful in helping historians to identify the trends and schools of thought in Texas history. However, placing biographies of Texas Rangers within that model can be somewhat problematic. Biographies of Texas Rangers tend to lend themselves easier to traditionalism than revisionism; many biographers of these men tended to have a favorable view of their subjects and saw them as important. Revisionists were more likely to avoid in-depth studies of people they already considered overrepresented in history and focused their criticism on the Rangers as a whole or wrote about members of groups that had not previously been discussed. Cultural constructionism is a relatively new phenomenon, and being more theoretical in nature, does not lend itself easily to biography.

However, there are several distinct schools of thought within the historiography of Ranger biography. The earliest Ranger biographies can be considered triumphalism. Triumphalists tended to be participants in battles with Indians or Mexico, many of them serving as Texas Rangers themselves, or were personally acquainted with their subjects. These biographers were mostly nonacademic historians and emphasized the heroic nature of the Rangers' struggle against what they saw as lesser civilizations. As products of their time, triumphalist authors often portrayed frontier conflict in stark black-and-white terms: the Rangers were the defenders of civilization and order while Mexicans and Indians were inferior people bent on destroying the advance of Anglo civilization. While many of their characterizations are uncomfortable and offensive to modern readers, triumphalist language reflected the attitudes of the culture in which they lived and wrote. In some cases their writing contained many colloquial elements and tried to reflect the dialect of frontiersmen.

In the early twentieth century, as participants in the early battles against Indians and Mexico were fading from the scene, academic historians began to take up Ranger biography. These authors can be considered academic traditionalists. They tended to focus on the nineteenth century, and they portrayed the Rangers as both the vanguard and protector of Anglo hegemony in Texas, pushing back the Indian frontier and protecting the southern border from treacherous Mexican bandits and insurgents. Although these biographers tended to be more balanced than their triumphalist counterparts, they still represented a top-down view of Texas history in which great Ranger leaders were representative of the entire community.

After the rise of revisionism in the 1960s, Ranger biography went through a largely dormant period before a renaissance of sorts in the 1990s and early 2000s. These new Ranger biographers will be referred to as updated traditionalists. They acknowledged many of the critiques of the revisionists but still largely viewed their subjects as heroic. They tended to be nonacademic historians and were able to utilize archival resources that had not been available to earlier historians. Updated traditionalists generally viewed Texas as more of a Western than a Southern state, and many of them published articles for *True West* magazine.

Finally, a smaller group of biographers will be referred to as synthesizers. These were academic historians who took a more critical view of their subjects while also acknowledging their importance. These biographers tended to emphasize Texas's southern origins and were more influenced by revisionism than the other schools of thought.

The earliest biographies of Texas Rangers were written in the triumphalist style. Many of the earliest biographers of Texas Rangers had been Rangers themselves and were personally acquainted with their subjects. Such is the case with one of the earliest Ranger biographers, John Crittenden Duval. A native of Kentucky, in 1835 Duval left college to fight in the Texas Revolution as part of a volunteer company commanded by his brother. He survived the Goliad Massacre in 1836 and shortly thereafter traveled back east to enroll in the University of Virginia. He returned to Texas in 1840 and worked as a surveyor before joining John C. Hays's Ranger company in 1845 where he served with the subject of his future biography, William "Big Foot" Wallace. After serving in the Confederate Army during the Civil War, Duval began to write, publishing his first book, *Early Times in Texas*, in 1867. Duval was referred to by historian Walter Prescott Webb as Texas's "first man of letters."[2]

In 1867, perhaps shortly after the publication of *Early Times in Texas*, Duval sought out his old comrade-in-arms William Alexander Anderson "Big Foot" Wallace at the latter's ranch in Medina County. He stayed with Wallace for two weeks, hunting, fishing, and recording recollections of his service as a Texas Ranger. Duval's account of Wallace's life was published in 1871 as *The Adventures of Big-Foot Wallace, The Texas Ranger and Hunter*. By his own admission, Duval was not as interested in recording completely factual information as he was with creating an impression of early frontier life. He wrote that he was "well aware that it will not stand the test of criticism as a literary production."[3] The book is typical of the triumphalist style; it is replete with derogatory references to racial minorities and depicts Wallace as a noble frontiersman reclaiming the frontier country from lesser people. Mexicans were frequent subjects for ridicule, being referred to as "swarthy, bandy-legged, contemptible 'greasers'" and "pumpkin-colored Philistines."[4]

Wallace continued to be a popular subject for biographers for decades. In 1899 Andrew Jackson "A. J." Sowell published *Life of "Big Foot" Wallace*. Sowell, born in Seguin in 1848, was a first-generation Texan. His grandparents had emigrated from Tennessee to De Witt's Colony in 1830 when his father, Asa Jarmon Lee Sowell, was 8 years old. Asa served as a Texas Ranger in Jack Hays's company and fought under Henry McCulloch during the Mexican War as well. By the 1850s the family had moved to Hays County and settled along the Blanco River in an area known as Sowell's Valley. Too young to fight in the Civil War, A. J. Sowell joined Company F of the Frontier

Battalion in 1870 and served until June 1871. In 1884 he published his first monograph, *Rangers and Pioneers of Texas*, followed in 1890 by *Early Settlers and Indian Fighters of Southwest Texas*. Both books are excellent examples of triumphalist literature.[5]

Sowell began working with Wallace in the late 1890s, near the end of the latter's long life. Apparently, Wallace was not satisfied with Duval's account of his life and undoubtedly would have known about Sowell from his earlier works as well as having served with Asa Sowell under Jack Hays. Sowell interviewed Wallace at the home of W. W. Cochran in Frio County (where the old Ranger was currently residing) and in 1898 accompanied him to a Ranger reunion at the Texas State Fair in Dallas. *Life of "Big Foot" Wallace* did not contain many of the tall tales found in Duval's earlier work, and Sowell's writing style, while still informal, was less colloquial than Duval's. It is still, however, a prime example of the triumphalist school. Wallace comes across as a noble, albeit rustic, figure protecting the frontier from brutally savage Indians and treacherous Mexicans.[6]

Sowell's account of Wallace's life, while free from the embellishments of Duval's earlier work, contains many of the same prejudices that tended to characterize triumphalist literature. For example, when describing the origins of Anglo Texas, Sowell wrote that "the Mexicans had become jealous and uneasy at the vast number that were coming in and therefore concluded to stop all further immigration of the Anglo-Saxon race and disarm those who had already come."[7] Of one of Wallace's earliest encounters with Indians, Sowell wrote, "These were Lipan Indians who made treaties and broke them at will. They were a branch of the Apaches and always treacherous."[8] One of the elements of Duval's biography that had apparently irritated Wallace was the explanation of how he acquired the nickname "Big Foot." Duval related that the nickname came from the Mier Expedition, while Sowell gave its origin earlier, having to do with an encounter with a Comanche of the same sobriquet.

One prominent biography can be considered a transition between triumphalism and academic traditionalism. In 1909 Albert Bigelow

Paine published a biography of Texas Ranger Captain Bill McDonald.[9] Paine was a native of New Bedford, Massachusetts, but had moved to Kansas as a young man, where he sold photographic supplies. In 1895 he moved to New York City to concentrate on writing and made a name for himself by writing children's books. Although not a trained historian, he quickly gained a reputation as a biographer. By 1901 he had been chosen by Thomas Nast to write the latter's biography, and in 1906 he began working with Mark Twain on a biography of the famous humorist that would eventually be published in four volumes in 1912.[10]

McDonald had been looking for someone to write his memoirs for some time, and he selected Paine for the job during the period in which Paine was recording Twain's reminiscences. The captain had recently left the Frontier Battalion, having been appointed state revenue collector by Governor Thomas Campbell in 1907. It seems likely that McDonald learned of Paine through his connections with politically connected people. Captain McDonald was a friend of political operative E. M. House and had famously accompanied President Theodore Roosevelt on a wolf hunt in Oklahoma in 1908.[11]

Like the earlier triumphalists, Paine relied primarily on interviews with his subject. However, he also placed McDonald within a broader framework, a hallmark of academic historians. Paine's theme, while relating the details of McDonald's career, was to emphasize the role the captain played in the transition of the Texas Rangers from frontier defense to a professional law enforcement agency. Paine stated his purpose at the beginning of this work, describing his book as the story of a man who "reduced those once lawless districts . . . to a condition of such proper behavior that nowhere in this country is life and property safer than in the very localities where only a few years ago the cow-thief and the train-robber reigned supreme."[12]

In addition to recounting McDonald's exploits in policing West Texas, Paine included many colorful quotes from the captain that would go down in Ranger lore. For example, McDonald's famous maxim, "No man in the wrong can stand up against a fellow that's in the right and keeps on a-comin'," was first recorded for posterity in Paine's monograph.[13] Others were misquoted. Paine described an incident in which McDonald arrived in Dallas to stop a prize fight. When the mayor asked where the other Rangers were, McDonald replied, "Hell! Ain't I enough? There's only one prize fight!" This was later misquoted in Ranger lore as "One riot, one Ranger."[14] *Captain Bill McDonald* still reveals the biases and racial attitudes of late nineteenth- and early twentieth-century Texans. Paine is honest about McDonald's world view and includes quotes replete with epithets modern readers would find offensive. The chapters concerning the Brownsville Riot of 1906 reveal McDonald's perspective that Black troops were solely to blame for the troubles in that town and that their officers covered up misdeeds.[15] The book also contained numerous factual errors.

By the turn of the twentieth century, the triumphalist school of historical writing in Texas was fading away. Many of the early Rangers had died, as had many of their colleagues who wrote about them.[16] In addition, the historical profession was becoming more professional. After the Civil War, young Americans who had studied in Germany returned to the United States determined to apply scientific methodologies to the study of history. These young scholars were instrumental in founding the American Historical Association (AHA) in 1884. Among the early (but not charter) members of the AHA was George P. Garrison, a graduate of the University of Edinburgh in Scotland who began teaching at the University of Texas in 1884, a year after that institution's founding. In 1897 Garrison was the driving force behind the formation of the Texas State Historical Association. Using the Wisconsin Historical Society as his model, Garrison wanted to combine academic and nonacademic historians under one organization. He wisely included such Texas luminaries as former governor Oran M. Roberts, former Texas Ranger and Confederate officer John S. "Rip" Ford, US senator John H. Reagan, and Dallas lawyer Dudley G. Wooten.[17]

This gave rise to academic traditionalism as a school of Ranger biography. This new generation of authors, like triumphalists, emphasized the heroic nature of their subjects. However, their treatment was more nuanced, and their writing was less colloquial. While many of these works relied on interviews with subjects that were still alive, many of them were beginning to utilize archival material as well. Perhaps more importantly, academic traditionalists were more concerned with putting their subjects into a larger historical context. This type of Ranger biography became prevalent after 1935 when historian Walter Prescott Webb published *The Texas Rangers: A Century of Frontier Defense* in 1935. Webb's seminal work on the Rangers was the first academic treatment of the force and was soon followed by a number of biographies of famous Rangers written by academic historians. The two best examples of academic traditionalists were two native Texans, Dora Neill Raymond and James Kimmins Greer.[18]

Dora Neill Raymond was born in El Paso and spent her formative years in San Antonio. She earned her BA and MA from the University of Texas in 1917 and her PhD from Columbia University in 1921. Her dissertation, "British Policy and Opinion During the Franco-Prussian War," was directed by Charles Downer Hazen and William A. Dunning. Dunning was the founder of the informal Dunning School, a group of historians who viewed Reconstruction, especially Black suffrage and political participation, as an unwise policy forced upon the South. Although this viewpoint had little effect on her early works on British history, one can detect elements of Dunning's influence in her biography of Texas Ranger Lee Hall. She soon began to write biographies, starting with works on British poets John Milton and Lord Byron before turning to her native state for inspiration. In 1940 she published *Captain Lee Hall of Texas.*[19]

Raymond employed a variety of sources in writing her biography of Hall. Hers was the first full-length biography of the Ranger captain, so she relied heavily on newspaper accounts and official documents. Much of her information came from interviews with Captain Hall's daughter and namesake, Jessie Lee Hall Keith. Like other traditionalist biographers, Raymond emphasized the heroic nature of Hall's service as a lawman and his bravery in taming lawless elements of the

Texas frontier. However, she did not leave out the negative aspects of Hall's life, including his unsuccessful tenure as ranch manager and his indictment and subsequent acquittal for embezzlement after a controversial term as agent for the Anadarko Indian Reservation in Oklahoma. Of his later years, spent in numerous unsuccessful business ventures in Mexico, Raymond wrote, "As his clothing grew threadbare and his dreams grew dim, drink became more necessary as a solvent for his doubts, and a stimulant to his imagination."[20] Raymond's writing style was less colloquial than earlier works and at times florid. Perhaps her style was influenced by the subjects of two previous biographies, John Milton and Lord Byron.

James K. Greer was born in Bosque County, Texas, in 1896. He earned his bachelor's, master's, and doctorate degrees from the University of Texas and later taught history at Texas Women's University in Denton; Howard University (now Samford University) in Birmingham, Alabama; and Hardin-Simmons University in Abilene until his retirement in 1959. Greer produced two valuable works on prominent Texas Rangers. He edited the memoirs of James Buckner "Buck" Barry, publishing it 1932 as *A Texas Ranger and Frontiersman: The Days of Buck Barry in Texas.*[21] Twenty years later Greer produced the first full-length biography of famed Ranger Captain John Coffee "Jack" Hays. Greer likely became interested in Hays while studying Barry, who served under the former in the Ranger service and the Mexican War.[22]

Although Greer was not able to employ interviews with people who knew Hays, like Raymond he employed a variety of sources, both archival and secondary. Although this was the first full-length study of Hays, many brief sketches and unpublished manuscripts of his life were extant at the time Greer was writing. According to Greer, "These have not been adequate even for their purpose, as the authors invariably fell into numerous errors of fact, copied each other's mistakes or neglected many activities of his life."[23] Greer's account of Hays's life and career, while emphasizing his importance in protecting the Texas frontier and his valuable service as a scout and counterinsurgent in the Mexican

War, lacks the hyperbole of the triumphalist biographies of the late nineteenth and early twentieth centuries.

Both Raymond and Greer represent a generation of academic historians that had been heavily influenced by traditionalist influences; Raymond had studied with Dunning at Columbia, and Greer had almost certainly taken classes with Charles Ramsdell, a Dunning School historian, at Texas. The next generation of academic historians did not seem to be very interested in Ranger biographies. During the 1950s and 1960s, a new approach to history called revisionism began to slowly dominate the profession. Scholars like Kenneth Stampp challenged traditional views of slavery, while other historians emphasized the need for a change in methodology from top-down studies to more inclusive scholarship that emphasized the contributions of common folk, Blacks, Latinos, and women. The timing was not surprising, as the academy was being influenced by the burgeoning Civil Rights Movement. Revisionist historians began to take a different view of the Rangers, the most notable being "*With His Pistol in His Hand*" by Américo Paredes and *Gunpowder Justice* by Chicano historians Julian Samora, Joe Bernal, and Albert Peña.[24] Both books were highly critical of the Texas Rangers and their portrayal as heroes by Webb, J. Frank Dobie, and others. The latter argued that the Rangers had always existed to protect the interests of the Anglo power elite at the expense of Mexicans, Indians, and Blacks. Over the next several decades, academic historians tended to eschew Ranger biographies. Since most famous Rangers of the nineteenth and early twentieth century had been white men, biographies of them might have been seen as unfashionable in the academy.

As a result, Ranger biography soon became the province of nonacademic historians again. After a long period when few Ranger biographies were published, the genre became popular again during the late 1990s and early 2000s. Several factors helped to contribute to this increased interest. In 1968 the Texas Ranger Museum opened in Waco. The Texas Legislature also designated this entity as the Texas Ranger Hall of Fame in 1973. The museum continued to grow and become a tourist attraction through the next several decades, aided by its location close to Baylor University and its visibility from Interstate 35. In addition, the Former Texas Rangers Association opened a museum in San Antonio and recently opened the Texas Rangers Heritage Center in Fredericksburg. This showed that Texans were still very much interested in the history of the Rangers.

Perhaps the most important event in the revival of interest in the Texas Rangers was the publication of Robert M. Utley's two-volume reappraisal of the Rangers. *Lone Star Justice*, published in 2002, focused on the Rangers from their creation to 1910, and *Lone Star Lawmen*, published in 2007, focused on the Rangers from 1910 forward. Utley's seminal work produced a renewed interest in the Rangers similar to the way that Webb's 1935 book had. Utley's purpose was to balance traditionalist Ranger history with new insights and perspectives emphasized by revisionists. After discussing the competing interpretations, Utley wrote, "Examples of confirming exploits undergird each interpretation. . . . Not surprisingly, the historical reality lies somewhere between the extremes."[25]

In the wake of Utley's two-volume history, Ranger biography began to experience something of a renaissance. This new biographical school can be considered updated traditionalism. Updated traditionalists tended to be nonacademic historians who generally viewed the Rangers in a positive light while acknowledging the atrocities they sometimes committed. They became more interested in twentieth-century Rangers than previous historians had been, and even nineteenth-century subjects tended to be from the period after the formation of the Frontier Battalion in 1874. Updated traditionalists also tended to be thorough in plumbing the depths of archival sources.

Even before Utley's groundbreaking work, nonacademic historians were beginning to expand into twentieth-century Ranger history. One of the earliest examples of an updated traditionalist was Brownson Malsch. Malsch, a journalist and local historian from Jackson County, Texas, published a biography of Manuel T. "Lone Wolf" Gonzaullas in 1980. Published only three years after Gonzaullas's death, Malsch's biography relied heavily on the Ranger's own personal scrapbooks. While it lacks an interpretive framework, *Lone Wolf* is a detailed account of Gonzaullas's long career, and when it was published it was one of the few biographies of a twentieth-century Ranger.[26]

One particularly prolific Ranger biographer has been Chuck Parsons. Parsons, a retired high school principal from the Midwest (Minnesota and Wisconsin) moved to Texas specifically to research and write about Texas outlaws and lawmen. He has been responsible for filling in gaps in Ranger historiography, writing biographies of important Rangers such as Leander McNelly, John B. Armstrong, and John R. Hughes, among others. An updated traditionalist, Parsons tended to view his subjects as heroic figures, forces for good in a harsh world, while acknowledging the atrocities and negative actions they sometimes undertook. Parsons's books were meticulously researched, and he included some sources hostile to the Rangers, such as accounts of their deeds from Mexican newspapers.

Parsons' biography of McNelly, cowritten by Marianne Little, was the first full-length study of the Ranger commander. A controversial figure, McNelly had typically been lauded by Anglo-Texans and vilified by Mexicans on both sides of the river. Parsons and Little did not avoid negative accounts of McNelly's Rangers, including their abuse of a Mexican ranchero who they refused to pay for forage and cursed before tearing down his fence as they left his property.[27] The authors also noted that McNelly's actions in crossing into Mexico to attack suspected cattle thieves were illegal while noting that McNelly himself did not see it that way. The same approach can be seen in Parsons's biography of one of McNelly's men, John B. Armstrong.[28] He was certainly critical of the Rangers crossing into Mexico and attacking the wrong ranch, but tempered that criticism somewhat by writing, "He [McNelly] had not only killed possibly innocent people but he had lost the element of surprise."[29] Nonetheless, Parsons made a real contribution to Ranger historiography by researching men who had often been mythologized but not seriously studied.

In recent years Ranger biographers have begun to pay more attention to twentieth-century subjects. Two biographies of Frank Hamer were published in the last several years, the most recent being John Boessenecker's *Texas Ranger: The Epic Life of Frank Hamer, the Man Who Killed Bonnie and Clyde*.[30] Boessenecker, a retired police officer and San Francisco trial lawyer, wrote several books on law enforcement in the Old West before producing his biography on Hamer. He did not shy away from issues of race and class, devoting an entire chapter to Hamer's clashes with the Ku Klux Klan during the 1920s and his unsuccessful attempt to protect George Hughes, a Black defendant, from a lynch mob in Sherman in 1930. Boessenecker was also willing to criticize Hamer. When discussing the 1930 Sherman race riot, he noted that Hamer, while being willing to shoot a white man to protect a Black man, made the decision not to fire on a mob surrounding the Grayson County jail, instead opting to wait for reinforcements from Dallas. Boessenecker added, "It was a convenient but wrong decision, for it resulted in one of the most horrific displays in America's sorry history of racial conflict."[31] His chapters on the hunt for Bonnie and Clyde are well researched and do much to dispel the mythology of that episode.

Bob Alexander, like Boessenecker a former law enforcement officer, expanded the breadth of Ranger biography into the twentieth century with his 2018 publication *Old Riot, New Ranger: Captain Jack Dean, Texas Ranger and US Marshal*.[32] Alexander also helped to fill in the gaps of Ranger historiography with his biography of nineteenth-century Ranger Ira Aten.[33] This excellent biography of an important Ranger who served in the ranks (Aten was a sergeant, but never a captain in the Frontier Battalion) was an upgrade over an earlier biography of Aten and will hopefully be followed by other biographies of Rangers serving in the ranks.

Finally, although most recent Ranger biographies in recent years have been written by nonacademic historians, their counterparts in the academy have produced some important works as well. These academic historians can be considered synthesizers.

Their works were important in incorporating the critiques of revisionism with more traditional views of the Texas Rangers. They were interested in placing their subjects within a broader historical context, and sometimes tended to view their subjects as products of the Old South more than the Old West.

Around the same time that Utley was researching and writing his groundbreaking volumes, fellow New Mexicans Charles H. Harris III and Louis R. Sadler were producing the first detailed study of Texas Rangers during the Mexican Revolution. In 2004 Harris and Sadler, history professors at New Mexico State University, published *The Texas Rangers and the Mexican Revolution: The Bloodiest Decade, 1910–1920.*[34] In 2010 they published a companion volume, *Texas Ranger Biographies: Those Who Served, 1920–1921.*[35] The latter work provides detailed information on the 1,782 men who served as Rangers during that decade. Harris and Sadler did not shy away from criticizing the excesses and brutality of the force during this period, while at the same time opposing some of the arguments made by recent critics of the Rangers. One of the most important contributions made by the authors was the untangling of the complex web of Regular Rangers, Special Rangers, and Loyalty Rangers during this period. Harris and Sadler's approach to the subject and their detailed analysis place them clearly in the synthesizer camp of Ranger biography.

Another important work that can be classified as synthesis is Paul Spellman's excellent biography of James Abijah Brooks, one of the Four Great Captains of the late nineteenth and early twentieth century.[36] Spellman, a professor at Wharton County Junior College, views Brooks as a product of his upraising in Kentucky during the Civil War and Reconstruction. He is also fair in his appraisal of Brooks's career as a Ranger, county judge, and a family man, praising some of his actions and being critical of others. Both of these characteristics—a view of their subjects as more Southern than Western and a willingness to both praise and criticize their subjects—are hallmarks of synthesizers. Spellman's biography of

John H. Rogers (another of the Four Great Captains) is a similarly impressive work of synthesis.[37]

Historian Harold J. Weiss Jr., a former professor at Jamestown Community College in New York, can be considered a synthesizer. In 2009 he published an updated biography of Bill McDonald.[38] Weiss utilized archival records that official biographer Paine had not a hundred years earlier. The result was a more nuanced and balanced view of McDonald that took into account his many strengths and weaknesses as a Ranger captain. He also examined his subject's career as a state revenue agent in a way Paine could not have done since McDonald was at the beginning of that job when Paine published his biography. Weiss was very frank about McDonald's racial views, writing, "McDonald would be called, by modern standards, a bigot in his beliefs about minority groups."[39] He goes on to add that while McDonald could be harsh with Black suspects, he was also capable of protecting Black prisoners from lynch mobs. Weiss attributed his racial attitudes to his upbringing in Mississippi during the mid-nineteenth century.

In 2011 Richard B. McCaslin produced *Fighting Stock*, the first biography of John S. "Rip" Ford since 1964.[40] McCaslin, a professor at the University of North Texas, viewed Ford as being shaped more by the South than the West, writing, "If nothing else, this book seeks to recover the complexity of Ford's career, and in so doing provide a useful perspective on Texas as not solely a frontier state, but also a Southern state."[41] He interprets many of Ford's actions as being in defense of slavery, including his time as a newspaper editor, leader in the secession movement, and Confederate officer. McCaslin wrote that although Ford never owned slaves, "his aggressive efforts, and those of others like him, made Texas a very Southern state in the nineteenth century."[42] This kind of reappraisal and rethinking of a noted Ranger as more Old South than Old West is an excellent example of synthesis.

In conclusion, over the past 150 years in which biographers have written about Texas Rangers, the historiography has progressed from triumphalism to academic traditionalism to updated traditionalism to synthesis. Early biographies were written by participants in wars with Indians and Mexicans and were mostly based on personal interviews with the subjects. In the early twentieth century, academic traditionalism became the dominant school of Ranger biography. These works tended to be written by academic historians and although they continued to view the Rangers as heroic figures, they were far better researched and employed numerous archival documents. Revisionism became a force in historiography during the 1950s and 1960s and forced a reappraisal of previously commonly held notions. Attitudes long deemed acceptable fell out of favor and Ranger biography shifted to accommodate this new paradigm. Although it is difficult to find any truly revisionist biographies of Texas Rangers, biographies from the 1980s forward tended to be updated traditionalism. These works were mostly the product of nonacademic historians and acknowledged the negative aspects of their subjects while still viewing them as mostly forces for good. Finally, academic historians writing Ranger biography in the past thirty years can be considered synthesizers. They acknowledged the criticisms that revisionists had of traditional views of Texas Rangers while attempting to understand their subjects in the context of their times.

So where does the field go from here? There is still plenty of fertile ground to be plowed by historians. Biographies of Rangers who served mainly after 1935 are still scarce, although some good examples exist. Further work remains to be done on the contributions of Black, Latino, and female Rangers. Although many of the great nineteenth-century figures have been written about, plenty of opportunities exist for fresh perspectives and reappraisals. Studies of individuals in the ranks are also scarce, at least in terms of individual biography. In short, although more words have been written about the Texas Rangers than any similar state law enforcement agency in the United States, the opportunities for new scholarship appear boundless.

Notes

1. Walter L. Buenger, "Three Truths in Texas," in *Beyond Texas through Time: Breaking Away from Past Interpretations*, ed. Walter L. Buenger and Arnoldo De Léon, (College Station: Texas A&M University Press, 2011), 1–4.
2. J. Frank Dobie, "Duval, John Crittenden," *Handbook of Texas Online*, updated October 16, 2020, http://www.tshaonline.org/handbook/online/articles/fdu33.
3. John C. Duval, *The Adventures of Big-Foot Wallace, The Texas Ranger and Hunter* (Philadelphia: Claxton, Remsen, and Haffelfinger, 1871), 6.
4. Duval, *Adventures of Big-Foot Wallace*, 179, 171.
5. Dorothy C. Ashton, "Sowell, Andrew Jackson," *Handbook of Texas Online*, updated March 23, 2019, http://www.tshaonline.org/handbook/online/articles/fso07.
6. A. J. Sowell, *Life of "Big Foot" Wallace: The Great Ranger Captain* (Austin: State House Press, 1989).
7. Sowell, *Life of "Big Foot" Wallace*, 7.
8. Sowell, *Life of "Big Foot" Wallace*, 21.
9. Albert Bigelow Paine, *Captain Bill McDonald, Texas Ranger: A Story of Frontier Reform* (New York: J.J. Little & Ives, 1909).
10. *New York Times*, April 10, 1937.
11. Paine, *Captain Bill McDonald*, foreword; Harold J. Weiss Jr., and Rie Jarratt, "McDonald, William Jesse," *Handbook of Texas Online*, updated October 8, 2023, http://www.tshaonline.org/handbook/online/articles/fmc43.
12. Paine, *Captain Bill McDonald*, 14–15.
13. Paine, *Captain Bill McDonald*, 79.
14. Paine, *Captain Bill McDonald*, 220.
15. Paine, *Captain Bill McDonald*, 328–29.
16. Duval died in 1897. While Sowell lived until 1921, he turned his attention to writing county-level histories such as *History of Fort Bend County* and *Incidents Connected with the Early History of Guadalupe County Texas*. Ashton, "Sowell, Andrew Jackson."
17. Richard B. McCaslin, *At the Heart of Texas: 100 Years of the Texas State Historical Association, 1897–1997* (Austin: Texas State Historical Association, 2007), 13–16.
18. Walter Prescott Webb, *The Texas Rangers: A Century of Frontier Defense* (Boston: Houghton Mifflin, 1935); Necah Stewart Furman, "Webb,

Walter Prescott," *Handbook of Texas Online*, updated October 18, 2016, http://www.tshaonline.org/handbook/online/articles/fwe06.

19. Agnes Wright Spring, ed., *The Arrow: Official Publication of the Pi Beta Phi Fraternity* 38, no. 4 (Spring 1922).

20. Dora Neill Raymond, *Captain Lee Hall of Texas* (Norman: University of Oklahoma Press, 1940), 336.

21. James K. Greer, *A Texas Ranger and Frontiersman: The Days of Buck Barry in Texas* (Dallas: Southwest Press, 1932). Dr. Greer, who died in 1998 at the age of 101, is actually buried next to Buck in the Barry Family Cemetery in Bosque County.

22. James Kimmins Greer, *Colonel Jack Hays: Texas Leader and California Builder* (New York: E.P. Dutton, 1952).

23. Greer, *Colonel Jack Hays*, 10.

24. Américo Paredes, *"With His Pistol in His Hand": A Border Ballad and Its Hero* (Austin: University of Texas Press, 1958); Julian Samora, Joe Bernal, Albert Peña, *Gunpowder Justice: A Reassessment of the Texas Rangers* (Notre Dame: University of Notre Dame Press, 1979).

25. Robert M. Utley, *Lone Star Justice: The First Century of the Texas Rangers* (New York: Oxford University Press, 2002), xii–xiii.

26. Brownson Malsch, *Captain M. T. Lone Wolf Gonzaullas: The Only Texas Ranger Captain of Spanish Descent* (Austin: Shoal Creek, 1980).

27. Chuck Parsons and Marianne E. Hall Little, *Captain L. H. McNelly, Texas Ranger: The Life and Times of a Fighting Man* (Austin: State House Press, 2001), 209.

28. Chuck Parsons, *John B. Armstrong: Texas Ranger and Pioneer Ranchman* (College Station: Texas A&M University Press, 2007).

29. Parsons, *John B. Armstrong*, 20.

30. John Boessenecker, *Texas Ranger: The Epic Life of Frank Hamer, the Man Who Killed Bonnie and Clyde* (New York: Thomas Dunne Books, 2016). The other recent Hamer biography is John H. Jenkins and Gordon Frost, *"I'm Frank Hamer": The Life of a Texas Peace Officer* (Austin: Pemberton Press, 1968). Boessenecker's book is a more exhaustive account of Hamer's life and career.

31. Boessenecker, *Texas Ranger*, 369.

32. Bob Alexander, *Old Riot, New Ranger: Captain Jack Dean, Texas Ranger and US Marshal* (Denton: University of North Texas Press, 2018).

33. Bob Alexander, *Rawhide Ranger, Ira Aten: Enforcing Law on the Texas Frontier* (Denton: University of North Texas Press, 2011).

34. Charles H. Harris III and Louis R. Sadler, *The Texas Rangers and the Mexican Revolution: The Bloodiest Decade, 1910–1920* (Albuquerque: University of New Mexico Press, 2004).

35. Charles H. Harris III, Frances E. Harris, and Louis R. Sadler, *Texas Ranger Biographies: Those Who Served, 1910–1921* (Albuquerque: University of New Mexico Press, 2009).

36. Paul N. Spellman, *Captain J. A. Brooks, Texas Ranger* (Denton: University of North Texas Press, 2007).

37. Paul N. Spellman, *Captain John H. Rogers, Texas Ranger* (Denton: University of North Texas Press, 2008).

38. Harold J. Weiss Jr., *Yours to Command: The Life and Legend of Texas Ranger Captain Bill McDonald* (Denton: University of North Texas Press, 2009).

39. Weiss, *Yours to Command*, 16–17.

40. Richard B. McCaslin, *Fighting Stock: John S. "Rip" Ford of Texas* (Fort Worth: TCU Press, 2011). For an earlier biography of Ford, see W. J. Hughes, *Rebellious Ranger: Rip Ford and the Old Southwest* (Norman: University of Oklahoma Press, 1964).

41. McCaslin, *Fighting Stock*, xv.

42. McCaslin, *Fighting Stock*, 36.

Chapter 5

Historiography of the Texas Rangers in Selected Periodical Literature and Book Chapters

Kenneth W. Howell

Professional historians have struggled to understand the Texas Rangers for more than a century. During this spate of time, some academics have heralded the Rangers as heroes, brave defenders of the frontier, and men of impeccable character, while others have portrayed them as bloodthirsty, racist murderers who were just as bad (if not worse) than the outlaws they sought to bring to justice. For professional historians these shifts in interpretation are not surprising. Like other scholars within the liberal arts, historians find it impossible to divorce themselves from the cultural beliefs of their own generation. In other words, historians are a product of their times, viewing the past through the filtered lens of the present and imposing cultural and social beliefs of their generation on historical events and figures. Even though they claim to maintain impartiality and objectivity, most historians will agree that they cannot achieve this lofty goal.

Instead, scholars justify their biases by claiming they are creating a "useable past"—one that either supports or rejects cultural trends of the present and leaves the general public wondering why their understanding of the past is at odds with that of trained scholars. Conversely, the questions raised by lay historians seem of little concern to professionals, who see little or no value in popular history, claiming that the general public's understanding of the past is shaped by "myths and legends." Therefore, tensions regarding historical interpretations ultimately erupt into heated debates between the general public and academics (as well as within the scholarly community itself), leading to confusion and distortion of the past.

The Texas Rangers serves as an excellent example of how one generation can proclaim a specific group of historical actors as heroes while subsequent generations can crucify them as scoundrels and murderers. This essay surveys the evolution of scholarly interpretations associated with the Texas Rangers by examining selected articles published in academic journals and popular magazines as well as specific book chapters included in edited volumes. An analysis of these publications reveals the strained relationship that historians have experienced for more than a century as they have attempted to unravel the complexities associated with the Rangers.

Between the 1840s and 1880s, writers occasionally wrote about the exploits of the Texas Rangers in newspaper articles and novellas, but it was not until the late 1890s and early 1900s that more extensive accounts of the lawmen's activities became prevalent in early history books and academic journals. These early publications marked an initial phase in the historiography of the Texas Rangers and established the "traditional" views of the organization and its men. Based primarily on oral traditions, the scholarship of this period defined the Rangers as noble and brave defenders of the Texas frontier, men "synonymous with the highest development of manliness and heroism."[1]

One of the earliest published histories of the Rangers was Wilburn H. King's "The Texas Ranger Service and History of the Rangers, with Observations on Their Value as a Police Protection," which appeared in Dudley G. Wooten's *A Comprehensive History of Texas, 1685 to 1897*.[2] Having served as the adjutant general of Texas between 1881 and 1891, King was well acquainted with the history of the early Rangers. Consistent with other works from this period, King attempts to capture the essence of what it meant to be a member of the Texas Rangers over time and space. The author lamented the fact that historical data related to the early history of the Rangers was lost to history because the office of the adjutant general of Texas was destroyed by a fire in the winter of 1853–1854, and in 1881 the same fate befell the state capitol. As a result, the fires destroyed important military documents, making it impossible to "procure authoritative original documents relating to military events between the years 1835 and 1881."[3] The absence of historical records explains why early Ranger historians primarily relied on oral histories and the early writings of frontier settlers, both of which left researchers with incomplete and mythical accounts on their subject. It also explains why there is still a debate over the creation and organization of the Rangers. Even in 1898 this point was made clear in Wooten's history of Texas when the editor summarized the main points of King's more detailed piece. He wrote, "The term 'Texas Rangers' is somewhat vague when sought to be historically applied to the various volunteer and irregular organizations that have figured in the frontier service of Texas. Even the exact date of its original application is involved in doubt."[4] Wooten continued by describing a brief history of the Rangers, tracing their activities during American colonization of Mexico, the republic years, the Mexican War, and the Civil War. Throughout this entire time, the Rangers primarily defended the Texas frontier against Indian depredations, but they also periodically quelled domestic upheaval. The only extended lapse in service was during Reconstruction when the State Police was created to maintain order on the domestic front and the US Army assumed sole responsibility for the protection of the frontier. In 1874 the state legislature created the Frontier Battalion to replace the State Police and augment the efforts of federal troops. This group, like the various categories of Rangers before them, defended the frontier. However, they also became more involved in the suppression of crime, particularly in Western and Southern locals.[5]

While King and Wooten provided one of the earliest histories of the Rangers, their writings also reflect the cultural beliefs of the late nineteenth century. Both editor and author maintained a bias in favor of the Rangers' activities and embraced an Anglocentric perspective. For example, Wooten states, "The deeds of daring, the midnight rides, and fearless encounters of these men with the desperadoes and border bandits of the Western and Northwestern Texas, as well as their aid in protecting the regular officers and tribunals of the law, would furnish abundant material for a romantic and thrilling history of adventure and bravery unsurpassed in the annuals of mediaeval knight-errantry." The editor goes on to explain, however, that a lack of historical documents and space limitations prevented King from writing "an account of the many exploits and achievements of the brave officers and men who have from time to time composed this unique and hardy fellowship of modern cavaliers."[6] Throughout his chapter King commented on the heroism and effectiveness of the Rangers. For example, he writes that "within and beyond this wide region [of the Texas frontier] lived and roamed the many bands and tribes of savages whose frequent forays upon the white settlements of Texas, with similar raids by the Mexicans, furnished the Rangers the occasions for exhibiting those qualities of readiness, tireless activity and endurance, fertility of resources, quickness of mind, and steadiness of courage and purpose in desperate situations which have carried their name and fame to far-distant lands, and made the title or term 'Texas Ranger' synonymous with the highest development of manliness and heroism." King further states, "In the singular and varying phases of political fortune and fellowship which have befallen Texas in the past sixty years . . . the Ranger organization was always needed and provided for with more or less liberality, and has always been found a safeguard to the lives, liberty, and property of the orderly, law-abiding people of Texas."[7] Such comments suggest that King was less than an objective chronicler of the early Rangers. It is possible even to trace the famous Ranger slogan "One Riot, One Ranger" to King's work. Using different phraseology, King writes, "Scores of cases might be adduced to show that a few Rangers—sometimes even one alone—could arrest without difficulty men of the most desperate character and condition, who could resist a sheriff unto death!" In fairness, King does acknowledge that the Rangers committed unspecified atrocities during their early existence, stating that it would be a mistake to think that they "always strictly [operated] within the exact limits of [their] legal authority." After this vague and brief admission, the author reinforces his original perspective by claiming that despite these "admitted follies and wrong-doings," a knowledge of the general character, conduct, and capabilities of this Ranger organization, and of the sum-total of its good work . . . will compel the admission that the value of its service is far beyond any estimate that can be made."[8]

King's article was unique among other Ranger publications at the turn of the twentieth century because it followed a comprehensive approach to the topic. Other accounts discussed Ranger activities within the context of early settlers' reminiscences on the Texas frontier. Many of these accounts derived from oral interviews conducted in the latter years of the settlers' lives or from surviving family members who provided second-hand information about their deceased elders. In other publications the articles were transcriptions of primary documents that were in some way associated with the Rangers. Like King, the authors of these early writings generally portrayed the Rangers as heroic defenders of Anglo settlers living on the wild Texas frontier. For example, in July 1901 George P. Garrison, the editor of the *Quarterly of the Texas State Historical Association*, published "Reminiscences of Capt. Jessie Burnam," a short piece that Mrs. Julia Lee Sinks obtained from Burnam's daughter, Miss Sada Burnam.[9] The article focused on her father's survival on the frontier, including descriptions of early battles with hostile Indian tribes in the early 1820s. The frontiersman claimed to have been involved in the first engagement between members of Stephen F. Austin's frontier militia (now considered to be the first Texas Rangers) and a nearby Indian tribe at Skull Creek. During this encounter the Rangers "killed fourteen Indians and wounded seven, who afterwards went and complained to the general government [in Mexico]."[10]

A few months following this initial encounter, Burnam replaced Robert Kuykendall as the captain of Austin's militia. The frontier captain's brief descriptions of his exploits reveal that these early "rangers" had to be ready at a moment's notice and had to constantly adapt to changing circumstances on the trail and the field of battle. During one incident a settler discovered a group of Native Americans was stealing horses from Burnam's homestead. Once informed of the theft, the frontiersman leaped from his bed and mounted his only remaining horse, "taking a pair of holster pistols and a rifle" with him.[11] Burnam overtook the hostiles less than a mile from his home. The captain dismounted and fired his weapons with no effect, so he remounted his steed and continued the chase. Realizing that his only chance was to stampede the horses, Burnam recalled that he "made a charge, yelling and shooting at the same time. The Indians stopped and prepared for me, thinking I would run through them." He continued, "Attention being drawn from the horses, they turned towards home, as I expected. No sooner was this done than I charged in between them and the Indians. They fired one gun and a number of arrows, but none hit me."[12]

Burnam's account was one of many published reminiscences that presented the Rangers as brave, heroic, effective frontier defenders. Most of these early articles are based on documents and firsthand accounts of specific events, especially those published in the *Quarterly of the Texas State Historical Association*.[13] The editors of the *Quarterly* included these types of documents for reasons beyond simply preserving the historical record of the state. At the turn of the century, the University of Texas at Austin was attempting to establish and build a reputable history department. One way to achieve recognition and notoriety was to develop a first-class archive for collections of primary documents, a depository that would attract scholarly attention across the nation. As such, the History Department at the University of Texas at Austin began an extensive campaign to collect any existing documents related to the history of Texas and the broader Southwest. To showcase their most prized collections, the editors of the *Quarterly* published excerpts from selected documents, especially those that highlighted characteristics and cultural myths that Texans embraced— including accounts about frontier life, the Texas Revolution, soldier experiences during the Mexican War and Civil War, the cattle industry, and the Texas Rangers.[14]

Although some of the early articles published in the *Quarterly* briefly mention the Texas Rangers, none of them provided a comprehensive examination of the organization.[15] Instead, these articles presented various accounts of life on the Texas frontier, revealing much about the circumstances and conditions in which the Rangers operated. Also, the publications offered key insights into the mindset of Texans regarding Native Americans, Mexicans, and Tejanos. Today the works offer interesting insights into the mindset of Rangers because there is no reason to believe that they held views contrary to their non-Ranger neighbors on the frontier. For example, the Rangers, like many Texans, believed that federal troops were ineffective in their defense of the frontier, especially in the post–Civil War era. Commenting on the aftermath of a joint Mexican and Indian raid on the southern border of Texas, Capt. John J. Dix stated, "He was not favorably impressed with the efficiency of US troops, under existing orders governing their movements; had more faith in one company of Texans . . . than a regiment of regulars." Dix continued, "Indian warfare [required that] a commanding officer should be clothed with discretionary powers." The captain's comments suggest that frontier justice sometimes required extralegal actions, especially when countering "atrocities [such as] the murder and mutilation of children and men indiscriminately."[16]

Examining the early period of Anglo settlement in Texas, many of the early settlers included in J. H. Kuykendall's series of articles titled "Reminiscences of Early Texas: A Collection from the Austin Papers" discussed the hardships of life on the frontier prior to the outbreak of the Texas Revolution. While each settler's recollection was unique, most discussed Indian encounters comparable to those experienced by

Jesse Burnam and detailed the activities of the volunteer militias that Stephen F. Austin formed to defend the colony against Indian raids. Because these militias used tactics embraced by later generations of Texas Rangers, it is not surprising that scholars have traced the origins of the Rangers to this period.[17]

In most of these early accounts, the Rangers and their predecessors were presented in favorable terms. Occasionally, the authors or editors might question the lawmen's actions, but at no time was their bravery, character, or abilities seriously challenged. Given that many of these early publications derived from firsthand accounts, the absence of any serious criticism is understandable. Also, if the conditions described in these sources bear any semblance to reality, the Rangers were indeed a unique breed of frontier warrior. Modern scholars do not have to agree with the tactics or motives employed by these early frontiersmen to understand that their primary goal was to protect their communities during extremely difficult times.

The 1920s ushered in a new phase of Ranger historiography. During this decade Walter Prescott Webb wrote several articles on the modern Texas Rangers that appeared in *The State Trooper: A Magazine of Law and Order*.[18] Though Webb wrote these articles in defense of the integrity and reputation of the Rangers, his editorials provide a unique glimpse into the activities and problems confronting their organization during the 1920s.

In one of his earlier articles, Webb attempted to place the modern Texas Rangers in proper historical context, explaining that the organization in the 1920s faced many of the same challenges that confronted Rangers during the late nineteenth century. Between 1874 and 1900, Webb recognized that there existed two types of Rangers—those protecting the Texas-Mexico border and those serving as policemen in the interior. Webb found the same distinction among the Rangers existed in the early twentieth century. Based on this structural dichotomy of the modern force, Webb highlighted the differences between Border Rangers and Interior Rangers, explaining that each type of lawman faced unique challenges as defined by the duties that they were asked to perform. Claiming that the Rangers were ideally suited for preserving the law on the border, he wrote, "The Mexicans, the smugglers, bootleggers, cattle thieves and all desperate characters have a respect and fear for them that they do not have for the United States soldier, customs inspector, or prohibition officer." He continued, "The Ranger has gained this respect by his fearlessness and boldness, and—it must be stated in truth—by his accurate aim." Webb concludes his assessment of the Border Rangers by stating, "The Texas Ranger does not take chances on the border—he cannot afford to. About the only instructions he carries is to take care of himself and bring in his man. A Border Ranger is a different type of man altogether from the Interior Ranger. He is a more dangerous man, and asks fewer questions than the interior man must ask."[19]

Webb also defined the duties of the Interior Rangers, commenting that they were men who "do the work which is familiar to the State Police everywhere. They run down bootleggers and auto thieves, disperse mobs, guard prisoners, attend court trials where violence is threatened, 'clean up' oil towns and camps that have fallen into the hands of the lawless element. In short, they move about over the state attending to the tasks that have become too big for the local police and county officers."[20] In the remainder of his article, Webb describes the nuts and bolts of the organization—command structure, recruitment, logistics of travel, officer pay, style of dress, and reputation. Based on his favorable comments, there can be no doubt that Webb was enamored with his subject.

Webb wrote seventeen more articles for the *State Trooper.* Serving more as a journalist than historian, he covered various episodes involving the Rangers in the 1920s, including the organization's efforts to break up bootlegger and gambling operations in San Antonio and Austin, the capture of bank robbers, the enforcement of law and order in the oil boomtown of Borger, and the arrest of corrupt public officials.[21] Additionally, Webb covered the political and legal problems confronting the Rangers. In the Fifty-Seventh Judicial District of Texas, John E. Elgin filed suit against Pat M. Neff, governor of Texas, and others. The plaintiff's attorneys argued the Ranger Law of 1919 was unconstitutional on grounds that "the statutory enactments were violative of the state constitution in rights they permitted the violation of private rights and conferred upon Rangers the powers and duties of constables and sheriffs." Judge R. B. Minor was swayed by the plaintiff's argument and issued an injunction against "all the defendants, excepting the defendant Neff, governor, from paying out, disbursing or receiving, any of the public funds of the state treasury of Texas, for the carrying out of any of the purposes or provisions of said Ranger law of Texas." In essence, the injunction temporarily shut the Rangers down. Interestingly, Webb speculated on the motives of the plaintiff by writing that "the injunction came as a culmination of a two years fight to secure the removal of Rangers from San Antonio."[22] His assertion was that the Rangers, who effectively closed many of the gambling and bootlegging operations in the city, became the enemies of the elites, including city officials, who invested and profited from such endeavors. Ultimately, Judge Minor's injunction would be overturned, but the appellate court was critical of the harsh tactics the Rangers employed during the preceding two years, casting continued doubt upon the organization's method of enforcing the law.[23]

If their legal issues were not enough, the Rangers also found themselves caught in the middle of a political feud between Pat Neff, the sitting governor, and his political rivals Jim and Miriam Ferguson. Governor Neff had used the Rangers extensively to enforce the nation's prohibition laws, especially in San Antonio. Conversely, Jim Ferguson, the former governor, and his wife were aligned with the liquor interest in the state. When Ma Ferguson was elected governor in 1925, she substantially weakened the Ranger Force by reducing their numbers to just thirty men and "removed all the captains but three." Sarcastically, Webb predicted that circumstances would ultimately improve for the Rangers, especially considering that Governor Ferguson regularly pardoned criminals. With so many lawbreakers being released back into the general population, Webb believed it was only a matter of time before the Rangers would be called back into service.[24] His comments proved prophetic because the next elected governor, Dan Moody, promoted a plan to revitalize the Ranger organization and to restore law and order to the state. As part of his reorganization plan, Moody removed three of the captains that had served under the Ferguson administration and replaced them with veteran Rangers: Frank Hamer, W. W. Sterling, W. L. Wright, and John H. Rogers.[25]

Other scholars writing in the 1920s followed more conventional methods of research methodology. Like earlier Ranger scholars, historians in the second decade of the twentieth century published articles that included the Texas Rangers within the historical context of other topics. For example, Lena Clara Koch's "The Federal Indian Policy in Texas, 1845–1860: Chapter III. The Rangers and Frontier Protection" compared the effectiveness of federal troops serving on the frontier with that of the Ranger force.[26] Koch provides the reader with a survey of Ranger operations on the frontier, noting various times when the state force worked closely with federal troops and other times when they operated independently. In some cases federal officers found that the Rangers sometimes had a tendency "to create hostilities, and rather endanger the peace of the frontier."[27] While Koch outlined the activities of the Rangers on the frontier prior to the outbreak of the Civil War, the real significance of her study was that it revealed similarities and differences in how state and federal authorities approached frontier defense. Frequently, the two forces worked together, but there were times when federal and state authorities did not trust each other to adequately protect the settlers on the state's southern and western frontiers.[28] One of the more interesting aspects of Koch's study is the brief examination of Indians serving with various Ranger companies. This was one of the earliest studies to recognize that Native Americans served with white Rangers in the protection of frontier settlements.[29]

In addition to Koch's article, Clarence P. Denman's "The Office of Adjutant General in Texas, 1835–1881" provided a detailed examination of the creation of the adjutant general's office, discussing topics such as the origins of the office and its evolution for more than four decades and highlighting the careers of the men who held the office. If researchers want to understand the upper command structure of the Texas Rangers after the creation of the Frontier Battalion in 1874, they will want to consult Denman's article.[30] For a brief period, the famous Ranger Captain John B. Jones served as the adjutant general between 1879 and 1881. On July 19, 1881, Jones died after suffering a long illness, and on July 25 the governor appointed Wilburn H. King as his replacement.[31]

Various stories about the Texas Rangers also filled the pages of popular magazines between 1920 and 1950. Of these publications, one of the more widely read was the *Frontier Times*, a monthly periodical devoted to preserving frontier history, border tragedies, and pioneer achievements. Every month the magazine featured the reminiscences or stories of settlers who lived on the frontier. Many of these published accounts incorporated tales of Ranger activities. Ed Carnal, for example, recounted his involvement in an Indian battle while he was serving as one of Major John B. Jones's escorts.[32] According to his story, Major Jones was cool and calm under fire, keeping his young troops steady as the battle continued to rage. Carnal stated that "rangers, as well as Indians, fought under the black flag. We asked no quarter and gave none. Whenever we met it was simply a case of outfight or outrun 'em, whichever could be done the best." He further explained, "When we fell into their hands they scalped us and frightfully mutilated our bodies, frequently cutting and hacking us to pieces. We didn't do as bad as that but scalped them just the same. Indian scalps in ranger camps were as common as pony tracks."[33] Other contributors to the magazine covered a myriad of encounters between the Ranger and their frontier nemeses, including the Battle of Antelope Hills, the famous Captain Arrington Expedition of 1879–1880, and the Battle of Dove Creek (1863).[34] Although the places and people involved changed from one battle to the next, a general theme emerged in all the pieces: the Rangers defended the frontier bravely against a savage foe who represented a continuous threat to the upstanding frontier settlers of Texas.

Additionally, *Frontier Times* offered its readers brief histories of individual Rangers, highlighting their careers and exploits. For example, in September 1927 an issue featured Captain June Peak, who served in Company B of the Texas Frontier Battalion. According to the piece, Captain Peak chased Sam Bass and members of his gang out of northern Texas in 1878 and fought numerous battles against Comanche and Kiowa Indians on the frontier. The article includes two reprinted resolutions that were written at the time Captain Peak retired. In the first resolution, the Concho Stock Association stated, "That in proficiency of service, in effectiveness of performance, in constant attention to duty, in vigilance of inspection, in courteous demeanor, in gentlemanly bearing, in noble generosity, in strictness of justice, tempered with true charity and correct judgement, and in real and true efficiency of discipline, Captain June Peak has shown himself to have no superior." The second resolution came from his former company. It stated, "In the camp and on the field he has always been prompted by a stem sense of duty, ever ready. Ever willing; that he was ever courteous, polite and gentlemanly; ever eager and bold, keen and quiet, urgent and energetic; never daunted, never uncertain, fearless in all things."[35] *Frontier Times* is replete with similar articles, describing the heroic exploits of various Rangers, including Captain Shapley P. Ross, S. P. Elkins, Vernon Wilson, Samuel Highsmith, and Frank Jones.[36]

During the mid-1930s, the articles in the *Frontier Times* began to cover the Rangers from a slightly different perspective. The publications were no longer simply placing the Rangers in a favorable light but now were providing a more strident defense of the lawmen's actions throughout their history. In part the magazine's editor, J. Marvin Hunter, was reacting to critics of Ranger tactics which had emerged in the years between 1910 and 1920 and reached a crescendo in the 1920s and early 1930s. In May 1935 the *Frontier Times* published a brief article titled "Texas' Once Famous Ranger Band Found to Have Degenerated." According to this piece, the Texas Senate commented that the "famous organization of man-hunters is losing 'its once fine reputation.'" The article continues to define the problem, stating that most of the wrongdoing associated with the organization was attributable to a group defined as "special" Rangers, who primarily consisted of "'official gun-toters,' serving as bouncers in night clubs, officers in gambling houses, traffic officers and guards at horse and dog race tracks." These special Rangers numbered more than 1,600. The article further argued that the regular Rangers, who numbered 36 at the time, had "been restive under the appropriation of their name by outsiders . . . [and claimed] there was elation all around when Governor James V. Allred ordered the revocation of all outstanding special commissions [for special rangers]." The article levied the charge that most of the "specials were issued during the administration of Governor Miriam A. Ferguson."[37] The solution was simple. The Senate committee recommended the abandonment of special commissions for Rangers unless unusual conditions at the local level merited the temporary additions to the regular force.

Following the *Frontier Times* editor's commentary on special Rangers, several articles appeared in 1935 that continued the magazine's defense of the Ranger force. One article stated, "From the Time of the organization of the first Texas Ranger company in 1842 down to the very present the Rangers have been a very effective force toward the establishment of law and order within the boundaries of our state." The article continued, "After subduing the hostile Indian tribes and driving Mexican bandits from the frontier, the aid rendered by Texas Rangers in the older and more conservative communities always produced a speedy and quiet return to lawful methods of setting all disturbances and local issues without much difficulty."[38] After providing several example of heroic deeds, the editor commented on the reorganization of the Rangers, stating that the "force is to undergo a complete reorganization, and will be combined with the State Highway Patrol, yet as we understand it, the Rangers will work as a complete unit." Then the editor stated his intended purpose of the article by writing, "We hope that under the new arrangement the efficiency of the Ranger force will not be crippled, for there is not an organization anywhere in the world that can compare, in point of loyalty, courage, efficiency, and tact, with the Texas Rangers."[39] Other pieces in subsequent volumes of the *Frontier Times* touted the courage and exploits of the Rangers and the leaders of the organization.[40] The editor wrote one final article in the 1940s titled "Texas Rangers Are Still Active." Correcting an insertion that the Rangers had lost their identity after being merged with the State Highway Patrol, the magazine quoted Captain R. W. Aldrich of the Texas Ranger Department of Public Safety, who stated, "The Ranger Force has not lost its identity and has not been merged with the Highway Patrol. The two organizations have no connection other than both being units of the Department of Public Safety."[41] Captain Aldrich was undoubtedly proud of his service to the agency and was quick to protect its identity and reputation. He was not the first Texas Ranger to stand up for the reputation and honor of the law enforcement agency, nor would he be the last.

The *Frontier Times* was significant to Texas Ranger historiography. Perhaps more than any other publication, the magazine influenced the interpretations of many historians, particularly those writing prior to 1970. The *Frontier Times* was instrumental in creating what some scholars refer to as the traditional narrative of the Texas Rangers, a perspective that has enjoyed an exceptionally long shelf life.

While the *Frontier Times* was significant in shaping the historic image of the Rangers, professional historians were also publishing various accounts indirectly related to the activities of the Rangers. In 1960 Henry W. Barton explained how the US Cavalry adopted many of the military strategies commonly used by the Texas Rangers, such as using small arms, like the Colt revolver, as their primary weapon, performing reconnaissance and counterguerrilla operations, perfecting their marksmanship with a variety of firearms, and developing superior horsemanship.[42] These tactics in part gave the US Army an advantage in the western Indian wars during the late nineteenth century.

Other historians, such as William L. Mann and George R. Nielsen, examined the lives and careers of individuals who served in Ranger companies during the Republic of Texas. Toward the end of his life, Mann published an article that focused on the exploits of James O. Rice, who served in a frontier Ranger company from Williamson County. Rice and his company gained notoriety when they confronted Manuel Flores along the banks of the San Gabriel River at Rice's Crossing on May 17, 1839.[43] Mann comments, "From the brief sketches available, [Rice] appears in his early life to have been a daring young man who had more than his share of excitement and many narrow escapes which would have caused others, more cautious, to turn back, but James O. Rice never ran from a fight."[44] Mann's article examined Rice in the same light that earlier scholars had portrayed other famous Rangers, such as John "Rip" Ford and John Coffee "Jack" Hays. Nielsen briefly examined the life and career of Mathew Caldwell, another man who served in ranging companies during the 1830s.[45] Nielsen defined Caldwell as a hero, stating that he "spent most of his time in the saddle fighting for his adopted country . . . he was at his best as the leader of small corps of frontiersmen where a situation demanded split-second decisions and a brave example. . . . Texas had many Caldwells, and he must be placed in proper perspective with the men of superb accomplishment of his day."[46] While both Mann and Nielsen provided informative and entertaining accounts of the Rangers, they continued to examine the lawmen from the same stereotypical perspective that earlier scholars and lay historians had developed during the previous decades.

Since 1970 Ranger historiography has experienced its most profound period of change. While the traditional views of the Rangers have continued to thrive during the past fifty years, some historians have questioned the actions and motives of the lawmen, portraying them as unapologetic racists and murderers. Other scholars have simply asked new questions about the Rangers and have focused their attention more on the organization's activities during the twentieth century. A third group of academics have attempted to redefine the Ranger identity, merging new perspectives with traditional interpretations of the law enforcement agency and its men.

One of the early criticisms of the Rangers that appeared in an academic journal came not in the form of an article but rather in a book review. Published in *Crime and Social Justice* during the summer of 1980, Larry Trujillo's review of *Gunpowder Justice: A Reassessment of the Texas Rangers* enthusiastically agreed with the conclusions that the book's authors reached concerning the lawmen, stating that the history of the Texas Rangers is a story of "racism, repression and resistance."[47] Trujillo concluded, "The fact that the Texas Rangers have been enshrined as heroes, while Texas Mexican resistance has been portrayed as 'bloodthirsty' and 'criminal,' speaks rather cogently to the racist dynamics of Anglo cultural hegemony."[48] The reviewer also finds that the Rangers were part of a larger cultural phenomenon of Anglo dominance. He states, "To understand fundamentally and dynamically the history of the Texas Rangers, it is crucial clearly to recognize their class control function and to analyze them in relation to the larger political economy of Texas." Trujillo continues, "Texas became part of the United States through conquest and annexation. The transformation to Anglo rule was accomplished by the rise and institutionalization of a state apparatus which maintained and legitimated Anglo ruling class hegemony. The Rangers, through force and intimidation (which included violent acts such as lynching and shooting of Mexicans), enforced this hegemony."[49] Trujillo's assessment of *Gunpowder Justice* was consistent with theses of numerous books that examined Chicano experiences in the American Southwest and identified Hispanics as the unfortunate victims of white supremacists. Though a select group of scholars, such as Américo Paredes at the University of Texas at Austin, had challenged the reputation of the Texas Rangers in book-length studies during the five decades prior to 2000, such criticism did not gain momentum in mainstream history journals until after the turn of the century.[50]

In 2003 William D. Carrigan and Clive Webb, in an article that examined the lynching of persons of Mexican origin or descent in the United States between 1848 and 1928, wrote that "lynching of Mexicans . . . often involved the active collusion of law officers themselves." In this regard, the authors declared, "The most systematic abuse of legal authority was by the Texas Rangers. Their brutal repression of the Mexican populace was tantamount to state-sanctioned terrorism. Although the exact number of those murdered by the Rangers is unknown, historians estimate that it ran into the hundreds and even thousands."[51] The following year the Harvard Law Review Association in an examination of the El Paso Salt War of 1877 argued that the Rangers under the command of Major John B. Jones contributed to the outbreak of violence by supporting Charles H. Howard, who planned to seize control of Mexican lands where locals had mined salt for their own needs and for trade.[52] In his study of Laredo Tejanos during the nineteenth century, Alexander Mendoza described the extralegal tactics and practices of discrimination of Rangers toward Tejanos living on the border. Mendoza explained, "The *Rinches* [Texas Rangers], as they were known to residents of Mexican descent along the Rio Grande, discriminated against Mexicanos and Tejanos with equal aplomb." He continued, "An 1885 gun battle between Rangers and respected Tejanos in Webb County and an interethnic election riot the following year only heightened the tension and mistrust that existed towards the law enforcement agency."[53]

Jason E. Pierce's recent publication, *Making the White Man's West: Whiteness and the Creation of the American West*, included a chapter titled "Enforcing the White Man's West through Violence in Texas, California, and Beyond." In this chapter Pierce summarized many of the criticisms leveled against the Rangers. He wrote, "Suspicion of the Tejano population in the state [Texas] endured throughout the nineteenth century and well into the twentieth century, and the task of dealing with the perceived threat of their treachery and deceit fell to the Texas Rangers." Pierce continued,

> While Anglos have long celebrated the Rangers as larger-than-life heroes, Tejanos and Mexicans had a very different view, seeing the group as staunch defenders of white supremacy who indiscriminately lashed out at innocent people because

of the color of their skin. Texas Rangers strove to protect their communities and those communities' values. Given that white supremacy was a community value, it is not surprising, then, that the Texas Rangers fought in defense of it. . . . Fears of Mexican raiders and the "terrifying image whites conjured up of cruel Mexicans" justified Ranger attacks on and intimidation of Tejanos, especially in the Rio Grande valley. . . . Once every generation or so, Rangers lashed out violently against Tejano and Mexican residents of the border, attacking both suspected criminals and civilians—the line between guilty and innocent often became too fine for the Rangers to distinguish.[54]

As criticism of the nineteenth-century Texas Rangers grew among academics, other scholars focused on the activities of the organization during the early twentieth century. In an article that examined the cooperation between powerful business interest and the state against the Longshoremen's Association during the Galveston dock workers' strike of 1920, William D. Angel Jr. revealed that Governor William Hobby sent in the Texas Rangers to protect nonunion workers on the docks. While the Rangers under the command of Captain R. W. Aldrich maintained the peace, they primarily cracked down on union organizers, suggesting that the state was willing to use the lawmen to suppress organized labor and keep Texas open to potential outside investors.[55]

Edward H. Phillips wrote a brief article on Ranger involvement in a 1930 riot that erupted in Grayson County at the courthouse in Sherman, Texas. After George Hughes, a local Black man, was taken into custody for allegedly assaulting the wife of his white employer, a lynch mob demanded that legal authorities release the prisoner to them. Fearing violence, local authorities requested Governor Dan Moody to send the Texas Rangers to aid in the protection of Hughes. The governor complied and sent two different groups of Rangers to the scene. Unfortunately, despite the presence of both Captain Frank Hamer and Sergeant Manuel "Lone Wolf" Gonzaullas, the Rangers were unsuccessful in quelling the riot. The mob forcibly removed

Hughes from the courthouse, tortured him unmercifully, and eventually suspended his lifeless body over a bonfire in the town's segregated Black neighborhood. It was one of the few times that the Rangers lost a prisoner.[56] Despite the stain on their record, the Rangers learned from their mistakes and made significant changes to the way they protected prisoners. These changes prevented similar miscarriages of justice from occurring in the future.

In an article that examined the Texas outlaw tradition, Mitchel Roth discussed the evolution of Ranger tactics during the modern era. Defining the 1930s as new age in Texas outlawry where criminals exchanged their horses, six-shooters, and Winchesters for automobiles, automatic pistols, and submachine guns, Roth explained that the Rangers had no choice but to adapt their strategies to meet the challenges facing them. He defines May 23, 1934, as the day the Rangers became a modern law enforcement agency. On this spring day, former Ranger Captain Frank Hamer and five other men ambushed the notorious Bonnie and Clyde south of Gibsland, Louisiana, on Highway 154, ending their pursuit of the notorious leaders of the Barrow gang. Based in part on the lessons learned while tracking Bonnie and Clyde, the Texas Rangers went through a major reorganization in early 1935.

Under the direction of Governor James V. Allred, the legislature created "the Department of Public Safety, the role of the Texas Rangers in law enforcement was greatly reduced . . . the Highway Patrol, which previously had been responsible for enforcing traffic and motor vehicle related laws, was given law enforcement duties on par with the Rangers." Additionally, "important steps taken to improve the quality of state law enforcement was the creation of the Headquarters Division at Austin," which served as a "central repository for fingerprints, photographs, and other data on felons and other outlaws convicted in Texas after 1935."[57] Hereafter, the Rangers became a modern police force able to properly deal with twentieth-century criminals.

Up to this point, scholarship primarily focused on how the Rangers carried out their duties. However, two important articles published during the modern era demonstrate the human side of the Rangers' story. In 1978 Gary Cartwright wrote a piece for *Texas Monthly* titled "Death of a Ranger."[58] Cartwright examined in detail the death of Ranger Bob Doherty, who was killed during a drug raid on February 20, 1978, in Argyle, Denton County. While the article attribute Doherty's death to key mistakes made during the raid, Cartwright captured the human toll of the event—the death of a Ranger, the anxiety and pain that Doherty's wife went through after learning that her husband had been shot, and the trial and conviction of Greg Ott, the college student and small-time drug dealer who killed Doherty. Perhaps more than anyone writing about the modern Rangers, Cartwright captured the essence of the fears, hardships, stresses, and sometimes heartbreak associated with being a Ranger or an immediate member of his family.

Similarly, but less tragic, Kemp Dixon provided a brief glimpse into the family life of Ranger Norman Dixon and his wife Leona Spellman Dixon. The account is based on a diary that Leona kept between January 1, 1938, and October 15, 1939. Throughout this period Leona described the long hours her husband spent away from home, her daily routines and chores that helped her to cope with his absence, and the relationships that she forged with the wives of other Rangers. While Leona's diary suggests that she and Norman enjoyed a loving and full marriage, it also identified the strains and hardships Ranger families endured.[59] Both Cartwright and Dixon remind readers that the wives and children of these famous lawmen are a vital part of Ranger history. Perhaps scholars will tell more of their story in future studies.

In the years following 1969, some scholars sought to modify the image of the Texas Rangers by reconciling modern criticism of the organization with the traditional Ranger narrative. In 1971 Llerena B. Friend published an article in the *Southwestern Historical Quarterly* titled "W. P. Webb's Texas Rangers," which examined the life and career of the Rangers' most recognized scholar.[60] While most students of Ranger historiography are well acquainted with Webb's

The Texas Rangers, they may not be familiar with how significant Texas's most famous frontier defenders were to his career. His fascination began with the writing of his MA thesis, continued throughout his professional career in the form of articles published in professional journals and popular magazines, and culminated in the publication of *The Texas Rangers*. In fact, Friend reveals that Webb's interest in the West, which led to the publication of *The Great Plains* in 1931, extended from his earlier research on the Rangers.

According to Friend, Webb, before his untimely death, came to realize that the Rangers were likely responsible for injustices committed against Mexicans and Tejanos on the southern border. As such, Webb had planned to revise *The Texas Rangers* but died before he started working on the revisions. Friend concludes, "What color or tone Webb's revisions would have taken on, we can never be sure."[61] Friend accurately described Webb's path to understanding the Rangers, but she also illustrated that his work provides an incomplete history of the organization—a supposition that Webb believed himself.

While Friend focused on the writings of Webb, other scholars attempted to redefine the identity of the Texas Rangers. Mark E. Nackman's "The Making of the Texan Citizen Soldier, 1835–1860" defined the early Ranger identity as being shaped by the forces of the frontier.[62] Nackman asked a simple question: "Who, then were the Texas Rangers?" His answer was equally simple: "The Ranger has for so long been a creature of folklore that there still is some temptation to think of the typical Texan as a gunman on horseback. Actually, in the years of frontier warfare before the Civil War, such a notion would have had some basis in fact. The Texas Ranger was none other than the *ordinary citizen soldier*." He continued, "Their adoption of the six-shooter in 1839 gave to the world the picturesque image of the Texan as gunfighter on horseback, and gradually, because Texas had so many volunteer rangers and so many occasions for their active operations, they became popularized as 'Texas Rangers.'"[63]

According to Nackman, "The reputation of these rangers as a unique breed of fighting men found only in Texas made them a legend in their own time."[64] Based on this reputation, the Rangers were viewed as an elite fighting corps, but according to the author, "this is something of a mistake. There was actually nothing unique or unusual about these rangers as Texans. In fact, they were mainly average fellows of their communities, but they had of necessity learned the arts of plains warfare in a manner that combined the most effective fighting qualities of their enemies." Nackman reminds his reader that the Rangers "never acquired official status as an organization proper . . . until the Texas legislature in 1874 created the Frontier Battalion under Major John B. Jones and the Special Force of Rangers under Captain L. H. McNelly."[65]

Though defined as hard fighting men who "appeared to have more in common with the red man they so despised than the with the white man whose civilization they advanced," these men were reflective of the antebellum society in Texas. Instead of an elite force, "they came from all walks of life . . . doctors, lawyers, poets, surveyors, and legislators . . . [with] farmers and ranchers . . . the most commonly represented."[66] Nackman concluded, "In the period up to the Civil War, there was no such thing as a career ranger. All who served had to have other occupations to make income and pay off debts contracted during their military engagement."[67]

Though antebellum Rangers might have lacked official organization, Robert M. Utley argued that the Texas Ranger tradition was established during this early era. In his "The Texas Ranger Tradition Established: Jack Hays and Walker Creek," Utley claimed that June 8, 1844, was "the defining moment, in the transformation of [Texas] mounted volunteers who performed 'ranging service' into Texas Rangers." He contended, "On this day, on an obscure stream named Walker Creek in the hills north of San Antonio, the qualities that would give singular character to the Texas Rangers came together in such an extraordinary and dramatic combination as to crystallize a tradition evolving loosely and sporadically since 1823."[68] The qualities that defined the Texas Rangers were leadership; personal character of the men as fighters; specialized skills as frontier warriors, including marksmanship with rifles and pistol; mastery of outdoor life; knowledge of their foe; and the introduction of a new weapon—Samuel Colt's revolver. All these traits came to bear on Rangers' victory over a superior number of Comanche Indians at the battle of Walker Creek. Outnumbered five to one, John Coffee "Jack" Hays exhibited extraordinary abilities as a leader during the battle, leading his men to an improbable victory. In the process Captain Hays became the "ideal Ranger, the one who above all others every Ranger strove to emulate."[69] Hays's men were hardened by frontier life and were veteran Indian fighters. Like the Comanche they "traveled swiftly and lightly, unencumbered by anything that could not be carried on horseback. They subsisted on Wild game . . . and slept in the open under a blanket with a saddle for a pillow."[70] Also, like their adversary, they excelled in horsemanship. Most importantly, they were trained marksmen with rifles and the newly acquired Paterson Colt, a revolving pistol that provided them superior firepower during battle. Taking full advantage of their resources, Hays and the fourteen men under his command routed approximately seventy Comanche warriors at Walker Creek, establishing in the process the founding traditions that came to define the Texas Rangers.

Providing a more balanced account of Texas Rangers, Harold J. Weiss Jr. traced the history of the organization, examining their evolution through three distinct periods. The earliest period spanned the years between 1823 and 1874. This phase was noted as the "heyday of the Rangers as citizen soldiers. Within this time frame ranging companies and other volunteer units engaged in a military struggle with Indian tribes and Mexicans for control of the land." The second period covered the years between 1874 and 1935 and was characterized as "the age of the Ranger as old-time professional lawmen." Beginning with the creation of the Special Force of Rangers and the Frontier Battalion in 1874, the Rangers evolved into a complex organization by the turn of the century, complete with a "chain of command and career-minded officers who carried out administrative duties and investigative work, from tracking criminals to collecting and analyzing evidence . . . the hallmarks of the old-style professional peace officers throughout the American West." The final period extended from 1935 to the present and represented "the Rangers as a new-style modern police." During this phase the Rangers became a modern state police force when they were placed with the Highway Patrol in the newly created Department of Public Safety.[71] This article does a masterful job of recognizing the limitations of Webb's *The Texas Rangers* as well as the scholarship that places the Rangers and Mexican Americans in "dichotomous relationships." According to Weiss, "Such opposing viewpoints, with each side emotionally defending its position, do not create an atmosphere that encourages asking new questions and seeking new answers in order to understand the complex world of modern law enforcement." He continues, "Viewing the Rangers in white hat–black hat terms will freeze their historiography in time, with more ties to local interest than regional and national concerns."[72] Weiss provides a brief but evenhanded account of the Rangers that incorporates modern criticism of the organization but also highlights the accomplishments of the agency as it evolved over time. He concludes, "The dichotomous views of some writers of Ranger roles—heroes or devils for military deployment as citizens soldiers against Amerindians and Mexican nationals, white hats or black hats for their actions as peace officers against desperadoes and Robin Hood bandits—cannot withstand the scrutiny of historical research. Yet the image of the Rangers will not really change until old stories are told in new terms."[73]

Expanding on Weiss's observations, Jody Edward Ginn presents the most recent addition to the discussion of Ranger historiography in his "The Texas Rangers in Myth and Memory," which is included in Light T. Cummins and Mary L. Scheer's edited volume, *Texan Identities: Moving beyond Myth, Memory, and Fallacy in Texas History.*[74] After providing his readers with a thought-provoking analysis of Ranger historiography and debunking some of the more common myths associated with the identity of the Rangers, Ginn demonstrates how traditional and modern myths continue to obstruct and shape our views of the Texas Rangers. He contends, "The truth of the matter, as is so often the case with history and memory, lies somewhere in between the two extremes 'in the realm of myths.'" Ginn continues, "Far more often, the myth and memory of the Texas Rangers has been perpetuated through the media, both popular and historical. Unfortunately, even the ostensibly historical treatments have often been lacking in depth, nuance, and, at times, basic factual accuracy."[75]

In closing, he argues, "Many scholars are now providing a more inclusive and balanced image of the Texas Rangers by moving beyond the romanticized and racially divisive rhetoric that has plagued much of Texas Ranger historiography, thereby pushing it into a new era." Optimistically, Ginn postulates, "These historians are including an examination of the perspectives of people and communities among whom the Rangers have served and are beginning to delve into a second century of their existence, a long overdue necessity for providing a well-rounded understanding of the overall history of this nearly two-hundred-year-old institution."[76] Both Weiss and Ginn make compelling arguments. If scholars are going to understand the history of the Rangers in any meaningful way, they must place the organization in its proper historical context and move beyond using the agency as means of social commentary. The Rangers must be understood in their own times before their history can provide any new insights into the present condition of law enforcement in the Lone Star State.

With a history that dates back to the earliest Anglo settlements in Texas, the Rangers have become a permanent cultural icon. The organization has served many functions during their existence—frontier defenders, Western peace officers, and modern-day professional lawmen. Their path to modernity has followed many winding trails, complete with courageous deeds, unthinkable hardships, and, at times, miscarriages of justice. Regardless of whether scholars view this distinct group of frontier defenders and lawmen as heroes or villains, the Texas Rangers will remain a vital part of the story of Texas. Given the past trends in Ranger historiography, it also seems likely that future scholars will continue to debate the merits of this select group of lawmen, predicating their interpretations of the Texas Rangers on the changing values and moral standards of each passing generation.

Notes

1. Dudley G. Wooten, ed., *A Comprehensive History of Texas, 1685 to 1897*, 2 vols. (Dallas: William G. Scarff, 1898), 2:335.
2. Wilburn H. King, "The Texas Ranger Service and History of the Rangers, with Observations on Their Value as a Police Protection," in Wooten, *Comprehensive History of Texas*, 2:329–67.
3. King, "Texas Ranger Service," in Wooten, *Comprehensive History of Texas*, 2:335–36.
4. Wooten, *Comprehensive History of Texas*, 2:329.
5. Wooten, *Comprehensive History of Texas*, 2:329.
6. Wooten, *Comprehensive History of Texas*, 2:329–30.
7. King, "Texas Ranger Service," in Wooten, *Comprehensive History of Texas*, 2:335.
8. King, "Texas Ranger Service," in Wooten, *Comprehensive History of Texas*, 2:366.
9. Sada Burnam, "Reminiscences of Capt. Jesse Burnam," *Quarterly of the Texas State Historical Association* 5, no. 1 (July 1901): 12–18.
10. Burnam, "Reminiscences of Capt. Jesse Burnam," 15.
11. Burnam, "Reminiscences of Capt. Jesse Burnam," 16.
12. Burnam, "Reminiscences of Capt. Jesse Burnam," 16–17.
13. In 1912 the journal was renamed the *Southwestern Historical Quarterly*.
14. Patrick Cox, "Eugene C. Barker," in *Writing the Story of Texas*, ed. Patrick Cox and Kenneth E. Hendrickson Jr., (Austin: University of Texas Press, 2013), 25–28.
15. For a modern overview of Texas Ranger history, see Jesse Sublett, "Lone on the Range: Texas Lawmen," *Texas Monthly*, December 21, 1969, accessed on December 5, 2019, https://www.texasmonthly.com/articles/lone-on-the-range-texas-lawmen. Note the date shown for this article is December 31, 1969. This is an incorrect date. According to fact-checkers at *Texas Monthly*, the article was a "web-exclusive" and was published circa 1997.
16. "The Mexican and Indian Raid of '78," *Quarterly of the Texas State Historical Association* 5, no. 3 (January 1902): 248.
17. J. H. Kuykendall, "Reminiscences of Early Texas: A Collection from the Austin Papers," *Quarterly of the Texas State Historical Association*

6, no. 3 (January 1903): 236–53; 6, no. 4 (April 1903): 311–30; 7, no. 1 (July 1903): 29–64; Eugene C. Barker, "The Government of Austin's Colony, 1821–1831," *Southwestern Historical Quarterly* 21, no. 3 (January 1918): 223–52. Barker was one of the first academics to examine the government of Austin's Colony. He provides a brief description of the militia system in this study. Barker published an earlier work that examined the Journal of the Permanent Council. In this article Barker examines the activities of Anglo-Texans in the immediate aftermath of the Texas Revolution, including activities of militia groups (ranging companies) in October 1835. For more see Eugene C. Barker, "Journal of the Permanent Council (October 11–27, 1835)," *Quarterly of the Texas State Historical Association* 7, no. 4 (April 1904): 249–78. Another article that examines frontier conditions is J. Fred Rippy, "Border Troubles along the Rio Grande, 1848–1860," *Southwestern Historical Quarterly* 23, no. 2 (October 1919): 91–111. However, like most of the writings of this period, the focus is not primarily on the Rangers but rather on the conditions along the southern border of Texas. The Rangers are mentioned only in relation to Juan N. Cortina's raids into Texas during the late 1850s. Nevertheless, as with most of the journal articles published prior to 1919, the significance of Rippy's piece is that it provided background information for subsequent generations of Ranger scholars.

18. In part the articles that appear in *The State Trooper: A Magazine of Law and Order* were a result of his 1920 MA thesis, completed at the University of Texas at Austin. Additionally, once Webb secured employment at UT Austin in 1923, Eugene Barker pushed him to continue to work on the Rangers. There is little doubt that Barker's encouragement prompted him to write brief articles on the Rangers throughout the 1920s.

19. Walter Prescott Webb, "Texas Rangers of Today: A Description of the Present Status of the Oldest Police Force in America," *State Trooper* 5 (March 1924): 5–6.

20. Webb, "Texas Rangers of Today," 6.

21. Webb, "Lawless Town Gets Ranger Justice: Cleanup of Law Breakers in San Antonio Is Object Lesson of Need of Strong State Force," *State Trooper* 5 (April 1924): 13–14; Webb, "Rangers Called in to Clean Up Austin: Texans Have Closed Forty San Antonio Gambling Dens," *State Trooper* 6 (November 1924): 21–22; Webb, "Lone Ranger Gets Bandits: Texas Officer Secures Surrender of Gang which Robbed

Banks and Shot Up One Town," *State Trooper* 7 (March 1926): 9–10; Webb, "Bank Robbers Slain: Texas Ranger Captain Takes No Chances on Escape of Two Desperadoes Taken in Crime," *State Trooper* 8 (November 1926): 7–8; Webb, "Oil Town Cleaned Up: Texas Rangers Summoned to Restore Order When Local Officials Could Not Enforce Law," *State Trooper* 8 (December 1926): 11–12; Webb, "Rangers Arrest Lawmakers: Texas Representatives Taken in Custody When One Accepts $1000 from Opponent of Measure," *State Trooper* 8 (April 1927): 11–12.

22. Webb, "Fight against Texas Rangers: A Discussion of the Motives Involved in the Suit to Enjoin Continuance of the Force," *State Trooper* 6 (July 1925): 11.

23. Webb, "Texas Ranger Case Important: Statement of Law Involved in Use of Force to Preserve State's Authority Is Comprehensive," *State Trooper* 6 (August 1925): 13–14, 20.

24. Webb, "Texas Rangers in Eclipse: Present State Administration Has Discredited Force by Policy of Interference with Its Duties," *State Trooper* 7 (January 1926): 13–14.

25. Webb, "Larger Texas Force: New Governor Expected to Increase Ranger's Strength to Combat Conditions of Lawlessness," *State Trooper* 8 (February 1927): 17–18; Webb, "May Increase Rangers: Texas Legislature Considering Measure Which Would Increase Force and Raise Rangers' Pay," *State Trooper* 8 (June 1927): 13–14; Webb, "Rangers Reorganized: Governor of Texas Appoints Captains to Replace Men Appointed in Ferguson Regime," *State Trooper* 8 (July 1927): 13–14.

26. Lena Clara Koch, "The Federal Indian Policy in Texas, 1845–1860: Chapter III. The Rangers and Frontier Protection," *Southwestern Historical Quarterly* 29, no. 1 (July 1925): 19–35.

27. Koch, "Federal Indian Policy in Texas," 28.

28. Koch, "Federal Indian Policy in Texas," 25–30.

29. Koch, "Federal Indian Policy in Texas," 34–35.

30. Clarence P. Denman, "The Office of Adjutant General in Texas, 1835–1881," *Southwestern Historical Quarterly* 28, no. 4 (April 1925): 302–22.

31. Denman, "Office of Adjutant General in Texas," 320–22.

32. Ed Carnal, "Reminiscences of a Texas Ranger," *Frontier Times* 1, no. 3 (December 1923): 20–23.

33. Carnal, "Reminiscences of a Texas Ranger," 24.

34. "The Battle of Antelope Hills," *Frontier Times* 1, no. 5 (February 1924): 11–14; J. Marvin Hunter, "Captain Arrington's Expedition," *Frontier Times* 6, no. 3 (December 1928): 97–102; Austin Callan, "Battle of Dove Creek," *Frontier Times* 24, no. 12 (September 1947): 542–44.

35. "Captain June Peak, Texas Ranger," *Frontier Times* 4, no. 12 (September 1927): 5–6.

36. "The Killing of Captain Frank Jones," *Frontier Times* 6, no. 4 (January 1929): 145–49; "Vernon Wilson Was a Texas Ranger," *Frontier Times* 6, no. 7 (April 1929): 257–58; "Captain Shapley P. Ross," *Frontier Times* 5, no. 11 (August 1928): 437–38; "Served as a Texas Ranger," *Frontier Times* 5, no. 11 (August 1928): 438–39, and 447; Maude Wallis Traylor, "Captain Samuel Highsmith, Ranger," *Frontier Times* 17, no. 7 (April 1940): 291–302. Of these works, Traylor's work on Captain Highsmith is the closest to a history of a Ranger captain. It is based on limited primary and secondary sources and attempts to chronicle the Samuel Highsmith's activities as a Ranger from the 1820s up to his death in the 1840s. Traylor's account was written later in the 1940s, which accounts for its deviation from the other accounts published in the *Frontier Times* during the 1920s.

37. "Texas' Once Famous Ranger Band Found to Have Degenerated," *Frontier Times* 12, no. 8 (May 1935): 363.

38. "The Texas Rangers Brought Law and Order," *Frontier Times* 12, no. 10 (July 1935): 425.

39. "Texas Rangers Brought Law and Order," 427–28.

40. Sarah Ellen Davidge, "Texas Rangers Were Rough and Ready Fighters," *Frontier Times* 13, no. 2 (November 1935): 125–29 (originally published in the *Galveston Tribune*); "Texas Rangers and Their Great Leaders," *Frontier Times* 15, no. 11 (August 1938): 471–76. The "Rangers and Their Great Leaders" piece covered many of the famous Rangers, including Jack Elgin, George Erath, Shapley Ross, Jack Hays, John Ford, Henry McCulloch, and others.

41. J. Marvin Hunter, "Texas Rangers Are Still Active," *Frontier Times* 22, no. 10 (July 1945): 294.

42. Henry W. Barton, "The United States Cavalry and the Texas Rangers," *Southwestern Historical Quarterly* 63, no. 4 (April 1960): 495–510. Two studies that reinforce the findings of Barton include Ernest C. Shearer, "The Callahan Expedition, 1855," *Southwestern Historical Quarterly* 54, no. 4 (April 1951): 430–51; and Kenneth F. Neighbours, "The Expedition of Major Robert S. Neighbors to El Paso in 1849," *Southwestern Historical Quarterly* 58, no. 1 (July 1954): 36–59.

43. William L. Mann, "James O. Rice: Hero of the Battle on the San Gabriels," *Southwestern Historical Quarterly* 55, no. 1 (July 1951): 30–42.

44. Mann, "James O. Rice," 30.

45. George R. Nielsen, "Mathew Caldwell," *Southwestern Historical Quarterly* 64, no. 4 (April 1961): 478–502.

46. Nielsen, "Mathew Caldwell," 478.

47. Larry Trujillo, review of *Gunpowder Justice: A Reassessment of the Texas Rangers*, by Julian Samora, Joe Bernal, and Albert Pefia, *Crime and Social Justice*, no. 13 (Summer 1980): 61.

48. Trujillo, review of *Gunpowder Justice*, 63.

49. Trujillo, review of *Gunpowder Justice*, 64.

50. For more on early criticism of the Rangers, see Américo Paredes, *"With His Pistol in His Hand": A Border Ballad and Its Hero* (Austin: University of Texas Press, 1958). For a more modern critique of the Rangers that questions whether the organization ability to function and exist in the modern era, see Robert Draper, "The Twilight of the Texas Rangers," *Texas Monthly*, February 1994, https://texasmonthly.com/articles/the-twilight-of-the-texas-rangers.

51. William D. Carrigan and Clive Webb, "The Lynching of Persons of Mexican Origin or Descent in the United States, 1848 to 1928," *Journal of Social History* 37, no. 2 (Winter 2003): 416–17. For a general examination of tensions along the Mexico-Texas border during the late nineteenth century, see Michael M. Smith, "General Rafael Benavides and the Texas-Mexico Border Crisis of 1877," *Southwestern Historical Quarterly* 112, no. 3 (January 2009): 235–60.

52. The Harvard Law Review Association, "Law, Race, and the Border: The El Paso Salt War of 1877," *Harvard Law Review* 117, no. 3 (January 2004): 941–63.

53. Alexander Mendoza, "'For Our Own Best Interests': Nineteenth-Century Laredo Tejanos, Military Service, and the Development of American Nationalism," *Southwestern Historical Quarterly* 115, no. 2 (October 2011): 144–45.

54. Jason E. Pierce, "Enforcing the White Man's West through Violence in Texas, California, and Beyond," in *Making the White Man's West: Whiteness and the Creation of the American West* (Boulder: University Press of Colorado, 2016), 218.

55. William D. Angel Jr., "Controlling the Workers: The Galveston Dock Workers' Strike of 1920 and Its Impact on Labor Relations in Texas," *East Texas Historical Journal* 23, no. 2 (October 1985): 14–27.

56. Edward H. Phillips, "The Sherman Courthouse Riot of 1930," *East Texas Historical Journal* 25, no. 2 (October 1987): 12–19.

57. Mitchel Roth, "Bonnie and Clyde in Texas: The End of the Texas Outlaw Tradition," *East Texas Historical Journal* 35, no. 2 (October 1997): 30–38.

58. Gary Cartwright, "Death of a Ranger," *Texas Monthly*, August 1978, https://www.texasmonthly.com/articles/death-of-a-ranger.

59. Kemp Dixon, "The Diary of a Ranger's Wife, 1938–1939," *East Texas Historical Journal* 54, no. 1 (2016): 7–17. For a more detailed account of Norman Dixon's career, see Kemp Dixon, *Chasing Thugs, Nazis, and Reds: Texas Ranger Norman K. Dixon* (College Station: Texas A&M University Press, 2015).

60. Llerena B. Friend, "W. P. Webb's Texas Rangers," *Southwestern Historical Quarterly* 74, no. 3 (January 1971): 293–323.

61. Friend, "Webb's Texas Rangers," 321.

62. Mark E. Nackman, "The Making of the Citizen Soldier, 1835–1860," *Southwestern Historical Quarterly* 78, no. 3 (January 1975): 231–53.

63. Nackman, "Making of the Citizen Soldier," 246.

64. Nackman, "Making of the Citizen Soldier," 247.

65. Nackman, "Making of the Citizen Soldier," 249.

66. Nackman, "Making of the Citizen Soldier," 252.

67. Nackman, "Making of the Citizen Soldier," 253.

68. Robert M. Utley, "The Texas Ranger Tradition Established: Jack Hays and Walker Creek," *Montana: The Magazine of Western History* 52, no. 1 (Spring 2002): 2.

69. Utley, "Texas Ranger Tradition Established," 4.

70. Utley, "Texas Ranger Tradition Established," 7.

71. Harold J. Weiss Jr., "The Texas Rangers Revisited: Old Themes and New Viewpoints," *Southwestern Historical Quarterly* 97, no. 4 (April 1994): 622.

72. Weiss, "Texas Rangers Revisited," 623.

73. Weiss, "Texas Rangers Revisited," 640. Three additional studies that examine the Ranger identity from a different approach are Michael T. Marsden, "Popular Images of the Canadian Mounted Police and the Texas Rangers," *Studies in Popular Culture* 16, no. 1 (October 1993): 1–14; Andrew Graybill, "Texas Rangers, Canadian Mounties, and the Policing of the Transnational Industrial Frontier, 1885–1910," *Western Historical Quarterly* 35, no. 2 (Summer 2004): 167–91; and Andrew Graybill, "Rural Police and the Defense of the Cattleman's Empire

in Texas and Alberta, 1875–1900," *Agricultural History* 79, no. 3 (Summer 2005): 253–80. Each of these studies provide a comparative study of the Rangers and the Canadian Mounted Police. While many similarities exist between the two organizations, the authors demonstrate that more differences separate the two agencies than bind them together, especially in tactics, strategies, and governance.

74. Jody Edward Ginn, "The Texas Rangers in Myth and Memory," in *Texan Identities: Moving beyond Myth, Memory, and Fallacy in Texas History*, ed. Light T. Cummins and Mary L. Scheer (Denton: University of North Texas Press, 2016), 87–120.

75. Ginn, "Texas Rangers in Myth and Memory," in Cummins and Scheer, *Texan Identities*, 115.

76. Ginn, "Texas Rangers in Myth and Memory," in Cummins and Scheer, *Texan Identities*, 115.

Chapter 6

In Their Own Words
The Autobiographical Way
Mitchel P. Roth

I t is a common conceit among Texas historians that except for the Alamo, the Texas Ranger is the most chronicled topic in Lone Star history. In terms of American law enforcement, Texas Rangers are probably the most iconic peace officers in America, on par with the London Bobbies and Canada's Northwest Mounted Police, but of the thousands who served on the force since it was created in 1823, very few Rangers have chronicled their experiences with pen and paper. Those who have either fashioned books, with help from editors, memoirs based on diaries they wrote (some passed down from generation to generation before coming into print), or dictated their Ranger lives to collaborators and coauthors. The paucity of accounts has been chalked up to several factors, ranging from poor education to an unwillingness to seek the limelight or self-promotion. According to one leading Ranger historian, "A Ranger needed a good gun, not good grammar." Bibliographer Jeff Dykes would have agreed, "noting they were fighters, not writers." The rarest period for Ranger autobiographies is prior to 1900. Perhaps it was because education was less valued in the era. One Ranger expert suggests that of the

170

approximately fifteen thousand Rangers who served before 1930, "most were probably poorly educated."[1]

Historians have consulted many firsthand Ranger accounts over the years. As primary source material, Ranger diaries, memoirs, and autobiographies have filled in the blanks for writers trying to humanize the Ranger experience. Also invaluable are official accounts, which can be found in letters, telegrams, and reports. It is common for researchers to compare autobiographies with official correspondence in order to check the validity of Ranger accounts, since most were written long after their service; it is not surprising that some accounts tend to be exaggerated, distorted, selective, and self-aggrandizing.

Autobiographies, Memoirs, Diaries, and Reminiscences

This chapter focuses on autobiographies, which in the case of the Rangers comes in a variety of forms. Each form of storytelling, or telling a nonfiction story, whether memoir, autobiography, or diary, has some unique characteristics. Purists will tell you an autobiography refers to an author recounting his or her life, usually written from a first-person point of view. As a source of history, there is usually some questions about the reliability of memory. Texas Ranger autobiographies were often written decades after the events. The retelling becomes even more complicated and questionable when a collaborator is brought in to "[impose] a certain 'linearity' and 'continuity' upon the dictation of the story."[2] A number of the following accounts suggest that since they were written so much later in life, they were a combination of accounts written by the Ranger himself and of the retelling by others assisted with the aid of memoirs, histories, fiction, and references to other writings—what one authority describes as the "intricate weaving of his memories, his self-citations, and the stories and memories and writings of untold number of other men."[3]

The Early Years

Few Rangers documented the service during its first century of exist-ence. By most accounts lawyer-author Samuel Reid's *The Scouting Expedition of McCulloch's Texas Rangers* (1847) was the "first book length treatment of the Texas Rangers," which went a long way toward establishing their "national reputation."[4] Based on a diary kept during a four-month period in 1846, it was probably also supple-mented by newspapers and other sources. It takes place against the backdrop of the Mexican-American War. Ranger historian Mike Cox asserts that the fact that it was written while the war was still in progress lends the tome credibility that offers "readers a genuine feel for the times."[5]

Texas folklorist J. Frank Dobie noted that in *The Scout and Ranger*, published in 1865, Texas Ranger James Pike "tells a bully story" that ranks among the best Ranger autobiographies. He goes on to suggest that while there are some exaggerations, "the fact that his narrative generally tallies with known facts lends authenticity to his personal remarks," but in some cases clearly "arrogated to himself the experi-ences of others." However, his accounts of two years of campaigning in various Indian wars are "among the most vivid on record."[6]

Shortly before the Civil War, Nelson Lee published *Three Years among the Camanches* [*sic*], which John Jenkins asserts "offers the best contemporary description of the life of the early Texas Rangers, and one of the few surviving eye-witness accounts of the life and activ-ities of the ferocious Comanche Indians." Texas historians suggest that this book, with almost half of its fifteen chapters devoted to Lee's captivity, and the rest covering the Rangers, the Mier Expedition, and the Mexican-American War, had been given short shrift by researchers. Texas Ranger historian Walter P. Webb wrote the introduction to the 1957 reprint, stating, "There is no better description of the life of the Texas Ranger than that by Nelson Lee."[7] That said, this account came under more scrutiny in 1991, when Gary Clayton Anderson's new foreword suggested the "the book is a unique brand of fiction/history, the embellished writings of a man who experienced part of what he claimed and added the rest based upon collected information."[8]

Andrew Jackson Sowell published *Rangers and Pioneers of Texas* and *Early Settlers and Indian Fighters of Southwest Texas* in 1884 and 1900, respectively. Sowell acknowledged in the earlier work he was "deficient in dates," a weakness shared by other early Ranger chroniclers. However, it benefits from the fact that he wrote it in his thirties, when he was relatively young, allowing him to present "many of the accounts an immediacy not available elsewhere." The 1884 volume is divided into three sections, with the last half of the book, concentrating on the 1870–1871 Wichita campaign, containing "his best prose, and leaves us a vivid account." His 1900 book is an entirely different work from his previous one, containing 132 accounts of early pioneers, mostly told to Sowell directly. Much of the writing covers Indian fights and the Texas Rangers. Jenkins asserts that the "material is fresh and does not seem to be included in other works from the era."[9]

1890s

Autobiographies from the nineteenth century are hard to come by, but those that did make it into print have been heavily utilized by researchers over the decades. What makes several of these so prominent was the fact that they were written by well-educated men with some type of journalistic backgrounds. Napoleon A. Jennings's *A Texas Ranger* has been reprinted numerous times since it was first published in 1899. Different editions have been supplemented by commentary from leading Texas historians, including J. Frank Dobie, Ben Procter, and Stephen Hardin.[10] Jennings was forthright when he answered the question as to why he wrote the book, commenting, "I am a writing man; I needed money; I had a story to tell; I told it."

Jennings was 18 and the scion of a mainline Philadelphia family when he became obsessed with going to Texas to seek his fortune. Instead he became a McNelly Texas Ranger. He provides what is considered the "earliest work dealing mainly with McNelly and his men."[11]

A Texas Ranger illustrates the challenges of hinging any Ranger debate on self-chronicled writings. Shortly after publication in 1899, its veracity was being challenged. In the words of J. Frank Dobie, "If his own eyes did not see every act he described, we may yet be sure that the stuff of the book, which is incidentally autobiography, came to him from eyewitnesses." This brings up the conundrum of whether using secondhand information should qualify as autobiographical writing. In the case of Jennings, "He probably telescoped some events; space and exigencies of narrative prevented his giving credit to every individual ranger who took part in the exploits recorded." Ultimately, Dobie noted, "Every writer who expects to be read must be selective, and many a historian who wanted to make the truth live has buried it in a dismal swamp of unselected facts."[12] Jennings wrote his book more than twenty years after the events, "a gap that weakened the authority of his account."[13]

Jennings tells his story through the eyes of a private. Moreover, what makes it valuable and interesting is the fact that it offers "a panorama of life in Texas in the old days" and is possibly more useful "than a dozen of the formal academic histories put together."[14] Conversely, the Texas historian Stephen Hardin asserted that his peers "must exercise caution if using as source." But he is confident that professional historians have enough training "that should have taught them to employ (a healthy dose of) skepticism toward any participant reminiscence."[15]

The 1890s saw the publication of a number of firsthand accounts. For the most part, they suffer from a certain amount of exaggeration. William Banta's *Twenty-Seven Years on the Texas Frontier*,[16] self-published in 1893, was written when he was 66, bringing into question its value, written so long after his Ranger service. In the book's preface, the modest former Ranger claimed he was not looking for fame but was recording his memories for future generations so they would "know what the pioneers of Texas suffered." Adding perhaps some credibility are the recollections also included in Banta's book by Ranger J. W. Caldwell's son, who noted he had "the assistance of rangers who were companions and eyewitnesses of my father."[17]

Alonzo Van Oden began keeping a journal after he joined the Texas Rangers in 1891 and is credited as "one of the few Rangers to record his actions and thoughts on a daily basis."[18] His journal contains an entry describing the death of his captain, Frank Jones. He was not present at the gunfight, but he probably spoke to some Rangers who were there since his account jibes with official reports. Diaries are not always the most reliable sources, particularly if, like Van Oden's, it is not a day-to-day journal and lacks specific dates. What remains clear is that the Ranger was literate and well-read. Some authors, recording their exploits decades after the fact, could at least square some of their observations with the adjutant general records houses in Austin. According to one historian, Van Oden's diary is most valuable when he mentions a Ranger casualty by name or described an incident that could be matched to a date in the Ranger records. Nonetheless, his lack of specific date keeping "in no way detracts from the value and interest of his diary."[19]

In 1898 the *Life of Robert Hall* was published by the pseudonymous Brazos.[20] It was not until 2013 that the real name of its author, Thomas A. Fagan, was identified.[21] This book is based on the reminiscences of an early settler who arrive in Texas shortly after the Battle of San Jacinto. The book has been targeted by critics for some of its exaggerated accounts of frontier life, while others found his writing "a casual, rambling style, often jumping back and forth in time and repeating parts of stories."[22] Still others critiqued it for being "always undocumented, and frequently no more than hearsay accounts."[23] But the author admits in the original editions that he did "not claim any literary merit for this book. It was written at a time I was in very bad health." According to Brazos, he was 80 at the time, and "often asking a dozen times as to some statement, I would still be in doubt as to whether I were recording the fact correctly or not."

This statement alone suggests that another writer was surely involved in the compilation of his account.[24]

In 1992 State House Press published a new edition of Hall's reminiscences with an introduction by Texan historian Stephen Hardin, who noted that the book was compiled after interviews with Rangers Hall and Bigfoot Wallace. Hall, according to folklorist J. Frank Dobie, "was part of the breed . . . characterized as 'authentic liars.'" But Hardin cautions readers, that despite questionable incidents that were clearly fabricated, "one should not be too eager to dismiss elements of Halls narrative that appear incredible—many are corroborated by contemporary sources."[25]

Early Twentieth Century Accounts

Captain Jeff Maltby's recollections, *Captain Jeff*, were published in 1906 and later reissued in a facsimile edition in 1967 with an introduction by Rupert Richardson. He chronicles his life in the Rangers during the Mexican-American War, the Civil War, and Reconstruction. Richardson suggests that the "organization and completeness of the book leaves much to be desired." The book shares the same weaknesses as other Ranger autobiographies, being written years, if not decades, after the incidents, leading to numerous errors in fact. His accounts were "nevertheless, essentially true." By most accounts the book is poorly organized and often disjointed. It also relies too much on more eventful episodes by giving short shrift to the mundane everyday Ranger life. The publisher's notice warns the reader ahead of time, noting that "the story is one continued thrilling incident after another from start to finish." Alas, life rarely moves forward in this fashion. The publisher suggests that the book will "[hold] the attention of lovers of fiction, romance and facts, and verifies the statement that facts are stranger than fiction." Moreover, it assures the reader that "all the tediousness is eliminated, and the story told in a brief, simple and convincing manner." Adding to its questionable value as a primary source is the addition of dozens of pages of filler material, including forty pages of newspaper extracts that add little to the tome.[26]

In 1909 Ranger sergeant W. J. L. Sullivan published *Twelve Years in the Saddle*. In his prefatory statements he acknowledged he was not offering "a history of my life" but instead aimed "to tell some of the exciting experiences" as a Texas Ranger.[27] Sullivan served under Bill McDonald and others between 1888 and 1900, "a period for which there are few surviving ranger recollections." Jenkins suggests that "his memoirs lack flavor, the wording obviously being provided by a person" more highly educated than Sullivan. The chapters in his firsthand account of Ranger activities in 1890s West Texas is curiously lacking chronological order, "but the dates are accurate enough to suffice." [28]

Prominent bibliographer Ramon Adams described Daniel Roberts's *Rangers and Sovereignty* (1914)[29] as "not the most important of these accounts," claiming most of the information on Sam Bass is wrong.[30] J. Frank Dobie declared the book poorly written, describing him "better as a ranger than as a writer." Conversely, Jenkins suggests that the book "gives a remarkable concise account of the service of one of the most active of all Texas Ranger units (Frontier Battalion) . . . the account is accurate, in the main, when dealing with events in which Roberts participated personally."[31] Historian Robert Wooster's new introduction to a combined facsimile edition of *Rangers and Sovereignty* and the recollections of Roberts's wife, Luvenia, *A Woman's Reminiscences of Six Year in Camp with the Texas Rangers*, asserts that "rare is the diary or reminiscence" or "rare is the case where two individuals left accounts of similar circumstances." This book in Wooster's eyes "fills the gap," providing perceptive observations of Texas Ranger life after the Civil War.[32]

When it comes to early Texas Ranger autobiographies, by most accounts James B. Gillett's *Six Years with the Texas Rangers* is at the top of the heap.[33] Written in 1925, it "never succumbs to the deification process."[34] A. C. Greene includes it in his *The 50+ Best Books on Texas* (1998), calling it "by far the best work ever done" on the Texas Rangers. Going further, Greene described the book as a "straightforward story of working in the days when the

Texas Rangers rode in companies, camped on the frontier." Moreover, the chronicle "came from the events themselves, not from an
overheated pen. His regard for honesty is evident throughout the
book."[35] Most criticisms of the book revolve around the inaccuracies concerning the killing of Sam Bass.

Few Ranger autobiographies of note were published in the 1930s
and 1940s. J. B. "Red" Dunn's *Perilous Trails of Texas*, edited by his
daughter, a prominent poet, was published in 1932. At the time Dunn
was considered the oldest living pioneer of the Corpus Christi area.
The introduction informs the reader up front that "in these sketches
they have been related exactly as they occurred, told in the simple,
direct style of the author, without any attempt to gloss over them."[36]

The memoirs of well-known Ranger Ira Aten saw publication
1945. In his first-person account he assures the reader no fiction
has been added to his chronicle of the years 1883–1889, and that
his memoirs would not have been published if not for the urgings of
iconic Ranger Captain John R. Hughes. His initial reluctance to write
his memoirs was due to his belief that a "person's memoirs should not
be released to the public only after his death so that there could be no
controversy with him over what he had written." But Aten relented
after his friends badgered him to write them to "release them while
I am still alive." One of the more curious decisions was his disincli-
nation "to mention the names of the many men we have hunted down
and arrested or to whom a worse fate came." He thought that not only
naming names but also the stigmatization that might have on families
and descendants was "cruel and unjust." If anyone doubted his veracity, he encouraged them to check the office of the adjutant general in
Austin for confirmation.[37]

The 1960s

The 1960s saw a recrudescence of Ranger-themed publications,
including autobiographical works. William Warren Sterling's *Trails
and Trials of a Texas Ranger* (1959) was among the most prominent

of these. Sterling claimed he had been told on more than one occasion, "You ought to write a book." At the time he was in his late sixties or early seventies. During his long career he held every position from Ranger to adjutant general. The author's stated aim was "to give a Ranger's eye view of the Service" in order "to relate some of the unheralded deeds performed by good Rangers whose names seldom appear in print."[38] The year before his death it was first privately printed by the author in Houston. It sold out quickly thanks to his prominence as a Texan and his folksy style. One of the biggest problems is the sheer number of characters in the book, so many, that "the book takes on some character of a subscription history as the names and most valiant deed of what must be every Ranger, friend and neighbor to cross paths with Sterling are mentioned, making the Index look like a county census roll."[39]

Ranger historian Mike Cox suggested that Sterling's book "remains one of the better Ranger narratives."[40] This might be so, but some of his claims do not stand up to scrutiny. He writes about his "harmonious relations with Mexicans," earned by his "fair treatment to people of all classes."[41] According to one Ranger, in 1915 "the Mexicans hate him, and I believe would kill [him at first opportunity]." Other historians suggest this as well, and other examples indicate that "his deeds did not match [his] admirable language."[42]

Sterling wrote his autobiography in the comfortable business headquarters of the McGill Ranches in Alice, Texas, where he took advantage of the office's excellent Texana collection. Recent historians have targeted his hypocrisy. He was quick to critique anyone he thought fell short of the standards that he expected. In his book he speaks disparagingly of a constable who he felt was "a blustering braggart." More recently, several historians suggested, "This description might well apply to Sterling himself," who was inclined to mythologize his exploits in his book when he wasn't selectively recounting his career.[43]

In 1962 historian Stephen B. Oates edited the memoirs of John Salmon "Rip" Ford, one of the most iconic Rangers of the nineteenth century. Ford had retired to San Antonio and begun writing his life story until he had amassed about 1,300 pages. His writing style has been described as "rich in detail," never placing himself in the spotlight. In 1885 he composed a "Statement of Purpose," that promised readers he would not "endeavor to become the hero upon all extraordinary events and [will] let the book speak of himself alone." According to one of his biographers, Ford didn't just include every great story he heard about the Lone Star State, but also "combed archives, interviewed former associates, and published a significant amount of history [found] in newspapers and other people's books."[44]

Ford had intended to see his memoirs between book covers sooner, but in 1897 he suffered a paralytic stroke and died several months later. The unpublished memoirs eschewed any concerns for arrangement or chronology and were rife with repetition. Moreover, his adopted daughter destroyed many sections, cutting out sections she felt were "indiscreet or indelicate."[45]

When it came time to publish his memoirs, which covered his entire life, his intention was to document every aspect of his career. According to one recent biographer, "Texans were not equally interested in all aspects of Ford's career." This perhaps explains why the entire memoir was never published in his lifetime. What excerpts that were published focused on his years as a soldier and Texas Ranger. Historian Richard B. McCaslin suggests that as a result of this focus on one small slice of Ford's life, he "became a one-dimensional archetype of the nineteenth-century Texan."[46] McCaslin noted that when the Oates-edited book was released, material was left out that was considered peripheral to his Ranger and military career. As a result, "The importance of his career and how it actually shaped Texas, both on the battlefield and off, became lost."[47] Ultimately, Ford's massive history was never published in its entirety. But to Oates's credit, he put the reminiscences "in logical, coherent, chronological order." What's more, Oates reorganized material into a connected narrative, integrated articles that covered the same topic, corrected grammatical errors, and so forth. His two main rules were to "preserve Ford's style" and not to tinker with sentences "that could be actually under-stood on first reading."[48]

Although his Ranger service dated back to the 1870s, George Durham's as-told-to autobiography was first published in 1962. It is "one of the few accounts of the McNelly's Rangers, told by a member of the force." He was the last surviving member of the storied unit when he died in 1940. Durham had become a legend in the 1930s and in the decade before he died, freelance reporter Clyde Wantland convinced him to tell his story, which he dutifully recorded. The book covers only two years he spent with McNelly (1875–76). The youngest member of McNelly's Rangers, Durham was able to dictate from memory years after his youth and his account "bears all of the marks of a truthful narrative."[49] After leaving the Texas Rangers, Durham was hired as foreman on the King Ranch, a position he held for decades. During this time he recorded his recollections and stored the pages in in a trunk in his home on the ranch.

The Modern Era (1980–2019)

In the 1980s and 1990s, several autobiographies (and biographies) of modern Rangers were published. They were very similar in tone and substance—not surprising because they were contemporaries. Several wrote two different volumes. Glenn Elliott with Robert Nieman in *Glenn Elliott: A Ranger's Ranger* (1999) covers twenty-six years in the service. Elliott claimed that he was asked to write down his recollections for his children and grandchildren. While he was flattered at first, it took Robert Nieman to convince Elliott to start writing, telling him, "Let's do a book." Elliott claimed that his coauthor and editor "gave [him] a completely free hand in choosing the cases related to the book." Nieman tried to assuage any doubts, writing, "In truth Glenn had a bigger part in the actual writing of the book than he is likely to ever admit." Nieman insisted that Elliott read every word and story, making sure they were "correct to the nth degree."[50] Elliott and Nieman followed up their first collaboration with *Still a Ranger's Ranger* in 2002.

In 1998 retired Ranger Captain E. G. Albers Jr. offered his account of life in the Texas Rangers. He stated upfront that "writing a book has not been an easy task for me." He goes on to explain that some of the information came from his reports and files, while some "come from memory which sometimes was vivid." He explains that he wanted to be careful and accurate but that "the crimes investigated and reported are accurate as to detail as I remember them." His Ranger career lasted from 1961 until retirement in 1974. This meant almost a quarter century passed before Albers wrote his memoirs. For some reason he decided to change the names of criminal suspects and perpetrators, leaving the reader to fill in the blanks.[51]

More recently, two historians point to two "significant works" that depict the Texas Rangers in the twentieth century.[52] *In the Line of Duty: Reflections of a Texas Ranger* covers the thirty-year Ranger career of Lewis C. Rigler. It was published in 1984 after he finally decided "to record my career for the benefit of my children and grandchildren." He would not be the first prospective autobiographer to do so, convinced he had a story to share. He apparently underestimated what was required to write a book; he "thought it would be easy." Most writers have some type of schedule and Rigler began imagining that he would just "sit down with daily reports, crime cases and letters and have a very fine time." He expected to complete "a chapter each day, and in a few days, I would have a book."[53]

The other significant book is H. Joaquin Jackson's bestselling *One Ranger: A Memoir*, published in 2005. To this could be added his sequel to the book, *One Ranger Returns*, in 2008, which functions as a bookend to his storied career.[54] In the first volume, he credits a cavalcade of "legendary Texas writers and journalists for opening their hearts, books and archives (and anything else we could rip off)."[55]

Over the past twenty years the Texas Rangers have grown in popularity, as demonstrated by the number of biographies and autobiographies. Although it covers 1887 and 1888, "a period for which there are few surviving ranger recollections,"[56] it was not until 2001 that *A Private in the Texas Rangers* was published. Abner Theophilus "A. T." Miller recorded daily entries into three diaries that were preserved and passed down in the family, until his great-grandson, John Miller Morris, published an annotated version of them. They begin with his recruitment in 1887 and detail his experiences in North Texas and Southwest Oklahoma, offering a unique portal into everyday life in a Texas Ranger company. What lends this work such authority is that it is not focused on the most spectacular incidents, "but rather the ordinary and tangible leanings of life."[57] Miller wrote his vignettes in a style that employed the "pleasant subtleties of archaisms and premodern speech patterns," utilizing words "keyed to the Upper Southern dialect of his youth with strong admixtures of western slang and criminal justice jargon."[58] Readers will find Morris portrays the constant excitement of Ranger life as more exaggeration than reality, where routine duties and paperwork were more typical than gunfights and rampant danger. This autobiography contrasts sharply with the other period memoirs that "string together one exciting incident or embellished anecdote after another."[59]

Texas Ranger Dispatch editor Robert Nieman has two other books on modern Texas Rangers to his credit: first, *Glenn Elliott: A Ranger's Ranger* (1999), now in its fourth printing, and more recently, *Ed Gooding: Soldier, Texas Ranger.*[60] His latest effort explores the life story of Edgar Dalton Gooding. A good portion of the book focuses on his experiences as a soldier during the Second World War. He sees death daily, experiences the hardships of every soldier (cold, fatigue, loneliness), and loses countless companions. It would go a long way to preparing him for the challenges he would face in in law enforcement. Like wartime, the lives of Highway Patrolmen and Texas Rangers were often full of danger, with death not uncommon.

In 2006 *Bill Callicott Reminiscences* was published as an e-book by the Texas Ranger Hall of Fame. But before that, 67-year-old William Crump Callicott was living in Houston in 1920 when Walter

P. Webb located him as he spread a wide net to capture Ranger interviews for his book in progress, *Texas Rangers: A Century of Frontier Defense* (1935). Callicott corresponded with Webb, offering in his own words his experiences on the Ranger force. By the time the two men began communicating, he was almost blind but still possessed a fine memory. By all accounts Callicott was not educated and wrote mostly phonetically, eschewing periods, commas, and punctuation entirely. According to Western historian Chuck Parsons, who transcribed and annotated *Bill Callicott Reminiscences*, each day the Ranger began one paragraph and continued writing the same paragraph until he had done his piece for the day. Callicott never promoted above private, meaning his name is rarely mentioned in any Ranger reports. He served six months under McNelly between 1874 and 1875. Parsons transcribed letters written in 1921, creating a narrative "for ease of reading, corrected spelling and added punctuation, without omitting any writing."[61]

In 2009 Doyle Holdridge published *Working the Border*, and in 2005 Ramiro "Ray" Ramirez's *They Call Me Ranger Ray* hit bookstores. It attained a certain amount of publicity for his account of bringing down the Austin Tower shooter, Charles Whitman. In 2013 one of the rare autobiographies by an African American Ranger was published by Lee Young and Nita Thurman, *Memoirs of a Black Seminole Texas Ranger*.[62]

There are other works that could have been added to the aforementioned, but the high points of Ranger autobiographical writings are all here. As long as there is a receptive audience clamoring for Texas Ranger recollections, there will surely be more autobiographies hitting bookstores and the internet in the coming years. No one knows for sure what memoirs, scrapbooks, and recollections reside in family libraries and estates. Likewise, there are probably Ranger firsthand accounts buried in various archival collections.

Notes

1. Mike Cox, *Texas Ranger Tales: Stories That Need Telling* (Plano: Republic of Texas Press, 1997), 289–90.
2. Mark A. Sanders, "Theorizing the Collaborative Self: The Dynamics of Contour and Content in the Dictated Autobiography," *New Literary History* 25, no. 2 (Spring 1994): 446.
3. Richard Hutson, "Ecce Cowboy: E. C. Abbott's *We Pointed Them North*," in *Western Subjects: Autobiographical Writing in the North American West*, ed. Kathleen A. Boardman and Gioia Woods (Salt Lake City: University of Utah Press, 2004), 132.
4. Samuel Chester Reid Jr., *The Scouting Expeditions of McCulloch's Texas Rangers* [. . .] (Philadelphia: G. B. Zieber, 1847). Reprinted in 1848, 1859, 1860, 1885, 1935, and 1970. See also Cox, *Texas Ranger Tales*, 302.
5. Cox, *Texas Ranger Tales*, 303.
6. James Pike, *The Scout and Ranger: Being the Personal Adventures of Corporal Pike, of the Fourth Ohio Cavalry, as Texas Ranger, in the Indian Wars* (Cincinnati and New York: J. R. Hawley, 1865). Dobie quoted in John H. Jenkins, *Basic Texas Books: An Annotated Bibliography of Selected Works for a Research Library* (1983; Rev. ed., Austin: Texas Historical Association, 1988), 533–34.
7. Nelson Lee, *Three Years among the Camanches: The Narrative of Nelson Lee* [. . .] (Albany, NY: Baker and Taylor, 1859). Reprinted 1871, 1957, 1967 and 1991. Webb cited in Jenkins, *Basic Texas Books*, 328. Jenkins points out that Webb's 1935 Ranger history, written two decades earlier, does not mention Lee at all.
8. Quoted in Cox, *Texas Ranger Tales*, 299.
9. Andrew J. Sowell, *Rangers and Pioneers of Texas* [. . .] (San Antonio: Shepard Brothers, 1884); Sowell, *Early Settlers and Indian Fighters of Southwest Texas . . . Facts Gathered from Survivors of Frontier Days* (Austin: Ben C. Jones, 1900).
10. Napoleon Augustus Jennings, *A Texas Ranger* (New York: Charles Scribner's Sons, 1899); Jennings, *A Texas Ranger*, with a foreword by J. Frank Dobie and introduction by Stephen L. Hardin (Norman: University of Oklahoma Press, 1997); and Jennings, *A Texas Ranger*, edited by Ben Procter (Chicago: Lakeside Press, 1992). Also reprinted in 1930, 1936, 1959, 1960, and 1961.
11. Chuck Parsons and Marianne E. Hall Little, *Captain L. H. McNelly, Texas Ranger: The Life and Times of a Fighting Man* (Austin: State House Press, 2001).

12. Dobie, foreword to Jennings, *Texas Ranger*, viii.

13. Dobie, foreword to Jennings, *Texas Ranger*, xi.

14. Stanley Babb, quoted in Jenkins, *Basic Texas Books*, 280.

15. Stephen L. Hardin, introduction to Jennings, *Texas Ranger*, xv.

16. William Banta, *Twenty-Seven Years on the Texas Frontier* (Austin: Ben C. Jones, 1893).

17. Cox, *Texas Ranger Tales*, 291.

18. Alonzo Van Oden, *Texas Ranger's Diary and Scrapbook*, ed. Ann Jensen (Dallas: Kaleidograph Press, 1936). Quote in Frederick Wilkins, *The Law Comes to Texas: The Texas Rangers, 1870–1901* (Austin: State House Press, 1999), 312.

19. Wilkins, *Law Comes to Texas*, 313.

20. Brazos [pseud.], *Life of Robert Hall, Indian Fighter and Veteran of Three Great Wars*, with an introduction by Stephen Hardin (1898; repr., Austin: State House Press, 1992).

21. Steve Mauldin, "Search for 'Brazos': The Mystery Writer of *Life of Robert Hall*," *Southwestern Historical Quarterly* 116, no. 4 (April 2013): 386–91. The excavator of the real Brazos was a master electrician from Helotes, Texas. He was inspired to uncover the actual writer after marrying a great-great-great-granddaughter of Ranger Lee Hall.

22. Jim B. Pearson, review of *Trails and Trials of a Texas Ranger*, by William Warren Sterling, *Arizona and the Southwest* 12, no. 4 (Winter 1970): 395.

23. Robert C. Carriker, review of *Trails and Trials of a Texas Ranger*, by William Warren Sterling, *Montana: The Magazine of Western History* 20, no. 2 (Spring 1970): 82.

24. Mauldin, "Search for 'Brazos.'"

25. Hardin, introduction to Brazos, *Life of Robert Hall*, xxix.

26. Captain Jeff Maltby, *Captain Jeff, or Frontier Life in Texas with the Texas Rangers* (Colorado, TX: Whipkey Printing, 1906; facsimile reprint with introduction by Rupert Richardson and Publisher's Notice by N. C. Bawcom, Waco: Texian Press, 1967).

27. Sergeant W. J. L. Sullivan, *Twelve Years in the Saddle: For Law and Order on the Frontiers of Texas* (Austin: Von-Boeckmann-Jones, 1909; facsimile edition, New York: Buffalo-Head Press, 1966).

28. Jenkins, *Basic Texas Books*, 526–27.

29. Daniel Webster Roberts, *Rangers and Sovereignty* (San Antonio: Wood Printing & Engraving, 1914). B. Roberts Lackey copied Roberts's book almost word for word for his book *Stories of the Texas Rangers* (San

Antonio: Naylor, 1955). When the publishers got wind of this, they placed an insert with a statement explaining that it was "to a large extent, a reprinting of *Rangers and Sovereignty.*" As it turned out Lackey had a copyright on the 1914 edition (Ramon Adams, *Six-Guns and Saddle Leather: A Bibliography of Books and Pamphlets on Western Outlaws and Gunmen* [repr., Cleveland: John T. Zubal, 1982], 378). A combined facsimile edition of *Rangers and Sovereignty* and Mrs. D. W. Roberts's *A Woman's Reminiscences of Six Years in Camp with the Texas Rangers*, with an introduction by Robert Wooster, was published in 1987 by Austin's State House Press.

30. Adams, *Six-Guns*, 542–43.
31. Jenkins, *Basic Texas Books*, 474.
32. Wooster, introduction to facsimile edition of *Rangers and Sovereignty*, vi.
33. James B. Gillett, *Six Years with the Texas Rangers, 1875 to 1881* (Austin: n.p. 1921; new ed., ed. Milo M. Quaife, New Haven: Yale University Press, 1925).
34. Cox, *Texas Ranger Tales*.
35. A. C. Greene, *The 50+ Best Books on Texas* (Denton: University of North Texas Press, 1998), 84.
36. John B. "Red" Dunn, *Perilous Trails of Texas*, edited by his daughter, Lilith Lorraine (Dallas: Southwest Press, 1932), v.
37. Ira Aten, *Six-and-One Half Years in the Texas Ranger Service: The Memoirs of Ira Aten* (Bandera, TX: Frontier Times, 1945).
38. William Warren Sterling, *Trails and Trials of a Texas Ranger* (Norman: University of Oklahoma Press, 1959), xi, xiii.
39. Carriker, review of *Trails and Trials*, 82.
40. Mike Cox, *Texas Ranger Tales II* (Plano: Republic of Texas Press, 1999), 135.
41. Sterling, *Trails and Trials*, 88.
42. Charles Harris III and Louis R. Sadler, *The Texas Rangers in Transition: From Gunfighters to Criminal Investigators, 1921–1935* (Norman: University of Oklahoma Press, 2019), 22.
43. Harris and Sadler, *Texas Rangers in Transition*, 21.
44. Cox, *Ranger Tales II*, 50; Oates, "Statement of Purpose," in John Salmon Ford, *Rip Ford's Texas*, ed. Stephen B. Oates (Austin: University of Texas Press, 1963); Richard B. McCaslin, *Fighting Stock: John S. "Rip" Ford of Texas* (Forth Worth: TCU Press, 2011).

45. *Rip Ford's Texas*, cited in Harris and Sadler, *Texas Rangers in Transition*, 50; Jenkins, *Basic Texas Books*, 165.
46. McCaslin, *Fighting Stock*, xi.
47. McCaslin, *Fighting Stock*, xiv.
48. Jenkins, *Basic Texas Books*, 165
49. Jenkins, *Basic Texas Books*, 127
50. Glenn Elliott, *Glenn Elliott: A Ranger's Ranger*, with Robert Nieman (Waco: Texian Press, 1999), viii.
51. E. G. Albers Jr., *The Life and Reflections of a Texas Ranger* (Waco: Texian Press, 1998), vii.
52. Bruce A. Glasrud and Harold J. Weiss Jr., "Introduction: In Pursuit of the Texas Rangers: The Twentieth Century," in *Tracking the Texas Rangers: The Twentieth Century* (Denton: University of North Texas Press, 2013), 4, 1–24.
53. Lewis C. Rigler and Judyth Wagner Rigler, *In the Line of Duty: Reflections of a Texas Ranger* (Houston: Larksdale, 1984).
54. H. Joaquin Jackson and David Marion Wilkinson, *One Ranger: A Memoir* (Austin: University of Texas Press, 2005); H. Joaquin Jackson and James L. Haley, *One Ranger Returns* (Austin: University of Texas Press, 2008).
55. Jackson and Haley, *One Ranger Returns*, 277.
56. Jenkins, *Basic Texas Books*, 526–27.
57. John Miller Morris, *A Private in the Texas Rangers: A. T. Miller of Company B, Frontier Battalion* (College Station: Texas A&M Press, 2001), 5.
58. Morris, *Private in the Texas Rangers*, 7.
59. Morris, *Private in the Texas Rangers*, 10.
60. Ed Gooding and Robert Nieman, *Ed Gooding: Soldier, Texas Ranger* (Longview, TX: Ranger Publishing, 2001).
61. William Callicott, *Bill Callicott Reminiscences*, transcribed and annotated by Chuck Parsons (Waco: Texas Ranger Hall of Fame, 2006).
62. Doyle Holdridge, *Working the Border: A Texas Ranger's Story* (Dallas: Atriad Press, 2009); Ramiro "Ray" Martinez, *They Call Me Ranger Ray: From the UT Tower Sniper to Corruption in South Texas* (New Braunfels, TX: Rio Bravo, 2005); and Lee Young and Nita Thurman, *Lee Young: Memoirs of a Black Seminole Texas Ranger* (McKinney, TX: Lee Young and Associates, 2013).

PART 3

Interpreting the Rangers

Their Historians and
Their Professional Writings

Traditionalists

Chapter 7

Chuck Parsons
Updated Traditionalist

Roy B. Young

This writer has been acquainted with Chuck Parsons for three decades, having first met him at a National Outlaw-Lawman History Association (NOLA) Rendezvous in Montana in the 1990s. We were walking toward one another in a hotel hallway when I recognized him from his picture that accompanied his monthly "Answer Man" columns in *True West* magazine. I was a newbie to Wild West–related meetings, having joined NOLA and Western Outlaw-Lawman History Association (WOLA) after the release of the blockbuster movie *Tombstone* on Christmas Eve of 1993. Chuck Parsons was one of the first persons I wanted to meet. After all, he was the "Answer Man!"

When asked the question, "Since you are a Yankee, how did you ever get to Texas?" Chuck will respond, "I am a Texan by choice. I listened to my heart and followed my passion for Texas history."[1]

He was born Charles Norman Parsons on July 23, 1940, on a 160-acre farm in north-central Iowa near the town of Laurens. His parents were William Thomas and Vera L. (Parker) Parsons. His ancestors were originally from England and came to North

America through Canada and then into the United States. He had one older sister, Wilma Leona, who was killed in a traffic accident in 1946, so his "growing up" was as an only child.

In 1950 the Parsons family left their rented farm in Iowa and Chuck's dad purchased a 240-acre farm in south-central Minnesota. In public school Chuck's extracurricular activities included track in the spring and marching and concert band year-round. In high school the budding musician was selected to be in the National Future Farmers of America band. Though Chuck never intended to be a farmer, he felt it only natural to take agriculture as a course and become an FFA member. The FFA national convention was held in Kansas City. Chuck attended the various scheduled activities, but the trip highlight was a visit to bookstores, and his purchase of the Ramon F. Adams book *Six-Guns and Saddle Leather: A Bibliography of Books and Pamphlets on Western Outlaws and Gunmen* for the extravagant sum of $12.50.[2]

Coming to resent having to live on a farm, Chuck discovered the game of cowboys and Indians. He related, "On Saturdays my parents went to town for groceries and I rarely got to attend a motion picture but, of course, the ones I did get to see were always westerns. I am sure that my initial interest in what is now termed the Wild West comes from those early years. One motion picture I recall seeing is *The Great Missouri Raid* about the James-Younger Gang starring Macdonald Carey and Wendell Corey. That must have been 1951 or 1952."

By then Chuck's passion was fixed, and later in the 1950s he found books by Ed Bartholomew, such as *Kill or Be Killed, Wild Bill Longley* and *Jesse Evans: A Texas Hide Burner.*[3] Another important title was *The Album of Gunfighters* by J. Marvin Hunter and Noah H. Rose.[4] He then collected other important titles of the current Wild West authors such as Carl W. Breihan and Harry Sinclair Drago. For the high school student in the1950s, there were few books that contained in-depth research, much less endnotes, a documentary device considered essential today.

Such titles as these and many others were the examples Chuck determined to follow as he began to develop in the recesses of his mind the idea that someday he would write and see published his own works of Western history. Chuck has related, "Even in those days I had the idea that I could write the 'definitive' biography of John Wesley Hardin and the all-encompassing history of the Sutton-Taylor Feud." By then he had discovered C. L. Sonnichsen's *I'll Die Before I'll Run: The Story of the Great Feuds of Texas*[5] and works related to the infamous feud. A half century later that vague dream started to become true.

After high school graduation, Chuck attended the University of Minnesota's Minneapolis campus, received his bachelor's degree, and then entered the field of teaching in the public schools. Next came graduate school, where he earned his master's degree in educational administration and supervision. For eight years he attempted to teach French to inner-city kids at a junior high school in Racine, Wisconsin. Those students' lack of interest in the subject matter was the main cause of his entering secondary school administration. As a high school principal in Barrett, Minnesota, and later, Silver Lake, Minnesota, he found that he looked forward to going to school every day and enjoyed every day's challenges.

In Minnesota in 1963, Chuck married his high school sweetheart, Aileene Evans, and with her had two sons, Anthony Charles Parsons and Timothy Jay Parsons, and is now grandfather to a grandson and a granddaughter.

In the summer of 1976, Chuck made his first trip to Texas. One of the main goals was to visit historian Barney Hubbs at Pecos. The two men had corresponded over a period of a year and learned they both had an interest in Clay Allison. Hubbs had already written a pamphlet on Allison and wanted to do another but had never found the time to do it. Chuck offered to help redo Hubbs's work, and the old gentleman, then nearing 80, agreed to the project.

Chuck recalled,

Hubbs' office was nearly as spacious as some people's homes but most importantly he gave me full access to his files on Allison and other western personalities. His office had a comfortable couch and the Pecos Restaurant was only a few blocks away, so I was set for writing. That office was my home for a week. Of course, most interesting for me was that behind the couch I slept on was the Clay Allison shotgun made of Damascus steel with his name plate showing the engraved owner: "R. C. Allison." I presume it is in the "West of the Pecos Museum" today.

At the end of one week, having worked about sixteen hours a day on it, Chuck was able to leave a neatly typed manuscript on Clay Allison for Mr. Hubbs. He was happy, Chuck was happy, and some months later it was in print entitled *Shadows along the Pecos: The Saga of Clay Allison, "Gentleman Gun Fighter."*[6] It was a forty-four-page pamphlet that was well received, thanks, in part, to Hubbs's promotion ability.

Being "well received" was great news to Chuck, as sometime later Barney Hubbs asked him about a reprint. Chuck's advice was to give him some time so he could do a more complete publication. It took several years, but the revised and enlarged work was published in 1983 by Pioneer Books of Seagraves, Texas, the publishing house of Ed Eakin, now based in Fort Worth. This edition was in hard cover and had additional photographs and an introduction by the late Dale T. Schoenberger, who had previously done significant research on Clay Allison, published as a single chapter in his book *The Gunfighters.*[7]

Chuck credits his Clay Allison work with getting him started on writing on outlaws and lawmen of the Wild West, especially Texas Rangers, and it was during this Clay Allison period that he started to put together his first book dealing with outlaw John Wesley Hardin. However, this book's focus was on Escambia County sheriff William Henry Hutchinson, the man who was responsible, at least in part, for the capture of Hardin in Florida in 1877.

Chuck related,

I had a praise-worthy manuscript ready for publication, with new material and hardly-ever seen photographs and submitted it to a Kansas publisher. I came to realize that just because John

Wesley Hardin spent a few months in Kansas did not make him a worthy subject for a Kansas publisher. Fortunately, historian and publisher Jim Earle of College Station, Texas was looking for a manuscript to start his series of biographies of Wild West characters. I sent the Hutchinson manuscript to him and he was interested. My title was unacceptable, though, and it soon became *The Capture of John Wesley Hardin* which, of course, was far superior than my original title, *The Life and Times of William H. Hutchinson*. Few people would recognize that title as a book dealing with the Wild West's most notorious outlaw. That biography came out in 1978 in run of 1000 copies, with fifty copies in a special collector's edition.

A book frequently needs a foreword by a recognized writer and scholar, and Jim Earle suggested that Chuck contact Dr. C. L. Sonnichsen, a historian, writer, and professor at University of Texas at El Paso. Chuck took Earle's suggestion and determined to call him. Chuck remembers, "I anticipated I would get to talk with Sonnichsen's secretary and that would be about the end of it, but lo! C. L. answered the phone. I explained who I was and what I wanted. He responded by asking me to send him a copy of the manuscript and he would write something. So I now had another biography, this time with a foreword by 'Doc' Sonnichsen. I felt elated as he was one of the most highly respected historians of the time."

Jim Earle continued publishing books on Western figures of import, such as Custer, Hickok, and a second title dealing with Hardin by Chuck and then-wife Marjorie Burnett Parsons, *Bowen and Hardin*.[8] This volume focused on Hardin's brother-in-law, Brown Bowen, whose carelessness resulted in Hardin and Bowen being captured, with Bowen ultimately going to the gallows for a senseless murder. Sheriff Hutchinson also captured Brown Bowen shortly after Sergeant John B. Armstrong captured Hardin.

Rather than making John Wesley Hardin a cottage industry, Chuck began to delve into the lives of Texas Rangers such as John B. Armstrong, John R. Hughes, Capt. Charles Brown McKinney, and the Sutton-Taylor Feud. Additionally, he has coauthored several biographies. With Jack DeMattos he did the most complete biography to date of Luke Short, *The Notorious Luke Short: Sporting Man of the Wild West*, with a foreword by Rick Miller.[9] Three years later the two historians again combined their research talents for *They Called Him Buckskin Frank: The Life and Times of Nashville Franklyn Leslie*, with a foreword by John Boessenecker.[10] That same year, 2018, proved to be a memorable year for Chuck as a biography he had earlier completed on Texas Ranger Jack Helm appeared: *Captain Jack Helm: Victim of Texas Reconstruction Violence*, with a foreword by Kenneth W. Howell.[11] In July 2018 his biggest book yet appeared, *Ben Thompson: Portrait of a Gunfighter*, written with Thomas C. Bicknell, who had researched Ben and Billy Thompson for decades.[12] Having a mutual interest in Texas history in general, and Hardin and Thompson in particular, was a natural outcome of their efforts. Limited by the University of North Texas Press to fifty illustrations and maps and a severe word-count, the book still ran up 665 pages.

In the latter years of his high school principal career of eighteen years, and the end of his first marriage in 1984, Chuck served as high school principal of Black Hawk ISD in South Wayne, Wisconsin. He recalled, "It was demanding: high school principal, then Director of Transportation added, and later Athletic Director added, all with additional compensation of course. I loved the work, looked forward to going to school every day, attended all the various school/sporting events, and usually had my Saturday's free to go to the State Historical Society of Wisconsin which was only an hour away. That Society had a wonderful collection of newspapers as well as books and journals devoted to western History."

In the early 1980s, while on a trip to Texas, Chuck met Gaines Kincaid, a historian living in Austin. The two had corresponded at some length about his going to Austin and spending a week or so with Kincaid while doing research at the Austin History Center. The main purpose of this research trip was to obtain all the letters and poems and other writings done by or about a Texas Ranger, originally from Virginia, who joined up with Captain McNelly's force in 1874 and served with him two years. His name was T. C. Robinson, though he signed all his contributions as Pidge. At the Austin History Center, daylight to dark, Chuck made copies of all Pidge's letters and poems from microfilmed newspapers. After determining something about Pidge's early life, he learned why he left Virginia and went to Texas, how for a short period he was a cowboy and then worked as a typesetter in the office of the *Austin Daily Democratic Statesman*. Pidge then joined McNelly, later resigning to go home to Virginia "to spend his pay." Actually he had a much more deadly reason, which is fully explained in Chuck's book. By 1985 Chuck had all the material on Pidge Robinson ready to publish, chose self-publishing, and Henington Publishing of Wolfe City, Texas, printed it.[13] Pidge became a virtual ideal subject for Chuck's first full-length book on a Texas Ranger. He divided the book into the three main parts: his early life and time spent as a cowboy/typesetter, the time he was with McNelly and submitting letters to the *Statesman*, and the time when he was still with McNelly but now sending his contributions to the *Austin Daily Gazette*. Chuck related, "Why the change from the *Statesman* to the *Gazette*, I never was able to determine. Actually I should not have listed myself as the author, but rather Robinson as the author and myself as the editor. All I contributed was an introduction, biographical sketch of his life and annotated the letters and poems he wrote. But the first edition was done . . . and years later, 2013, Texas A&M asked if the book could be reissued."

Continuing to fulfill his dreams with visits to Texas, in 1987 Chuck made an excursion to the small town of Gonzales, site of the first shots of the Texas war for independence. There he met Marjorie Lee Burnett, a Texan by birth who had studied her county's history and that of surrounding counties for many years. She had already published a book on the Sutton-Taylor Feud, and that is, in part, what drew the two together. Her book *The Taylors, The Tumlinsons, and the Feud*, published in 1986, had sold out fairly quickly, and she published a second, revised edition in 1988.[14] The two historians became friends that soon developed into a serious correspondence that led her to ask Chuck to provide an introduction for her second volume. Eventually, this developed into a writing partnership based on their intense interest in the Sutton-Taylor Feud and its many interesting characters besides the Taylors and the one Sutton for whom the feud was named. Their relationship developed into the decision to get married on July 7, 1990, at Gonzales. The couple settled into Chuck's home in South Wayne, Wisconsin, and there the jointly authored book *Bowen and Hardin* was written. Their book was launched at the Old Jail Museum in Gonzales during their annual Come and Take it Days. They signed and sold many copies of that book, in part because many of the people who went that day to the old jail did so because they had known Marjorie and her parents for many years and wanted the event to be a success. At that point, Chuck says, "Nobody knew me, other than being Marjorie's husband!"

Upon retirement from his occupation of high school principal, the couple moved to Texas, settling a few miles outside the little community of Smiley. However, in April 1996 this second marriage ended in divorce and Chuck moved to Luling, Texas, the county seat of Caldwell County.

All during his years of college, graduate school, teaching, and administration, as well as marriage and the raising of two sons, Chuck never let go of his passion for history. He had written a few short articles dealing with education but knew his heart was in studying and writing about America's Wild West history, especially aspects of Texas history such as the Sutton-Taylor Feud and the gunfighter John Wesley Hardin. He stated, "So much of history cannot be separated from other aspects; if you focus on Texas Rangers you are obligated to concern yourself with the fugitives they chased; and vice versa: if you focus on certain outlaws you can hardly ignore those who will eventually pursue them and hunt them down."

Chuck has never been simply a historian sitting at a computer Googling names and events, or one who would read a stack of books written by others from which he would borrow research and employ it as his own. With his move to Luling, he was closer to the Texas

State Archives in Austin and the San Antonio Public Library. Many days were spent studying the adjutant general reports of the 1870s period in Austin, as well as the San Antonio newspapers of the 1870s in the Alamo City. Being single again, he traveled some, not on any romantic cruises or flights of fancy but going to certain places where some noted action had occurred involving an outlaw or lawman or a Texas Ranger. He visited such sites as the Taylor-Bennett Cemetery south of Cuero, and the McCrabb Cemetery, almost in the city limits of Cuero, where William P. "Buck" Taylor and the Meadors are buried. In addition to his participation in NOLA and WOLA, he became active in history groups such as the Texas State Historical Association, the East Texas Historical Association, the West Texas Historical Association, and lesser-known groups including the Edwards Plateau Historical Association and the South Texas Historical Association. Locally, he became a member of the Caldwell County Genealogical and Historical Association with headquarters in Luling. He credits these organizations and their publications with giving him an outlet for immersion in is his own writing and research.

Another local historical society in which Chuck was active in this period was the Rancho Nixon Historical Society, then headed by Donald Hoffman, a descendant of John Wesley Hardin. In a short time after his move to Smiley, Texas, Chuck was elected vice president of this society. Ostensibly, the society's goals were the study and preservation of the history of Hardin. Soon, however, the society determined it would initiate a project to have Hardin's body exhumed from its burial location in the Concordia Cemetery in El Paso, Texas, and moved to Nixon, Texas, one of Hardin's old haunts and the home of Mr. Hoffman.

As the discussion of exhumation progressed, Chuck insisted upon proof that the remains in the grave marked for Hardin at Concordia were actually his, seeing that his grave was unmarked for seventy years, from 1895 to 1965, and the grave location determined only by a local cemetery caretaker. To obtain exact proof would involve scientific technology to identify the remains as Hardin's. Concordia had no intention of giving up Hardin's remains nor granting permission for an exhumation. That cemetery board was well-pleased with what they had accomplished in marking a grave for Hardin and the resulting attraction it became for Wild West historians and curious tourists.

In 1995 Hoffman and several other members of Rancho Nixon Historical Society made the impetuous decision to stealthily enter the Concordia grounds in a secret mission to exhume the remains in Hardin's grave and transport them to Nixon for reburial. Though their plan ultimately failed, the whole nefarious episode caused Chuck to rethink his membership in the society and to resign his position as vice president.[15]

The year 2001 saw the publication of Chuck's first extensive biography of a Ranger captain, Leander H. McNelly, coauthored with Marianne E. Hall Little.[16] Deemed by eminent historian Robert Utley as the "definitive work" on McNelly, the foreword was penned by Texas governor Dolph Briscoe Jr.[17] In this volume Parsons and Little, as is Chuck's regular practice, dug into previously untapped records, gleaning a considerable amount of McNelly's previously unreported activities. Though McNelly was a respected Ranger, both by fellow Rangers and outlaws alike, Chuck did not hold back in showing his proclivities and faults. From McNelly's early years as a sheepman to his first soldiering experiences in 1861 with the Confederate 5th Texas Cavalry, from serving as captain of the Texas State Police and invaluable service as a Ranger in the 1870s Sutton-Taylor Feud to his waning and final days as a lawman, documentary evidence was used to establish a biography that is both readable and dependable.

In 2004 Chuck contributed a chapter in *Legendary Watering Holes: The Saloons that Made Texas Famous*, which he credits with his success in later books of his own authorship being published by university presses.[18] Chuck's first published article for which he received payment ($65) was on the little-known figure of the Sutton-Taylor Feud George Culver Tennille, who was killed in a gun battle with Gonzales County lawmen in July of 1874. He had been accused of stealing a horse and resisting arrest. Chuck recalled,

"I wrote everything I could find about him, submitted it to *Frontier Times*, the then companion magazine to *True West*, and Joe 'Hosstail' Small deemed it worthy of publication!"[19] He had previously been published in the *Quarterly of the National Association for Outlaw and Lawman History*, with an article "'Wild Bill' Hickok Killed Two Men in Abilene" about the death of gambler Phil Coe and the accidental killing of deputy Mike Williams, both occasioned by Hickok. Another of his articles, "Destroying the Hardin Gang," was the sketch of two brothers who served under Captain John R. Waller in Company A of the Frontier Battalion.[20] This Ranger group pursued members of the John Wesley Hardin gang after his killing of Deputy Charles Webb in Comanche in May 1874. The article was included in an anthology entitled *The Best of NOLA: Outlaws and Lawmen of the Old West*.[21]

In 2006 Chuck met and married a lovely lady by the name of Patricia D. Baker. The couple lives in Luling and are members of the historic Prairie Lea Baptist Church. There they were married, Chuck was baptized and plays the piano for worship assemblies, and Pat teaches Sunday School. They have also researched and written the congregation's history.

Chuck considers the Texas Rangers an important part of Texas history. His focus is not so much the early years, or those of the twentieth and twenty-first centuries. Primarily his interest begins in the 1870s, when the Frontier Battalion was organized in 1874. He says,

> You can't ignore the early decades. There were Tumlinsons, fighting Rangers of the 1820s and 1830s, and even in the early 1870s you have old Captain Joe Tumlinson still involved in fighting—not Indians but members of the Taylor faction; Captain Joe belonged to the Sutton faction. The early Rangers were not so much the law enforcement body they later became and remain today, but they were protecting the frontier of early Texans. Of course we see that the Indian fighting was the equivalent of one civilization destroying another for the land, but that was really no different from the Comanche destroying other tribes

to populate the same land. History is basically one group taking from another, whether on a small or large scale.

Chuck considers some of the Rangers to be much more fascinating than others, though if the complete story of each of them was known we would find them more or less equally fascinating. He believes B. L. "Baz" Outlaw remains a prime example. Of Baz Outlaw Chuck says, "He had the potential to become not only a captain but conceivably one of the four 'Great Captains' although some may argue that point. But that eluded him completely because he was susceptible to drink, so much so that drunkenness ruined his career and eventually his life. Shakespeare could have made a great five-act tragedy about Baz Outlaw."

Chuck's book on Captain John R. Hughes, published in 2011, presented a challenge.[22] Dr. Paul N. Spellman had already written biographies of two of the four Great Captains, John H. Rogers and J. A. Brooks, but chose not to tackle Hughes. Dr. Harold Weiss was working on Captain Bill McDonald, and that left the opportunity for Chuck to complete the quartet. Hughes had served more time in the Rangers than any other, and Chuck was glad to have the opportunity to chronicle his life.

For the foreword of the Hughes book, Chuck chose eminent Wild West historian Robert K. DeArment. DeArment states, "Here for the first time is the complete story of the man who, because of his length of service and extraordinary achievements, could well be called THE greatest Texas Ranger captain."[23] As Parsons has always done with Ranger accounts, he again was interested in more than "what happened when" and probed deeply into obscure records, newspaper accounts, and personal reminiscences of Rangers who were there and who experienced the episodes of Hughes's life that are covered in this biography. From Hughes's early life hunting buffalo, driving cattle, and living among the Osage Tribe to his move to Texas, Chuck was able to learn the man's early story, the bulk of which was fully covered for the first time.

In Texas Hughes was introduced to Ranger Ira Aten and Chuck explains, with documentary evidence, how Hughes first became a Ranger. With riveting detail, in an easy-to-follow chronological fashion, Chuck covers both the highlights and the everyday experiences of a nineteenth-century Ranger through twenty-eight years of service. Upon the forced retirement of Hughes in 1915, the old Ranger began to make himself available for newspaper interviews. In most instances Hughes was careful to let the historical record speak for his Ranger years. Because Chuck Parsons well knows the ins and outs of research, he was vigilant in examining every known aspect of Hughes's Ranger life. In plain English with easy-flowing text, and in a scholarly approach with detailed endnotes, Parsons's work on Hughes is a fitting compliment to the work of Spellman and Weiss to complete the biographies of the Four Great Captains.

With books on the four Great Captains in print, Chuck turned to a biography of Texas Ranger Captain Jesse Leigh Hall, who began his career as a lawman in Grayson County, then joined with Captain Leander H. McNelly, eventually being selected to replace McNelly.[24] Hall continued in the Ranger service until he resigned in 1880. Chuck further believes there are yet other important Rangers who need an updated biography, including George Arrington, Neal Coldwell, and the Sieker brothers. The appealing thing to Chuck about Arrington, whose only biography was by Jerry Sinise in 1979, was that he began his career as a wanted man, fled the country, and changed his name and became an outstanding lawman. Frank Canton, he says, did the same, eradicating his life as Joe Horner the outlaw to become the adjutant general of the state of Oklahoma. Chuck states, "I feel that these individuals who were so comfortable on both sides of the law hold more fascination than the ones who always were on the right side of the law. Richard C. Ware gained fame as being the Ranger whose bullet ended the life of desperado Sam Bass. He then became a United States Marshal, but he does not have a full-length biography (some would say George Herold ended the life of Bass but that is an argument which will never be fully ended for everyone)."

Thanks to the Former Texas Rangers Association of Fredericksburg, Texas, many graves of Texas Rangers are being marked by an iron cross, even though there may already be a headstone at their grave. Chuck has attended several of these events and has been a public part of two markings. The first was that of Lowe R. Hughes (1852–1881), a Ranger who served under N. O. Reynolds, "The Intrepid." His grave is marked in the Bagdad Cemetery, near Leander in Williamson County. The second was James Maddox Bell (1865–1897), who was an Austin police officer prior to joining Captain John R. Hughes's Company D. Bell was the great-great-uncle of Chuck's wife Pat. The goal of the Former Texas Rangers Association is to mark the graves of all Texas Rangers, and once the grave is located, it is only a matter of time before the grave is marked.

Chuck says,

There are plenty of Rangers who attract me but there are so many and so little time. Charles L. Nevill who became Captain of Company E of the Frontier Battalion after N. O. Reynolds resigned; George Herold and Richard C. Ware both had fascinating lives as Rangers and as lawmen wearing other badges and each need a solid biography, but as yet only little sketches of their lives are available. I would like to delve into Mexican records to research various Rangers of Mexican descent, such as Lino Saldana and Jesus Sandoval who were on McNelly's payroll, albeit for a short period during the mid-seventies. A project which I have often considered is dealing with that famous photograph of the Texas Rangers sent to El Paso to stop the prize fight. In it appear all four "Great Captains" and Adjutant General Mabry, standing in the front row, with the remainder of the Rangers behind them on the steps of the court house. Virtually all the Rangers at that time were in El Paso and in one photograph! Only a few were absent from the photograph. An article, or small book, on that photograph with a sketch of the life of each Ranger would be an important contribution. Fortunately, they are all identified. These men all performed an important service. These are basically all "rank and file" and, with the exception perhaps of Sergeant Sullivan, who later wrote his own reminiscences, remain just a name.

While Texas Rangers and outlaws and lawmen of other fields have long been of great appeal to Chuck, other things have popped up that took time and energy but for which he has no regrets. In 2011 he took the complete handwritten manuscript of Cal Polk, annotated it, and submitted it to the *Plum Creek Almanac*.[25] Polk was a Caldwell County native, born in 1863, quit school at a very early age and became a cowboy, drove cattle up the trail, managed to get to New Mexico during the Billy the Kid years, helped chase that outlaw down, then moved to Oklahoma and became a lawman himself. Chuck added a great many endnotes explaining who the people were that Cal Polk met along the way. Historian and author Frederick Nolan of England wrote the foreword, and Chuck received permission to use a painting by San Antonio artist Donald M. Yena, "Dollars on the Hoof," on the cover of the *Plum Creek Almanac*. He was also able to use as illustrations photographs of Tom O. Folliard and Charles Bowdre and the drawing of the "Capture of Billy the Kid" from Pat Garrett's biography, as well as photographs of Polk and members of his family. He has stated, "It was all a wonderful experience for me: Frederick Nolan, Donald Yena and Cal Polk all together in one publication."

In 2013 Chuck and writing partner Norman Brown completed a long-standing writing project of Chuck's on John Wesley Hardin titled *A Lawless Breed: John Wesley Hardin, Texas Reconstruction, and Violence in the Wild West*.[26] Leon C. Metz, a renowned Hardin historian, wrote the foreword. As in all of Chuck's books on historical characters, readers soon notice in this biography that he goes far beyond simple facts and figures gleaned from newspapers and the writings of other historians. This book, like his several books on Texas Rangers, delves deeply into the background of his main character, including his siblings and friends, providing readers with genealogical and biographical information of interest.

While recognizing the groundbreaking work of Hardin biographers Richard Marohn and Leon Metz, even assisting them in their research and gathering illustrations, Chuck dug deeply into remote resources to discover new information and previously unpublished photographs that justified and warranted a new biography of the man considered by many to have been the West's most deadly gunman. Chuck and Norman took nothing previously published on Hardin, even the man's own autobiography, at face value. Every alleged incident was reexamined, resulting in a more accurate picture of Hardin and his associates. Of the book Chuck humbly stated, "In spite of once contemplating the definitive biography of Hardin, in our maturity we realize there is no such thing." This attitude is part of what keeps Chuck motivated to continue to ferret out tidbits and follow rabbit trails that will, hopefully, lead to new information on his characters.

Chuck considers that one of the best things to have happened to him during his Wild West history years was being chosen to be the "Answer Man" for *True West* magazine. One day he received a call from the new editor of *True West* with an invitation to join the magazine's staff. The announcement of Chuck's appointment appeared in the November 1982 issue, stating that beginning with the January 1983 issue of *True West*, "Chuck Parsons, who has spent more than twenty-five years researching the Old West, will attempt to answer your questions." The plan was that readers would send in their questions, the editor would send them to Chuck, and he would answer them. For the next seventeen years, Chuck conducted "The Answer Man" column for a total of 204 columns. The column came to an end only when the publication was sold to new owners.

How does one assess the contributions of a historian of the caliber of Chuck Parsons? A literal assessment is based on neither his many years in the field of Wild West history nor his involvement in various history-related organizations, nor his long-standing relationships with other historians. It is based on what he has written, what has been published, and what has stood the test of time.

Chuck Parsons is a straightforward historian. No one should refer to him as a "traditionalist." He is a fact finder who tells what happened, how it happened, and why it happened and relates it all with words and phrases that are in the common vernacular. He doesn't need a copy of Rodale's *The Synonym Finder*[27] at hand to flower up his statements. When you read a statement from Chuck, it is backed up with sound documentation. He rarely uses words such as "probably," "possibly," "likely," "could have," or other terms that lead the reader into imaginary scenarios.

He has taken up topics, especially in the realm of Texas Rangers, that others had either ignored or thought less worthy than others. His presentation of the lives of N. O. Reynolds, John R. Hughes, John B. Armstrong, L. H. McNelly, C. B. McKinney, and other luminaries of Ranger history, such as his 2020 book on Jesse Leigh Hall, have made a major contribution in the way of preserving true Ranger stories that to this day, and long into the future, will illuminate, inform, and instruct students of the remarkable history of Texas law enforcement.

Chuck Parsons's contributions to Texas Ranger history are monumental and complement those of such pioneer writers as A. J. Sowell, John Henry Brown, and Benjamin Highsmith, who sought out living Rangers and told their first-person accounts. They rank alongside those of Walter Prescott Webb, Robert Utley, Louis Sadler, Charles H. Harris III, and other renowned Ranger historians who did deep on-site research in dusty archives, dark and dank courthouse basements, weed- and snake-infested cemeteries and battlegrounds, and dug until they found all the history available. Their countless hours in public and university libraries came before today's readily available internet resources, ancestral websites, and the many avenues for reading scanned, word-searchable historic newspapers.

We who love Texas Ranger history are fortunate to have men such as Chuck Parsons to research, write, and publish accounts of the lives of early Rangers and tell without amplification or supposition their contributions to what has made Texas great.

Notes

1. All quotations attributed to Chuck Parsons via emails to author in 2019.
2. Ramon F. Adams, *Six-Guns and Saddle Leather: A Bibliography of Books and Pamphlets on Western Outlaws and Gunmen* (Norman: University of Oklahoma Press, 1954).

3. Ed Bartholomew, *Kill or Be Killed* [. . .] (Houston: Frontier Press of Texas, 1953); Bartholomew, *Wild Bill Longley: A Texas Hard-Case* (Houston: Frontier Press of Texas, 1953); Bartholomew, *Jesse Evans: A Texas Hide Burner* (Houston: Frontier Press of Texas, 1955).

4. J. Marvin Hunter and Noah Rose, *The Album of Gunfighters* (n.p.: Hunter and Rose, 1951).

5. C. L. Sonnichsen, *I'll Die Before I'll Run: The Story of the Great Feuds of Texas* (New York: Harper & Brothers, 1951).

6. Barney Hubbs and Chuck Parsons, *Shadows along the Pecos: The Saga of Clay Allison, "Gentleman Gun Fighter"* (Pecos, TX: West of the Pecos Museum, 1977).

7. Schoenberger, Dale T., *The Gunfighters* (Caldwell, Idaho: Caxton Printers, 1971).

8. Chuck Parsons and Marjorie Lee Burnett, *Bowen and Hardin* (College Station, TX: Early West, 1991).

9. Jack DeMattos and Chuck Parsons, *The Notorious Luke Short: Sporting Man of the Wild West* (Denton: University of North Texas Press, 2015).

10. Jack DeMattos and Chuck Parsons, *They Called Him Buckskin Frank: The Life and Times of Nashville Franklyn Leslie* (Denton: University of North Texas Press, 2018).

11. Chuck Parsons, *Captain Jack Helm: Victim of Texas Reconstruction Violence* (Denton: University of North Texas Press, 2018).

12. Thomas C. Bicknell and Chuck Parsons, *Ben Thompson: Portrait of a Gunfighter* (Denton: University of North Texas Press, 2018).

13. Chuck Parsons, *"Pidge": A Texas Ranger from Virginia* (Wolfe City, TX: self-published, 1985); Chuck Parsons, *"Pidge," Texas Ranger* (College Station: Texas A&M University Press, 2013).

14. A third, revised edition was published with authorship showing "Marjorie Burnett Hyatt," under the title *Fuel for a Feud* in 1990. For a contrary view of the Sutton-Taylor Feud and the role of Hardin by Parsons and others, see the book by James Smallwood that changed the feud into a violent crime ring in Texas, *The Feud That Wasn't: The Taylor Ring, Bill Sutton, John Wesley Hardin, and Violence in Texas* (College Station: Texas A&M Press, 2008).

15. This information summarized from a letter by Parsons to Mr. Hoffman, August 30, 1995, via a copy in the Robert G. McCubbin Collection, Wild West History Association, Safford, AZ.

16. Chuck Parsons and Marianne E. Hall Little, *Captain L. H. McNelly, Texas Ranger: The Life and Times of a Fighting Man* (Austin: State House Press, 2001).

17. See Robert M. Utley, *Lone Star Justice: The First Century of the Texas Rangers* (New York: Oxford University Press, 2002), 329.

18. Richard Selcer, ed., *Legendary Watering Holes: The Saloons That Made Texas Famous* (College Station: Texas A&M University Press, 2004).

19. Chuck Parsons, "George Culver Tennille," *Frontier Times*, December–January 1977.

20. Chuck Parsons, "'Wild Bill' Hickok Killed Two Men in Abilene," *NOLA Quarterly* 1, no. 1 (1975): 9; "Destroying the Hardin Gang," *NOLA Quarterly* 5, no. 4 (July 1980).

21. Robert K. DeArment, ed., *The Best of NOLA: Outlaws and Lawmen of the Old West* (Laramie, WY: NOLA and University of Wyoming, 2001).

22. Chuck Parsons, *Captain John R. Hughes, Lone Star Ranger* (Denton: University of North Texas Press, 2011). To some, Hughes was the best gunman of the Four Great Captains.

23. Parsons, *Captain John R. Hughes*, ix, x.

24. Chuck Parsons, *Texas Ranger Lee Hall: From the Red River to the Rio Grande*. (Denton: University of North Texas Press, 2020).

25. Chuck Parsons, ed., "Life of C. W. Polk," *Plum Creek Almanac* 29, no. 2 (Fall 2011): 7–74.

26. Parsons, Chuck; Norman Wayne Brown, *A Lawless Breed: John Wesley Hardin, Texas Reconstruction, and Violence in the Wild West* (Denton: University of North Texas Press, 2013).

27. J. I. Rodale, ed., *The Synonym Finder* (Emmaus, PA: Rodale Books, 1961).

Chapter 8

Stephen L. Moore

Factual Purveyor

Matthew M. Babcock

H ow did the Texas Rangers originate and develop prior to
1846? In eight major works written over the last two decades,
Stephen L. Moore, a sixth-generation Texan and Stephen F. Austin
State University graduate, thoroughly addresses this critically important question. Moore, whose family has owned land in present-day
Anderson and Houston Counties since 1835, was drawn to this topic
from an early age because he has several ancestors who were nineteenth-century Texas Rangers. Focusing primarily on the role of the
Rangers during the tumultuous years of the Texas Revolution and
Republic of Texas from 1835 to 1845, Moore has meticulously uncovered the forgotten history of the earliest Ranger companies in Texas
history prior to the 1840s, which he points out has "received far less
acclaim" from scholars because of the records lost in the 1855 fire
in the Texas adjutant general's office and the 1881 fire in the Texas
State Capitol.[1]

In addition to describing the unit's major structural and tactical
changes from 1822 to 1846 and their efforts to protect the Texas
frontier in military engagements against Indians and Mexicans,

Moore has served the needs of historians and genealogists alike by conducting diligent primary research to uncover the names of the individual members who served in these early frontier ranging companies and to more deeply explore the lives and service records of Ranger officers, from his ancestor Captain William Turner Sadler to Captain John Coffee "Jack" Hays. Overall, Moore exhibits a traditionalist perspective on the Texas Rangers. His outlook broadens over the course of his writings, however, to include more insight into the motivations and cultures of Indians and Mexicans, and he even exposes a few Ranger faults in some of his more recent works. Moore's single best synthesis on the early Texas Rangers is his fast-paced narrative and exceptionally well-written book *Texas Rising: The Epic True Story of the Lone Star Republic and the Rise of the Texas Rangers, 1836–1846* (2015), which is the official nonfiction companion to the History Channel's *Texas Rising* series. He was contacted by the History Channel's publishers, William Morrow / Harper Collins of New York, during the summer of 2014 because "one of their senior editors had seen my previous books on the Texas Rangers and San Jacinto campaign and felt that I was a good fit." After signing nondisclosure agreements, Moore was able to "review the complete script for the series," focus on its "key elements," and draw from his prior research to "offer a broader view of the Texas Revolution and the events leading up to it."[2]

Specialists and genealogists should consult Moore's exhaustively researched, encyclopedic four-volume *Savage Frontier: Rangers, Riflemen, and Indian Wars in Texas* (2002–2010) series, which he was compelled to research and write to find out more about his ancestors who served in the 1830s Ranger companies. According to Moore, Rangers had both Hispanic and Anglo influences; however, he focuses squarely on the Anglo influences, defining them as a group of self-armed, nonuniformed squad of male civilians "who operated independently from a regular military organization" to protect "the outer frontiers of a settled area" from Indian hostilities. Linking Texas Rangers to early English colonial rangers, Moore distinguishes "volunteer rangers" from "regular army" troops. Moore acknowledges that "loosely organized ranging companies had operated in conjunction with the Texas Militia since 1822," and he credits Stephen F. Austin with first using the term *rangers* in 1823. According to the author, however, the unit was not officially created until 1835, when Captain Robert Coleman organized "the first Texas Ranger company" and battalion, which were "legally recognized by the provisional government of Texas in October."[3]

One of Moore's most significant accomplishments is detailing the members and service periods of so many Ranger companies from records in the Texas State Archives. Working in conjunction with Donaly Brice and his staff, Moore consulted the original service papers filled out by these men, which enabled him to more precisely determine the locations of Ranger units, include eyewitness accounts of Indian engagements, and even reconstruct muster rolls of companies whose original records had been lost. That said, the author's most efficient way of presenting this material is in tables. Although certain genealogists and military historians will appreciate knowing the names and personal background of every member of every known Ranger company ever mustered into service in the Lone Star State, providing such a high level of detail within the text bogs down the narrative flow of Moore's story and at times simply serves as a way to fill up space when little information is known about a particular unit's actual campaigns.

Some readers may also be taken aback by the title of Moore's quadrilogy, *Savage Frontier*, which reflects an exceedingly one-sided perspective on the Rangers and the frontier warfare of this era. On the one hand, this is not so surprising, given that Moore was initially attracted to this time period to research his own family history, including several ancestors who served in the Texas Rangers and Texas Militia, and that he consulted Texas military records, memoirs, newspaper reports, county histories, as well as other early secondary accounts that were often written by former Texas Rangers and Indian-hating settlers. As the author plainly describes, in the general council's own words, its 1835 resolution to create a corps of Rangers was done to "protect the inhabitants" of Texas "from the savage scalping knife."[4]

But this does not mean that reproducing an exclusively nineteenth-century Anglo-Texan perspective in which "blood-thirsty" Indians commit "savage depredations" on "helpless" Texan settlers and "pillage" their settlements is still acceptable today.[5] Modern ethnohistorians and borderlands scholars recognize that Texas is made up of multiple cultural frontiers that have at least two sides and that Anglo-Texans originally settled in a province, not a wilderness, which had been inhabited by Native American and Hispanic families for centuries. Moore acknowledges that early Anglo-Texan settlers "who ventured into the prairies did so at their own risk" and that "those starting homes or farms farther north and west were venturing into territories long considered that of the local Indian tribes," but the use of "local" diminishes the extent of Indigenous territoriality in the region.[6]

This point is brought home even more clearly in *Taming Texas: Captain William T. Sadler's Lone Star Service* (2000), which Moore revised and expanded from a short biography he originally compiled from stories told to him by his grandmother Evaline Kolb Moore and her cousin, former Texas land commissioner Jerry Sadler, in seventh grade. The author explains that in 1822 his great-great-great grandfather William Sadler "camped near the village of the Ioni Indians," that Nacogdoches was "named for the Nacogdoche Indians who had originally inhabited the area," and that "the future state of Texas derived its name from the local Tejas Indians."[7] What connects these seemingly disparate statements is that Ionis, or Hainais, and Nacogdoches were both Caddos and subgroups of the Tejas, or Hasinai Confederacy. Even though the Caddos were experiencing population decline from disease by the early nineteenth century, they remained one of the oldest, largest, and most politically sophisticated Indigenous cultural groups in early East Texas.

In his works prior to *Texas Rising*, Moore could also say more about the destructive impact that Texas Rangers had on Indigenous land and resources. As Moore explains, many Ranger units lived off the land when they were in the field, killing game and eating honey, but in doing so, they competed for the same resources with surrounding Indian tribes. Building and sustaining their forts, which were generally situated in river valleys and included Forts Parker (Sterling), Houston, Milam (Viesca), Saline, and Kickapoo, depleted precious timber, water, and wildlife resources. Beyond this Texas Rangers also posed a direct threat to Indians when they were off duty because they received extensive land grants, and many Ranger officers, from William T. Sadler to Jack Hays, worked as surveyors, facilitating frontier settlement and the eradication of Native American homelands.[8]

Contrary to popular belief, early Texas Ranger units experienced few military successes against Indians or Mexicans. According to the author, in August 1835 Colonel John Henry Moore led a five-company Ranger battalion in "the first true Texas Ranger campaign against the Indians" from Parker's Fort to the forks of the Trinity River, but the "large and ill-formed force" confronted more "mud bogs and swollen streams" than Indians.[9] In general Moore contends that Lieutenant George C. Kimbell's Gonzales Mounted Ranger Company was the only force to respond positively to William Travis's call for help at the Alamo, with thirty-two men arriving on March 1, all of whom perished in the ensuing battle. As the author explains, "There were few trained soldiers who fought for the Texan cause. They were farmers, lawyers, merchants, preachers, businessmen, and teenagers, many who had lost loved ones at the Alamo or Goliad."[10]

The Rangers' most significant contribution during the Texas Revolution came in conjunction with Texas militia and army troops at San Jacinto. In *Eighteen Minutes: The Battle of San Jacinto and the Texas Independence Campaign* (2004), Moore reveals that Texas Ranger companies "would contribute more than eighty new men" to General Sam Houston's army. Although General Houston's decision to assign so many Rangers to guard the baggage wagons and tend to the sick at Harrisburg was very unpopular, many still proved their worth as scouts for the cavalry and as soldiers in combat at San Jacinto. Captain William Sadler and seven of his former Rangers from the Fort Houston settlement near modern Palestine, for example, fought as private soldiers in Captain Hayden S. Arnold's Company of Nacogdoches Volunteers and guarded Mexican prisoners afterward.[11]

Overall, Moore contends, previous Ranger scholars have underemphasized the importance of frontier ranging corps during the Texas Revolution. "The General Council of Texas," the author maintains, "legally created three separate ranging systems" at that time, which included the four-district superintendent system, Major Robert Williamson's three-company ranging corps, and the ranging battalion under Colonel Jesse Benton. As commander of the Texas Army, Major General Sam Houston held supreme authority over all of them. None of these systems were fully developed during the war, Moore acknowledges, but they were still significant for the protection they provided Texas residents during the absence of regular army troops.[12] Houston, too, Moore compellingly argues, has been mischaracterized as "cowardly" for allegedly retreating during the San Jacinto campaign, when in fact "he had intelligence from the Texas Secretary of State that he might be able to rendezvous with US troops to support his cause" and decisively defeated a much larger force at San Jacinto.[13]

Interestingly, Moore also has Cherokee family ties, as his ancestor William C. Moore married a Cherokee woman in Texas in 1848.[14] This connection most likely reveals why Moore offers the most evenhanded portrayal of Anglo-Indian relations when discussing the Cherokees throughout his works and helps explain his motivation to examine this turbulent relationship in more depth in *Last Stand of the Texas Cherokees: Chief Bowles and the 1839 Cherokee War in Texas* (2009). Moore also has two ancestors who fought on the Texas side of the 1839 battles at Battle Creek and the Neches Rivers, which he convincingly argues were the turning point in President Mirabeau Lamar's effort to drive Chief Bowles's tribe from Texas to the Indian Territory. Involving more than 1,600 participants, including more than

400 Texas Rangers, Moore maintains that the July 16 Battle of the Neches was the most significant battle ever fought between Texans and American Indians and "the largest sustained battle in which the Texas Rangers participated." In an effort to contribute to both sides of this conflict, Moore organized an archaeological search team that identified the sites of conflict in the July 16 battle and donated artifacts "to the American Indian Cultural Society that maintains the Cherokees' Neches battleground property and to the Texas Ranger Hall of Fame and Museum in Waco" for historic preservation.[15]

Although the author appears to hold the Cherokees in high regard, he demonstrates in *Savage Frontier*, volume 2 (2006), that the vast majority of Texas Rangers, soldiers, and settlers clearly did not. After his death in the battle of the Neches, Chief Bowles's "lonely skull and skeleton were reportedly still visible in the spot for years." Seeking battlefield trophies and souvenirs, Texans callously used their knives to "cut away pieces of his body," with one man taking "a strip of skin from Chief Bowles' back" for use as "a razor strap and good luck charm."[16] Furthermore, it is tough to feel empathy for Texas troops accidentally discharging their weapons and wounding themselves when they were burning every Indian village and cornfield that they saw in the midst of an Indian expulsion.

In contrast to the large battles Texas Rangers took part in at San Jacinto and the Neches River during the late 1830s, in their frontier engagements against Indians farther west during the 1840s they tended to be undermanned but very well-armed. As Moore explains in *Savage Frontier*, volume 3 (2007), because of President Lamar's reliance on the Frontier Regiment of the Texas Army to protect Texas's northern and western frontiers, "By the end of 1839 only three companies of Texas Rangers remained in service." This remained the case until February 1841, when the Texas Congress authorized the formation of twenty special county minuteman companies of which only fifteen actually formed. Although traditional Ranger companies "had been commissioned to serve for three to six months," these new units could only stay in the field for a maximum of fifteen consecutive days and their men for a maximum of four months per year.[17] As Moore shows in the final volume of the *Savage Frontier* series, for the majority of the period 1842–1845, Captain Jack Hays commanded "the only company of Rangers in service for Texas." During 1843 and 1844, Hays's company was "the only government-authorized Ranger company," and during 1845 it remained the largest of five companies.[18]

The author also argues that the adoption of the Colt repeating pistol by the Texas Rangers during the early 1840s "marked a major change in frontier warfare."[19] Without question the Colt five-shot revolvers carried by Jack Hays and his fifteen Rangers eventually worked to their advantage amid incredible odds against Chief Yellow Wolf and more than sixty Comanches at Walker's Creek on June 8–9, 1844. The Comanches retreated after the third round of fire and in two days of fighting suffered twenty-three dead, including Yellow Wolf, and thirty wounded, with only one Ranger killed and at least four wounded.[20] Moore has also carefully researched the use of the Colt five-shooter by Texas frontier military units from 1840 forward; however, his argument exaggerates the pistol's effectiveness in Comanche engagements prior to the Walker's Creek battle. As Moore himself acknowledges, due to the lack of an action account or contemporary newspaper reports, it is unclear whether Hays's legendary 1841 solo battle with Comanches at Enchanted Rock ever even happened, and the author's evidence indicates that the five-shooter's role in the infamous March 19, 1840, Council House Fight was far from decisive. Although some of Colonel Lysander Wells's cavalry present in San Antonio that day had Colt Patent Revolvers, this group was "not immediately part of the proceedings with the Comanches," and even though one cavalryman did use his pistol to kill a Comanche, Colonel Wells was "ill-trained on how to shoot this new pistol" and his weapon "would not fire."[21]

During the late 1830s and early 1840s, Ranger personnel diversified to include Native American and Tejano members. This trend began in the fall of 1838 in East Texas under Major General

Thomas Rusk, who "allowed his militia brigades to maintain small battalions of mounted rangers," when Captain Lewis Sánchez and Captain Panther of the Shawnees respectively organized companies of mounted Tejano and Shawnee Rangers. Captain James H. Durst's mounted Ranger company was composed primarily of Cherokees and also included Caddos and Shawnees.[22] As Texas Ranger manpower and number of units declined during the 1840s, this trend of ethnic diversification intensified. In 1841 Captain Antonio Pérez commanded a fifteen-man Ranger company in San Antonio, all but one of which consisted of Tejanos, and the July 1–August 31, 1841, muster roll for Captain Jack Hays's forty-three-man company of Bexar County Minutemen includes Chief Flacco's seven Lipans and eight Tejanos from Captain Pérez's company.[23]

In addition to confronting Indians, Texas Rangers increasingly targeted Mexicans in the disputed Nueces–Rio Grande borderlands during the early 1840s. The evidence indicates that Jack Hays's company routinely followed policy by targeting Mexican bandits; however, other minuteman units formed in 1841, such as Captain James Ownby's San Patricio Rangers, repeatedly seized the goods of Mexican traders or, as in the case of Captain Alanson Miles's San Patricio company, simply robbed Mexican residents indiscriminately. Given such ruthlessness, it is not surprising that Mexican troops captured and imprisoned some of these individuals for their own bandit-like behavior.

In the same way that many Civil War officers fought previously in the US-Mexican War, Moore concludes that many Texas Rangers who served in the US-Mexican War came of age during the Republic of Texas era. As seasoned frontiersmen they put to good use against Mexican forces not only their "scouting and fighting ability" but also their experience "living off meager supplies." In 1845, following the Texas Congress's vote in favor of annexation by the United States, Major Jack Hays led a Ranger battalion responsible for scouting and providing intelligence for the US Army "while keeping Indian resistance in check." He then headed the first of three Texas Mounted

Riflemen regiments in 1846, helping General Zachary Taylor's troops seize Monterrey in September, where, Moore contends, Hays and his men "gained a national reputation."[24]

In conclusion, Moore's most significant achievements are the yeoman-like work he did to reproduce the muster rolls of forgotten early Texas Ranger companies in combination with a single-volume readable synthesis of the Texas Rangers during the decade of the Lone Star Republic. Moore has also shed further light on the major events and significance of the 1839 Cherokee War, particularly the Battle of the Neches. As thorough as Moore's research is, since it has been conducted primarily from an Anglo-Texan historical and genealogical perspective, the opportunity still exists for scholars interested in pursuing Native American and Hispanic viewpoints to utilize his works as sources for their own further research. What prompted Cherokees, Shawnees, Lipans, and other Indians to serve as Texas Rangers, and what influence did they have on those units? For Lipans the opportunity to join military forays against their longtime Comanche enemies and obtain spoils from battle were clearly important factors. Prior to his untimely death in 1843, Chief Flacco the Younger commanded a fifty-man Lipan "Corps of Observation" force to report on Mexican troop movements in the disputed Nueces strip and developed a close friendship with Captain Jack Hays while scouting for him, helping Hays to become a better tracker.[25]

And what about Hispanic cultural influences on Texas Ranger units? How, if at all, do Ranger units relate to the Spanish military's use of presidial, mounted militia companies, and Indian auxiliaries to protect New Spain's northern frontier? Stephen F. Austin's employment of smaller mounted twenty to thirty-man militia forces to protect the Texas settlement frontier from Indian attacks in 1826 is very reminiscent of the Spanish employment of highly mobile flying companies or Light Troops during the 1770s. Both innovations also represent an effort to move away from heavier mounted cavalry to counter Indigenous mobility and confront Native groups on their own terms.[26] If Moore privileges the Ranger and Anglo-Texan perspective and sometimes exaggerates the superiority of their firearms in his depiction of frontier violence, then he also deserves credit for not blindly eulogizing the Rangers as infallible heroes and for periodically acknowledging their faults.

Notes

1. Stephen L. Moore, *Taming Texas: Captain William T. Sadler's Lone Star Service* (Austin: State House Press, 2000), 3; Moore, *Savage Frontier: Rangers, Riflemen, and Indian Wars in Texas*, 4 vols. (Denton: University of North Texas Press, 2002–2010), 1:viii; Deborah Kalb, "Q&A with Stephen L. Moore," May 18, 2015, http://deborah-kalbbooks.blogspot.com/2015/05/q-with-stephen-l-moore.html.
2. Kalb, "Q&A with Stephen L. Moore."
3. Moore, *Texas Rising: The Epic True Story of the Lone Star Republic and the Rise of the Texas Rangers, 1836–1846* (New York: William Morrow, 2015), 18, 25; Moore, *Savage Frontier*, 1:8–9, 14, 21; Kalb, "Q&A with Stephen L. Moore."
4. Moore, *Savage Frontier*, 1:ix, 35; Moore, *Savage Frontier*, 2:xii.
5. Moore, *Taming Texas*, 2, 93, 131.
6. Moore, *Savage Frontier*, 1:3;
7. Moore, *Taming Texas*, 4, 11, 14, 25; Kalb, "Q&A with Stephen L. Moore."
8. Moore, *Taming Texas*, 27–34, 41, 145–46; Moore, *Savage Frontier*, 1:63–65, 123; 2:212; Moore, *Texas Rising*, 252.
9. Moore, *Savage Frontier*, 1:25; Moore, *Texas Rising*, 16–17.
10. Kalb, "Q&A with Stephen L. Moore."
11. Moore, *Eighteen Minutes: The Battle of San Jacinto and the Texas Independence Campaign* (Dallas: Republic of Texas Press, 2004), 82–83, 103, 119, 152; Moore, *Taming Texas*, 39–49, 53, 66, 77.
12. Moore, *Savage* Frontier, 1:123; Moore, *Texas Rising*, 47, 55–56, 58, 61.
13. Kalb, "Q&A with Stephen L. Moore."
14. Stephen L. Moore, *Last Stand of the Texas Cherokees: Chief Bowles and the 1839 Cherokee War in Texas* (Garland, TX: RAM Books, 2009), 5–6.
15. Moore, *Last Stand of the Texas Cherokees*, 3–4.
16. Moore, *Savage Frontier*, 2:281, 285.
17. Moore, *Savage Frontier*, 3:x–xi.

18. Moore, *Savage Frontier*, 4:viii–ix.

19. Moore, *Savage Frontier*, 3:xiii.

20. Moore, *Savage Frontier*, 4:148, 150, 152; Moore, *Texas Rising*, 333–34.

21. Moore, *Savage Frontier*, 3:24, 28, 341–48; 4:2.

22. Moore, *Savage Frontier*, 2:x, 106, 109.

23. Moore, *Savage Frontier*, 4:181, 184, 322, 324.

24. Moore, *Savage Frontier*, 4:ix, 204; Moore, *Texas Rising*, 336–37.

25. Sherry L. Robinson, *I Fought a Good Fight: A History of the Lipan Apaches* (Denton: University of North Texas Press, 2013), 192, 197, 206; Thomas A. Britten, *The Lipan Apaches: People of Wind and Lightning* (Albuquerque: University of New Mexico Press, 2009), 188, 192–93.

26. Nathan A. Jennings, "Ranging the Tejas Frontier: A Reinterpretation of the Tactical Origins of the 8 Rangers," *Journal of South Texas* 27, no. 2 (Fall 2014): 72–91, esp. 80–81.

Chapter 9

Bob Alexander
Popular Chronicler
Paul N. Spellman

> I have made my investigation, formed my opinion, and will not be
> hesitant to reveal it. Readers may now draw theirs.
>
> —Bob Alexander, *Sacrificed Sheriff*[1]

ob Alexander possesses the remarkable gift of a relentless
B passion to pursue the facts in whatever case or project or
research in which he is engaged. In addition, and in some ways even
more importantly, he has never forsaken the colloquial vernacular in
his writing style that sets him apart from nearly all his fellow nonfiction Western writers. The combination, then, of these two propelling
factors—unparalleled investigative pursuit and unpretentious idiomatic discourse—bear witness to a unique personality and a compelling background and career that have honed these talents over many
decades. The evolution of this Texas Ranger historian is the subject of
this chapter.

The Law Enforcement Career

The progression of Alexander's investigative pursuit of the facts, his raison d'être, if you will, presents no real mystery. Bob's forty years of dedicated service to his state and his country were largely based on investigative responsibilities at nearly every available level.

Bob Alexander's career in law enforcement began as a tenderfoot officer in the Garland, Texas, Police Department, where he served six years on duty, promoted to detective and then detective sergeant, and began his lifelong love affair with criminal justice and investigation. "The law enforcement bug bit me," he would say.[2] During that same period of time, Bob attended East Texas State University in nearby Commerce, Texas, driving an hour each way between the campus and his grandfather's Rockwall ranch while at the same time working night and weekend shifts as a Garland police detective, toughening himself up for the long haul of adulthood as he ultimately earned his bachelor of science degree in 1970. His interest in expanding his career in law enforcement then led him to engage in special training programs offered through the US Treasury Department in Washington DC, and in 1971 he was designated a special agent for the treasury's Alcohol, Tobacco & Firearms Division (ATF).

Special Agent Alexander was assigned first to Little Rock, Arkansas, where he worked for three years, much of it as an undercover agent dealing with the illegal gun runners and moonshiners in the Hot Springs area. Here he became accustomed to the undercover lingo associated with the more than often high-risk stakes of that game. "Walk the deal," the signal to keep your undercover status for the time, and "Buy with gold," make the arrest, became part of the agent's everyday discourse. After his three-year hitch, Bob was reassigned to the Dallas area ATF office, where he worked for five years. Because of the national expanse of illegal firearms and the pursuant investigation, Alexander found himself on specific cases that would take him for short periods to Seattle, New Orleans, Tulsa, New York City, and Albuquerque.

During these trips, and as part of his off-duty routine, Bob became an avid reader of Western literature, both fiction and nonfiction.

He not only enjoyed the read in and of itself as a distraction from the serious duties of the career he loved, but also his own passion for investigation, for following leads, and for closing a case all fit neatly into the stories he eagerly absorbed. He could read about the sheriffs and marshals of the Old West pursuing the outlaws and fugitives, and enjoy a deeper understanding than most readers of the challenges that confronted law enforcement, the difficulties of an often-corrupt legal system in an ornery land, and the satisfaction of rounding up that elusive cow thief or killer—or witnessing his bounty's grave being dug.

Alexander's third assignment with the ATF was as supervisor of a law enforcement metro group in Los Angeles, California, a position he held for one year. He explains, "I was responsible for the implementation of [Federal] Bureau [of Investigations] programs, policies, and ATF criminal enforcement activities for metropolitan Los Angeles." This included Hollywood, Watts, and East Los Angeles. "That year I supervised Special Agents and their individual criminal investigations . . . and coordinated Bureau activities with other Federal, State, County, and City law enforcement agencies."[3]

In the late 1970s Alexander began a twenty-one-year assignment back again with the Dallas, Texas, district of the ATF, assigned a myriad of duties over those two decades with special emphasis on white-collar and organized crime that would take him deep into the field of investigation, from surveillance to undercover work to the arrest and subsequent testimony in front of grand juries at both the state and federal levels. It was arduous but generally satisfying work that grew the passion inside of him, a career of more than forty years since that first day on the Garland police force that earned him distinctive praise and recognition, including five US Treasury Awards, for Special Achievement (1986, 1988, and 1989), Adopted Suggestion (1988), and a Special Act Award in 1990. Bob's 4,044 hours of continuing education and development time—hours as recognized by the Texas Commission on Law Enforcement Standards and Education—had meanwhile qualified him for the prestigious Master Peace Officer Certification.

In 1996 ATF Special Agent Bob Alexander retired from active service and duty, carrying home with him the Treasury Department's coveted Albert Gallatin Award for distinguished service to the nation. His passion for law enforcement and investigative pursuits, and his passion for the Old West that had become part of his persona, in tandem, had only just begun.

Prolific Western historian Bill O'Neal recalls a visit from the just-retired Treasury man: "Bob drove 200 miles to the campus of Panola College to talk with me about the craft of writing history books about the Old West. We met in the college library, where I pointed out a number of reference books he would find useful. When I had to go to class I left Bob at a table taking notes, and when I returned late in the day he was surrounded by books and note cards."[4] The game was on.

Early Historical Work

Bob Alexander, fascinated by the tales of law enforcers of the Old Southwest, had read bits and pieces about the Silver City, New Mexico, story and of men like Sheriff Harvey Whitehill and "Dangerous Dan" Tucker. But another setting had also captured the ATF agent's imagination: Tombstone, the infamous and legendary Western town only 150 miles southwest of Silver City. Established in Arizona Territory in 1879 as part of the silver rush, Tombstone's nascent days and infamous name were initiated by miner and soon-to-be millionaire Ed Schieffelin. In just two years the boomtown boasted a population of ten thousand, dirt streets lined with banks, churches and mercantiles alongside 120 saloons, brothels, and gambling halls. There were the Earps, Wyatt and Morgan and Virgil, the Clantons and the disputable OK Corral shoot-out, and Sheriff John H. Behan, reportedly the scurrilous mortal enemy of the Earps. And then there was Dave Allison, an Arizona Ranger and law enforcer who eventually made his way to Texas and joined the Frontier Battalion there.

And the lawless, cold-blooded murderers who roamed the territory with arrogant impunity—they too leaped from the pages as Bob Alexander soaked up every anecdote, every tale. Johnny Ringo was there, and Doc Holliday, Curly Bill, John Kinney, Bronco Bill Walters: the list seemed unending and, ultimately, absolutely fascinating to the ATF agent.

Four years removed from retirement in the year 2000, and employed now as an adjunct instructor of criminal justice courses at Navarro College in Waxahachie, Texas, Alexander was determined to write his own version of the Old West history he had been reading for years, a version that bared the facts, separated them from the myths and legends, and told the real story of real men who flashed the blemishes of mortality, from good to evil, in the environs where they had landed. Living on a small working ranch at the outskirts of Maypearl, Texas, south of Dallas and not too far from the campus where he taught and also served as a campus security officer, Bob and Jan Devereaux, an award-winning writer in her own right, made their home together in the comfortable country atmosphere of Days Gone By.[5] It proved a perfect environment for the aspiring writer to gain a foothold for his idiomatic writing style—"I can't write it any other way," he would tell you—while relying on those forty years of investigative experience to do the painstaking but ultimately satisfying research upon which his book would be built. This is where he would start his artful journey— telling the stories of Silver City, New Mexico Territory.

But where to begin? Alexander was especially fascinated by the three enforcers of the law in that region of New Mexico and Arizona territories—Behan, Tucker, and Allison—for he saw in them a need for history to get it right. They had obviously played a significant role in the evolution of territorial law and order in the Southwest of the late 1800s, but their names, individually and collectively, had been set aside in the heap of "other characters" and overshadowed by Wyatt Earp and Billy the Kid and others. Bob Alexander was determined to set the historical record straight. Johnny Behan had taken the worst of it, as far as Alexander was concerned. The Tombstone lawman had taken the historical rap for being the enemy of the Earps, as Hollywood History had rewritten their legacy, and every previous version that Bob read implied the same, that Sheriff Behan was the bad guy. But Bob's in-depth research told him a far different story.

The same with Dan Tucker. He was an asterisk at the bottom of the imaginative tall tales of the Earp brothers, who had been unevenly portrayed for decades as heroic enforcers of the law, larger than life characters on the Western plains, riding hard after the outlaws and shooting straighter and faster than any. But as Bob kept digging into the stories, digging deeper than most academics ever had done, and certainly with more clarity of the facts than any movie screenwriter, Tucker and Behan began to rise in his estimation and above the superficial accounts printed and produced for a century. Someone had to tell their story, and tell it right and true, and let the saloon hall dominoes fall where they may.

Every author, large and small, has to begin somewhere, write that first sentence, suggest that initial theme, pick a chapter title, a middle, and an ending. Retired special agent and adjunct instructor Alexander decided to look for encouragement and support for the peculiar direction he had set out for himself, to "write" the wrong of Western historicity. And why not start at the top? Two recognizable names of historians at the turn into the twenty-first century, and of eminent respect in their fields, were El Pasoan Leon Metz, the most prolific Western writer of his moment in time, and Paula Mitchell Marks, distinguished professor at Austin's St. Edwards University. Would they have an encouraging word for this neophyte author, something to hang his Stetson hat on? You bet they would!

"Alexander spent months in New Mexico reading old letters," wrote Metz, "digging through old newspaper files, carefully checking court and census records, talking with the descendants of people who might have known Dan Tucker, comparing each account against other chronicles, and then going back over everything again, in the process piecing together a compelling story. He is a tough, diligent researcher, and an admirable writer."[6]

Recalls Paula Mitchell Marks, "Bob first contacted me while researching and writing his first book, *John H. Behan, Sacrificed Sheriff*. To tell the truth, I really didn't want to deal with him, having grown quite weary of all things Tombstone. But he won my interest with his thoughtful, fresh approach to the life of this much-maligned nineteenth-century lawman. I watched him diligently uncover evidence, apply careful reasoning and judgment, and seek to set the record straight."[7]

Nearly two decades after the fact, the now-himself prolific writer of the West would happily acknowledge the encouraging words from Metz and Marks: "I wouldn't have gone on writing without their support at that time."[8]

Research tools in hand, time assigned around his ranching duties at Maypearl and his CJ courses at Navarro, and founts of information awaiting from Tucson to Santa Fe to Austin, Alexander began his due diligence of piecing his research notes together, the stories that would reveal the truth about Tombstone's *Sacrificed Sheriff* Johnny Behan (2002); Silver City's *Dangerous Dan Tucker* (2001) and *Sheriff Harvey Whitehill* (2005), each with his own biography; and *Fearless Dave Allison* (2003), who served as an Arizona Ranger, a New Mexico police chief, and a Texas Ranger. Alexander was crisscrossing the Southwest, unknowingly at the time making his way ultimately back to Texas.

Over the next six years, Bob Alexander published nine studies of the characters of the Southwest, adding titles such as *Six-Guns and Single-Jacks* (2005), *Desert Desperadoes* (2006), *Lynch Ropes & Long Shots* (2007), and two volumes of *Lawmen, Outlaws, and S.O.Bs* (2004, 2007). Author and historian Robert K. DeArment, who had previously met Bob at a history conference in Arizona, recalls, "Bob said he was doing a book on a western gunfighter and had been inspired to do so by a chapter on the fellow in one of my books."[9] In his introduction to *Sheriff Harvey Whitehill: Silver City Stalwart* (2005), DeArment noted, "Bob Alexander's specialty, searching beyond the sometimes overworked Western literature and the cyclically repeated stories. This roster of good men, bad men, and extraordinary ne'er-do-wells, apart from being fascinating reading, is a bona fide contribution to Texas and New Mexico borderland history. I don't know how he does it, but he has my admiration and earnest hope he will continue."[10]

That "continuation" would range across the Southwest as Alexander literally tracked lawmen and outlaws from Arizona to New Mexico and, ultimately, like Fearless Dave Allison, into Texas.

Texas Rangers

"The demarcation line moving Texas Rangers from service as part-time warriors bent on chasing and chastising Indian adversaries to that of law enforcers in an altogether new arena is relatively easy to discern. Certainly the overall and generalized story of the Texas Rangers is rich, the outfit's history—legitimate history—dating to the pre-Republic of Texas epoch. Though there are scattered anomalies, for the most part, the actual transition from soldierly actions to civil policing duties was a mid-1870s phenomenon."[11]

"The right of the people to be secure in their persons, houses, papers, and effects, against unreasonable searches and seizures, shall not be violated, and no Warrants shall issue but upon probable cause."[12] If there is a foundation to the law enforcement philosophy of Bob Alexander, special agent or writer, it may be found here within the concrete bounds of the Constitution's Bill of Rights. The internal motor that drives Alexander forward in all his thinking and writing, and earlier in his investigative work for the government, is energized by the very basis of the system of law in the United States, delineated in the amendments themselves and in operation for more than two centuries and counting. Whether the case be from the files of the Dallas District of the ATF in 1988 or lifted from the annals of a time a century before, Bob builds his work in the sincere belief that law and order must hold accountable the very essence of what this nation understands as most dear, and the persons sworn to uphold that law must never waver from their appointed task. Bob Alexander rides straight and true in that belief, in his life, in his career, in his writing.

In a February 2018 letter to fellow author Darren L. Ivey (*The Ranger Ideal*, 2 vols.), Alexander expanded on the theme of frontier law enforcement evolving, in this case, through the early decades of the Texas Rangers: "Evolution into a wholly unfamiliar realm was unavoidably wrought with tribulations—and occasionally even overt resistance and, at times, purposeful wrongdoing. Putting it mildly, there was a learning curve. In the broadest sense—on the whole Texas Rangers passed the test—adaptability being a hallmark of their survivability." Continuing his argument, Bob noted that "during the Frontier Battalion's earliest days, management was prohibited from forcing any Texas Ranger into 'detective work' . . . it was at first a strictly voluntary undertaking. . . . As an investigator the individual Texas Ranger had to shape and sharpen his skills as an interrogator and crime-scene analyst."[13]

In the summer of 2007, Bob Alexander sat in an interview with Candy Moulton, editor for *Roundup* magazine and at that moment asking questions for a *True West* magazine piece. They discussed Bob's work on Billy the Kid, the Salt War, Silver City, and the recent publishing of *Desert Desperadoes*. At the end of the brief exchange, Candy asked Bob about his next project in the offing, to which Bob replied, "I want to get down in the trenches and talk about what I would call the everyday working [Texas] Rangers," with one eye set on Company D of the Frontier Battalion. Moulton opined, in what would ultimately be considered a majestic understatement, "With his attention to detail and his manner of building a case through writing, Bob Alexander is sure to put a new spin on the Texas Rangers."[14]

Alexander's interest in the Texas Rangers stemmed not only from his own occasions to work alongside the contemporaneous investigators while an ATF agent but also as far back as his research on Dave Allison. He had had cause to reference Rangers such as Captains Frank Jones and John R. Hughes, the prototypical undercover Ranger Ira Aten, J. B. Townsend, Sgt. A. Y Baker, and Allison's investigative work alongside Company D. The thought of shifting his attention onto Texas law enforcement had been a constant for years.

Although the precise thread of communication may be a bit thin, Candy Moulton's published interview somehow made its way to the Denton offices of University of North Texas Press and its editor, Ron Chrisman, who immediately knew a good thing when he saw it. His contact with Bob led to a symbiotic working relationship that would begin early in 2008 and last for a decade and still. The first fruit of this congenial harvest was *Winchester Warriors: The Texas Rangers of Company D, 1874–1901*, published by UNT Press in 2009.

In the preface comments, Alexander was, as expected, straight to the point: "The method of attack for this volume is simple," he wrote. "Explore why Texans demanded a Frontier Battalion in the first place, and then follow its transition from an organization of Indian fighters to crime fighters. Tracking the personnel and performance of just one early day Texas Ranger troupe, Company D, has been the tactic adopted for such a project."[15] What is distinctive about Bob's approach in this, his first Texas Ranger book, is what might be called a holistic approach—that is, rather than focusing on the administrative leaders of a Ranger company, whose exploits would be generally noteworthy if not always stellar, or instead of focusing on individual incidents that might have made the front page of a Texas newspaper, Alexander chose to look at the whole unit as just that, a whole. The evolution of Company D, a microcosm of the Frontier Battalion itself, provided a lesson in group dynamics, personnel management, and a way "to put a human face on those remarkably fascinating fellows, who, regardless of their place in the pecking order, did their part to stabilize the elusively expanding frontier in nineteenth-century Texas."[16]

Chapter One of *Winchester Warriors*, "A Carnival of Crime and Corruption," begins with an anecdotal look back to 1873 and an incident in Lampasas that evolved from the murder of a town sheriff to the arrival of a State Police unit and a second main street shootout with the local toughs, to the dissolution of that same police force shortly thereafter and a call for a more effective agency of law enforcement in then late Reconstruction Texas. From the catastrophic gunplay in Lampasas that left ten dead and state officials bewildered, a new force would rise from those ashes, the two-headed Special Force and Frontier Battalion: the rebirth of the Texas Rangers, if not in name, then in repute.

By the next year, post-Reconstruction Democrat governor Richard Coke signed into existence a Special Force under Captain Leander McNelly to quell the borderland violence in spots like DeWitt County and along the dangerous environs of the Upper Nueces River. The Frontier Battalion, given over to Major John B. Jones, was to take on the continuing Indian threats of the Apache in the southwest and the Comanche and Kiowa to the north. As the Indian threat quickly diminished in Texas after 1875, the Frontier Battalion turned its attention to criminals and fugitives on the run from county constabularies who had no jurisdiction outside their county line. The battalion was divided into six companies, A through F, with an initial recruitment of seventy-five men for each company. Company D was first commanded by Blanco County's own Cicero Rufus "Rufe" Perry.

In the ensuing fifteen chapters, Alexander explores the assimilation of the hundreds of recruits over the next twenty-seven years as they became a cohesive unit of law enforcement across Texas, through individual incidents and often turbulent times, growing up together around a starlit campfire or hitched together in a saloon shootout watching each other's back. There are heroics and embarrassments alike, moments of individual or collective courage, and disappointments of lives lost, discipline squandered, and whiskey-laden casualties.

Specific names crop up as would be necessary to tell the story: the commanders of Company D who followed Perry—Roberts, Moore, Sieker, and the more recognizable Frank Jones and John R. Hughes; and the most notable of the company men—Ira Aten, Neal Coldwell, William Scott Cooley, Ben Lindsey, and the enigmatic Baz Outlaw. (Three of these men of Company D would eventually be the focal point of later Alexander books.) But throughout the treatise, the author remained determined to keep the focus on the company as a whole, moving and changing and evolving as a single body of law enforcement.

Even tackling a whole new genre, Alexander remained true to his cowpoke vernacular and maintained that "zest and fire" in his writing. On the jacket cover of *Winchester Warriors*, a reviewer captured an essential quality of Bob's writing gift: "When finished, the reader will feel as if they had been there riding alongside the boys, firing away at the brigands, wrestling with the daily trials of the Texas frontier, often successful but not always. *Alexander wants to tell you—just you, it feels like—a story, and a darn good one at that.*"[17] To wit, in chapter 3, "I'm Shot, Sure as Hell": "Two days earlier, on the tenth, Comanches skipped an Agency headcount and jumped the reservation, dashing across the Red River into Texas. It wasn't a social call. There they raided the Oliver Loving ranch, killing a cowhand, John Heath, and also making off with a band of white-eyed and badly frightened saddle-horses. The Indians left a plainly readable trail to follow. Iron horseshoe dints interspersed with unshod hoof prints in soft ground and plopping piles of manure make damn good clues."[18]

And the photographs. One of Alexander's truly significant contributions to the Old West literature, although usually overlooked in lieu of the hearty research and wonderful verbosity, has been his consistent inclusion of photographs from that antiquated era. Drawing from private collections and archives across the Southwest, Alexander's literally thousands of photos have adorned all but the first two of his books; it wasn't until *Fearless Dave Allison*, his third rendering, that the photos began to appear. Many of them are printed for the first time on his pages, and in several of his books they are set in several galleries rather than scattered throughout. In any case, as a singular perspective they put faces to names and portraits to the landscape of his storytelling. Accompanying the publishing of Bob's work on Company D, *True West* magazine emphasized the importance of Bob's offerings when they reproduced many of the *Winchester*

Warriors photographs in their April 2012 issue and repeated that article with twelve of their favorites in January 2019.[19]

In Alexander's second volume of *Lawmen, Outlaws, and S.O.Bs*, in chapter 9, "The Saloonkeeper Reached for His Gun," the dramatic shootout in the streets of Richmond, Texas, on August 16, 1889, is colorfully illuminated over five rapid-fire pages. At the center of the downtown gunplay, both literally and figuratively, stood Ira Aten, Company D's sergeant, and three privates, intent on quelling the violence if possible. "One riot, one Ranger" notwithstanding, it wasn't possible, and seeing the deadly consequences before them, the Rangers withdrew from the debacle. The legendary Jaybird-Woodpecker War raged on for hours until ammunition was exhausted and bodies lay strewn for blocks.[20]

It may have been the only recorded instance when Ira Aten backed out of a fight, but it likewise demonstrated the sensible intelligence of the man who had already become one of the most famous figures in Texas Ranger lore: no need to die in an unwinnable fight! Aten's name adorns hundreds of pages of Ranger books, and the Ranger monthly records account for Aten's remarkable career in law enforcement over decades. Though never aspiring to any administrative responsibilities, preferring to do the gritty work of law enforcement both face-to-face and in the often even more dangerous undercover world, Aten's name was nevertheless associated with the great commanders of his era— Brooks and Rogers and McDonald—and Aten himself helped recruit the young John R. Hughes, who would later command Company D.[21] That being said, only one biography had been published about the singular Ranger, a brief and apparently unsatisfying 1960 treatise by Harold Preece, *Lone Star Man, Ira Aten: Last of the Old Texas Rangers*.

With *Winchester Warriors* completed, on the bookshelves and selling rapidly, Bob Alexander knew it was time to redress that situation and write the definitive biography of Ira Aten. "If anybody of the frontier policing fraternity had a gritty tale worth telling," wrote Alexander, "it surely was Mr. Austin Ira Aten."[22] Because of Aten's participation in some of the most sensationalized incidents on the frontier, "objectively peering at Ira Aten's life story does, assuredly, expose much more than [the] narrative of but one man." Even more dear to this researcher's heart was Aten's seminal work of investigative prowess. "When four bodies—a quadruple homicide—were found floating in the Rio Bravo, Ira Aten was tasked with the criminal investigation," Alexander explains in his preface. "[He] exhaustively built an airtight criminal case based largely on circumstantial evidence. Interestingly, for the time and place, Sergeant Aten employed a forensic technique, the first time it was used in Texas—*possibly* in the United States."[23] This was a man built right in Bob Alexander's wheelhouse. Telling Aten's story— the real and factual account, not some whitewashed apologue—was a task this author could not ignore.

With encouragement from both a growing readership base and a supportive UNT Press, in 2011 *Rawhide Ranger, Ira Aten; Enforcing Law on the Texas Frontier* became a hardbound reality and tour de force. At 450 pages, 50 more than his first Ranger tome and by far his longest writing venture at that point, Bob's story of the dynamic Ranger flew off the pages with the now-expected passion of its author. It was a page-turner that satiated the hungry readers looking for that unusual style that only Bob Alexander seemed to be able to produce, but it satisfied the academics at the same time with its exhaustive research and plainspoken facts. Over one thousand endnotes attest to the integrity of the information, and dozens of remarkable photographs adorn its pages. In June of that same year, the Wild West Historical Association published Bob's accompanying article on Aten ("Square Deals and Real McCoys"), and summarily awarded Alexander with their recognition of *Rawhide Ranger* as their Book of the Year. It was Bob's fifth literary award in five years.[24]

Magazines and Journals

Alongside his prolific book writing and publishing, over the years Alexander also engaged in penning shorter articles for professional journals and Western magazines. Several of these would accompany or presage one of his books being published simultaneously, and others were invitations to tackle specific topics or Wild West figures. Finishing up his first two books with High-Lonesome Press in Silver City, Bob opened the *Quarterly of the National Association for Outlaw and Lawman History* journal in the summer of 2002 with "An Outlaw Tripped Up by Love," a tightly knit account of cowboy turned Sheriff Thomas Decatur "Tom D." Love. Its eight pages of narrative were adorned with five old photos of that era, and no less than eighty-three endnotes to substantiate his story.[25] Three years later Alexander was invited to write an article for the *Western Outlaw-Lawman History Association Journal*, "Guns, Girls & Gamblers, Silver City's Wilder Side."[26] The article's inspiration was a speech Bob had given earlier that year at the Annual WOLA Shootout Conference in Santa Fe, as he parceled a condensed version of his Silver City research into a manageable presentation.

As Alexander transitioned over to his Texas Rangers work, *True West* magazine came hunting for him no less than four times in four years. In addition to the two previously mentioned contributions of Bob's favorite Ranger photographs, twice in 2010 Bob contributed to the renowned frontier periodical, coauthoring "Trumpeting Elephants & Kicking Asses: Republicans and Democrats, New Mexico Style" with Jan Devereaux, and "Hellfire & Hot Tamales," the story of Dave Allison's capture of Pascual Orozco Jr. in 1915.[27] In 2013 Bob wrote a poignant but exciting narration of the death of Ranger William Emmett Robuck, the first Ranger Force casualty in the borderlands, which was taken in part from *Riding Lucifer's Line*, the next book on tap from Alexander.[28]

Texas Rangers, Continued

In the introduction to *Riding Lucifer's Line: Ranger Deaths along the Texas-Mexico Border,* Texas Ranger Hall of Fame & Museum executive director Byron A. Johnson wrote, "Alexander's research is meticulous. His reasoning is logical and the interpretations are impartial. Bob pays attention not only to 'what happened' but also places an incident in its appropriate historical context. These Texas Rangers had a compelling story and Alexander, in his relaxed and easygoing style has told it well."[29]

On the one hand this telling seemed a departure from Bob's projects to this point, but at closer inspection it couldn't have been more on target for the evolving Ranger historian's perspective. Writing an entire book about Rangers who were killed on duty might have seemed depressing to some at first glance, but the mortality of the frontier lawman was frail at best, and the frontier itself deadly by definition. These hardy souls lived and died in their West, some by bullet, some by the bottom of a whiskey bottle, but few after what anyone would consider a long and happy life. Telling the stories of the twenty-five Rangers who were killed between 1875 and 1921—a self-enforced boundary line by the author, else the book would have grown even larger—emphasized the dangerous existence they chose to live, under the dire conditions they knew would defeat them at the end. But they chose the path of law enforcement in spite of the danger, knowing the odds and braving the environs. Many more outlaws and fugitives fell at the hands of these Rangers, or from a scaffold on a Texas town square; only two dozen Rangers felled over forty-six years may have beaten the odds after all.

Alexander began this tale of tales right where he had left off with *Rawhide Rangers*: at his idiomatic best. "The Texas-Mexico border is trouble," he muses in the opening preface remarks. "Like a Black Widow seductress the borderland is at the same time alluring, deceitful—and heartless. Haphazardly splashing across the meandering Rio Grande into Mexico is—or at least can be—risky business, hazardous to one's health and well-being. On the border nonchalant inattention to geographical surroundings and any childish naivety about inhumanity can get one killed."[30] Pleonasm aside for a moment, Bob defines the purpose of *Riding Lucifer's Line*—a title he created on his own—as "in a narrowly focused approach, to survey the personal tragedies of one body of men, Texas Rangers, as they scouted and enforced laws throughout borderland counties adjacent to the [Rio Grande]."[31]

But Alexander proffers a deeper context for these stories as well, an arena he had suggested in earlier writings but without specific definition. "Individually these are but mini-biographical tales," Bob suggests, "profiles, sketches: Strung together they offer *societal commentary.* . . . Collectively those boys dying along the tough Texas border offer pieces of *sociological insight* into the ceaseless turbulence and turmoil allied with enforcing the laws and apprehending *mal hombres* on the line: We are but products of place and time."[32] Here, in his most serious tone and sans the populist prose, Alexander explored the wider context of the psychological and emotional toll of living on the American frontier, the courage to live and die by one's convictions, and the debt that is ultimately paid to the unforgiving land that, finally, is left untamed. This is a side of Bob Alexander that is as real, as genuine, as the convivial cowpoke author who is more often displayed on his written pages. Perhaps it is the poignancy of death— that every chapter in *Riding Lucifer's Line* ends in the violent death of a lawman—that brought to the surface, albeit briefly, the man whose own personal convictions are inextricably tied to the vital nature of the rule of law, and whose own lifelong sense of duty has propelled him ever forward.

Since his days exploring the Ranger records for *Winchester Warriors,* Bob had had an itching to carve out at least three of those characters in his own telling; he had been eminently successful with his rendering of Ira Aten in 2011, but Frank Jones and Baz Outlaw still awaited his direct and focused attention. Those biographies would come, but they would have to wait a bit longer, for *Bad Company and Burnt Powder: Justice and Injustice in the Old Southwest* was up next.

Building upon the sociological perspective of his just-completed book, Bob took an even dozen figures from the files and folders of his previous Ranger research and told their stories as adventures and misadventures on the Texas frontier. Each could stand on its own—"each exemplifying a thrilling Wild West narrative." Collectively, however, Bob was more interested is approaching the uneven evolution of "the practical application and implementation of a criminal justice system in the nineteenth and early twentieth century American Southwest." For some of these characters, the system worked, the law prevailed, the criminal was justly and fairly convicted. But for others the law betrayed them, as crooked judges, biased juries, and just plain bad luck let the criminal off the hook and left the lawman either helpless or lifeless or both. And in a connection of past and present, Alexander suggests that "if the past really is prologue, then this Old West compilation facilitates the cracking open of a doorway—just a little bit—*shining a clear spotlight on humankind, its compassions and cruelties.*"[33]

Often overlooked in his books once more, but truly significant to the academic field at large, there was a plethora of wonderful and engaging photographs scattered throughout *Bad Company*, over a hundred of them, and a thousand endnotes to typically finish off the treatise. Bob began with a somewhat unusual tip of his Stetson to women and more specifically mothers of the Old Frontier—their courage, their endurance, and their collective contributions of civility, stability, and routine in an untethered environment. The dozen stories that follow reverberate with Bob's infectious storytelling skills.

"There is no real public appetite for a cold and bland menu of humdrum history," he declares in his preface remarks to *Bad Company and Burnt Powder*. "Old West narratives—fiction and nonfiction— spin on an axis of conflict. The wide-ranging readership—many discerning academics included—want true-life chronicles served steaming hot, liberally peppered with raw meat violence and basted with bloodshed."[34] While most of the characters on this stage are relatively unknown to modern Western readers, they nonetheless breathe life into that epoch as they live, and often die violently, in a world of occasional justice and too-often impartial injustice.

With his momentum at full throttle in 2014, Alexander now aimed his full attention at Captain Frank Jones, the respected, beloved commander of the Frontier Battalion's Company D. Frank Jones's story was one that had been oft told in chapters and snippets and magazine articles, and even Alexander himself had on several occasions illuminated Jones's leadership, courage, and untimely, violent death on the Rio Grande. Jones appears in both volumes of *Lawmen, Outlaws, and S.O.Bs*, and certainly throughout *Winchester Warriors* and *Rawhide Ranger.* Now it was time to give the man his due.

Six-Shooters and Shifting Sands: The Wild West Life of Texas Ranger Captain Frank Jones, the fifth collaboration with UNT Press, and with a marvelous introduction by now retired Ranger chief Kirby Dendy, was another tour de force for Bob Alexander, and was correspondingly received eagerly by a now-insatiable Alexander readership. Photographs by the dozen pop up throughout this engaging biography of one of the most famous Rangers of all time, and for all of his passion and obvious love for this character and his story, Bob still held true to his intentions, to write "an unbiased and factual treatment based on incredibly detailed references."[35] Facts over fiction notwithstanding, Jones's story still reads like a Hollywood script, as Bob simply lets the truth unwind in its own fashion, exciting, heart-pounding, dramatic, frustrating, and satisfying at the same time.

The closing pages of Jones's story and life are as dramatic and violent as any Texas Ranger story told, and Bob Alexander told it with all the passion he could muster, cold and bland facts be damned. The hunt for the notorious Olguin Clan along the Texas-Mexico border near Ysleta in June of 1893 ended in one of the most explosive shootouts in Ranger history, situated near the top of any list with such as the 1889 debacle on the streets of Laredo or the Connor fight in East Texas. Bearing down on the Olguin hideout on the banks of the Rio Grande, Jones and his platoon were cut to pieces by snipers who lay in wait. The captain, bearing the brunt of the charge into the withering fire, also took the brunt of the cloud of bullets that dropped him to the sandbar in the middle of the river. "I'm all shot to pieces," those who survived the gunfire recalled their captain's words later, and then soon after came the ravaged cry, "Boys, I am killed!" Wrote Bob in epitaphic fashion, "There on the shifting sands of Pirate Island lay the lifeless and bloody body of Frank Jones: His biography a closed book. Penning words for successive chapters would not be furthering the fallen Texas Ranger's story."[36] For the author this had become personal. For the reader *Six-Shooters and Shifting Sands* became a masterpiece.

Soon upon the heels of *Six-Shooters and Shifting Sands* came *Whiskey River Ranger: The Old West Life of Baz Outlaw* (2016). Even Jones himself may have laid out the path for Bob's next tome when he described his company's top sergeant as "a man of unusual courage and coolness and in a close place worth two or three ordinary men."[37] Similar perhaps to the remarkable story of Ira Aten, how could a Ranger historian pass up this Company D man? At the same time as the glowing accolades spotlighted this irascible Ranger, Bob Alexander—and surely Captain Jones—knew the dark side of Bazzell Lamar "Baz" Outlaw as well. For here was mortal man in the flesh, driven, courageous beyond any expectations, fearless, and yet self-destructive in ways that defied correction. In Alexander's simplest characterization, "He was a problem solver and in not just a few cases *the* problem." Bob expounds, "Baz Outlaw fit the Wild West profile perfectly: he could be a fearless and a crackerjack lawman, as well as an unmanageable maniac. . . . He was his own worst enemy."[38] The story was just too good to pass up, and Bob acknowledged the fact, admitting that "promoting the preservation of Baz Outlaw's story [was] fun."[39]

Not unlike other mortals who donned the badge of law enforcement to tame an untamable land, Baz Outlaw fell victim to the seduction of a whiskey bottle, ravaging himself finally to death, and given to such a schizophrenic personality that oftentimes he turned on his own fellow lawmen, acted so reprehensibly as to terrify the very citizens he had sworn to protect, and found himself on the wrong side of the arrest warrant. "Baz Outlaw, his mind sometimes numbed by tarantula juice," summarized the author, "fought hard to keep from going under—drowning—in that remorseless *whiskey river* of despair, hopelessness, and craziness."[40] And ultimately failed.

On the one hand, the Baz Outlaw story was something of a departure for Alexander: a Ranger gone bad rather than the heroic figures the author had researched heretofore. But the acknowledgment of less-than-admirable lawmen with a Ranger badge had always been a part of the stories: Wood Saunders and Ernest St. Leon (*Riding Lucifer's Line*), Captain James Monroe Fox and his "bad company" (*Texas Rangers: Lives, Legend, and Legacy*, pp. 354–61), and so on. In *Winchester Warriors* Alexander notes, "Good men deserve good leaders. Sadly, this was/is not always the case. . . . Some (Rangers) were unpleasantly arrogant and self-centered, bellicosely belligerent and overbearing, sneaky backbiters and jealously covetous, while several were the wretched prisoners of strong drink. Some were even downright mean."[41]

By the end of 2016, *Whiskey River Ranger* had become yet another in the unfolding list of Texas Ranger bestsellers for Bob Alexander, and he wasn't finished yet. Not by a long shot. Bob Alexander and his cohort, the redoubtable Donaly Brice, former chief archivist of the Texas State Archives in Austin, explain in the preface of their compendious *Texas Rangers: Lives, Legend, and Legacy*, the project that would be the next step in Alexander's evolution as a Texas Ranger historian, when on "June 4, 2013, the Texas Department of Public Safety Commission by thoughtful process of a formally crafted Resolution designated the Texas Ranger Hall of Fame & Museum at Waco as the professional representative and officially sanctioned steward for the forthcoming Texas Ranger Bicentennial celebrations, an endorsement of foremost significance. . . . [The] Museum's staff sought outside input from a cadre of nonfiction writers and researchers. And, within that framework is genesis for the book in hand, the authors having been privileged to sit in on those informative discussions and exchange of ideas."[42]

The project was not only worthy of the best efforts of Alexander and Brice but it would also necessarily be a straightforward approach to the nineteen decades of Ranger history that shaped the ideology of law enforcement in Texas from its Mexican colonial days through the republic years and 170 years of Texas statehood. The chronology was in place and no one better attuned to its complexities than these two researchers/writers. The greater challenge was twofold: how to fit two centuries of anecdotes into a manageable volume that would not quantitatively overload its potential readership, and what specific approach should be taken to assure a panoramic that would please both the critical academic and the uncritical casual audience. Knowing that their own colleagues and peers would dive into the final product as a matter of intellectual course, Bob and Donaly mused, "Were a vacationing family from Newark visiting the museum for the very first time, what messages and/or impressions about the Texas Rangers would we want them to take back to New Jersey?"[43] Consequentially, the resulting *Texas Rangers: Lives, Legend, and Legacy*, published in 2017 after four years of collaboration between the authors and the museum staff and others, was met with considerable fanfare at its debut and continuing acclaim, even, presumably, in New Jersey.

Midway through *Texas Rangers*, in chapter 13, "Spiking the Legacy," the authors relate an anecdote in reference to the investigation by Ranger Company D Captain Jack O. Dean of the stunning and dramatic assassination of District Court Judge John H. Wood in 1979. The subsequent hunt for Wood's killer by the FBI was aided, if not salvaged altogether, by Captain Dean's on-site investigation and local knowledge that eventually led to the arrest and conviction of Wood's killer, Charles Harrelson, who would spend the rest of his life in prison. The point of the story here was to underscore the behind-the-scenes work that Dean engaged in to bring this otherwise sensational front-page story to its fruition, rather than a moment to simply highlight "the Texas Rangers in action" stereotype.

"But for [Dean's] lead, the FBI might never have ended the case. Yet the media spotlight fixed solely on the FBI, which never let the public know that Dean or any other state or local officers had been involved."[44] For the Texas Rangers of today, that was no slight; rather, their unmatched investigative work of the past eight decades, more so than their Main Street shootout reputation of the past, has been the imprint they have preferred to leave to their legacy.

Bob Alexander had his next project already in hand, as he noted in a 2019 interview: "I never had to drum up a topic. Something always came up in the work I was doing at the time." One year after the collaboration with Brice, Bob and UNT Press unveiled *Old Riot, New Ranger: Captain Jack Dean, Texas Ranger and U.S. Marshal.* The longest and most contemporaneous of Bob's several biographies, at over five hundred pages this volume not only looks into the life and career of a modern era lawman in its finest sense—Dean retired in 2004 after forty-three years in law enforcement—but also explores the continuing and broadening evolution of law enforcement in the Southwest, the thread that has connected Alexander's projects from the beginning tales of a Silver City sheriff.

"I Work at It!"

Prolific author and Texas Ranger historian Bob Alexander is creating a legacy of academic excellence and prodigious historiography to an unprecedented degree, his bookshelf offering to readers of the West and Southwest a wide range of engaging information, notwithstanding fact and legend and myth roiled together, in a demotic writing style that is both unique and immensely popular to his readership.[45] "While reading many of the books he has authored," wrote Texas Ranger chief Kirby W. Dendy in his foreword to Alexander's fifth Ranger book, "it was apparent that Bob was not presenting a personal agenda or making predisposed statements by shading his canvas in tones most aligned with individual preferences, unless one would consider truth and objectivity as the focus of that work. Because, that's exactly what I've seen in every book I've read that Bob Alexander has written: An unbiased and factual treatment based on incredibly detailed references." And, Dendy continues, "His writing approach reminds me fondly of my days as a young boy sitting in my grandfather's barber shop, listening with fascination to the tales of hunting, war, and everyday life told by his colorful clientele."[46]

Or sitting around a late-night campfire on the open range, swapping tall tales and old favorite stories with the other cowpokes. Or taking turns reading Zane Grey passages at a book club soirée.

For twenty years Bob Alexander has inexorably followed the jouncy trail of frontier justice across the wide expanse of the American Southwest, from Tombstone to Silver City to Santa Fe, and from El Paso to Midland to Austin to Laredo, utilizing his investigative experience and raw-cut writing style to engage the Western reader in a straightforward, often violent, take on how the West was, if not won, if not tamed, at least confronted by both the law and the outlaw. "A career peace officer during the Wild West era—or even today," Bob argues, "might have proficiently carried out 1000 safe arrests never seeing his/her name in print. When things go right, there's zilch to write about. It is when conditions go haywire—usually in but a fractional second—that the journalists and tabloid writers start cranking the presses of awareness." And the indefatigable Bob Alexander goes to work. "When retelling of a spine-tingling incident to fellow officers"—or to an avid readership hungry for the sensationalized details that Bob Alexander brings to their table— "the comments are typically predicated with an alert: 'Then, it turned Western.'"[47] Sure as shootin'.

Notes

1. Bob Alexander, *John H. Behan: Sacrificed Sheriff* (Silver City, NM: High-Lonesome Books, 2002), 5; and other statements as well. Here he is admonishing other writers—"Some recount the Behan story as they wished it were, rather than the way it is"—and sticking to primary sources for his information.

2. Interview with Bob Alexander, April 18, 2019, LaGrange, TX. A delightful six hours of conversation led to much of the career material included in this chapter.

3. Interview with Alexander, April 18, 2019. Bob was disinclined to give much personal information, preferring to accentuate his career as it contributed to his approach to his writing.

4. Alexander interview, April 18, 2019.

5. See for example, Jan Devereaux's wonderfully researched and beautifully written *Pistols, Petticoats, & Poker: The Real Lottie Deno: No Lies or Alibis*, introduction by Robert G. McCubbin (Silver City, NM: High-Lonesome Books, 2009).

6. Leon Metz, in Alexander, *Dangerous Dan Tucker: New Mexico's Deadly Lawman* (Silver City, NM: High-Lonesome Books, 2001), 5. Metz notes with acumen that Bob "himself toted a badge for thirty-five [*sic*] years" and "as a sleuth himself he understood the processes of investigation. He knew what it was like to lay his life on the line."

7. Correspondence from Paula M. Marks to Spellman, August 14, 2019.

8. Interview with Alexander, April 18, 2019.

9. Correspondence from Robert K. DeArment to Spellman, August 2, 2019.

10. Robert DeArment, in Alexander, *Sheriff Harvey Whitehill: Silver City Stalwart*, introduction by Robert K. DeArment (Silver City, NM: High-Lonesome Books, 2005), 2. Alexander's first eight published books went to press with High-Lonesome Books and Glia Books, both out of Silver City. Says DeArment, "For the most part, the personalities Alexander profiled have long been overlooked. Thankfully they have now found a voice."

11. Letter, Alexander to Darren Ivey, February 6, 2018.

12. Fourth Amendment, Constitution of the United States

13. Letter, Alexander to Ivey, February 6, 2018

14. Moulton, "A Ranger War & Billy the Kid," *True West*, July 2007, 75.

15. Alexander, *Winchester Warriors: Texas Rangers of Company D, 1874–1901* (Denton: University of North Texas Press, 2009), xii.

16. Alexander, *Winchester Warriors*, xi–xii. "There is a glaring downside, however," Alexander admits. "Scant attention will be given to happenings not directly affecting Company D, nor is this a format for mini genealogical profiles of Texas Rangers."

17. Paul N. Spellman, in Alexander, *Winchester Warriors*, emphasis by author.

18. Alexander, *Winchester Warriors*, 39.
19. Alexander, "The Best Texas Rangers Photos Ever," *True West*, April 2012, 34–41; Alexander, "The Best of the Texas Rangers in Photos," *True West*, January 2019, 24–31.
20. Alexander, *Lawmen, Outlaws, and S.O.Bs: Gunfighters of the Old Southwest*, vol. 1, introduction by Chuck Parsons (Silver City, NM: High-Lonesome Books, 2004), 184–88.
21. Alexander, *Lawmen, Outlaws, and S.O.Bs*, xi. Alexander makes a pointed contrast between Aten and the more famous, media-aggrandized Wyatt Earp, "a sociological commentary on how the entertainment media can and has warped history."
22. Alexander, *Rawhide Ranger, Ira Aten: Enforcing Law on the Texas Frontier* (Denton: University of North Texas Press, 2011), vi.
23. Alexander, *Rawhide Ranger, Ira Aten*, vi–viii.
24. Alexander, "Square Deals and Real McCoys," *Wild West Historical Association Journal* 4, no. 3 (June 2011): 32–52; Alexander won the Western Outlaw / Lawman History Association award for best book in 2003 (*Fearless Dave Allison*), 2004 (*Lawmen, Outlaws and S.O.Bs*, vol. 1), and 2006 (*Desert Desperadoes*), the National Outlaw and Lawman Historical Association award in 2003 (*Fearless Dave Allison*), and the Wild West History Association award in 2011 (*Rawhide Ranger, Ira Aten*). The WWHA also awarded his 2009 article "Tucker X Texas = Trouble" as their Best Journal Article of the Year.
25. Alexander, "An Outlaw Tripped Up by Love," *Quarterly of the National Association for Outlaw and Lawman History* 26, no. 3 (July–September 2002): 1, 7–16.
26. Alexander, "Guns, Girls & Gamblers: Silver City's Wilder Side," *Western Outlaw-Lawman History Association Journal* 14, no. 4 (Winter 2005): 12–20.
27. Alexander and Jan Devereaux, "Trumpeting Elephants & Kicking Asses: Republicans and Democrats, New Mexico Style," *True West*, January/February 2010, 27–31; Alexander, "Hellfire & Hot Tamales," *True West*, September 2010, 61–63.
28. Alexander, "Death on the Line," *True West*, May 2013, 24–31.
29. Byron Johnson, in Alexander, *Riding Lucifer's Line: Ranger Deaths along the Texas-Mexico Border* (Denton: University of North Texas Press, 2013), xii. Bob also takes things in stride, according to an anecdote shared by Ranger Museum research librarian Rusty Bloxom: "When a newly-discovered primary source contradicted some of the

common assumptions Bob had written, he shrugged and chuckled, 'Wish I'd had this when I was writing the book.'" Correspondence, Bloxom to Spellman, August 2019.

30. Alexander, *Riding Lucifer's Line*, xiii.
31. Alexander, *Riding Lucifer's Line*, xv. Quoting the estimable Walter Prescott Webb: "Lead sinks more men in the Rio Grande in a year than gold does in a decade." *The Texas Rangers: A Century of Frontier Defense,* (Austin: University of Texas Press 1965), 508.
32. Alexander, *Riding Lucifer's Line*, xix.
33. Alexander, *Bad Company and Burnt Powder: Justice in the Old Southwest* (Denton: University of North Texas Press, 2014), xviii–xix (emphasis author's).
34. Alexander, *Bad Company and Burnt Powder*, viii–ix. In a follow-up conversation between the author and Alexander (September 6, 2019), Bob says simply, "Nobody's going to read it if everybody just does their job and no one gets shot."
35. Kirby Dendy, in Alexander, *Six-Shooters and Shifting Sands: The Wild West Life of Texas Ranger Captain Frank Jones* (Denton: University of North Texas Press, 2015), xiii.
36. Alexander, *Six-Shooters and Shifting Sands*, 348–57.
37. Alexander, *Six-Shooters and Shifting Sands*, 281; Captain Jones to Adjutant General W. H. Mabry, June 21, 1892, Adjutant General Records, Texas State Archives, Austin, Texas.
38. Alexander, *Whiskey River Ranger: The Old West Life of Baz Outlaw* (Denton: University of North Texas Press, 2016), vii.
39. Alexander, *Whiskey River Ranger*, xi. Alexander explains, "Recapping escapades of players on the real Wild West stage, apart from offering worthwhile historical value or thoughtful conclusions that may be drawn, has thus far indisputably served as an entertaining platform for furthering both breathtaking fictionalized and tamer nonfiction narratives." Fun.
40. Alexander, *Whiskey River Ranger*, xiii. "His biography in every sense of the word is a full-fledged Western. Readers will not be shortchanged."
41. Alexander, *Winchester Warriors*, xi.
42. Alexander and Brice, *Texas Rangers: Lives, Legend, and Legacy* (Denton: University of North Texas Press, 2017), viii. Adds Ranger Museum research librarian Rusty Bloxom, "Bob includes each staff member in the acknowledgments of every book that has drawn from sources at the [Texas Ranger Hall of Fame and] museum. He tells them

and the world that each one of them has played a role in the completion of his work." Correspondence, Bloxom to Spellman, August 2019.

43. Alexander and Brice, *Texas Rangers*, ix. But, they admit, "resolving such a wide-ranging concern seemed—at first blush—uncomplicated. Upon sober and unhurried reflection the matter proved much more complex."

44. Alexander and Brice, *Texas Rangers*, 381n15; Robert M. Utley, *Lone Star Lawmen: The Second Century of the Texas Rangers* (New York: Oxford University Press, 2007), 280.

45. And respected by his peers: prolific coauthors Charles Harris and Louis Sadler's newest contribution to the Ranger story, *The Texas Rangers in Transition: From Gunfighters to Criminal Investigators, 1921–1935* (Norman: University of Oklahoma Press, 2019), is dedicated "to Bob Alexander, Ranger Historian."

46. Kirby Dendy, in Alexander, *Six-Shooters and Shifting Sands*, xii-xiii.

47. Alexander, *Bad Company and Burnt Powder*, ix.

Revisionists

Chapter 10

Robert M. Utley
New Standard Bearer

Harold J. Weiss Jr.

Of constabularies around the world, only the Royal Canadian Mounted Police compete with the Texas Rangers in nearly universal name recognition. The Mounties began in 1873 as a frontier force designated the Northwest Mounted Police and evolved into a national institution admired for their scarlet tunics, precision drill, and efficient policing.

By contrast, the Texas Rangers began in the 1830s as a tradition rather than an institution. Officially they bore the Ranger designation only sporadically for decades. Not until after half a century fighting Indians did they evolve from sometime-citizen soldiers into full-time lawmen. In both incarnations, they disdained uniforms and all other military attributes.

Aside from these differences, the two institutions display another significant contrast. The Mounties have projected a consistently favorable image, prompting widespread admiration. The Rangers have displayed varied images, but most conspicuous have been polar images almost from the beginnings in the 1830s to the present day. At the one pole the image is firmly positive, at the other firmly negative. Thus, unlike the Canadian Mounted Police, the Texas Rangers are either idolized or deplored.[1]

T he author of this expressive statement—Robert M. "Bob" Utley—has impacted the historical writings with the Texas Rangers. Although he did not have an extensive body of published works on the life and times of the Rangers, nevertheless Utley moved the historical field forward. His numerous historical writings dealt with the frontier military institution, Indian tribes, and law and order in the American Southwest. But his authoritative two-volume history of the Texas Rangers, well researched and elegantly written, made him stand out among Ranger historians at the turn of the twenty-first century.

The relationship of an author to the field of Ranger history turns the researcher into a modern detective. The process calls for an investigator who can keep an open mind and gives a balanced appraisal. The search for factual evidence can result in a storyline that is favorably received by an audience. The message should also call for a level of excellence that becomes a lofty goal for other Ranger historians to attain.

Robert Utley, known as the Old Bison, passed away in June of 2022. Accolades from historians and friends about his career in the national parks and his numerous publications appeared in magazines, newspapers, and on the internet. As a person he was described as being generous with his time and expertise. As a writer and historian, Utley received praise for setting a high bar to work toward. He left a lasting legacy of achievement and gained immortality through the printed page. Utley has been called the Dean of Western Historians, and the profession might not see his like again.

Robert Utley wrote his own obituary. After a thoughtful reminiscence he said, "By the time you read this, I will have checked out and perhaps had my ashes scattered over the big rock in Logan Canyon, Utah, where Melody [his second wife] and I first connected in 1973. When and how I died will have to be filled in after I die."[2] Utley, suffering from hearing loss and wheelchair-bound, passed away from heart failure in his 90s.

Utley's Evolving Public Career and Scholarly Writings on the American West

Born in 1929 in Arkansas, Robert Utley had an eventful life. He joined the National Park Service and rose to be its chief historian. He studied history at two institutions: Purdue University and Indiana University at Bloomington. He published authoritative historical works on western America. In the process Utley won numerous honors, from book awards and university honorary degrees to being president of the Western History Association.[3]

In his youthful days Robert Utley became enamored with the life of George Armstrong Custer and the movements of the US 7th Cavalry with the Sioux and other Indians at the Battle of the Little Bighorn in 1876. This happened for two reasons: reading books and watching Errol Flynn play Custer in the movies. In fact in the late 1940s, Utley saved enough money to take a trip to the Custer Battlefield National Monument in Montana. For several years thereafter, he worked as an aide to guide visitors around the battlefield during the summer months.

In the early 1950s, after taking historical courses at Purdue University, Robert Utley entered Indiana University at Bloomington to work on a master's degree in history under the direction of Oscar Osborne Winther. Professor Winther specialized in the transportation frontier and was one of the leading lights in American western historiography. Utley wrote, "I found him gentle, kind, and likable, but not especially helpful." Yet Utley left Indiana University with a degree and a master's thesis on the historiography of the Battle of the Little Bighorn from 1876 to 1900. Winther's scholarship and standing in the historical profession was such that Utley "benefited from the label of 'Winther student.'"[4]

For the most part, the career of Robert Utley dealt with government service. In the mid-1950s he was drafted into the United States Army. He went through a hard-nosed basic training to be an infantry rifleman. Utley applied to officer candidate school (OCS) and graduated with distinction as a second lieutenant. This propelled him into a position with the historical section of the Joint Chiefs of Staff of the US military. Here he learned even more about "style, clarity, precision, handling of evidence, and readability" in historical writing.[5] In addition Utley joined the Potomac Corral of Westerners, where he met the top brass of the Park Service and talked about Custer at their monthly dinner meetings. As Utley's military career came to an end, he had a choice: either return to Indiana University to work on a doctoral dissertation dealing with the Sioux in the 1890s or rejoin the National Park Service. He chose the latter.

In 1957 Robert Utley entered the National Park Service and stayed until he took early retirement at the start of the 1980s. He began his career in New Mexico, worked on historical projects, and became historian of the Southwest Region, which included all or parts of six states. Utley ended his career in the state of Virginia as chief, Division of Historical Studies. Here he learned the "ways of the Washington bureaucrat."[6] Utley also pointed out, "I regarded myself as a historian first and a Park Service official second. I sought to maintain my professional independence as a historian, and over the next three decades I succeeded."[7] In retirement Utley had the time to spend on being an author, as he followed his wife, Melody Webb, in her career moves within the Park Service.

As a professional historian Robert Utley has tried to "keep one foot in each of two worlds."[8] One pathway dealt with the popular field, which included the amateur writers and those employed in historical societies, museums, and parks. The other field of study encompassed the academic community of scholars found in the nation's colleges and universities. A golden opportunity for Utley came when these two diverse camps joined together to form the Western History Association in the 1960s. He took a leading role in its formation and enjoyed being with both the buffs of the Corrals of Westerners and the scholarly historians from the higher educational institutions.

The published works by Robert Utley in academic and commercial presses were varied, vivid, and memorable. He tried to tell believable stories that pointed to larger themes. His research and writing dealt mainly with the military experience and violent epochs in the American West. These studies fell into four categories: the frontier army, Custer in fact and fiction, the Indian frontier, and law and order in the Southwest. In time Utley worked with an agent and received monetary advances in the tens of thousands against royalties from the presses.

Robert Utley enjoyed digging into research files, organizing notes, and presenting the findings in elegant prose. Among his numerous books, several stood out. He published a two-volume history of the frontier army in the nineteenth century that has become standard works.[9] Equally important, he finally penned an award-winning biography of George Armstrong Custer.[10] At the urging of Ray Billington, the dean of western historians, Utley put together a volume on the Indian frontier in the late 1800s.[11] An earlier study of the Sioux in the 1890s, based on notes for his doctoral dissertation, established Utley as a talented nonfiction author.[12] These were followed by his praiseworthy and award-winning biographies of Sitting Bull and Geronimo.[13] Many of these publications are still in print.

Years before Utley wrote his history of the Rangers, he mentioned them as a military body in his books on the US Army, the Mexicans, and the Indian tribes. He did this in two ways: first, the Rangers fired and popularized Samuel Colt's six-shooter in the US-Mexican War; second, Utley pointed out the use of the Rangers by Texas in Indian fighting in the late 1850s and how the federal government enlisted and paid for Rangers at the start of the decade for frontier service.

In the 1980s Robert Utley and his wife traveled to Lincoln, New Mexico. They toured landmarks and talked about its violent past. "Having devoted three decades to Indians and soldiers," Utley wrote, "I was seeking fresh fields to plow. I found them in Lincoln, a setting for a cast of vivid characters in dramatic conflict and a case study in frontier violence."[14] After researching records found inside and outside the state, Utley penned two volumes, one dealing with the Lincoln County War and the other a biography of Billy the Kid.[15] These books did not turn out the way the author thought. He spent less time in researching and writing about Billy the Kid, but the biography outsold the volume on the Lincoln County War. The book about the Kid, Utley reminisced, "soared in sales and accolades beyond anything I had ever written."[16] He learned a lesson as a narrative historian: people are more interested in stories of particular individuals who have earned a place in fact and fiction.

Utley and His Ranger Histories in Thought and Deed

At the turn of the twenty-first century, a number of historical writers tried their hand at composing a history of the Texas Rangers. When Melody Webb retired from the National Park Service in the 1990s, she and Bob Utley moved to Georgetown in the Texas Hill Country. Surrounded by source material in archives and libraries, Utley realized that a history of the Rangers had become an "appealing project."[17] In the end he wrote a two-volume Ranger history, with 1910 being the start of the twentieth century. Putting together books, articles, and essays in print and giving speeches at historical meetings and with the public at large, Utley became a pacesetter for the Texas Rangers.

In the annals of Ranger writings, the general histories published by Robert Utley have been praised for their scholarly research and insightful narratives. His titles aptly caught the Ranger aura and showed their long-standing role in Texan affairs: *Lone Star Justice: The First Century of the Texas Rangers* and *Lone Star Lawmen: The Second Century of the Texas Rangers*. Utley's first volume covered the military and early law enforcement periods to 1910. By this date, he wrote, the "Rangers were closing out the era of the Old West and verging on another incarnation altogether."[18] This twentieth century remake took place in a culture that involved world wars, the Great Depression, the rise of an industrial Texas, and the modernization of the Ranger service. In Utley's view these modern Rangers "kept the name of the old and clung to the history, the traditions, and even the legendary that had gained pride and renown for the old."[19] In putting these volumes together, the author used archival records, printed primary source materials, and historical accounts written by American and Hispanic writers. One criticism of this process has been that Utley's use of Mexican records needed to be more diverse and meaningful.

Several words come to the mind when reading critiques of Utley's Ranger histories: fair-minded, thorough, balanced, and always interesting. One reviewer of his second volume expressed these thoughts in vivid language: "The strengths of Utley's book are several. He can handle a breadth of material with clarity; he is a good writer of action scenes in particular; he updates Ranger history; he is fair-minded but does not pull his punches; and, unlike Walter Prescott Webb in his 1935 history of the Rangers, he closely examines and passes judgment on issues of Ranger integrity and conduct."[20] Those who put together review essays recognized that Utley dealt with the Texas Rangers as both saints and sinners.

Robert Utley saw his days researching and writing about the Texas Rangers as a gratifying experience in his life. He remembered his two volumes in this way:

> I greatly enjoyed researching and writing my two Ranger books. The first, dealing with the first century of the Rangers, got the most publicity and sales, but I have always believed that the second, dealing with the second century, was the best and the greater contribution to history. There is some competition, I know, but I would be less than human if I thought they were better than mine. In 2015, the Western Writers of America held their annual conference in Lubbock. I gave the keynote address: "The Texas Rangers Then and Now." Judging from the standing ovation, the Rangers still resonate in the word beyond Texas.[21]

Robert Utley used two organizing themes in his books on the life and times of the Texas Rangers. One thought pattern dealt with the Ranger captains in the field and at central headquarters. The other framework covered the administrations of the governors of the state. As a scholarly leader Utley handled both courses of action with sensitivity and thoroughness.

In putting together the first volume on the nineteenth century, Bob Utley emphasized the role of Ranger captains. This procedure had become standard since the days of Walter Prescott Webb. The author first covered the faint beginnings of ranging the Texas lands against Indian tribes and Mexican nationals, especially by Robert M. Coleman and Robert M. "Three-Legged-Willie" Williamson. These citizen-soldier endeavors built more a Ranger tradition of service rather than a permanent organization. During the military era Utley stressed in detail the usual figures in thought and deed: John Coffee "Jack" Hays; the McCulloch brothers, Ben and Henry; Samuel H. "Sam" Walker; and John S. "Rip" Ford. They took part in events like the Great Comanche Raid and the US-Mexican War in the 1840s and the violent troubles with the Comanche in the north and Juan Cortina along the border in the following decade. As the need for military action decreased in Texas in the 1800s, the Rangers turned to face gunslingers, outlaw gangs, and other criminal elements.

In the last half of his first volume, Robert Utley wrote about the Rangers as law officers. It all started with the creation in 1874 of the Frontier Battalion (later called the Ranger Force) under the capable leadership of John B. Jones and the birth of the controversial ranging force led by Leander H. McNelly. The day-by-day operations of the Rangers as peace officers gave them institutional continuity. The author then covered the personal makeup and actions of the Four Great Captains: J. A. Brooks, John R. Hughes, William J. "Bill" McDonald, and John H. Rogers. Dramatic episodes took place before, during, and after the Ranger careers of these officers: the killing of Sam Bass, the capture of John Wesley Hardin, the Sutton-Taylor Feud, the Salt War, the Brownsville Raid, and the shooting of Captain Frank Jones. "For the last quarter of the nineteenth century," Utley wrote, "the lawmen of the Old West did battle with stock thieves; stagecoach, train, and bank robbers; fence cutters; belligerents in the political, ethnic, and family feuds that rocked many counties; and the bad men, both Mexican and Texan, who made the international border a perpetually turbulent zone extending from Brownsville to El Paso."[22] These happenings occurred under the watchful eyes of Adjutant Generals William Steele, Wilburn H. King, and Woodford H. Mabry.

The Rangers and other western peace officers in the late nineteenth century worked within the confines of what Utley called a "six-shooter culture." He went on to say in one essay, "They not only set high value on mastery of the Winchester repeater and Colt six-shooter but admired men who had validated their skills against human targets. The culture embraced physical strength, courage, and fearlessness as well as a readiness to apply violence where deemed necessary. A frontier lawman needed all these qualities, but if not kept in check they could easily drift into excess."[23] In this atmosphere Rangers attained high marks for tracking and capturing fugitives, mediating between contentious factions, taming boomtowns, and protecting courtrooms. Utley concluded in his first volume, "In quelling riots, controlling rowdies, calming feuds, and keeping the peace in excited communities, the Rangers did exceptionally well. In sending bad men to the penitentiary, they went down to defeat in a defective criminal justice system."[24]

Robert Utley used a different format for the second volume on the twentieth century. He covered Ranger happenings tied to the administrations of the Texas governors. This happened for several reasons besides personal choice: the lack of archival Ranger records for the early 1900s; the response of Texas to national events like the Mexican Revolution, the two world wars, and the Great Depression; and the ups and downs of the leadership of the Ranger companies in the field and at central headquarters. Even with this complex scenario, Utley was still able to put together in several hundred pages the first comprehensive history of the modern Texas Rangers in the twentieth century.

During the first half of the twentieth century, Robert Utley researched and wrote about the governors who supported law and order and the involvement of the Rangers. He also pointed out the chief executives of the state who allowed their personal beliefs and a political agenda to undermine Ranger operations. The low point in the Ranger service came with Governors James E. "Pa" Ferguson and Miriam A. "Ma" Ferguson. They hindered Ranger operations by cutting budgets and appointing political hacks. More in line with law and order and the deployment of the Rangers were the gubernatorial administrations of Pat M. Neff, Daniel J. "Dan" Moody, and James V. Allred. In the days of Governor Allred, the desire to stop political interference and the need to modernize the Rangers made the state legislature create the Department of Public Safety (DPS) in 1935.

During these eventful time periods, new Ranger leaders emerged to bring back a degree of respectability to the Ranger force. Their names became household fixtures: Manuel T. "Lone Wolf" Gonzaullas, who tamed oil boomtowns and became a first-rate criminal investigator; Francis A. "Frank" Hamer, with his memorable roles in the Sherman Riot and the gunning down of Clyde Barrow and Bonnie Parker; Thomas R. "Tom" Hickman, who gained a reputation with his publicized encounters with bank robbers; William W. Sterling and his part in the bridge controversy with Oklahoma; and William L. "Will" Wright, who served long and honorably along the border against smugglers, rustlers, and the rowdies in the towns. They resemble old-time Rangers before 1900, but their operations occurred in the modern era of automobiles, radios, rapid-firing weapons, urban centers, and new technologies in the investigation of criminal behavior.

Director James B. Adams of the DPS characterized the Rangers as "felony investigators" in the 1980s.[25] That they were. By the opening of the twenty-first century, Rangers as crime fighters and troubleshooters took part in high-profile cases. New names appeared on Ranger rolls, as, for example, E. J. "Jay" Banks, Robert A. "Bob" Crowder, Jack O. Dean, H. Joaquin Jackson, and Clint Peoples. They had encounters with prison rioters, robbers, and murderers like Gene Paul Norris. In addition, in the late 1900s the Ranger service became more inclusive, as Blacks, Hispanics, and women joined the organization in greater numbers. By the end of the twentieth century, two high-profile cases gained state and national attention. In one episode the Rangers investigated the violent clash between federal agents and the Branch Davidians with David Koresh. In the other affair the Rangers became involved, especially Captain Barry Caver, with stopping the spread of the Republic of Texas movement in the state. Continuity and change have become one of the hallmarks of the Texas Rangers for two centuries.

Robert Utley emphasized the key remakes in the traditional story of the Rangers. In the passage from the nineteenth to the twentieth centuries, three watershed moments changed the nature of the Ranger service. A milestone in the struggle between the Rangers and the Comanches occurred at Walker's Creek in 1844. Here the Rangers under Jack Hays effectively used their five-shot Paterson Colts and warfare in the American Southwest would never be the same. Another crucial dividing line took place in 1874 with the creation of the Frontier Battalion under Major Jones. At the time the intermittent citizen-soldier Rangers came to an end and the organizational continuity of the Rangers as peace officers came into being. The third significant modification happened with the formation of the DPS in 1935. This new agency housed the Rangers, the Highway Patrol, and administrative bureaus and a crime lab. The ability to adapt to a changing culture became one of the hallmarks of the Ranger service for two hundred years.[26]

Revisionism took many forms in the Ranger writings that came from the pen of Robert Utley. In one way he updated the traditional story about military and police operations. In his volume on the nineteenth century, for instance, Utley wrote about lesser-known groups like the Frontier Forces of 1870–1871. These ranging companies included both Anglos and Hispanics, with a number of Mexican American captains. After several pages on their operations, Utley concluded that the Frontier Forces "played a brief but creditable role."[27]

Equally important, with his study of the twentieth century, Robert Utley stressed the vital role played by Director Homer Garrison of the DPS in modernizing the Ranger service. This included better training, an improved communications network, and a more efficient crime lab. In their criminal investigations, often in support of local lawmen, the Rangers at this time operated differently in West Texas than the eastern portions of the state. The former called for old-style Rangers to handle smuggling and cattle rustling in the vast regions. The latter, especially in the rising urban areas, needed "concrete Rangers" who operated like city detectives. Utley ended by saying, "In the twentieth century, Colonel Homer Garrison has no peer. In his thirty-year reign as director of DPS (1938–68), he not only saved the Rangers from likely extinction but molded them into skilled professional crime fighters."[28]

The main contributions by Robert Utley to Ranger historical writings were his revisionist thoughts and his vivid pen-and-ink descriptions. He saw the Rangers as a product of their own time and space. All sides in the triad—Ranger-Indian-Mexican—had to be dealt with fairly without partisan feelings when they carried out heroic deeds and dastardly acts. Like other historical writers, Utley noted the bad behavior with intimidations and killings by the Rangers in the US-Mexican War in the 1840s, the Mexican Revolution of the early 1900s, and the agricultural struggle in South Texas in the 1960s. In these eras rogue Ranger Captains J. Monroe Fox, Mabry B. "Mustang" Gray, and Henry L. Ransom carried out violent actions that dishonored the organization. Even Captain A. Y. Allee in the farm problems in the Rio Grande valley in the 1960s used strong-arm methods that gave the Rangers a bad name.

Overlooked in this violent saga has been Robert Utley's perceptive thoughts on the interactions between Rangers and those of Mexican descent. In clear and precise words he wrote:

> The revisionist case seems built on four supports. The first is the well-documented atrocities of the Mexican War and McNelly's border operations. The second is an interpretation of such incidents as the San Ambrosia affair of 1885 (chap. 13) and the Cerda killings of 1902 (chap. 15) that brushes

aside all uncertainty and ambiguity, uncritically embraces the popular Mexican belief of what happened, and assumes that they occurred regularly. The third is the popular belief itself, unquestionably a deeply held belief passed from one generation to the next, but rooted in folklore and a scattering of anecdotes. The fourth, which undergirds the popular belief as well as the conclusions of the revisionists, is a tendency to tar the Rangers of two centuries with the actions of some in the twentieth century. The border excesses of 1915–1919 and the strike-breaking operation of the 1960s against Mexican agricultural workers are but two of several twentieth-century grievances resented by Mexicans.[29]

The revisionist impulse demonstrated by Robert Utley led to a balanced treatment of the Rangers and their foes. He did not try to whitewash events to make all Rangers strong, brave, and honorable. Neither did he endorse the belief that the Rangers as military and law officers filled their ranks with demonic individuals who killed systematically. These blanket images in Utley's view can be found in historical works like those of T. R. Fehrenbach and Américo Paredes. Utley applied the brakes to extremism with the doings of the Ranger service. His dictum: "The Rangers have both a black side and a white side but mostly, like all institutions composed of people, a range of grays separating the two. Sound history records the range as well as the poles."[30]

Robert Utley ended his writing days about the Texas Rangers by recording and trying to understand the ties between myth and reality. Oral and written myths can be viewed as the fabled tales about the origins of the human race. At the same time, legendary stories about individuals, which might have a historical base in fact, appear in exaggerated forms. The enduring legend of the Texas Rangers came from fiction writers in print and film in the popular culture of the nineteenth and twentieth centuries. Even some Rangers like William Alexander Anderson "Bigfoot" Wallace and Bill McDonald added their touches to the folk epic. In essence this added up to what one newsman said in the early 1880s: "The Texas Ranger can ride harder,

fight longer, live rougher, and makes less talk about it than anybody
else that walks on two feet."[31]

Robert Utley realized that this image might not fit the historicity of
living Rangers like Captains Jack Hays and Frank Hamer. But it surely
fitted the fictional world of the *Lone Ranger* on radio and in the movies
and television. "That the legend has so profoundly and for so long
flourished in the public mind," Utley wrote, "is a consequence of major
proportions. That people the world over know of the Texas Rangers,
no matter how false or distorted the image, endows the Rangers with a
significance eclipsing their influence on the course of history."[32]

To his credit Robert Utley saw the Rangers as "legendary heroes
and legendary knaves."[33] His historical knowhow about the Ranger
service—their changing roles, organization, and personnel—will be
cited by historians in the years to come. In many ways Utley, like
Walter Prescott Webb, made an impact on the historical profession in
Texas and elsewhere. But his books and articles are not the last word
on the Texas Rangers. Future historians will use them as a springboard
to new ways of thought and expression.

One avenue of research and writing that Robert Utley pursued
will become more important in the decades to come: tying Ranger
history to the American way of life. In the military era of Ranger
operations, their relationships on and off the battlefield with the
US Armed Forces need to be explored in depth. As law officers the
Rangers had numerous intergovernmental relations in the American
federal system, notably with sheriffs, US marshals, and state
troopers scattered throughout the country. In reality and myth, as
heroic figures and dastardly individuals, the Texas Rangers became
regional icons and national and international celebrities. In a review of
Ranger books, Mitchel Roth, a noted historian of the police and justice
system, made a compelling case: "Before there were Pinkertons,
the Secret Service or the New York Police Department, there were
the Texas Rangers. Celebrated in story, song and movie, the Rangers
are one of the few police forces in the world to have been elevated to

the role of regional, let alone international, icons. Besides Canada's Mounties and England's bobbies, it's doubtful that any other force approaches their elevated status."[34]

Utley's Descriptive Know-How

Besides being able to write insightful narratives of Ranger personnel and their ongoing actions, Robert Utley had the knack to draw a pictorial image of Ranger characters. He made them come alive in the reader's mind. This happened whether the Rangers acted as military figures, served as an early law enforcement body, or joined the DPS as a detective force.

Most historians agree that Jack Hays played a pivotal role in leadership, the use of Colt's revolver, and the fighting in the US-Mexican War. Utley described Hays in an unforgettable way:

> Jack Hays hardly looked the part of frontier fighter, or even out-doorsman. Slim, only five-eight in height, with wavy brown hair, brushy eyebrows, and smooth- shaven face, he impressed on observer as a "delicate-looking young man." Outdoor life turned his fair complexion to tawny and weather beaten, while the demands of leadership in an environment fraught with danger gave him "a thoughtful and care-worn expression" and a "habitual frown." Unprepossessing in appearance, he exhibited a like temperament. Modest, quiet, soft-spoken, thoughtful, a man of few words either spoken or written, he had no need to boast: his actions told all.[35]

By the end of the nineteenth century and the turn of a new era, the Texas Rangers became peace officers with the creation of the Frontier Battalion. A name change—the Ranger Force—occurred in 1901. At that time two of the Four Great Captains, John Hughes and Bill McDonald, captured the public imagination. Both chased felons and carried out detective work. McDonald, though, understood and contributed to the popular culture of modern times. This especially happened when his actions in the field became the basis of the "one riot, one Ranger" story. Utley expressed this view in these words:

"Captain Bill" possessed courage, bravery, dedication, persistence, mastery of horse and gun, and criminal investigative skill. Six feet tall, wiry, lithe of movement, he projected authority with riveting blue eyes deeply set in a face framed by big ears and adorned with a mustache merging into muttonchop whiskers. More than any other captain, he was a showman, a colorful character, a self-promoter who reveled in notoriety. He cultivated politicians and newsmen and made certain that his exploits received public acclaim, often at the expense of his men.

McDonald gained a merited reputation for talking down mobs. "I used to tell him," recalled one of his men, "Cap, you're going to get all of us killed, the way you cuss out strikers and mobs." "Don't worry, Ryan," was the response. "Just remember my motto." He repeated his motto often enough to bequeath it to all successive generations of Rangers: "No man in the wrong can stand up against a fellow that's in the right and keeps on a'comin.'"[36]

Not as colorful or given to theatrics as McDonald, John Hughes ably served in a long-lasting role: captain of Ranger Company D in West Texas. In fact he was the best gunman of the Four Great Captains. Utley gave Hughes high marks for being a Ranger:

"A braver or cooler officer has never been commissioned," observed the editor of a Pecos newspaper. To those expected qualities Hughes brought others. He had a sharp mind, rugged physique, vigor and endurance, and unquenchable zest for rangering. He was a skilled out-doorsman, especially adept at tracking. Service at Shafter and Presidio had given him an understanding of the unique demands of the border. Of prime importance, Hughes selected his recruits with great care and exacted high standards of performance. Like successful captains since Jack Hays, he led by example rather than edict. His men accorded him respect, affection, and loyalty, which he returned in full measure. "Folks trust John," observed on of his men. In short, John Hughes loved his job and did it incomparably.[37]

By the middle of the twentieth century, the Texas Rangers moved from the adjutant general's office over to the DPS. By that time two Rangers became household names: Frank Hamer and Manuel Gonzaullas. The former has been seen as the prototype for the modern Ranger. The latter rose through the ranks to be a Ranger captain and the initial head of the crime lab in the newly formed DPS. Utley described Hamer as a "tough muscular giant weighing 230 pounds and standing an impressive six feet three."[38] He went on to say:

Hamer excelled as a marksman with every type of firearm, hand and shoulder. His trademark was a powerful swing of the right arm that smashed the flat of his hand against an opponent's ear. "Captain Hamer's open palm always took the fight out of the hardiest ruffian," observed a colleague, who also marveled at his mastery of foot fighting; "few antagonists could stand up under his mule-like kicks." Stolid, given less to words than action, he would emerge in coming years as a skilled criminal investigator, a fiercely effective lawman, and while hardly peaceful, the most widely admired peace officer in Texas.[39]

Manuel Gonzaullas became a more complex Ranger than Hamer. Different historical accounts have surfaced about his birth and upbringing. He appeared on the Ranger stage in the 1920s. Utley described all his intricacies:

Manuel Gonzaullas not only displayed professional distinction but personal as well. Of medium build but muscular and strong, he dressed and groomed impeccably, loved fancy guns and cars, and harbored a well-deserved high opinion of his talents. Resembling Captain Hickman in vanity, he nevertheless treated all but lawbreakers with courtesy. Like the famous Captain John H. Rogers, he was a devout Presbyterian and carried a pocket Testament. Toward lawbreakers he harbored a visceral hatred that granted no mercy. His two pistols, with trigger guards removed, rested in special holsters that exposed the triggers for instant action. During his long career he is said to have shot and killed twenty-two men and in turn received seven wounds. Although an extrovert, he kept his plans secret and preferred to work along. "I went into a lot of fights by myself," he recalled, "and I came out by myself, too." Mexican bandits labeled him "El Lobo Solo," and the sobriquet stuck. "Lone Wolf" Gonzaullas became a legend in his own lifetime.[40]

Lone Wolf Gonzaullas had one more distinction. He studied criminalistics and became the best-known Ranger detective of his generation. The Texas Rangers had come of age. Utley talked about this happening:

Manuel T. Gonzaullas, the dashing "Lone Wolf" of earlier times, served DPS in Austin for five years, 1935–40. As chief of the Bureau of Intelligence, he combined his talents as criminal scientist and criminal investigator to erect an exceptional unit. With his mastery of ballistics, fingerprinting, moulage casting, handwriting, documents analysis, and microscopic examination of human hair, blood, shreds of fabric, and any other specimen that might offer evidence, he had developed a staff whose capabilities were the envy even of the FBI. At the same time, he supervised a small cadre of criminal investigators operating mainly as undercover detectives. In their first year alone, his men solved 140 of 142 cases, including 56 murders.[41]

A Comparison: Utley, Webb, and the Modern Historians

In presenting his findings in his two-volume history of the Ranger service, Robert Utley did not want to revise the classic work on that organization done by Walter Prescott Webb. He wanted to replace it. Utley did several things better than Webb: (1) Utley was able to use more primary and secondary materials than Webb had to work with in his generation; (2) Utley presented more factual information and analytical thoughts than Webb had put in his historical study; (3) Utley gave a more balanced view of Anglos, Indians, and Mexicans than the Anglo-centric beliefs stressed by Webb; (4) Utley covered the complexity of events in the twentieth century and the rise of the pop-culture Rangers that did not appear in the research and writing done by Webb. With his ability to cover the heroic Rangers and the dastardly Rangers in fact and fiction, Robert Utley deserves the title of the New Standard Bearer.

A number of modern historians have tried to write general histories of the Texas Rangers. They include Bob Alexander (with Donaly Brice), Mike Cox, Stephen Hardin, Charles Robinson III, Robert Utley, Walter Prescott Webb, and Frederick Wilkins. They all had extraordinary work habits. They all wrote in different formats, basically one or two volumes, with Wilkins putting his thoughts in four books. They all received accolades for their accomplishments. They all had strengths and weaknesses: as the best storytellers—Cox and Hardin; for the use of the vernacular language—Alexander and Brice; for stressing the Rangers in their horseback days—Robinson; for emphasizing the lives of field captains—Webb, who has been called the Dean of Ranger Historians; and for combining the scholarly approach with popular culture—Utley, who has been elevated to Dean Number Two.

Notes

1. Robert M. Utley, "Images of the Texas Rangers," chap. 24 in *The Way West: True Stories of the American Frontier*, ed. James A. Crutchfield (New York: Forge, 2005), 257.
2. *Roundup Magazine* (Western Writers of America), October 2022, 4.
3. Utley, *Custer and Me: A Historian's Memoir* (Norman: University of Oklahoma Press, 2004).
4. Utley, *Custer and Me*, 40.
5. Utley, *Custer and Me*, 55.
6. Utley, *Custer and Me*, 109.

7. Utley, *Custer and Me*, 62.
8. Utley, *Custer and Me*, 87.
9. Robert M. Utley, *Frontiersmen in Blue: The United States Army and the Indian, 1848–1865* (New York: Macmillan, 1967); Utley, *Frontier Regulars: The United States Army and the Indian, 1866–1891* (New York: Macmillan, 1973). See also Utley, *The Commanders: Civil War Generals Who Shaped the American West* (Norman: University of Oklahoma Press, 2018).
10. Robert M. Utley, *Cavalier in Buckskin: George Armstrong Custer and the Western Military Frontier* (Norman: University of Oklahoma Press, 1988).
11. Robert M. Utley, *The Indian Frontier of the American West, 1846–1890* (Albuquerque: University of New Mexico Press, 1984).
12. Robert M. Utley, *The Last Days of the Sioux Nation* (New Haven: Yale University Press, 1963).
13. Robert M. Utley, *Geronimo* (New Haven: Yale University Press, 2012); Utley, *The Lance and the Shield: The Life and Times of Sitting Bull* (New York: Henry Holt, 1993). See also Utley, *The Last Sovereigns: Sitting Bull and the Resistance of the Free Lakotas* (Lincoln: University of Nebraska Press, 2020).
14. Robert M. Utley, *Four Fighters of Lincoln County* (Albuquerque: University of New Mexico Press, 1986), vii.
15. Robert M. Utley, *High Noon in Lincoln: Violence on the Western Frontier* (Albuquerque: University of New Mexico Press, 1987); Utley, *Billy the Kid: A Short and Violent Life* (Lincoln: University of Nebraska Press, 1989). See also Utley, *Wanted: The Outlaw Lives of Billy the Kid and Ned Kelly* (New Haven: Yale University Press, 2015).
16. Utley, *Custer and Me*, 198.
17. Utley, *Custer and Me*, 229.
18. Robert M. Utley, *Lone Star Justice: The First Century of the Texas Rangers* (New York: Oxford University Press, 2002), x.
19. Robert M. Utley, *Lone Star Lawmen: The Second Century of the Texas Rangers* (New York: Oxford University Press, 2007), x.
20. James T. Bratcher, "The Texas Rangers: From Blood on Their Boots to Branch Davidian Onlookers," *Journal of the West* 46 (Summer 2007): 75.
21. Robert Utley to author, Dec. 2, 2019.
22. Utley, *Lone Star Lawmen*, 4–5.
23. Utley, "Images of the Texas Rangers," 260–61.

24. Utley, *Lone Star Justice*, 301.
25. Utley, *Lone Star Lawmen*, 265.
26. Utley, *Lone Star Justice*, chap. 1 (Colts), chap. 8 (Frontier Battalion); Utley, *Lone Star Lawmen*, chap. 10 (DPS). The chapter on Hays and the Colts, "The Texas Ranger Tradition Established: Jack Hays and Walker Creek," was reprinted in *Montana: The Magazine of Western History* 52, no. 1 (Spring 2002): 2–11.
27. Utley, *Lone Star Justice*, 137–42, quotation on 142.
28. Utley, *Lone Star Lawmen*, chap. 12 and pp. 331–41, with quotation on 331.
29. Utley, *Lone Star Justice*, 292–93.
30. Utley, "Images of the Texas Rangers," 257–63, with quotation on 263; Utley, *Lone Star Justice,* 289–95. See also Utley, "Tales of the Texas Rangers," *American Heritage* 53, no. 3 (June/July 2002): 40–47.
31. Mike Cox, *Texas Ranger Tales II* (Plano, TX: Republic of Texas Press, 1999), 230.
32. Utley, *Lone Star Justice*, 295–302, quotation on 298.
33. Utley, *Lone Star Justice*, 302.
34. Mitchel P. Roth, "Rangers in a Strange Land," *Austin-American Statesman,* April 13, 2008.
35. Utley, *Lone Star Justice*, 5.
36. Utley, *Lone Star Justice*, 256–57.
37. Utley, *Lone Star Justice*, 266–67.
38. Utley, *Lone Star Lawmen*, 93.
39. Utley, *Lone Star Lawmen*, 94.
40. Utley, *Lone Star Lawmen*, 126.
41. Utley, *Lone Star Lawmen*, 199–200.

Chapter 11

Louis R. Sadler and Charles H. Harris

Border Footprints

Timothy P. Bowman

W hat Texas history needs most is a return of "common sense"—
at least, according to historian Ty Cashion. In his recent
assessment of Texas historiography, *Lone Star Mind*, Cashion argues
that a state as diverse as twenty-first century Texas requires academic
and lay historians to bridge the gap between the former's emphasis on
innovative scholarship with the latter's desire for accessible narratives.
"The stereotypical shortcoming of scholarship," writes Cashion,
"begins with an unrealistic emphasis on social history at the expense
of such familiar topics as political, military, and economic history as
well as contextual matters that reinforce traditional ways and values."[1]
Historians who can bridge such a gap would then effectively bring
Texas history into the modern era, constructing a useful metanarrative
that will hopefully reflect the deep diversity of the Lone Star State.

One could argue that such a divide has certainly characterized
Texas Ranger historiography for nearly a century. For example,
historians such as James Sandos and Benjamin H. Johnson have
published studies of South Texas's 1915–1916 Plan de San Diego
revolt, leading the way in publicizing mob violence against Mexicans.

More recent efforts, such as William D. Carrigan and Clive Webb's *Forgotten Dead*, Monica Muñoz Martinez's *The Injustice Never Leaves You*, and the important public history advocacy work of the Refusing to Forget initiative, have only further advanced public knowledge of anti-Mexican violence in the South Texas borderlands, much of which Texas Rangers themselves perpetrated.[2] Such works have collectively provided a corrective to a traditional body of historical literature far less critical of the Rangers, a veritable cottage industry dating back to the 1935 publication of Walter Prescott Webb's classic study, *The Texas Rangers: A Century of Frontier Defense*.[3]

More recently, Charles Harris and Louis Sadler have sought to find an intellectual middle ground between what might be termed (if imperfectly) traditionalists and revisionists over the course of their extraordinarily productive more-than-forty-year careers. Harris and Sadler, both of whom spent their careers at New Mexico State University, are arguably the most all-time prolific chroniclers of Texas Ranger history. As this essay will demonstrate, Harris and Sadler—both highly credentialed, well-published academic historians—have increasingly sought to provide what they consider to be a middle ground between critical academic assessments of Texas's most famous law-enforcement body and the more apologetic, celebratory histories by lay historians. In so doing the two have never backed down from controversy, often lobbing intense intellectual barbs—with the occasional *ad hominem* attack—at their fellow academic historians. Harris and Sadler have continued their productive careers through to the present, with no signs of slowing down.

Harris and Sadler's earliest works during the 1970s and '80s were undoubtedly pathbreaking. Many historians had long been critical of histories of the Mexican Revolution prior to Alan Knight's 1986 magisterial two-volume history, *The Mexican Revolution*. Mexican historian Michael C. Meyer commented in 1988 that much of the previous work consisted of "tired generalizations that hide much more than they reveal." Meyer lauded Harris and Sadler's early works, though, claiming that they had shown "that the corpus of available primary documentation . . . is incredibly rich and must be carefully studied."[4] Harris and Sadler's earliest work effectively highlights the centrality of the US-Mexico border to the Mexican Revolution of the 1910s, pointing the way forward for scholars who would, in fact, write similar histories. Perhaps naturally, the Texas Rangers would be among the central actors in some of the ensuing published works. In the April 1980 edition of the *Southwestern Historical Quarterly*, which is the premier historical journal in Texas, the duo published "The 1911 Reyes Conspiracy: The Texas Side." The conspiracy's story itself had been told elsewhere. Bernardo Reyes was a general who had served as Minister of War under Porfirio Díaz, who was dictator of Mexico from 1876 to 1911. Díaz had been toppled from power by Francisco Madero in 1911. In response, Reyes set himself up in San Antonio, Texas, with plans to overthrow Madero. The authors rightly acknowledge that the Reyes conspiracy had been covered elsewhere, yet they also argue that it deserved new scrutiny due to recently declassified Federal Bureau of Investigation (FBI) documents that shed light on Reyes's activities in San Antonio.[5] Thus, "The 1911 Reyes Conspiracy" represented Harris and Sadler's dual-sided early career mission: recentering the Mexican Revolution on the border by focusing on underutilized or ignored primary sources.

Harris and Sadler's careers as Ranger historians thus date from this early period. Oscar Colquitt, Texas governor during the start of the Mexican Revolution, needed the defunct law-enforcement group to protect the border against the possibility of revolutionary violence spilling northward. The problem, as Harris and Sadler note, is that Colquitt ran his 1910 gubernatorial campaign on the promise of curtailing Ranger activity, due to the organization's sometimes violent reputation. In early 1911 Colquitt had reduced the force to a mere fourteen men, but he made quick appeal to President William Howard Taft to subsidize expanding the Ranger force in order to protect the border. The extraordinary nature of such an event aside—the federal government underwriting the costs associated with running a state police force—Harris and Sadler noted 1911 as a turning point in Ranger history, concluding that it "was the Mexican Revolution that gave the Texas Rangers a new lease on life." Nonetheless, though, the authors were not yet ready to tackle the Rangers head-on at this early point in their careers. Part of this is because the organization's role in the Reyes conspiracy proved to be relatively minor. Colquitt remained concerned with the border, detaching the Rangers to Laredo, but federal officials really proved the true force in stopping the Reyes faction. Little could Harris and Sadler have known at this point how the arch of their careers would eventually lead them to becoming arguably the most widely read and punctilious historians of the Texas Rangers.[6]

It makes sense that the Rangers would remain only a passing concern in Harris and Sadler's earliest writings, given their collective emphasis on recentering the Mexican Revolution along the border as well as uncovering underutilized primary materials. Some of this may have been reflective of the Rangers' tangential roles to their earlier focus. In a 1982 article published in *The Americas* titled "The 'Underside' of the Mexican Revolution: El Paso, 1912," Harris and Sadler note that the Ranger force fell to its pre-Reyes conspiracy size by January of 1912 due to the general perspective in Texas that the border appeared relatively pacified.[7] Almost surprisingly, the Rangers make no appearance in an earlier 1978 article published in the *Hispanic-American Historical Review* on the Plan de San Diego, an irredentist uprising in South Texas during the Great War; many historians, including later Harris and Sadler, would later grapple with the violently controversial roles that the Rangers played.[8]

Harris and Sadler produced a slew of other studies during this early period on other subjects primarily by utilizing newly available primary sources, such as studies on Pancho Villa's famous 1916 raid on Columbus, New Mexico, and even a short 1986 article on US government archives and the Mexican Revolution more broadly.[9] The duo thus proved themselves adept at archival sleuthing. Although these perspectives on uncovering newly available documents would remain important to Harris and Sadler over the course of their careers, the Texas Rangers still waited on their collective intellectual horizons.

The two would go on from these humble beginnings to have storied careers as historians. Notably, their monographic output after this series of early articles would contain books on subjects *other* than the Texas Rangers. Of these works two stand out. In 2003 they published *The Archaeologist Was a Spy: Sylvanus G. Morley and the Office of Naval Intelligence* with the University of New Mexico Press. Morley, a noted archaeologist, covertly gathered intelligence for the US Navy about German activity along the Central American and Mexican coastlines during the Great War. Twelve years later, in 2015, Harris and Sadler released *The Great Call-Up: The Guard, the Border, and the Mexican Revolution* with the University of Oklahoma Press. *The Great Call-Up* is an exhaustive study of the National Guard's mobilization along the US-Mexico border during the Mexican Revolution that relates more clearly to their earlier article-based work than *The Archaeologist Was a Spy*. Both of these works enjoyed widespread academic and popular appeal.[10]

Harris and Sadler's monographic output on the Rangers began appearing in the early twenty-first century. In 2004 the authors published what would undoubtedly prove to be their most influential study: *The Texas Rangers and the Mexican Revolution: The Bloodiest Decade, 1910–1920*. With the publication of this book, Harris and Sadler set their uncompromising agenda of becoming the most ambitious Texas Ranger historians of all time. The careful depth of their archival research first became introduced to the literary public; in fact their historical agenda would be split over multiple volumes on the Rangers that often stretch to significant page lengths. As such, Harris and Sadler's Ranger writings would prove a bit nontraditional in the academic sense. None of this is to say, however, that Harris and Sadler's individual works eschew the more traditional approach of making a direct argument, encapsulated by a thesis statement that is then proven over the course of a book-length study; rather, Harris and Sadler set as their approach striking a balance between heroic portrayals of the Rangers with those historians more critical of the force, the latter largely populated by Mexican American and borderlands historians. The authors address this positioning in the book's introduction: "But viewing everything strictly within a racial context is a bit simplistic, ignoring the socioeconomic and political differences within the Hispanic population. Chicanos' accounts of the Rangers tend to be as stereotyped as anything one can find among Anglo writers, which is surprising among those who themselves are so sensitive to stereotyping. Chicano writers are also prone to portray Chicanos in the same overly heroic light that they decry in [Walter Prescott] Webb's treatment of the Rangers."[11] Juxtaposing Mexican American and borderlands histories against Webb's 1935 classic, *The Texas Rangers*, Harris and Sadler suggest a middle ground that is, in their view, necessary in order to move the organization's history forward. Much of the rest of their work spoke to this perceived tension; it would also, however, provide a source of criticism controversy.[12]

Harris and Sadler thus set out in *The Texas Rangers and the Mexican Revolution* "neither to justify nor to condemn but rather to paint as accurately as possible a portrait of the Rangers, warts and all."[13] This is a laudable historiographical goal, indeed, if sometimes resulting in more deeply descriptive analysis as opposed to having an argument-driven focus. Of course the authors never dispel the organization's violent history, which dates back to the tumultuous years of the Texas Republic and the US invasion of Mexico in 1846. A number of "Ranger" forces, oftentimes violent ones, dotted Texas history throughout the remainder of the nineteenth century, until a state law reconstituted the Rangers in 1901 to protect the frontier— or the Texas-Mexico borderlands—against supposed lawlessness. These early twentieth-century Rangers were usually poorly supplied and funded. What becomes clear in the book's earliest pages is two primary elements: Harris and Sadler's attention to detail is second to none, and their writing style is clear and engaging:

[The Texas Adjutant General] proposed on August 31, 1910, that the Ranger appropriation for the 1910–1911 fiscal year be doubled—to $50,000 a year. In justifying this mind-boggling increase, he stated that at present the Ranger Force consisted of four captains, four sergeants, and eighteen privates, but it should be increased to at least fifty officers and men. Requests for the Rangers' services were so numerous that they could be granted in only the most serious or urgent cases. There was enough work to keep 100 or more Rangers busy. During the previous two years the organization had made 1,017 arrests, 458 of them for felonies, the remainder for misdemeanors. The Rangers had traveled a total of 277,871 miles and had recovered thousands of dollars of stolen property.[14]

Harris and Sadler thus paint a large picture of Ranger activities during the early 1910s, including evidence about individual men who served in the force.

Nonetheless, Harris and Sadler display a penchant for controversial stances even early in *The Texas Rangers and the Mexican Revolution*. In 1910 in the town of Rocksprings, a mob—which the authors note "was reportedly composed of Anglos and Hispanics"—lynched a man named Antonio Rodríguez. The authors note that Rodríguez "had raped and shot to death in front of her children the wife of a rancher in Edwards County because she 'spoke roughly' to him," and that after his apprehension the next day "he readily admitted his guilt." Harris and Sadler go on to note that the state sent in the Rangers to "assist the sheriff in protecting the town from Mexicans," and that the incident exacerbated ethnic tensions in Texas while also becoming a cause for concern for the Mexican government.[15] Because of their concern with striking a balance between those critical of the Rangers with historians who celebrate them (not to mention their mission of providing a sweeping overview of the institution itself during the Mexican Revolutionary era), Harris and Sadler fail to consider certain larger questions about the incident that later historians would make their primary focuses. For one, was Rodríguez even truly guilty? Historian Nicholas Villanueva Jr. would certainly cast doubt on such an assumption, not to mention pointing out that the Rodríguez lynching would do a lot more than simply "exacerbate[e] ethnic tensions" as Harris and Sadler characterize; namely, it touched off mob violence against ethnic Mexicans across the borderlands. Secondly, such violence, as historian Monica Muñoz Martinez argues, would serve to fracture Texas communities and become a point of contention for people who lived with the memory of this troubling era of anti-Mexican violence for over a century into modern times.[16] Despite, then, their laudable goal of providing a centrist take on Ranger histories, Harris and Sadler would still by implication draw accusations from later Mexican American historians that their historical positioning did not take into account the bottom-up perspectives of ethnic Mexicans in the borderlands who found themselves the victims of brutal violence.

Harris and Sadler do little in the book's early pages to dispel any concerns that readers have about their hoped-for centrism. A. Y. Baker, a deeply controversial and problematic figure in early twentieth-century Texas-Mexico borderlands history, is introduced as "a man not to be messed with." In May of 1902, Baker, along with another group of Rangers, happened upon a man named Ramón de la Cerda in a subsection of the King Ranch, where he was in the process of branding a stolen calf. The authors report that Cerda and Baker fired at each other simultaneously; the former shot the Ranger's horse in the head, while Baker shot Cerda himself in the head. Cerda's brother, Alfredo, proceeded to issue threats against Baker in and around the border town of Brownsville. Harris and Sadler write that "Alfredo Cerda was evidently naïve enough to think that Baker would simply sit around waiting to be dispatched. Imagine his surprise when Baker killed him."[17]

The authors' writing style, while clearly merely an attempt to convey a dramatic narrative with appealing, action-packed prose, runs the risk of contributing to the outsized "one Ranger, one riot," larger-than-life mythos. This, however, was not the authors' intention. Harris and Sadler note coverage of the incident in Julian Samora, Joe Bernal, and Albert Peña's 1979 study, *Gunpowder Justice: A Reassessment of the Texas Rangers*, which in their view omits Ramón de la Cerda's name in an alleged effort to make Baker seem more like a ruthless killer. On the other hand, both Walter Prescott Webb in his aforementioned classic study and William Warren Sterling in his 1959 book, *Trails and Trials of a Texas Ranger*, say little about Baker's killing of Alfredo de la Cerda, "presumably because it doesn't fit the noble Ranger image."[18] Harris and Sadler's writing about the Cerda killings thus deserves to be read carefully. Any reader lacking a critical or discerning eye might read this passage with the presumption that Harris and Sadler fall more into the traditional category of Texas Ranger historians.

These concerns aside, *The Texas Rangers and the Mexican Revolution* proceeds like a densely packed novel. Efforts at border monitoring, frustrations at their inability to chase bandits across the Rio Grande, even their international stardom—the adjutant general in charge of the Rangers began receiving inquiries on the organization's training efforts from Chinese officials, who sought to create a "Mongolian ranger" force to protect the Chinese republic against bandits from inner Asia—are retold with exhaustive detail. Moreover, Harris and Sadler's work is important because the larger context of Texas history is often amplified to great degrees.[19] For example, the ascent of James "Pa" Ferguson to the governor's mansion in 1915 ushered in a new downturn in Ranger history. Some Rangers were fired, while others quit the force in disgust due to widespread knowledge of the governor's corruption (Ferguson would, in fact, find himself impeached and kicked out of office in 1917).

Worthy of brief note here is the Plan de San Diego revolt, which Harris and Sadler explore in chapter 8. The revolt rested upon a document that outlined an irredentist uprising among South Texas Mexicans that was to begin at 2:00 a.m. on February 20, 1915. Essentially, the plan involved breaking the Southwest off from the United States through military force, killing all males over the age of 16, and establishing independence for Mexican Americans, Apaches, and African Americans. Harris and Sadler take aim at historian Benjamin Heber Johnson, whose 2003 study, *Revolution in Texas*, they argue, "portrays the rebels in a heroic light [in an attempt] to explain the genocidal clause in the Plan de San Diego." They continue their accusations against Johnson, stating that "since genocide is politically incorrect, if the rebels were running around advocating genocide it would tarnish their heroic image."[20] Such attacks on other historians continue throughout their discussion of what the authors refer to as "the Bandit War," or the resulting conflict between Euro-Americans and ethnic Mexicans that emerged from the Plan de San Diego rebellion. Chapter 9 opens with the statement that "the principle targets of the Plan de San Diego's announced war without quarter—Anglo males over sixteen—were too obtuse to realize their deaths would be both legitimate and necessary, [and] as Rodolfo Acuña would have us believe, they obstinately refused to be massacred."[21] This passage references Acuña's classic study *Occupied America: A History of Chicanos*, which launched Mexican American history to academic prominence at the height of the Chicano Movement. Acuña's study no doubt came from a perspective that prized a bottom-up view of the past; nonetheless, its standing as more of an academic relic by the early twenty-first century seems an odd point of attack for Harris and Sadler, whose study appeared over three decades later in 2003.[22] Such preoccupation with launching attacks at other historians serves as an unfortunate distraction in an otherwise beautifully written and carefully researched study. Decisions to attack other historians aligned with the social-history outlooks of the Chicano era oftentimes detract from Harris and Sadler's mission at striking a more moderate tone on Texas Ranger history.

Still, Harris and Sadler make important other claims regarding ongoing controversies surrounding Ranger history, perhaps none more so regarding the Special Rangers—volunteers who joined the force—during the Plan de San Diego revolt. The authors note that some "writers have tended to broad-brush the killings of Hispanics during the Bandit War by blaming everything on the Rangers," citing Paul J. Vanderwood and Frank N. Sompanaro's 1988 volume, *Border Fury*. Harris and Sadler proceed to note that there were few regular Rangers in the area, and that some of the Special Rangers who partic-ipated in murders and lynchings of ethnic Mexicans no doubt did so as members of vigilante groups like the Law and Order League, along with other municipal and county officers who also participated in the killings. Critics of this position would no doubt consider this a moot point regarding the overall character of the Rangers along the border during the 1910s; nonetheless, such argumentation does speak back to the authors' larger point that as an institution the Rangers deserve a more critical appraisal as opposed to a sweeping dismissal.[23]

The rest of *The Texas Rangers and the Mexican Revolution* covers the turbulent 1910s with a level of detail unforeseen in previous studies. The book concludes with the famous 1919 legislative inquiries into the force led by representative J. T. Canales of Brownsville, which many historians credit for drastically reducing the size and the scope of the force as the 1920s dawned. Harris and Sadler take a somewhat more measured approach, arguing that "their numbers were reduced because World War I was over (the US Army was drastically reduced in 1919 for exactly the same reason)."[24] Readers could clearly take for granted that a sequel volume, covering the Rangers during the 1920s, was forthcoming. For now, though, Harris and Sadler had established themselves as authoritative and bold—if not sometimes controversial—voices on Texas Ranger history.

Any widespread survey of the Rangers after 1920 would have to wait for a few years after the publication of *The Texas Rangers and the Mexican Revolution*. Nonetheless, Harris and Sadler stayed extraordinarily productive in the intervening years. Although the Rangers wouldn't always be in the starring role—Harris and Sadler, are, to be fair, Southwestern historians who focus broadly on military and diplomatic history—Texas's most famous law-enforcement group would always at least be looming in the shadows.

Certain thematic elements stemming from Harris and Sadler's dogged dedication to archival work run throughout the rest of their books. Six years after the publication of *The Texas Rangers and the Mexican Revolution*, they published *The Secret War in El Paso*. The duo make a point implicit in their first book: the Mexican Revolution wouldn't have succeeded without the US-Mexico border's influence. Moreover, newly accessible FBI records provided for an almost "day-to-day picture of Revolutionary intrigue in places such as New York City, Washington, D.C., New Orleans, San Antonio, El Paso, and Los Angeles, among others." El Paso is of critical importance, though, because it was "the base of operations for constant intrigue involving US and Mexican authorities, Mexican Revolutionists, and others."[25] As such, this populous border hub, to the authors, serves as a case study for an examination of Mexican Revolutionary intrigue if done on other parts of the border.

Perhaps particularly because Harris and Sadler rely heavily on FBI documents, *The Secret War in El Paso* thus focuses little on the Rangers. Most of their appearances in the book can be described as anecdotal. For example, the authors note that a Ranger detail including John Hughes and John H. Rogers—"two of the great Ranger captains of that era"—worked with a federal security force to ensure the safety of President William Howard Taft when he met with Mexican dictator Porfirio Díaz in El Paso on October 16, 1909.[26] Later that year, Hughes worked on a tip from federal agents to crush a local *reyista* cell that was making homemade hand grenades; his posse of officials included Rangers, a US marshal, and two other federal officials who made fourteen arrests. Around this same time, the Rangers also played a role in crushing a local group devoted to the Partido Liberal Mexicano, an anti-Díaz group founded by the anarcho-syndicalist brothers Enrique and Ricardo Flores-Magón, who were in exile in the United States.[27]

Given *The Secret War in El Paso*'s general scope, it comes as little surprise that the Rangers only play supporting roles in the narrative. This, arguably, lends itself to a more complete picture in the city's goings-on during the revolutionary period. Nonetheless, Harris and Sadler weren't done with the Rangers—even in the Mexican revolutionary period. The same year that the duo published *The Secret War in El Paso*, they also published something of a companion volume, entitled *Texas Ranger Biographies: Those who Served, 1910–1921*. Harris and Sadler's stunning attention to detail is fully on display in this volume, which contains the biographical information of all 1,782 men who served in the organization along the Texas-Mexico border during those deeply troublesome years. *Texas Ranger Biographies* thus stands as a compendium for any researchers interested in basic details on the enforcement body during this period.

The book, though, isn't without its own perspective. Harris and Sadler's evolving views on the Rangers can be read both in the book's foreword and in its preface. Then director of the Texas Ranger Hall of Fame and Museum in Waco, Texas, Byron A. Johnson, authored the foreword. Although Harris and Sadler still sought to carve out the historiographical middle ground as laid out six years previously in their first book, Johnson's perspective is much more sympathetic with the Rangers. Johnson notes that until recently, many historians had believed that the Ranger force was restricted to southerners of Anglo-Saxon descent; Harris and Sadler's work, however, has shown that "in reality, issues of mutual defense, survival and political expediency often made allies and countrymen of racially and culturally disparate groups—at least in the short term." Johnson goes on to rightly note that ethnic Mexicans have served as Rangers since the 1820s. He next informs readers that "claims that Texas Rangers were 'blood enemies' of all Native Americans are equally dispelled by the historical record," seemingly implying by inference that the existence of Spanish-surnamed individuals in the organization's ranks might somehow dispel arguments by other historians that Rangers engaged in widespread acts of racial oppression or even, as noted earlier, ethnic cleansing.[28] One could forgive readers if such positioning in the book's foreword lent the impression that Harris and Sadler were dismissive of claims that Rangers engaged in brutal activities.

Harris and Sadler's own views are more nuanced and sophisticated. They also clearly lay out the authors' ongoing research agenda. One signpost for future work is included in the authors' discussion of the Plan de San Diego uprising of 1915, which, as shown, appeared in their earliest article work as well as in *The Texas Rangers and the Mexican Revolution*. Harris and Sadler note here that "the Rangers' role in these events is the most controversial episode in the organization's history," nodding to other historians' critiques of the Rangers as having committed atrocities and acts of ethnic cleansing in the revolt's reprisal killings. Harris and Sadler argue that the plan was, in fact, a secret ploy by the regime of Mexican president Venustiano Carranza, whom, they claim, called off the plan after receiving diplomatic recognition from the United States in 1915. Carranza then allegedly revived the plan the following year to force the US government to withdraw federal troops that had entered Mexico in pursuit of Pancho Villa after his famous raid on Columbus, New Mexico.[29] Harris and Sadler in fact went on to author an entire book on this subject in 2013, entitled *The Plan de San Diego*, in which they utilize Mexican sources to argue that Carranza was behind the plan all along. In making this argument, the authors attack numerous other historians, perhaps most notably Benjamin H. Johnson, who highlight that South Texas Mexicans had arguably good reason to support actions such as the plan due to decades of repression at the hands of Anglo-Americans in the borderlands (the authors go as far as accusing Johnson of perpetuating "politically correct" narratives, echoing unfair personal accusations against him noted earlier in this essay).[30] Harris and Sadler's aforementioned attempts at carving out the historiographical middle ground seemed to bring them more into conflict with social historians as opposed to Ranger apologists. *The Plan de San Diego* thus stands as a bold, combative, and strange side note to their voluminously productive careers.

One important contribution that Harris and Sadler make in *Texas Ranger Biographies* that is not present in any of their other writings is answering the question of what or who constituted a Texas Ranger. Perhaps not surprisingly, the authors' approach remains explicitly empirical. Captain Leander McNelly, for example, who led a notoriously violent group of "rangers" along the Rio Grande in 1877 that the legislature termed "special state troops," was not really a Ranger at all, because his group was not a part of the Frontier Defense Battalion, which Harris and Sadler provide as the Ranger force's official name from 1874–1901. Nonetheless, Walter Prescott

Webb, arguably the most widely read Texas Ranger historian of all time, argued that "because McNelly considered himself a Ranger, acted like a Ranger, and people thought of him as a Ranger, he was a 'real Ranger.'" Likewise, important among Ranger lore is Frank Hamer, who famously played a central role in the ambush that killed the outlaws Bonnie and Clyde in 1934. Hamer, however, was a *former* Ranger by this time, who in 1934 instead found employment in the Texas prison system. Clearly, then, although Harris and Sadler cast doubt at this point that the Rangers committed acts of mass murder against ethnic Mexicans during the 1910s, to their credit they also refrain from including more celebrated characters like Hamer who would otherwise cast the Rangers in a more heroic light.[31] Their original intellectual mission of carving out a historiographical middle ground was still very much in play.

Perhaps Harris and Sadler's strongest point in *Texas Ranger Biographies* is their statement against blanket criticisms of the entire organization for the crimes of the few. Noting "a pronounced tendency by historians of the Texas Rangers to focus on a literal handful of men who acquired formidable reputations—usually exaggerated—while ignoring the ninety-nine percent of Rangers who served in virtual anonymity as members of what is arguably the most famous law enforcement organization in the world," the authors imply (without naming any specific historians this time) that those who focus on extralegal killings or lynchings depict the Rangers as a body uniformly meant to terrorize Mexicans and Indians during the late nineteenth and early twentieth centuries.[32] Undoubtedly, this is fair: as *Texas Ranger Biographies* shows, nearly two thousand men served in the force, the majority of whom did so honorably and without any engagement in controversy. Nonetheless, perhaps one could argue the problematic decade of the Mexican Revolution deserves to be understood in its own right apart from the Rangers' longer history. Questions about how historians characterize the Rangers as a whole are clearly subjective.

One of Harris and Sadler's singularly most important achievements is 2019's *The Texas Rangers in Transition: From Gunfighters to Criminal Investigators, 1921–1935.* Not only is the prolific duo's keen-eyed sense of detail once again present, but this most recent book also offers a broader interpretive element: in particular, *The Texas Rangers in Transition* shows how the gunfighters of the Old West gave way to a modern crime-fighting force. The book itself serves as a sequel to the volume on the revolutionary years. Also, *The Texas Rangers in Transition* marks a refreshing turn in Ranger historiography. Texas from 1921 to 1935 was still a violent place, "awash in booze and oil," note the authors. Indeed, examining the 1920s and '30s certainly gives fresh perspectives on classic elements in Texas history—namely, the prohibition years and the lesser-studied chaos of oil boomtowns. Also, the period under study has received relative neglect by Ranger historians in particular; the reasons for this are unexplored in the text, but one can perhaps assume that the Rangers are more associated with Old West among a lay audience and, clearly with the border and the Mexican Revolution, among a scholarly one. Nonetheless, *The Texas Rangers in Transition*, in Harris and Sadler's words, traces a transformative chapter in the organization's history "mirroring Texas's transition from an essentially rural to a rapidly urbanizing state."[33] Fewer frameworks for broad studies of Texas history during this time period could prove any more instructive.

Harris and Sadler address the issue of Anglo racism more directly in *The Texas Rangers in Transition* than in their previous books. "Virtually all the white men we deal with in the following pages," they write in the book's introduction, "were racists." Frank Hamer, they note, was typical for his time—a white supremacist who believed that ethnic Mexicans were just above African Americans in the supposed racial hierarchy. Texas, many of the Rangers examined in this volume would have believed, was a member of the "Solid South"; the state was also filled with "Yellow Dog" Democrats, who would sooner vote for a yellow dog than a Republican, due largely to the Republican Party's legacy stemming from the Civil War.[34]

Alongside a more detailed accounting for the culture of white supremacy, *The Texas Rangers in Transition* reconstructs the nuances of violence in the modern period. Booming oil production throughout the state, combined with the illicit production and sale of alcohol after the Volstead Act, meant that the scope for law enforcement would have to spread northward from the Texas-Mexico borderlands. Some of that liquor would flow north across the border from Mexico, though, meaning that the agency could not afford to entirely lose sight of the US-Mexico border, despite improved US-Mexico diplomatic relations. Oil boomtowns, however, dotted the state, from South Texas hundreds of miles north to the Texas Panhandle. The "rough-and-tumble" nature of such settlements meant that the Rangers faced a much wider scope of activities.[35] How Texas governors utilized the Rangers against Mexicans during the Revolution (ultimately the first book's focus) is obviously important. Harris and Sadler's shifting focus in this book, however, shows how the Ranger force became a modern bureaucracy, "one in which administration and logistics were of critical importance," due to the wider scope of the state's law-enforcement activities.[36]

Although *The Texas Rangers in Transition* offers a nuanced departure from *The Texas Rangers and the Mexican Revolution*, Harris and Sadler still don't back down from positions that might be deemed controversial in their quest to provide a centrist perspective on Ranger history. For example, as already mentioned earlier, Representative J. T. Canales from Brownsville led an investigation into Ranger violence against Mexicans in 1919. Characterizing Canales as likely a "mouthpiece for [Jim] Wells"—a corrupt political boss from South Texas—Harris and Sadler portray Canales's investigations of the Rangers as unreasonable attempts to "cripple the organization by slashing its numbers," and unfairly "including a demand that Adjutant General James A. Harley be fired." Nonetheless, though, Canales "did perform a valuable service by publicizing the dark side of the Ranger force—racism, brutality, abuse of authority, drunkenness, summary executions, and political favoritism." Such passages are worded much more carefully than similar ones in their previous books. Relatedly, Harris and Sadler concede that the clear downturn in Spanish-surnamed individuals joining the force during the 1921–1935 period is surely explained by the brutality of the 1910s.[37]

The Texas Rangers in Transition offers a number of fascinating glimpses into the state's uneasy lurch toward modernity. Concerning oil boomtowns, Rangers often sent in undercover agents to gather intelligence regarding potential illegal activities before raids. None of this is to say, though, that Harris and Sadler lose sight of their flare for the Old West–style justice. For instance, the authors chronicle J. W. McCormick's shooting of "Bad Bud" Ballew in Wichita Falls on May 5, 1922. Ballew had arrived in the city "bent on mayhem," but "McCormick confronted him and, in an echo of the Wild West, beat him to the draw."[38] Even still, other elements placed the Rangers straight into the modern era. The same year as Ballew's killing, the Rangers faced the enormous challenge of a statewide railroad workers strike, which, aside from being an episode that seems emblematic of the Gilded Age or Progressive Era, placed manpower and financial burdens on the organization. Also, the Rangers worked to stave off some lynchings of African Americans during the early part of the period, but the fact of there being only one lynching in Texas during the year of 1924 might indicate that the state was finally leaving the past—along with its frontier-style justice and racial terror against African Americans and ethnic Mexicans—behind.[39]

Harris and Sadler certainly strike a tone in the book that appeals to both lay and academic audiences. Both, obviously, find much to engage in: The Ku Klux Klan were widely popular among Anglos in the state (as elsewhere in the country), much to the chagrin of law enforcement. Miriam "Ma" Ferguson's election to the governorship twice during this period of Ranger history (in 1925 and 1933) represented a major step forward for Texas women, despite controversy surrounding her tenure (stemming largely from her husband, ex-governor James "Pa" Ferguson, who as noted earlier was ousted from the office in 1917). Also, Ma Ferguson's relationship with the Rangers was often tenuous at best. Finally, as mentioned before, oil boomtowns, such as Borger, in the Texas Panhandle, brought in crime and intrigue that hearkened back to the Old West, though this time stemming from modern discoveries in the oil industry.

The Texas Rangers in Transition caps off what has been an extraordinarily productive career for Harris and Sadler. Clearly, the duo are nowhere near close to being finished; the middle and late twentieth centuries in Ranger history almost beg for their careful eye for detail. Not only are the two a collective anomaly in the sense of their prodigious output, but Harris and Sadler also stand unabashedly apart from lay historians and other academic historians in charting a path forward that they feel is honest as well as correct, despite any criticism of their work from fellow historians (and despite the occasional unfortunate and unnecessary attacks against other historians). Harris and Sadler clearly stand apart from the rest of the pack—but, as they might hope and suggest, somewhere in between.

Notes

1. Ty Cashion, *Lone Star Mind: Reimagining Texas History* (Norman: University of Oklahoma Press, 2018), 161.
2. See, for example, James A. Sandos, *Rebellion in the Borderlands: Anarchism and the Plan of San Diego, 1904–1923* (Norman: University of Oklahoma Press, 1992); Benjamin Heber Johnson, *Revolution in Texas: How a Forgotten Rebellion and Its Bloody Suppression Turned Mexicans into Americans* (New Haven: Yale University Press, 2003); William D. Carrigan and Clive Webb, *Forgotten Dead: Mob Violence against Mexicans in the United States, 1848–1928* (Oxford: Oxford University Press, 2003); Monica Muñoz Martinez, *The Injustice Never Leaves You: Anti-Mexican Violence in Texas* (Cambridge, MA: Harvard University Press, 2013); and, "Refusing to Forget," accessed October 31, 2019, https://refusingtoforget.org.
3. Walter Prescott Webb, *The Texas Rangers: A Century of Frontier Defense*, 2nd ed. (Austin: University of Texas Press, 1965). Several decades later, however, Webb noted that his Anglocentric book failed to account for acts of violence committed by Rangers against Mexicans. For more see Martinez, *Injustice Never Leaves You*, 246.
4. Michael C. Meyer, "Introduction," in *The Border and the Revolution: Clandestine Activities of the Mexican Revolution, 1910–1920,*

by Charles H. Harris III and Louis R. Sadler (Silver City: High Lonesome Books, 1988), 3.

5. Harris and Sadler, *Border and the Revolution*, 29.

6. Harris and Sadler, *Border and the Revolution*, 31, 35–52. Quotation on page 31.

7. See Harris and Sadler, "The 'Underside' of the Mexican Revolution: El Paso, 1912," chap. 3 in *Border and the Revolution*, fn10.

8. Charles H. Harris III and Louis R. Sadler, "The Plan of San Diego and the Mexican-United States Crisis of 1916: A Reexamination," *Hispanic-American Historical Review* 58, no. 3 (August 1978): 381–408.

9. See, for example, Charles H. Harris III and Louis R. Sadler, "Pancho Villa and the Columbus Raid: The Missing Documents," *New Mexico Historical Review* 50, no. 4 (Oct. 1975): 335–46; and Harris and Sadler, "United States Government Archives and the Mexican Revolution," *New World: A Journal of Latin American Studies* 1 (1986): 108–16.

10. Charles H. Harris III and Louis R. Sadler, *The Archeologist Was a Spy: Sylvanus G. Morley and the Office of Naval Intelligence* (Albuquerque: University of New Mexico Press, 2009); Harris and Sadler, *The Great Call-Up: The Guard, the Border, and the Mexican Revolution* (Norman: University of Oklahoma Press, 2015).

11. Charles H. Harris III and Louis R. Sadler, *The Texas Rangers and the Mexican Revolution: The Bloodiest Decade, 1910–1920* (Albuquerque: University of New Mexico Press, 2004), 5.

12. For more on Webb's career, see Michael L. Collins, "Walter Prescott Webb," in *Writing the Story of Texas*, ed. Patrick L. Cox and Kenneth E. Hendrickson Jr. (Austin: University of Texas Press, 2013), 43–66.

13. Harris and Sadler, *Texas Rangers and the Mexican Revolution*, 8.

14. Harris and Sadler, *Texas Rangers and the Mexican Revolution*, 46.

15. All quotations in Harris and Sadler, *Texas Rangers and the Mexican Revolution*, 51.

16. See, for example, Nicholas Villanueva Jr., *The Lynchings of Mexicans in the Texas Borderlands* (Albuquerque: University of New Mexico Press, 2017), 53–78; and Martinez, *Injustice Never Leaves You,* 30–35.

17. Harris and Sadler, *Texas Rangers and the Mexican Revolution*, 57.

18. Harris and Sadler, *Texas Rangers and the Mexican Revolution*, 58.

19. Harris and Sadler, *Texas Rangers and the Mexican Revolution*, 120.

20. Harris and Sadler, *Texas Rangers and the Mexican Revolution*, 210–21.

21. Harris and Sadler, *Texas Rangers and the Mexican Revolution*, 248.

22. For example, see, Rodolfo F. Acuña, *Occupied America: A History of Chicanos*, 8th ed. (London: Pearson, 2014).

23. Harris and Sadler, *Texas Rangers and the Mexican Revolution*, 289–90, 612n68.

24. Harris and Sadler, *Texas Rangers and the Mexican Revolution*, 460.

25. Charles H. Harris III and Louis R. Sadler, *The Secret War in El Paso: Mexican Revolutionary Intrigue, 1906–1920* (Albuquerque: University of New Mexico Press, 2009), x.

26. Harris and Sadler, *Secret War in El Paso*, 15.

27. Harris and Sadler, *Secret War in El Paso*, 66.

28. Charles H. Harris III, Frances E. Harris, and Louis Sadler, *Texas Ranger Biographies: Those Who Served, 1910–1921* (Albuquerque: University New Mexico Press, 2009), viii.

29. Harris, Harris, and Sadler, *Texas Ranger Biographies*, xii.

30. Charles H. Harris III and Louis R. Sadler, *The Plan de San Diego: Tejano Rebellion, Mexican Intrigue* (Lincoln: University of Nebraska Press, 2013).

31. Harris, Harris, and Sadler, *Texas Ranger Biographies*, xiii.

32. Harris, Harris, and Sadler, *Texas Ranger Biographies*, xv–xvi.

33. Charles H. Harris III and Louis Sadler, *The Texas Rangers in Transition: From Gunfighters to Criminal Investigators, 1921–1935* (Norman: University of Oklahoma Press, 2019), 3.

34. Harris and Sadler, *Texas Rangers in Transition*, 3–4.

35. Harris and Sadler, *Texas Rangers in Transition*, 4–5, 5–6.

36. Harris and Sadler, *Texas Rangers in Transition*, 7.

37. Harris and Sadler, *Texas Rangers in Transition*, 9–10, 30–31, 41–62. Quotations on pages 9–10.

38. Harris and Sadler, *Texas Rangers in Transition*, 63–82. Quotation on page 82.

39. Harris and Sadler, *Texas Rangers in Transition*, 83, 152–61.

Dual Format
Traditionalists/Revisionists

Chapter 12

Frederick Wilkins

Early Practitioner

Leland K. Turner

F rederick Wilkins made a definitive and significant contribution to
Texas Ranger history. However, he was not trained in the practice
of professional history. He was a citizen historian with a particular
interest in the nineteenth-century history of the Texas Rangers.
He was, in fact, a career army officer who after his retirement published
four books that, not surprisingly, were essentially military history.
The books addressed Ranger history from 1823 to 1901—a time when
the Rangers resembled militia organizations or paramilitary forces
rather than the police and detective organization the Rangers became
in the twentieth century. His stated purpose was to record, rather
than interpret or revise, Ranger history. Wilkins believed that Ranger
history had too often been a subject of mythology and by the 1990s a
subject of revisionist, and not necessarily positive, interpretations.[1]

It is not surprising that Wilkins took an interest in Texas history
and the history of the Texas Rangers during what can be considered the
paramilitary years. He was born Frederick John Wilkins Jr. in Dallas,
Texas, on October 2, 1916. The young Wilkins attended North Dallas
High School and was enrolled at Southern Methodist University

in 1935. Certain high school and college extracurricular activities suggested Wilkins held interests in military and martial pursuits. In high school he earned a position as a ROTC second lieutenant. At SMU Wilkins joined the fencing club and received nominations for athletic honors.[2] Wilkins soon joined the United States Army. After his service in World War II, Wilkins married in January of 1945 a Miss Frances Lutcher Semaan. The couple enjoyed a remarkably varied social life, particularly in San Antonio. His obituary makes no mention of surviving or predeceased children, so apparently the couple were childless.[3] He retired from the US Army as a lieutenant colonel who spent his career in information services. And apparently he was good at his craft. He won in 1962 an Army Special Act award for writing and producing two television programs that examined the history and traditions of the US Army.[4] When he retired in the 1980s, Wilkins was already an accomplished researcher, writer, and producer. He led a diverse life with various interests beyond his efforts to chronicle the history of the Texas Rangers. Though he was not a professionally trained historian, his research in primary and secondary sources is professional and exhaustive. Wilkins was not simply a retired military officer pursuing his interest in the Rangers as a military force. He and his wife were routinely involved in community affairs. The couple collected Middle Eastern art and were invited to discuss the Romance and Beauty of Oriental Rugs for a local San Antonio audience in 1975.[5] He maintained interests in gardening and was a member and officer of the Magnolia Green Garden Club in San Antonio.[6] Moreover, as a public information specialist for the Fourth Army he was, during his military days, known as the "village historian" for Fort Sam Houston in San Antonio, Texas.[7] Wilkins's interest in history was apparent, abiding, and not just a hobby in his retirement years.

His four-book series stands as a chronology of nineteenth-century Texas Ranger history. He did not, however, write the books in chronological order. His first book, *The Highly Irregular Irregulars: Texas Rangers in the Mexican War* (1990), begins with a brief history of the early Rangers. Much of the book then relates the story of Ranger forces and their accomplishments throughout the Mexican-American War. In his second book, *The Legend Begins: The Texas Rangers, 1823–1845* (1996), Wilkins's story returns to the early Ranger years. It is a much more detailed story of the Rangers and the motivations to create the force and its various manifestations during the colonial and republic years. The final two books address the second half of the nineteenth century. *The Law Comes to Texas: 1870–1901* (1999) considers the changing organizational structure and mission of the Texas Rangers in response to expanding settlement. New and improved technology enabled the expansion of a growing economy as well. Wilkins analyzes the disappearance of the Texas frontier and how expansive settlement began the slow but certain transition of the Rangers from militia to a state-supported paramilitary. That transition continued in the late nineteenth century as the beginnings of a police and detective organization began to emerge. Finally in his last book, *Defending the Borders: The Texas Rangers, 1848–1861* (2001), Wilkins addresses the era between the Mexican-American War and the American Civil War. It was a time when Texas leaders and federal authorities battled over the question of which entity was ultimately responsible for frontier defense.

Texas Ranger history is certainly rife with mythology, and Wilkins's stated purpose was to write straightforward Ranger history. He proposed that his books would simply present the facts of history without the interpretations and revisions common in modern academic circles. Likewise, he suggested he did not intend to embrace the folklore and mythology that pervaded the traditional practice of Texas Ranger history. He wrote, "Recording history deals with the painstaking task of dealing with myth and fable" to uncover reality. What may have been taken for true and settled history when Walter Prescott Webb published his *The Texas Rangers: A Century of Frontier Defense* in 1935 may be, he insisted, discovered in 1996 to be myth and fables. "I am not," he continued, "attempting revisionist history . . . but it is time to retell the Ranger story."[8]

The entirety of Wilkins's Ranger series is written in the narrative, a style that had fallen into disfavor in the 1990s, the era in which

Wilkins published his Ranger histories. He wrote those books during a time that the New Western History dominated historiography and interpretations of American West history, and to a lesser extent, Texas history. The narrative was condescendingly considered archaic history in the tradition of Webb and Frederick Jackson Turner. Prominent New Western Historians Richard White, Patricia Nelson Limerick, Donald Worster, and others in the 1990s vehemently denied Turner's frontier thesis and actively promoted a new interpretive history in which region and place dominate the story rather than an interpretation, such as Turner's, which emphasizes Manifest Destiny and a consistent westward march of American civilization. Other than *The Highly Irregular Irregulars*, Wilkins writes about a settlement frontier persistently moving westward and removing or eliminating the Indian population along the way. Yet he does not invoke Turner's frontier thesis. It may, however, be applied to his work. Wilkins's stated intent was to avoid interpretation and revision. Nonetheless, his work focuses on frontier conquest and western expansion and as such may well be interpreted as a Turnerian approach to settlement history.

For reasons that are not obvious, Wilkins's works were rarely reviewed in academic journals. Given his meticulous research, new sources, and at least an attempt at impartiality, Wilkins's books deserved professional attention. Such inattention is not uncommon in academic circles with a prejudice against the traditional narrative and the fact that Wilkins was a citizen historian rather than one academically trained in the field of history and its contingent historiography. Nonetheless, in the words of Light Cummins in his review of *The Law Comes to Texas*, "Wilkins's straightforward and well-written narrative tells the story of the famed Texas Rangers . . . [his] book offers a solid survey treatment of the organization. The author writes with a lively flair that provides numerous anecdotes and historical color to the exploits of the Rangers. Moreover, the book rests squarely on comprehensive research in the records of the state government in Austin."[9]

Similar statements apply to the remaining three works in Wilkins's Ranger series. He exhibited certain tendencies obvious in each. The books fixate on detail and specifics, whether his topic is weaponry, campaign and battlefield tactics, or military recruiting and organization. Two topics tend to dominate most of Wilkins's work—weaponry and leadership. He dedicated at least two separate chapters to the Colt revolver. He emphasized the importance of tactics developed by Rangers to effectively use Kentucky rifles from horseback and argued that Rangers revolutionized warfare through certain innovative rifle and pistol tactics. On the other hand, leadership is a theme woven through each book. His work is particularly focused on four to five Ranger captains and their leadership styles. The focus on weaponry and leadership should be no surprise. Wilkins spent a career in the military and wrote books that are essentially military history.

Because his books were not widely reviewed, a short review of each is in order here. In the preface to *The Legend Begins* he wrote, "The Texas Rangers have always been a mixture of fact and fancy with history and fable so blended it is difficult at times to separate [the two]."[10] Wilkins argued that the Rangers were, in the beginning, just ordinary militia organizations. In 1823 Mexico simply did not have the resources to provide permanent or effective security for its newly established colonies in Texas. The colonists were, he insists, quite ready, willing, and, in many ways, able to defend themselves in most circumstances. The typical American immigrant was generally acquainted with militia organizations, and many had served in militias or similar organization. What colonists wanted, according to Wilkins, was some amount of permanent, professional, and compensated security. For his part, Stephen F. Austin offered employment to ten men to serve as "rangers" in support of local militia units. Apparently his was the first use of the term *ranger* in Texas.

The Legend Begins addresses very little colonial Texas history and places a larger focus on the republic and its defense requirements. Ranger activity, Wilkins argues, was somewhat limited until the newly established Republic of Texas faced pressure from both Indians in the east, north, and west and the Mexican government to the south.

His narrative is brief and lacking the extensive detail common to most of his work until page 16. There he begins an extensive analysis of the early Tumlinson Ranger unit and its work on the Colorado River frontier.

The remainder of *The Legend Begins* is a quite straightforward yet in-depth narrative that addresses frontier security and the weapons employed in such defense. Having established a new republic, Texans faced pressure from most border regions. As mentioned before, Wilkins carefully analyzed Ranger weaponry. He devoted an entire chapter to the "Tools of the Trade." He first considers the use of rifles rather than muskets and, in particular, the Kentucky rifle. It was a shorter weapon than the musket, much more accurate, and easier to operate. The Kentucky was a rifle most southern immigrants had likely mastered because of its effectiveness in hunting game, an essential practice in frontier survival. Most Rangers carried at least one pistol, but not yet the repeating pistol, and a large knife that was later known as the iconic and legendary Bowie knife. Despite an array of weapons, Wilkins argues that in the earliest days, the rifle was the Ranger's most dependable and preferred weapon. He asserts that frontier defenders learned to operate the rifle effectively from horseback and in so doing revolutionized frontier combat.

Finally, in *The Legend Begins* Wilkins reflects on the security issues confronting Anglo-Texans and Tejano settlers. Particularly problematic were the Comanche and their South Plains allies and adversaries, the most aggressive and active raiders on the northwest frontier. Nonetheless, other Indians such as the coastal Karankawas and the eastern tribes clashed with early settlers. The conflict increased considerably, and in 1839 Governor Mirabeau Lamar required all counties to raise an armed company in response to Indian conflicts and border bandits, essentially a militia for local protection. The quite real threat of Mexican invasion is the subject of Wilkins's chapter simply titled "Invasion." In 1842 alone Mexican General Adrian Woll invaded and sacked San Antonio on two occasions. A third invasion targeted a small outpost at Corpus Christi.

The young republic—without international support and absent internal intrigue in Mexico—could not maintain the integrity of its border or frontiers. Comanches and other Indians raided incessantly from the north, and invasion by Mexican forces remained a tangible threat.

The answer, Wilkins asserts, especially to the Comanche threat, was well-equipped and hard-riding Rangers under excellent leadership. Wilkins examined Ranger leadership in the chapter "Hays Makes a Name" in *The Legend Begins*. It is not a stand-alone chapter about Hays, but it does reveal Wilkins's affinity for the Ranger leader. Moreover, the chapter dedicated to the Colt revolver and its emergence within and spread throughout the Ranger forces is not merely about the gun. Wilkins used the various themed chapters to create a chronological narrative about the rise and importance of the Ranger tradition in the early years of the Republic of Texas.

The eventual annexation of Texas meant certain war with Mexico. Wilkins asserts that Texans had anticipated war and many advocated for such. Politicians, settlers, Tejanos, and Rangers alike believed that to join the Union and then to defeat and marginalize a powerful enemy to the south would render the security that the people of the colonies, the republic, and the state had long desired. Victory was not a given, but most Texans, especially the Rangers, were confident and ready. Most Rangers served as irregulars not officially attached to the army, while others served in various mounted and infantry units. Wilkins's first Ranger book but the second in the chronology addresses the irregular units that served in the Mexican-American War.

Once again, Wilkins in *The Highly Irregular Irregulars* does a splendid job telling the military history of the war, generally from the Ranger perspective, but often he wrote about the Rangers in the larger scheme of battle tactics, operations, and morale. He emphasizes the Ranger scouting prowess that proved quite valuable to General Zachary Taylor's campaign in the north. In extensive detail he examines the recruiting processes and the organization needed to outfit and transport Rangers to the theater of war. He is also quite particular when detailing the movements of Rangers on scouting missions, their performance during battles and skirmishes, and the Ranger overall contribution to battlefield success. He routinely highlights the valor of the Rangers and their honorable actions after the violence of battle, whether that conflict was with the regular army or guerilla warriors. Wilkins paints suspenseful stories of Rangers on scouting missions and explores both the drudgery of escorting supply trains and the frenzy of full-fledged combat.

Much of the story surrounding the northern campaign to capture Monterrey and Saltillo considers the relationship between General Taylor and Ranger Captain Ben McCulloch. It was often a prickly relationship. Taylor did not care for the "wildness" of the Rangers but appreciated their tenacity in fights with renegade guerillas seeking plunder. More importantly, he respected their ability to reconnoiter enemy positions and determine enemy strength and battle readiness. On the other hand, McCulloch and his Rangers did not particularly care for Taylor's dismissive nature and the disdain shown by regular army officers. Nonetheless, Wilkins argued, Taylor and the army regulars always wanted the Texas Rangers to join the fight. Wilkins painstakingly recounts Ranger significance in the overthrow of Mexican defenses in Monterrey. He suggests that without a certain scouting mission by McCulloch and his Rangers, Taylor would have been blind to Mexican troop and artillery numbers and, most importantly, location. Wilkins credits McCulloch with producing for Taylor the reports that allowed him to win the Battle of Buena Vista and to return to his honored position as an American military hero.

Despite his victory at Monterrey, Taylor had fallen into disfavor with military men, politicians, the public, and, more importantly, newspaper writers. Following a resounding victory at Monterrey and an opportunity to take the entire Mexican garrison, Taylor arranged a truce. The resulting armistice allowed Mexican forces under the command of General Pedro de Ampudia to march away from certain defeat with weapons in hand. Taylor explained away his decision, saying that the United States was at war with the Mexican government, not the Mexican people. Wilkins argues that Taylor believed that such philanthropy might very well win over the people of northern Mexico and cause a break between the northern provinces and the central government. Nonetheless, his decision did not bide well with the Ranger irregulars and others. The Texans had volunteered to fight, had fought valiantly, and through intense combat had put themselves in a position to annihilate Ampudia's army. "Diplomacy," Wilkins suggests, "was not the Rangers' forte."[11]

With Taylor firmly in control of the north, the battle for Mexico shifted to the south. There Captain John C. Hays emerges as a central figure in Wilkins's narrative of Ranger actions in Central Mexico. Hays and other Rangers performed similar duties in Central Mexico to those of Rangers in the northern campaign. Once again Wilkins argues Ranger forces were integral to American success at the battle of Puebla. That conflict culminated in US military success in Central Mexico that effectively ended the war.

It was in Central Mexico, Wilkins argues, where Rangers were in contact with larger civilian populations and many more guerilla fighters. Outlaws with little political agenda but intent on plunder waited constantly in ambush, which earned the guerrilla fighters a reputation for murder and mayhem in the city and countryside. The demographics and geography of Central Mexico put Rangers in closer proximity to civilians and guerrillas and thus more conflict and violence. In *Highly Irregular Irregulars*, Wilkins acknowledges that certain accusations of Ranger atrocities in the north and a Ranger raid in Mexico City that became known as the Cutthroat Retaliation were deplorable. Wilkins, however, defends the Rangers, arguing that some were with certainty wild and rowdy and often dismissive of authority and regulations but had not committed the atrocities of which they were routinely accused. He makes a sincere effort to restore the reputation of most Rangers who were just different, he said, from other soldiers. To his credit he does chronicle several instances of atrocities instigated by discreditable Rangers. Wilkins does, however, interpret the atrocities as isolated instances.

With the campaigns and war essentially over, most irregulars were mustered out of service immediately, including almost all the Rangers. With the war over and victory realized, many Texans hoped for peace, or at least some enhanced security, along the border. The war was won but the border was not tamed in the process, neither were the Comanches and their allies. Conflict and violence along the northwest Indian frontier and the Rio Grande border are the subject of Wilkins's next monograph. The period between the Mexican-American War and the Civil War, according to Wilkins, has largely been ignored and overlooked by Ranger historians. Yet the importance of Ranger frontier and border defense did not diminish. His book *Defending the Borders* is his answer to that perceived gap in Ranger historiography.

The first chapter, "Roads West," initially seems strangely irrelevant. It includes stories of the escapades of famous Rangers Jack Hays, John Ford, and others. Those Rangers were involved in expeditions to help the army find a route to El Paso del Norte—a route that was suitable for a wagon road, which the US Army desired. Nonetheless, it does make sense as a prelude to the final book in Wilkins's Ranger series. The expansion into West Texas changed the frontier, its economy, and its population.

Most of the content in *Defending the Borders*, however, considers the debate between the government of the United States and that of Texas. Which entity is ultimately responsible for frontier and border security? Moreover, expectations went even further. Many settlers expected and demanded that the federal government punish Mexico for harboring and offering refuge to runaway slaves. Wilkins argued that most Texans expected the federal government to fund border and frontier security. Texas was, after all, a legitimate member of the Union and should be afforded the same security and advantages other states enjoyed. Throughout their collective experience as a colony and a republic, Texans were plagued by Indian raids along the frontier and in the interior and by bandits operating out of Mexico. Wilkins also acknowledges that Texas had its own criminals and outlaws with which to contend on the border and frontier.

The debate concerning responsibility for security and defense becomes a critical subject in *Defending the Borders*. Secretary of War C. M. Conrad, in a dismissive response to Texas governor Peter Bell, advised the governor that criminal activity was a civil matter and policing the border was inherently the state's responsibility. Additionally, he informed Bell that the federal government had no money to expand the army. The scenario that Wilkins presents suggests that in terms of border and frontier security, Texas was hardly in better shape than before annexation. Yes, the US Army assumed responsibility for border defense in the case of a Mexican or other foreign invasion. Border bandits and other outlaws, on the other hand, were a Texas problem. In response Texas Ranger companies formed, and Texas paramilitary troops were once again responsible for security along the border and frontier. It is in this era that John "Rip" Ford built a legendary reputation. Wilkins does not challenge that legend to any degree.

In *Defending the Borders*, Wilkins acknowledges that because of past difficulties and at times outright failure, it was necessary for the Rangers to make tactical changes to defense and policing strategies. Wilkins argued that the passive defense and the reactionary vengeance of the past made way to proactive policies. Eventually state funding provided resources to outfit a Ranger expedition to take the battle to the Comanches. Governor Hardin P. Runnels in 1858 authorized an expeditionary force under John Ford's leadership. Unfortunately the expedition had limited success in dispersing the Comanche threat and was hardly more effective than federal troop tactics. Moreover, Wilkins suggests, pressure from relentless migration westward exacerbated the problems not only with the Comanche and other Southern Plains tribes but also with all Indians. Very little changed regarding the defense of the southern border and the northwest frontier in the years between the wars. Secession changed the reality for Rangers and settlers on the frontier. Federal troops vacated the Texans frontier and borderlands, while more Texans joined the Confederate Army or were conscripted. The result was an increase

in violence and conflict along the vast frontier that stretched from
the rolling plains to the Big Bend. Once again, with the outbreak of
Civil War, Texans and their Rangers were alone in their mission to
respond to pressure from Plains Indians in the north and raiders from
the south.

Wilkins writes nothing about the Texas Rangers during the Civil
War. That conflict fundamentally changed Texas for various reasons.[12]
In *Law Comes to Texas*, Wilkins chronicles the most famous era of
Texas Ranger history. He exams the extensive changes in Texas: its
growing diversity, its booming population, its expansive economic
growth, and the changing nature of the Texas Ranger forces.
Technology, Wilkins suggests, brought significant and permanent
change to Texas. Once Ranald Mackenzie and his troops cleared
the West Texas grasslands and the Panhandle of hostile Indians,
cattlemen and investors rushed in, eager to take advantage of the
open range. The railroad followed and brought barbed wire, windmills, and other technology that would transform what was once a
hostile frontier into a productive agricultural region. Rangers were
yet needed to hunt down murderers, cattle thieves, bank robbers, and
other outlaws, often in groups of only one or two Rangers rather than
more sizeable companies. Once again, the structure and mission of
the Texas Rangers necessarily adapted to massive changes within
the state.

Given the relatively insufficient federal support during the Reconstruction years, Texan leaders endeavored to employ Texas Rangers
once again for frontier defense. Governor Edmund Davis in 1870
addressed the need to protect the vulnerable Texas frontier. Davis
requested the Texas Legislature fund a Frontier Force. However,
the legislation that created the force was not sufficient to make the
force a reality. It was generally underfunded despite the legislation
requiring such funding. At times provisions were plentiful and at times
not. As was the tradition, Ranger companies came and went with
regularity. Such problems were all too familiar to Ranger veterans.
The 1874 General Act, promoted by Governor Richard Coke, proposed

a permanent frontier defense. Nonetheless, the traditional temporary or short-term Ranger companies were allowed to muster in response to emergencies. With certainty, according to Wilkins, Governor Coke and the legislature desired a permanent presence on the northwest and southern frontiers. The Ranger companies formed as military forces of the state of Texas. Democrats in Reconstruction Texas were hostile to the Reconstruction-Era state police department. The Frontier Battalion formed, and a more formal command structure emerged. However, Wilkins asserts that by 1875–1876, a smaller Frontier Battalion was adequate to the state's role in frontier defense because of a stronger response by the federal army. The US Army launched a coordinated and eventually successful campaign against the Southern Plains Indians, the Comanches in particular.

The US Army's successful Red River campaign against the Comanches and last Southern Plains holdouts, according to Wilkins, made a paramilitary organization like the Frontier Battalion increasingly unnecessary. The Rangers still had a role to play in Texas. Bandits still plagued the border, and groups of Rangers such as Captain Lee H. McNelly and his men—the McNelly Boys—continued to perform traditional Ranger work along the border. Famous outlaws made their way to Texas. The Apache continued their raids in the Big Bend region. Texas, though, was changing. The Texas Rangers started out as common militia, grew into a paramilitary organization, and in the Mexican-American War fought as regular and irregular soldiers. With the oil strike at Spindletop, an era featuring law enforcement replaced the long tradition of a partisan or paramilitary role for the organization. The Texas Rangers of the twentieth century became a police and detective institution

Wilkins wrote in the introduction of *Law Comes to Texas*, "When it is all examined, the Rangers appear as neither the villains nor the superman which some writers have chosen to portray."[13] Wilkins did not entirely realize his promise to write only the truth without embellishment, interpretation, or sustaining and perpetuating Ranger myth, folklore, and legend. He made concentrated efforts to remain neutral, but he does at times reinforce the legend through his praise of certain Ranger leaders, especially John Coffee Hays. Wilkins endeavors in *Highly Irregular Irregulars* to rehabilitate the reputation of Texas Rangers who fought in the Mexican war. Some deserved the Texas Devils moniker, and he does admit such. He in fact adds a section, "Battles—or Legends," at the end of *Legend Begins*. In that section he questions the veracity of Hays's epic lone stand on Enchanted Rock. Remember, his writings show Wilkins is quite impressed with Hays. Wilkins also questions the sources of the Bander Pass story. Legend suggests some thirty or so Rangers repulsed over one hundred Comanches in an early 1840s battle. That particular fight has been touted as a legendary feat in the course of chronicling Ranger history. Wilkins did not find evidence of the battle or have confidence in the stories repeated in support of such action.

Wilkins's reverence for the Texas Rangers, including the various iterations of the organization and certain leaders, is clear. His writing for the most part is what he proposed it to be—just the facts. In many ways Wilkins lives up to his pledge to "retell the Ranger story" and to not employ "revisionist history." Yet he too often ignores the vigilantism and arbitrary violence practiced by select Rangers and contributes to the legend and lore of the Texas Rangers. Nonetheless, when Frederick J. Wilkins Jr. died on December 15, 2004, he left a Ranger legacy of his own in four well-crafted Texas Ranger histories.

Notes

1. Frederick Wilkins always recognized Donaly Brice, formerly of the Texas State Library, in his acknowledgments for his valuable assistance in the intensive researched required for this Rangers Series. I want to thank Donaly as well. He found obscure documents to put together what details were available to provide a sketch of Wilkins's life before his career as a Ranger author.
2. "Fencing," *Rotunda*, Southern Methodist University Yearbook, 1938, 214.
3. "Obituary: Frederick J. Wilkins, Jr.," *San Antonio Express-News*, December 17, 2004.

4. "Fourth Army Writer Wins Citation," *San Antonio Light*, July 8, 1962.
5. "Oriental Rugs to be the Topic," *San Antonio Express*, Thursday, April 10, 1975.
6. "Gardeners to Cruise River," *San Antonio Express*, Thursday, May 4, 1972.
7. "Action Line," *San Antonio Light*, Wednesday April 23, 1967.
8. Frederick Wilkins, *The Legend Begins: The Texas Rangers, 1823–1845* (Austin: State House Press, 1996), xi.
9. L. T. Cummins, review of *The Law Comes to Texas: the Texas Rangers, 1870–1901*, by Frederick Wilkins, *Choice Review* 36, no. 11 (July 1999).
10. Wilkins, *Legend Begins*, xii.
11. Frederick Wilkins, *The Highly Irregular Irregulars: Texas Rangers in the Mexican War* (Austin: Eakin Press, 1990), 103.
12. Wilkins does not address the Civil War years in any of his books. But a good reference for those years is David Paul Smith's *Frontier Defense in the Civil War: Texas' Rangers and Rebels* (College Station: Texas A&M University Press, 1992).
13. Frederick Wilkins, *Law Comes to Texas: the Texas Rangers, 1870–1901* (Austin: State House Press, 1999): xii

Chapter 13

Mike Cox

Prolific Hybrid Author

Rusty Williams

S ome write Texas Ranger history as mythology, exaggerated accounts intended to explain the foundational nature of Texas, its values, and its culture. Others write about the Rangers as poets might, evoking an imaginative awareness or emotional response. Some write of Ranger history in an academic style, fact and speculation put forward in support of a premise to be maintained or proven. Still others write as movie scriptwriters, with history serving only plot, character, and action.

Texas author Mike Cox writes as a journalist, recounting the news of Texas Ranger history and presenting it with a storyteller's skill. Mike Cox grew up hearing stories about the Texas Rangers; most Texans do. But most Texans don't have a grandfather like his. Cox acknowledges granddad L. A. Wilke as a major influence on his love for storytelling and his early knowledge of the Rangers.

"I spent hours sitting in Granddad's home office," Cox recalls, "listening to him reflect on his newspaper days and the colorful characters he encountered." Granddad Wilke started in the newspaper business in the days of the Mexican Revolution, when much of West

Texas was still frontier country. During the Prohibition, gangster, and oil scam years of the 1920s and 1930s, he was a reporter or editor in Corpus Christi, San Antonio, Fort Worth, Dallas, and Houston. Wilke would spin out stories for hours to a captivated grandson about Rangers such as Hamer, Hickman, Gonzaullas, and Hughes.[1]

Wilke's home office was littered with papers, clippings, a typewriter, stacks of old magazines, and bookshelves crammed with a considerable collection of Texas-related books. "One of those books had a yellow and blue dust jacket," Cox remembers. "The spine held its partial title, *The Texas Rangers*, followed by the single word, 'Webb' and the name of the publisher, Houghton Mifflin Company."[2]

"Later, of course, I absorbed the book," Cox says. The narrative of Walter Prescott Webb's 1935 *The Texas Rangers: A Century of Frontier Defense* (along with its strengths and shortcomings) and Granddad Wilke's stories remained with Cox for years, inspiring his best-selling definitive history of the Texas Rangers.

Mike Cox was born and bred to write. His father was a longtime Amarillo newspaperman sent to Sweetwater to cover a murder-for-hire trial. The woman who was covering the trial for the Sweetwater newspaper was young, pretty, and smart. Cox's father was smart, too. Smart enough to marry her and start a family.

"Thanks to a murder," Cox says, "I was literally born into journalism."[3]

Both parents were writers, selling articles to magazines, writing books, and wringing every dollar possible out of the true stories they researched and wrote. Along the way they tutored their son on the craft.

And he was eager to join the profession. While attending Angelo State University, Cox worked full-time as a reporter for the *San Angelo Standard-Times* before transferring to Texas Tech and getting a job with the *Lubbock Avalanche-Journal*. By the time he joined the staff of the *Austin American-Statesman* in 1970, he was building a freelance writing career and well on his way to writing his first book, a biography of Fred Gipson, the esteemed Texas author of *Old Yeller*.

"My journalism background has served me well in almost all aspects of my career," Cox says. "A good reporter learns how to research, how to organize that research, and how to transform that research into something readable." But there's more to it than that: Students in every news writing class and reporters in every newsroom are inculcated with an ethical journalism code. The words may vary from place to place, but the codes—every one of them—are based on principles of truthfulness, objectivity, accuracy, accountability, and fairness.[4]

For an old-school newsman like Mike Cox, writing nonfiction (on any subject and in any genre) carries some special obligations. Truthfulness separates nonfiction from fiction; in nonfiction there should be no made-up events or scenes, no reinvented quotes or conversations (unless clearly disclosed to the reader). Objectivity requires that the writer lay out salient facts and allow the reader to reach his own conclusion. Accuracy means seeking out primary sources, providing more credence to sources who witnessed (or were closest to) the events described than those who interpreted later. A journalist should be able to exhibit the source of every quote, event, or conclusion; by that he is accountable to his reader. To show fairness to both reader and story, the journalist should provide a context for events that might seem wholly unsuited to the current time or culture.

Cox spent the first two decades of his career adhering to those journalistic principles of truthfulness, accuracy, accountability, and fairness. The code remains a part of everything he writes.

Mike Cox took a new job in 1985. After twenty years as a newspaperman, Cox left the open collars and Keep Austin Weird vibe of the *Austin American-Statesman* newsroom for a new job at a state agency: media spokesperson for the white-shirt-and-tie Texas Department of Public Safety.[5]

The most storied division of the DPS is the Texas Rangers, and Cox found himself responding to reporters, researchers, out-of-staters, and curious schoolkids asking to know more about the organization. As the DPS marked its fiftieth anniversary in 1985, queries were only increasing in volume. The department's current printed mail-out piece about the Texas Rangers—this was in the days before email, Dropbox, or websites—was a bit shabby and out of date, so Cox wrote a tight, new, 5,500-word history of the law enforcement body. The DPS kept the twenty-eight-page illustrated booklet—titled *Silver Stars and Sixguns: The Texas Rangers*—in print and distributed it for the next twenty years, and still includes the text on the Ranger division website.

Silver Stars and Sixguns is as close to an "official" history as it gets. It begins by acknowledging the romance and culture of the Rangers, then pivots neatly to a chronological history. The history name-checks some of the better-known Rangers—"Big Foot" Wallace and Frank Hamer, among others. It provides a context for the famous "One riot, one Ranger" saying, and the origin of the "No man in the wrong" Rangers' creed. *Silver Stars and Sixguns* doesn't shy away from controversy, including the 1917 Mexico incursions and the shame of the Ferguson administration years. Yet there's none of the "Throw your hands in the air, boys!" fanciful dialogue found in some of the lighter Ranger histories; there are none of the complex syllogisms found in some academic writing.

Cox brought a reporter's sensibilities to *Silver Stars and Sixguns*. The short history is just facts—who, what, where, when, why, and how—and good storytelling, tight and compelling from the first page to the last. Several years after Cox joined the DPS, he received a call from Ed Eakin, owner of Eakin Press. Eakin asked if Cox would write a children's history of the Texas Rangers, an offer Cox, at first, turned down.

"He did kinda have to talk me into it since I'd never written for children before," Cox said. The former newspaperman was uneasy with the need to create dialogue, a practice common (and often required) in children's literature but foreign to his journalistic ethos. Assured that he wasn't expected to make up facts about Rangers or cases, Cox enrolled in a children's writing workshop at Our Lady of the Lake University in San Antonio.

The Texas Rangers: Men of Action and Valor (1990) serves up a brief history of Texas Ranger operations using ten stories, "true incidents from the annals of the Rangers."[6] The first is about a boy who meets up with Ranger Captain John J. Tumlinson Jr. (son of the first Texas Ranger to die in the line of duty) when Indians shoot the family cow full of arrows. The final story involves detective work by a modern Ranger chasing thieves who dig up and steal rare dinosaur tracks. A helicopter, the regional radio net, the crime lab, and two helpful ranch boys assist the (pseudonymous) Ranger in tracking down the culprits.

The book contains plenty of gee-whiz action, much of it with plucky youngsters landing in the middle of Ranger exploits. It's all good fun, but in the book's preface, Cox betrays a hint of discomfort at straying from strictly journalistic nonfiction: "Dialogue has been added to make these stories interesting to read, but I'm satisfied it has the ring of authenticity, and that anything in this book that didn't happen at least could have happened."[7]

As successful as *Men of Action and Valor* was, Cox has yet to write another nonfiction children's book.

In 1995 Cox began *Texas Ranger Tales: Stories That Need Telling* (1997). In some ways it's a version of *Men of Action and Valor* for grown-ups, but the twenty-seven Ranger tales are denser, having a greater mass per unit. The tales, arranged chronologically, are packed with historical narrative, context, realistic local color, and Ranger humor. "I aimed my literary Winchester at two kinds of stories," Cox said. "First, the stories had to be interesting. Second, I wanted to concentrate on lesser-known Ranger stories."[8]

In the book's introduction, Cox quotes J. Frank Dobie as saying that a story belongs to the person who tells it best. By that measure Mike owns these stories. He takes an interesting, lesser-known story, then adds another twist. He caps it all with a sharp quote or poignant fact, giving the narrative even more weight. These are campfire stories—entertaining, informative, and told by a masterful storyteller.

For instance, the first chapter, "Samuel Walker's Last Fight," opens with a brief biography of Samuel Walker, for whom Samuel Colt named the Walker Colt six-shot revolver in 1846. Cox follows Walker's rangering and regular army career through his combat death during the Mexican War in 1847. His death was national news, and Walker's remains were eventually returned for a hero's burial in the Oddfellows Cemetery in San Antonio. So far, it's an interesting take on a storied early Ranger.

But Walker's "Last Fight" wasn't his fatal one in Mexico. Instead, it occurred a century and a half later when an attempt was made to move his remains from San Antonio to the grounds of the Texas Ranger Hall of Fame and Museum in Waco. Cox paints a war of words between San Antonio and Waco almost as vicious as that between Rangers and Comanches in Walker's day. Then he caps the tale with a quote from an old-time Texan: "Walker was a Texas Ranger, and if he'd a-wanted to go to Waco, he'd a-walked."[9]

That last quote typifies another element of Cox's storytelling: Ranger humor. "You show me a man that doesn't have a little tinge of humor in his make-up, and I'll show you a man who has a problem," Cox quotes a retired Texas Ranger as saying. "That goes for a Ranger or anyone else."[10]

The final chapter of *Texas Ranger Tales*, "Rangers Make 'Em Die Laughing," is made up of the dark, just-between-us stories old Rangers might tell one another quietly over morning coffee. Most of the anecdotes in this chapter appear to have been shared (anonymously) by contemporary Rangers; he seines others from old documents, articles, and early daybooks.

Taken as a whole, *Texas Ranger Tales: Stories That Need Telling* is not a full-on Texas Ranger history. (That would come later.) Rather, it projects the aura of the Texas Rangers, showing them as individuals of all stripes throughout the two hundred years of the storied organization.

No person who has written as much about the Texas Rangers (and very few have) has had as much access to the Texas Rangers organization as Mike Cox. During his fifteen years with the DPS, Cox worked alongside and on-scene with many of the modern Rangers and, as chief of media relations for the DPS, became close friends with several of them. "There's a cultural difference between law enforcement officers and a non-law enforcement officer," he says. "At first, a lot of [the DPS officers] tended to view me as a reporter—they didn't like to give me information; there were turf concerns."

Trust can be a slow-growing crop, but Cox demonstrates how he cultivated acceptance by law enforcement officers in *Stand-Off in Texas: "Just Call Me a Spokesman for the DPS"* (1998). This is a Texas Ranger book, but it's equal parts memoir and contemporary history. Cox was media point man for the DPS during three headline-grabbing criminal events of the 1990s: hostage-taking by Republic of Texas separatists in West Texas, the siege of the Branch Davidians in Waco, and the Killeen Luby's Cafeteria mass murder. *Stand-Off in Texas* describes Cox's involvement in these events and how he helped translate the tight-lipped Texas Ranger ethos into informative and compelling front-page news. "My time with the DPS helped me understand the modern Ranger culture," Cox said. "And I came to a special appreciation of the mythology and history of the Texas Rangers."[11] But even as his face appeared on televisions around the world describing events of the separatist standoff, *Texas Ranger Tales* was generating good reviews and plenty of reader enthusiasm. The publisher asked Cox to do a follow-up volume.

Texas Ranger Tales II (1999) delivers what the original delivered, and more of it. Twenty-two new Texas Ranger stories—interesting, little-known, and reading more like fictional short stories than mini-history lessons—comprise the bulk of the book. Again, they are organized chronologically, but Cox has skewed his story selection to the more contemporary accounts, which provide clues to the planning and operations of modern Rangers. "The Sherman Riot" relates a gruesome and disgraceful mob action in 1930 that confronted Texas Rangers with a moral Hobson's choice; "Cowboy Tom Hickman" is a concise biography of one of the most likable Rangers of the twentieth century, a lawman who became chairman of the Texas Public Safety

Commission, the same policy body that had once fired him from law enforcement; and "The 'Eyes of Texas' on the Balinese Room" reveals the political obstacles Rangers encountered when cracking down on mob-related vice operations in the 1950s.

Meanwhile, there was always the memory of that book on his grandfather's crowded bookshelf years before. The book with the yellow and blue dust jacket. The book with *The Texas Rangers* and "Webb" on the spine.

Over the years Cox had read, reread, and referenced Walter Prescott Webb's 1935 *The Texas Rangers: A Century of Frontier Defense*. At the beginning of the twenty-first century, Webb's book was the standard definitive history of the Rangers, but it was hopelessly outdated, and its faults glowed like neon. "Webb's history stops deader than an outlaw with a Ranger bullet in his heart with the creation of the Department of Public Safety in 1935," Cox says. "The book ends with Webb's incorrect prediction that the formation of the agency marked the end of the Rangers." Webb's treatment of Mexicans and Mexican Americans is arguably racist, and his 1930s scholarship is limited by a lack of access to many autobiographies and primary documents that have become available since Webb completed the book.[12]

Cox got a book contract from a New York publisher and began eight years of research into original documents, correspondence, early newspaper coverage, theses, dissertations, oral histories, unpublished manuscripts, and personal interviews. However, he wasn't the only author set on bringing Texas Ranger history into the twenty-first century. He was four years into researching and writing his own history when Oxford University Press published *Lone Star Justice: The First Century of the Texas Rangers* (2002), the first of two volumes of an updated Ranger history by Robert M. Utley. At first Cox was tempted to file away his own project in a bottom drawer. "Utley is a solid historian," Cox said. "He's one of those academics who manage to transcend the academy and write good, readable history." But Cox realized that the book Utley wrote was different from the one he was writing. "I wanted to be less of a teacher, to avoid moral conclusions.

I wanted my readers to develop their own opinions from the facts
I gave them."[13]

Originally planned as one overarching volume, the publisher
eventually released Cox's updated history as two books: *The Texas
Rangers: Wearing the Cinco Peso, 1821–1900* (2008) and *Time of the
Rangers: Texas Rangers, from 1900 to the Present* (2009). Despite all
the research (or, more likely, because of it), Cox relates a complete
linear history of the Texas Rangers through storytelling. The structure
of his two Texas Rangers volumes eschews thematic chapters,
dense analysis, academic proofs, didacticism, and grand conclusions.
Instead, the books are readable reportage written with appropriate
context, vivid scene-setting, and (where possible) the Rangers' own
words or other contemporary accounts. The result is a straightforward
narrative that extends from Stephen Austin's first encounter with
Texas Indians in 1821 through the Rangers' 2009 role in helping
prevent cross-border violence due to vicious drug wars in Mexico.[14]
"Over the years, people have asked me why I wrote my two-volume
history when another publisher also released a two-volume work,"
Cox said. "These are two different types of books, the proverbial apple
and orange."[15] To date *The Texas Rangers: Wearing the Cinco Peso,
1821–1900* and *Time of the Rangers: Texas Rangers, from 1900 to the
Present* are Cox's best-selling books.

Gunfights and Sites in Texas Rangers History (2015) came about
largely by accident. *True West magazine* commissioned Cox to write
a piece on traveling to historic sites in Texas connected to the Texas
Rangers. The article sparked an idea that led to a book designed
for Texas road trippers. *Gunfights and Sites* divides Texas into five
geographic regions, then alphabetically by county. Each of the 107
included counties contains at least one Ranger-related historical site
(and many counties feature a half dozen or more.) The book leads the
explorer to some interesting destinations: down a dusty country road
to the Big Foot Wallace Museum (Frio County); to the house of the
Jaybird-Woodpecker shootout and the death of Ranger Frank Schmidt
(Fort Bend County); and to a site on Santa Anna Peak that served as an

Indian lookout and reunion camp for many of Texas's early Rangers
(Coleman County).

Gunfights and Sites is more than a book of lists. Each site comes
with a story explaining its historical significance and, when needed,
detailed directions to the location. (The especially ambitious tourist
will also find an appendix giving directions to more than a hundred
Ranger-related historical markers. As a bonus, another appendix lists
the twenty-eight Texas Rangers who have Texas counties named
for them.)

Twenty years after *Texas Ranger Tales: Stories That Need Telling*
appeared, the corporate successor to the original publisher proposed
that Cox combine that book and the sequel, *Texas Ranger Tales II*, into
one book and introduce it to a new generation of Texas Ranger reading
enthusiasts. *Texas Ranger Tales: Hard-Riding Stories from the Lone
Star State* (2016) includes a revised version of all the stories from both
original volumes.

"When I first wrote them, the internet was just a wisp of smoke
compared to what it is today," Cox said. "I was able to learn new
things about some of the people and events I had written about."[16]
Hard-Riding Stories contains new illustrations and a new chapter.
"Space Rangers Defend a New Frontier" describes where modern
fiction—books, movies, television, comics—have taken the Texas
Rangers legend: into outer space. The world's fascination with the
Ranger myth endures, no matter where they range.

Mike Cox continues to write about Texas Rangers, Texas history,
Texas cities, Texas outdoors, and Texas characters. He's a prolific writer,
likely one of the most commercially successful professional writers of
historical Texas nonfiction. Pile every book Cox has written—thirty or
more, so far—one on top of the other, and the stack would reach your
belt buckle. The pile would include biographies, true crime books,
oversized coffee-table picture books, an as-told-to memoir, four books
of true Texas tales, several illustrated city histories, a round-up of
Texas disasters, and, of course, his Texas Ranger books. Add to the
pile the hundreds of magazine, newspaper, and journal articles, and

essays he's written about Texas, the West, history, and the outdoors, and the stack would reach your shirt collar. (And that doesn't include the hundreds of stories—politics, crime, government, books, business, and more—that he's written for his full-time media employers or the chapters he's contributed to scholarly anthologies.) "The storytelling, or narrative, or popular history brings the past alive," Cox says. "Some writers tell; I like to show."[17]

As many pages as Cox has written, however, it's difficult to discern any overriding school of study or interpretation in his books. He certainly doesn't recognize a consistent historiographical theme or approach in his writing about Texas Rangers. Some could argue he's a traditionalist; Cox perfumes some of his Rangers writing with notes of Texas exceptionalism. Others call him a revisionist, and Cox hasn't been shy about chipping the gold plate off some earlier Rangers to see the base metal beneath. Put simply, however, Cox is a storyteller writing in the journalistic tradition. And that, occasionally, can be both a strength and a drawback.

Of the five basic elements of good storytelling—context, color, character, motivation, and resolution—the first two are most available to a writer willing to do thorough research. And Mike Cox is a thorough researcher. He pans for story nuggets in the usual streams: historical archives, libraries, and the yellowing pages of old newspapers. But you'll also find him in the backroom of a rural county lock-up studying an 1880s jailer's logbook. Or bumping along a rocky trace near the Rio Grande in desolate Presidio County in a four-wheel-drive vehicle with Texas Ranger Joaquin Jackson—both men gunned up— as Cox searches out a site where, in 1915, two Rangers were killed in an ambush by Mexican bandits.

Sometimes his reliance on documented fact—or lack of facts— can put Cox on the wrong side of Texas Ranger orthodoxy. In *The Texas Rangers: Wearing the Cinco Peso*, Cox writes that three famous fights supposedly involving Ranger Captain John C. Hays—Bandera Pass, Enchanted Rock, and Paint Rock—may never have happened at all. Conclusive evidence is lacking for all three of these encounters, and the stories about them may be nothing more than legend, he writes. He's willing to let the reader reach his or her own conclusion.[18]

But the most captivating stories are the tales of people— characters—with inner lives and hidden thoughts that motivate their actions. We sometimes find it difficult to understand the thoughts and impulses of those closest to us in the present, much less persons of a century or two before. Absent diaries or other first-person accounts, the feelings, motives, and individuality of historical characters are sometimes lacking in the works of a writer adhering to a journalistic style. For example, the "Los Sediciosos" chapter of *Texas Rangers, from 1900 to the Present* (which documents the troubles on Texas's borders from 1915 to 1919) begins with an introduction to Basilio Ramos Jr., notorious for setting forth the Plan de San Antonio. Cox provides little background on Ramos and no indication of his motivation in the main text. Likewise, Mexican border bandit Chico Cano is no more than a one-dimensional predator in the book's text. These antagonists are hollow men, seeming hardly worth the attention given them by scores of Rangers and other lawmen. (Interestingly, the characters of both Ramos and Cano are fleshed out in the chapter's notes. There, Ramos's political motivation is made clear, and Cano is painted as "Big Bend's most infamous bandit."[19] It's typical of Cox's exhaustive research that there's rarely a bloody scalping or a case of campfire flatulence that isn't sourced in his text or notes. Cox's search for facts often nets new stories, stories that don't fit his main narrative. Quite often, those sidebar stories find their way into the notes, as well.)

For storytellers, the resolution usually refers to the consequence(s) of the actions occurring during the story. While academic writers seem to find it easier to assert and argue causation and effect than do journalists, Cox often describes related events, but seldom—unless quoting a source—claims that those events resulted in a changed circumstance. The "Assist Civil Authorities" chapter in *Wearing the Cinco Peso, 1821–1900*, for example, tells of the 1883 legislation intended to halt rampant fence-cutting on West Texas ranches, a type of economic warfare that was costing millions of dollars a year. Cox describes incidents of enforcement by Rangers throughout the remainder of the 1880s, but neglects to tell whether the enforcement efforts halted the practice. (A chapter note suggests it did not.)

Cox's *Texas Ranger Tales: Hard-Riding Stories from the Lone Star State* is a better demonstration of the storyteller's skill. The standalone stories that comprise the chapters each balance the elements of context, color, character, motivation, and resolution and represent popular history that engages while it informs.

Cox's facility at storytelling within the journalistic tradition—his objectivity, credibility, and popular acceptance—has earned him the respect of his peers. In 1993 he was elected to membership in the Texas Institute of Letters, a prestigious organization whose members include such Texas literary lights as Larry McMurtry, Cormac McCarthy, James Michener, Bill Moyers, and Light T. Cummins. In 2011 he received the A. C. Greene Award for lifetime achievement.

Authors Glenn Dromgoole and Carlton Stowers included three Mike Cox books (including the two volumes *Wearing the Cinco Peso* and *Texas Rangers, from 1900 to the Present*) in their *101 Essential Texas Books* (2014). Cox is the only author in the book with multiple titles.

"I sold my first magazine article when I was in the eighth grade for thirty-five dollars to *The Cattleman* magazine," Cox says. "I thought I was rich, and that fame would soon follow. I was wrong about both."[20] Whether or not Cox is rich today is up to him and his banker to decide, but there are a lot of people who say he's well-known due to his readings, seminars, and book signings around the state, and for the articles he contributes to such magazines as *True West, Texas Highways, Texas Parks & Wildlife Magazine,* and *Texas Sportsman.* For more than four years he also found time to edit a quarterly magazine, *Wild West History Association Journal.*

But he's best known for his Texas Ranger books and activities. He's an associate historian with the Former Texas Rangers Association and an active contributor to the Former Texas Rangers Foundation.

And he's always ready for a road trip to the farthest corner of Texas to learn a new Texas Ranger story.

"Granddad told me stories about the Texas Rangers," Cox says, "and somewhere along the way, I realized the best way to convey history is through storytelling. If you can connect a reader to a good story, especially one with a universal theme, people are going to enjoy it more."[21]

Notes

1. Cox, *The Texas Rangers: Men of Action and Valor* (Austin: Eakin Press), vii.
2. Cox, *The Texas Rangers: Wearing the Cinco Peso, 1821–1900* (New York: Forge Books, 2008), 13.
3. From correspondence with Mike Cox, April 2019.
4. For examples, see David Craig, *The Ethics of the Story: Using Narrative Techniques Responsibly in Journalism* (Lanham, MD: Rowman & Littlefield, 2006) or Society of Professional Journalists Code of Ethics, revised September 6, 2014, https://www.spj.org/ethicscode.asp.
5. Unless otherwise cited, biographical material comes from written information provided by Mike Cox and from biographical notes he provided to his book publishers.
6. Cox, *Men of Action and Valor*, vi.
7. Cox, *Men of Action and Valor*, ix.
8. Cox, *Texas Ranger Tales: Stories That Need Telling* (Plano: Republic of Texas Press, 1997), x.
9. Cox, *Stories That Need Telling*, 16.
10. Cox, *Texas Ranger Tales: Hard-Riding Stories from the Lone Star State* (Guilford, CT: Lone Star Books, 2016), 345.
11. Author interview with Mike Cox, March 15, 2019.
12. Cox, *Wearing the Cinco Peso*, 14, and author interview with Mike Cox, March 15, 2019.
13. Author interview with Mike Cox, March 15, 2019.
14. *Cinco Peso* and *Time of the Rangers: Texas Rangers, from 1900 to the Present* (New York: Forge Books, 2009) are both extensively footnoted. In addition to providing sources, the notes sometimes provide biographical information, added context, or alternative versions of better-documented stories related in the main text. At least

one critic commented favorably that the voluminous notes constitute a
third volume of Cox's two-volume history.

15. From correspondence with Mike Cox, April 2019.

16. Author interview with Mike Cox, March 15, 2019.

17. Author interview with Mike Cox, March 15, 2019.

18. Cox, *Wearing the Cinco Peso*, 390n65. See also Cox, "Battle of the Painted Rocks: Scraping off the Layers," *West Texas Historical Association Year Book* 78 (October 2002): 151–69. Though Cox allows that absence of evidence is not evidence of absence, his skepticism of accounts of those battles has led to some criticism of his journalistic methodology.

19. Cox, *Texas Rangers, from 1900 to the Present*, 394n7.

20. "Lone Star Listens: Mike Cox," interview by Kay Ellington, *Lone Star Literary Life*, December 18, 2016, https://www.lonestarliterary.com/node/807.

21. Rebecca L. Bennett, "Reviving History through Storytelling," *Hill Country View*, May 1, 2017.

Cultural Constructionalists

A New Vista

Chapter 14

Gary Clayton Anderson
Reframing Indian-Anglo-Ranger Relations

Roger Tuller

If all the books written about the Rangers were put one on top of the other, the
resulting pile would be almost as tall as some of the tales they contain.

—Américo Paredes, *"With His Pistol in His Hand"*

Acontroversial version of Texas and Texas Ranger history emerged
for a wide audience with the 2005 publication of *The Conquest
of Texas: Ethnic Cleansing in the Promised Land, 1820–1875* by
Gary Clayton Anderson. Jacket blurbs from distinguished historians
Jesus De La Teja and Richard White warned readers that Anderson
found "Texas to have been an exceptionally violent place precisely
because its leaders embraced coercive means to rid the state of people
who did not meet Anglo-American standards of civilization," and that
the book would "make Texans who are devoted to the Ranger version
of history howl in pain." And, in case prospective readers missed the
use of "ethnic cleansing" in the subtitle, the inside front flap revealed
that *The Conquest of Texas* "portray[ed] nineteenth-century Texas as
a cauldron of racist violence." Clearly this was not a traditional view
of Texas history.[1]

Born in 1948, Gary Clayton Anderson earned a BA at Concordia College, an MA from the University of South Dakota, and his PhD from the University of Toledo. He was a member of the history faculty at Texas A&M University (College Station) from 1981 to 1991 before moving on to the University of Oklahoma, where he is professor emeritus in American Indian history and ethnohistory. It his extensive publication record, however that has brought him the most attention. Among his many books, two became finalists for the Pulitzer Prize in History. The first, published in 1984, was *Kinsmen of Another Kind: Dakota-White Relations in the Upper Mississippi River Valley, 1650–1862*. The second, *The Conquest of Texas: Ethnic Cleansing in the Promised Land, 1820–1875*, was published in 2005. This far more controversial work places Texas Ranger history in a global context and challenges traditional notions of mythological frontier heroes and triumphant Anglo advancement through the contemporary lens of ethnic cleansing.[2]

The Conquest of Texas was not, however, Anderson's first foray into Lone Star territory. His previous regional emphasis on the northern plains had shifted focus with the 1999 publication of *The Indian Southwest, 1580–1830: Ethnogenesis and Reinvention*. Writing about "the native peoples of the southern plains and its periphery," Anderson joined contemporary ethnohistorians to reach beyond "the simplistic dualism . . . so prevalent in older historical literature." Following European contact, he argued, many of the native bands of the Southwest "altered themselves culturally to forge unity with other groups, abandoning languages, social practices, and even economic processes to meet the needs of the new order." Rather than characterize these people broadly as the "neophytes" and "barbaros" of earlier histories, he portrayed them as "actors rather than perpetrators or victims . . . people determined to survive and quite willing to reinvent culture or to join other, stronger groups if necessary to do so."[3]

In the brief epilogue of *The Indian Southwest*, "The Southern Plains Milieu, 1810–1830," Anderson laid the groundwork for *The Conquest of Texas*. "After Mexico's war for independence broke out in 1810," he wrote, "the southern plains attracted a host of new people, Native American, American and a mixture of ethnic backgrounds." By the early 1820s American trade with Santa Fe and the influx of both Anglo and "immigrant Indian" settlers from the United States brought new economic and political pressure to the region. Empresario Stephen F. Austin and the settlers in his colony soon recognized that the surrounding tribes, a "handful of Tonkawas" and "the more populous Wichitas" living to the northwest "viewed the Americans as intruders." "Rather than negotiate with them or make a reasonable effort to purchase their lands"—options apparently more obvious to Anderson than to either the Anglo settlers or traditional Texas historians—Austin instead surprised a small Tonkawa band accused of rustling colonists' livestock. He forced the leader to punish the perpetrators, then ordered the Tonkawas to "leave the Colorado River valley and never return."[4]

The concepts underlying that incident, and so many more, were fully developed in *The Conquest of Texas*. Certainly, Professor Anderson's interpretation of the first fifty years of Anglo–Native American relations in Texas challenged most traditional and revisionist historiography of Texas and the Texas Rangers, as well as that of Texas Indians. But his evident bias in favor of Native Americans was nothing new under the sun. Nor was he the first to apply twentieth-century analytical constructs to nineteenth-century history; since the Columbus Quincentenary of 1992 and even before, a growing number of studies had advanced and debated the idea of genocide against Native Americans, using language and concepts that only came into general usage during the 1940s. Indeed, Anderson anticipated and countered such potential criticism with an endnote to his introduction: "To those readers who believe that 'presentist' arguments are unfair, I would suggest that as an explanatory model, ethnic cleansing sheds much useful light. And it is well understood."[5]

Somewhere beyond the provocative advertising copy and historiographical controversy, Anderson crafted a thoroughly documented, if biased, narrative of Anglo expansion at the expense in Native Americans in Texas, often carried out by the Texas Rangers and viewed through the lens of ethnic cleansing. Not without its flaws, *The Conquest of Texas* nevertheless earned the attention of serious scholars of Texas history and the more general reading public.

The intellectual scope of Anderson's book is more comprehensive than many of his predecessors. In his work the historiography of Texas and Texas Rangers merges with ethnographic and anthropological studies of multiple tribes. Previous authors writing about Anglo pioneers and Texas Rangers often devoted little research to their Native American "adversaries," which complicated analysis of Ranger-Anglo-Indian relations. Conversely, chroniclers of Indian history frequently showed more concern with Indigenous cultural anthropology than they did with discussing Anglo suffering or Ranger heroics. In addition, several ethnohistorians conflated the actions of Texas Rangers with the (mis)deeds of militia troops, the Texas Army, and civilian mobs, while Ranger adherents continued to draw sharp distinctions between all these groups, relieving the Rangers of responsibility for at least some atrocities.

Early accounts of the Texas frontier presented a much simpler picture. Written by white participants in the battles to expand Texas or based on their memoirs, these books adopted a triumphant and often racist stance toward the Indigenous population. Pioneer minister John Wesley Wilbarger's *Indian Depredations in Texas*, first published in 1889, exemplified the genre. This 672-page tome comprises a patchwork of reminiscences, interviews, and accounts written by "others, who were either cognizant of the facts themselves or had obtained them from reliable sources." Alongside 250 separate depictions of Anglo–Native American combat, judged "the most complete compilation of accounts of Indian warfare in nineteenth-century Texas" by one historian, Wilbarger found time to discuss the origins of the Texas Rangers: "A sort of State militia was formed, composed of laboring men, hunters and trappers, and were known as 'Texas Rangers' . . . thoroughly posted and 'up to the tricks' of the cunning red man, they were a host unto themselves, and the timid felt assured of safety whenever a 'ranger' was on hand." As for the "cunning red man," Native Americans emerged from these chronicles as "irredeemable savages," such as the Rangers' Tonkawa scouts, who "fleeced the flesh off" Comanche and Waco corpses, "which horrid booty the cannibal monsters bore away with them to their camp, in which, doubtless a revolting, ghoulish feast was celebrated." Clearly, the good reverend "showed little sympathy for their culture or motives."[6]

Similarly, contemporaneous captivity narratives showed little understanding for the Indian captors—nor should such understanding be expected. Wilbarger witnessed his own brother's scalping, and some female captives experienced infanticide, rape, and torture. These were immediate, traumatic experiences burned into the authors' psyches. In addition, the social and "scientific" beliefs of the nineteenth century supported ideas of racial superiority and inferiority; why would white Anglo-Saxons not consider themselves superior to the "cannibal monsters" who consumed human flesh in their rituals? Balanced, academic understandings of Ranger-Indian contact lay in the distant future.[7]

The earliest academic studies of Anglos, Rangers, and Indians retained much of the flavor of the pioneer narratives, establishing what historian Walter Buenger dubbed "traditionalism" in Texas history. More rigorous and systematic scholarly standards replaced simplistic recapitulations of old-timers' memories, but the pro-Texas bias and implications of Anglo superiority remained. Professional historians such as George P. Garrison and Eugene C. Barker wrote broad histories and laudatory biographies about Texas, portraying the state's history as *A Contest of Civilizations*, or Stephen F. Austin's life as *A Chapter in the Westward Movement of the Anglo-American People*, who, "naturally," emerged victorious.[8]

By the 1930s their students were producing their own studies. In 1933 Rupert Norval Richardson produced *The Comanche Barrier to South Plains Settlement*, a somewhat more balanced saga that

combined available anthropological sources and actual criticism of
some Anglo and Ranger actions with a narrative that continued the
pioneer storytelling style. Richardson described the whites who first
encountered the Comanches on the South Plains as "bold, aggressive,
intolerant, and with little understanding of the Indians or sympathy
for them." When Ranger Captain John S. "Rip" Ford attacked a
"Comanche village of seventy lodges north of the Canadian" in 1858,
his report did not "state the number of women and children among the
seventy-six Indians slain, for that was no matter to Texas people . . .
the fact that these hostilities resulted in the death of Indian women and
children did not, as they thought, detract from the propriety or justice
of the war." Yet Richardson also included Ford's testimony favorable
to those Comanches on the two small reservations in Texas. During
the spring of 1858 the Rangers had "watched [them] closely . . . but
nothing occurred that gave any foundation" to local alarm regarding
their presence, which conveyed a degree of balance absent from most
earlier (and many contemporary) accounts. Still, the perspective
remained Anglo-centric: Native Americans perpetrated "massacres"
while Anglos fought "battles"; Texas "citizens organized into 'ranger
companies'" as Indians formed "war parties."[9]

Two years later the Texas Rangers found their academic champion
in Walter Prescott Webb. His *The Texas Rangers: A Century of Frontier
Defense* (1935) solidified the heroic Ranger image with scholarly
authority. His idealized Ranger "[stood] alone between a society and
its enemies," in this case "the Indian warrior, Mexican bandit, and
American desperado." Like Richardson, Webb sought to balance
his account of Indian-Anglo-Hispanic relations with some degree of
fairness. "It is not the purpose here, or anywhere in this volume, to
praise the Indian or to condemn him, but rather to understand him," he
claimed. But his "understanding" characterized Native Americans as
possessing a "primitive nature" and "ferocious cunning." When at war
they "killed the men, took the women, and adopted into the tribe the
children who were too young to run away." Webb, a Garrison student,
structured his book around a three-way "Conflict of Cultures" between

the archetypical "Indian Warrior, Mexican Vaquero, and Texas Ranger."
The valiant Rangers—and their "race"—would, of course, triumph in
the end. In addition to recognizing such broad racial generalizations,
Gary Clayton Anderson categorized Webb's interpretations (along
with those of Barker and Richardson) as "little different from the story
of the American frontier—as part of nation building" then current in
academia. Many of the depictions in *The Texas Rangers* would appall
twenty-first-century readers, especially those interested in Amerind
or Hispanic cultures. But Webb wrote in the twentieth century, under
the tutelage of nineteenth-century historiography. Many ethnocultural
resources—and more tolerant viewpoints regarding ethnicity—were
not widespread in his era.[10]

Revision of Ranger history arrived comparatively late, as it did
for Texas history in general. The most direct attacks on the Ranger
myth addressed their mistreatment of Tejanos and Mexicans but not
Native Americans. Both *"With His Pistol in His Hand": A Border
Ballad and Its Hero*, by Américo Paredes (1958), and *Gunpowder
Justice: A Reassessment of the Texas Rangers*, by Julian Samora, Joe
Bernal, and Albert Peña (1979), criticized—excoriated, in the case
of Samora, Bernal, and Peña—the Rangers for abuses of Latinos, as
both individuals and a group, and for the political corruption of the
force. The modern treatment of Native Americans in Ranger histories
varied but generally included a more sympathetic tone and reflected
some of the trends in contemporaneous ethnohistory. Yet despite
more acknowledgment of their excesses than earlier accounts, the
protagonists of these neotraditional accounts remained Texas Rangers,
(generally) stalwart examples of Texan courage and manhood fighting
to protect civilization from attack. The most ambitious of all was
American West generalist Robert Utley's 2002 updating of Webb,
Lone Star Justice: The First Century of the Texas Rangers, which
attempted to stake out a middle ground between the adulation of
Webb and the condemnation of Samora, Bernal, and Peña. Largely
successful in his aim, Utley still maintained a degree of bias in favor
of his subjects; the same could be said of most historians.[11]

Native American history regarding Texas has seen more growth and greater diversity of methodologies and analytical constructs since the middle of the twentieth century. Earlier accounts followed the pattern of revised Ranger history, traditional Texas history modified by expanding understanding drawn from the burgeoning discipline of ethnohistory. An early illustration of this trend was *The Comanches: Lords of the South Plains*, coauthored by Ernest Wallace and E. Adamson Hoebel and published in 1952. More than a simple account of Comanche-Texan conflict, this book covered cultural subjects to a greater extent than Indian fights. Drawing on anthropology, archeology, the authors' fieldwork interviewing Comanches, and traditional Texas History sources, *Lords of the South Plains* comprised more information about Comanche culture than any previous historical accounts. The Texas Rangers did not even enter the narrative until page 265 of the total 381. The historical perspective, however, was the standard Turnerian, nation-building version, with "natives mak[ing] the Texas frontier unsafe for white settlement" until they were confined to a reservation. Then, "the white settlements in Texas advanced more in the decade from 1874 to 1884 than in the fifty years preceding," a clear triumph in the authors' minds. Still, Wallace and Hoebel, along with Richardson, "will remain our best sources about prereservation Comanche life from a Comanche perspective" according to ethnohistorian Morris W. Foster.[12]

Comanches were not the only Native Americans fighting Texas Rangers, of course. *The Kiowas* received somewhat more favorable analysis from University of Texas anthropologist Mildred Mayhall in 1962. While acknowledging the real conflicts between Plains tribes and Texans, her cultural history shifts more—but certainly not all—of the responsibility to the Anglos. "The Texans mobilized militia and later developed the Texas Rangers to guard their frontiers" in response to the "fear and dread" caused by Kiowa raiding. Yet "Texans continued to drive the Indians from their best hunting grounds, in violation of treaties and without compensation." After the Texas Revolution, the Kiowas "need[ed] guns and ammunition, especially against the

Texans, who were free of Mexico in 1836 and pushing a war of extermination or removal of the Indians from Texas." The narrative transformed to the point that by 1970, Marian T. Place included these remarks in her *Comanches and Other Indians of Texas*, intended for the state's secondary school libraries: "Nowadays apologists try to prove that all the blame for Indian-white conflicts were [*sic*] caused by the whites. This is not true in regard to the Comanches. Both sides shared the blame."[13]

Whether or not students of Native American history and culture "apologized" for such historical conflicts, they intensified cross-pollination of social sciences into their research during the late twentieth and early twenty-first centuries. In 1991 Dianna Everett's *The Texas Cherokees: A People between Two Fires, 1819–1840* viewed that people's experience in Texas from their first arrival until their expulsion through the lens of their social and political culture. The Texas Rangers are referenced only once, for their discovery of documents that would help launch the Cherokee War of 1839. *Being Comanche: A Social History of an American Indian Community*, by Morris W. Foster, used multiple sources and methodologies—archival records, books, observation, interviews, ethnographic studies, and historical studies—to paint a sociological portrait of the Comanches from 1706 to 1990. "The image of ruthless Comanche warriors killing and taking captive the Anglo settlers," Foster charged, "was used to justify first Anglo occupation of their lands and later the establishment of an independent Anglo-American government and militia to protect the frontier better." Kevin Mulroy attributed even more ulterior motives to the Rangers in *Freedom on the Border: The Seminole Maroons in Florida, the Indian Territory, Coahuila, and Texas*. In this ethnohistory he argued that in the mid-1850s Rangers crossed into Mexico "under the pretext of pursuing Lipans and other hostile Indian bands . . . but the weight of the evidence supports the notion that their main intention was to break up the Seminole maroon settlement and return fugitive blacks to their Texas owners." Thomas Kavanagh returned to prereservation political analysis with his *Comanche Political History: An Ethnohistorical Perspective, 1706–1875* in 1995.[14]

Three years later, Kelly F. Kimmel used "world-system theory" as an analytical framework for *The Conquest of the Karankawas and the Tonkawas, 1821–1859*, a complex theoretical, sociological inquiry into the process and outcomes of conquest. The author noted that "The Anglo-Texans had used the belief that the Karankawas were cannibals . . . to justify their 'wars of extermination' against them in the 1820s." Yet the Texans would use the same "element of terror— the [in this case real] threat of cannibalism . . . [by] their Tonkawa allies" against other tribes. In the only reference to Texas Rangers, Kimmel suggested that "the likely borrowing of leadership styles by the Texas Rangers from the Tonkawas, Lipans, and Comanches lies within the larger debate surrounding the American Indian influence on Anglo-American institutions." He traced this idea to a comment by Webb in *The Texas Rangers* over sixty years before. Also in 1999, Gary Clayton Anderson structured *The Indian Southwest, 1580–1830: Ethnogenesis and Reinvention* around "the process by which distinct ethnic cultures recreate themselves as new cultures over time." Yet another sociological study of the Comanches emerged in 2002 with *Comanche Society: Before the Reservation*, by Gerald Betty. His stated goal was to create a "comprehensive understanding of the . . . Comanche Nation." Once again Anglo-Texans, although not their Rangers specifically, bore greater responsibility for frontier conflicts than in traditional versions, generally refused to interact with the Indians, and took a relatively hostile stance toward them. This situation "led to a great deal of suspicion between Comanches and Texans, resulting in numerous robberies, abductions, and other hostilities." Clearly, the interpretive pendulum was swinging in new directions.[15]

By the early 2000s, other ethnohistorians were incorporating interpretive models from the growing field of genocide studies to their research, including Anderson. Many, however, advanced their arguments regarding Indian removal, warfare, and reservation policies beyond the idea of ethnic cleansing; they argued instead that Euro-Americans perpetrated full-blown genocide against the Indigenous population of North America, a perspective by no means universally accepted. Historian David Stannard's *American Holocaust: Columbus and the Conquest of the New World* and anthropologist Russell Thornton's *American Indian Holocaust and Survival: A Population History since 1492* were early examples of this approach. More recent examples included Robert H. Jackson and Edward Castillo, *Indians, Franciscans, and Spanish Colonization: The Impact of the Mission System on California Indians*; controversial author/activist Ward Churchill's *Struggle for the Land: Indigenous Resistance to Genocide, Ecocide and Expropriation in Contemporary North America* and *Kill the Indian, Save the Man: The Genocidal Impact of American Indian Schools*; and Barbara Alice Mann, *George Washington's War on Native America*.[16]

In contrast, Gary Clayton Anderson argued that these genocidal interpretations "turn isolated events into trends and blame all Euro-Americans for consequences that chronologically span four centuries and involve a multitude of factors." As historian Norman Naimark reminded his readers, "Ethnic cleansing and genocide are two different activities, and the differences are important." Almost all definitions of genocide include the idea of intentionality; "the murder of a people . . . is the objective." "Ethnic cleansing," on the other hand, intends "to remove a people . . . from a concrete territory . . . and to seize control" of the land they inhabited. Significant loss of life often results from ethnic cleansing, but that is not its primary goal. Rather "its purpose is to remove a specific population from land that a more powerful group covets."[17]

The Conquest of Texas: Ethnic Cleansing in the Promised Land, 1820–1875 revealed Anderson's positions on the history of Texas, its Rangers, and Native Americans, as well as on ethnic cleansing, with an introduction titled "Demythologizing Texas." He picked up the narrative thread where *The Indian Southwest, 1580–1830* ended, setting the stage with a cautionary reminder that "Texas was not a wilderness open for the taking," noting an Indigenous population of thirty thousand people in 1820. As he continued Anderson almost casually expressed opinions likely to infuriate many Texans. For example, "rather than a fight for liberty," the Texas Revolution was "a poorly conceived southern land grab," fueled by Texans' desire to expand slavery, thereby increasing their profits from cotton production. In defending his overall interpretation of violence against Native Americans as ethnic cleansing, he noted that "the ethnic conflict in Texas continued because Anglos wanted it to." Thus, the violence resulting from Anglo expansion "can be seen for what it was: an Anglo-Texas strategy and a policy (at first haphazard, debated, and even at times abandoned) that gradually led to the ethnic cleansing of a host of people, especially people of color."[18]

To bolster this argument, Anderson drew parallels between Texas Rangers and Yugoslavian paramilitary organizations as "agents of ethnic cleansing." He went on, writing that "the paramilitary groups that forced removal or committed the occasional genocidal act were an extension of the Texas political system." That system encouraged Texas Rangers, the enforcement arm of Texas policy, to attack Indian villages filled with women and children—the usual victims of ethnic cleansing. Rangers killed indiscriminately; they robbed, and they raped. Their goal was to spread terror so that neighboring Native American groups would leave. As in Yugoslavia, they were quite successful at their business.

Yet not all Rangers fit the same mold in Anderson's analysis. "Some rangers were fine troops: well mounted, well led, and disciplined," he acknowledged. Others stayed in their home counties, "strutting" in front of local young women. But there was a third category of Ranger, renegades "filled with hatred and malice" who served for the plunder they could acquire, whether it be property or scalps. In Anderson's final analysis, then, Texas Rangers "could be brave defenders of the republic, rather harmless stay-at-home showoffs, or (more often than not) brutal murderers." The parenthetical comment was telling; it clearly revealed the author's bias against the "agents of ethnic cleansing" in nineteenth-century Texas.[19]

Anderson began his narrative with the Indigenous, the tribes present before the "American Invasion," a logical foundation for a cultural and ethnohistorian. He introduced Americans as a minority, outnumbered by Native Americans, "immigrant Indians" from the United States, and Tejanos. A distinct creed developed among the Americans, most of whom hailed from the slaveholding South, "founded on the belief that that certain races were more accomplished and more justified in inheriting the land than were others." As Anglo-Texan numbers grew, the "Texas creed" evolved to include the idea that "Anglos were justified in using violence . . . to create and sustain Anglo dominance." Beginning with Stephen F. Austin's first colony along the lower Brazos and Colorado Rivers, Anglo settlers asserted both that creed and their claim to those lands. Thus, an aggressive, racist minority began their expansion.[20]

"As soon as he possessed the men," according to Anderson, "Austin commissioned the first militia or 'ranger' companies along the Colorado River." In 1823 these Rangers surrounded an "unsuspecting" Karankawa village and opened fire; they "murdered" approximately two dozen people, "men, women, and children alike," then scalped the dead and looted the village. "The massacre . . . set the tone for the handling of nearby Indians" by Austin's colony. While Rangers cleared Karankawas and Tonkawas from the lower Brazos and Colorado valleys, Austin kept Mexican authorities alerted to his perceived threats from other tribes. By 1826 the Karankawas, Tonkawas, Wacos, and Tawakonis had been pushed westward. "Austin," Anderson posited, "must have been pleased." Depicting these actions with carefully chosen and clearly biased vocabulary, the author stated his perceptions clearly: With the support of government officials, the Father of Texas had begun to implement ethnic cleansing as a policy.[21]

The Rangers themselves played a smaller role in Anderson's version of the Texas Revolution, although Rangers at Gonzales ignited the struggle with the legendary "Come and Take It" skirmish over an "old cannon." The general values they reflected, however, remained prominent among Anglo-Texans. In closing his final chapter on the revolution, the author prophesied that "a cancer" was already overwhelming the new republic. Texans would now "embrace a nearly endless pattern of conflict." Soon a "culture of violence would stalk the land . . . plunging Texas into decades of despair."[22]

During the brief lifetime of the newly founded republic, Texas struggled with intransigent Indians and inconsistent Indian policies, ultimately adopting ethnic cleansing as an official policy. While President Sam Houston pursued a policy of diplomacy with Indians, his successor, Mirabeau B. Lamar, advocated for expansion of the republic and expulsion of the Indigenous population. Addressing the Texas Congress following the "Cherokee War" of 1839, President Lamar announced that "the proper policy toward the barbarian race is absolute expulsion from the country." Anderson noted that such rhetoric had been used in the past, yet "never had it come from a chief executive, and never had military expulsion become state policy." Presented with the options of peaceful coexistence or aggressive expansion, according to Anderson, Texans had chosen the latter course. This cycle of violence would continue even after Texas joined the Union.[23]

With statehood came war with Mexico, followed by decades of westward expansion and increasing conflicts against the Plains tribes (primarily Comanches), with both state and federal governments struggling—often against each other as much as the tribes—to find a workable Indian policy. Despite sometimes noble attempts at a peaceful resolution, "the majority of Anglo-Texans . . . supported ethnic cleansing in one fashion or another." As the Anglo population (along with Germans in the Hill Country) pressed west, Indian depredations increased. Reports of these raids were almost always exaggerated by Texas newspapers, then used to support requests for federal troops or Texas Rangers to provide protection. Federal troops and officials often dismissed the exaggerated claims as Texas newspapers and   politicians decried the inefficiency and ineptitude of the army and Congress. Nonetheless, those requests almost inevitably led to more military action, thus paving the way for still more expansion and resultant depredations. Attempts to create a boundary between settlers and Native Americans were foiled by the sheer volume of immigrants; Anderson called the plans "a fiasco." Creating two small reservations in the upper Brazos River region ultimately resulted in the expulsion to the Indian Territory of their occupants and the murder of their agent, Robert Neighbors. Following the Civil War, US Cavalry troops, often adopting Texas Ranger tactics, drove the last Comanche warriors out of the Panhandle in 1875. "This violence," Anderson concluded, "was the tool used to cleanse Texas of unwanted ethnic groups. The job mostly had been completed by 1875," when "only a few thousand" Native Americans remained for "their last stand." Despite the fact Texans "had many opportunities to end the violence," by 1875 the state had been ethnically cleansed.[24]

Gary Clayton Anderson's account of Texas history and his assessment of the Texas Rangers were, to be sure, "not your grandfather's tale of how a courageous few made a righteous conquest of a wild land." *The Conquest of Texas* demonstrated bias and adopted a controversial—although not unprecedented—analytical framework. It often emphasized Native American culture and events over the Anglo-Texan tales that readers may have found more familiar, or reevaluated those commonly known stories from an Indian perspective. The infamous "Council House Fight" of 1840, for example, became the "Council House Massacre" in Anderson's retelling. His characterizations of some Texas icons were often unflattering and the conclusions sometimes jarring. But the book nevertheless remained a noteworthy study by an important author, and an indispensable alternative to the traditional, heroic, and—to be blunt—racist versions of Texas history (or heritage?) of the not-so-distant past.[25]

Anderson's book betrayed many of the biases one might expect from an ethnohistorian who spent over twenty-five years reading and writing the cultural history of Native Americans. Most American historians, no matter their interpretive school—most Americans, for that matter—would agree that Indians suffered egregiously at the hands of Europeans and their descendants from 1492 onward. Having immersed himself in their history and culture for so long, Professor Anderson's empathy was clear and virtually unavoidable. When he shared his deeper understanding of Indigenous lifeways with readers, he often did so to the exclusion of similar explications of the "dominant culture," thus creating a bias in favor of the Indians. But he did not express this academic bias dishonestly: he included graphic descriptions of Native American acts of violence, including scalping, infanticide, and torture, as well. Objectivity stands as a laudable goal, but often an elusive one—indeed, some historians would argue an unattainable one in its purest form. Although Anderson displayed these biases, he contained them and presented a more multifaceted portrait of Indians, as well as Anglo-Americans, than many of his predecessors.[26]

The criticism that Anderson obviously anticipated most and attempted to counter at the outset of *The Conquest of Texas* was presentism, analyzing and judging the past in terms of the present. In his classic application of logic to historical thinking, *Historians' Fallacies*, the esteemed David Hackett Fischer criticized "the *fallacy of presentism* [as] a complex anachronism in which the antecedent is falsified by being defined or interpreted in terms of the consequent." For Fischer the driving of Native Americans from Texas in the nineteenth century would be "falsified" by defining it as "ethnic cleansing," a concept not available to scholars until the mid-twentieth century. Neither Texans in 1835 nor Texans in 1875 possibly could have known that they were practicing ethnic cleansing; indeed, they used different terminology—"drive from the country," or even "exterminate"—to conceive and describe their actions. If the goal of professional history is, in the words the venerable German historicist Leopold von Ranke, to describe events "as they really were," then "ethnic cleansing" would be of little use in analyzing the events of nineteenth-century Texas. Such an analytical framework could arguably "falsify" the motives and perceptions of Anglo-Texans and distort our interpretations of their actions.[27]

Which alternative, then, is most important: to analyze past events "as they were," following strict rules of logical historical practice, or to employ the "new concepts . . . to understand [those events] in the present"? If individuals in the past followed patterns of behavior that mirrored more recent actions, is it necessarily fallacious to use the more contemporary terminology to describe the past actions? Serbian paramilitary organizations attacked Bosnian Muslims to drive them from their lands in the early 1990s, Anderson would argue, in much the same way that Texas Rangers drove Indigenous tribes from the territory they sought to settle from the 1820s to the 1870s. The nomenclature changed across time, but the behavior remained fundamentally the same. If both instances were essentially similar in motive, action, and result, as Anderson posited, did calling them both "ethnic cleansing" really "falsify" history, especially if it helped us to better understand the actions in Texas or to have seen them as part of broad trends in world history? Clearly Anderson would answer no; he would rather accept the pejorative label of presentist if such analysis allowed him "to create a new paradigm for understanding the violence that dominated the Texas history, especially along its frontier."[28]

"I'm the moderate here," Anderson could plausibly argue at the 2007 Battle of San Jacinto Symposium. Between the historiographical poles of triumphant conquest on one side and deliberate genocide on the other, ethnic cleansing occupies a legitimate analytical middle ground, even when applied to nineteenth-century Texas. Twentieth-century ethnic cleansing could not have occurred without the "direct involvement and connivance of political leaders." And so it was in Texas over a century ago. Leaders of the Texas Republic and the state, many of them former Rangers themselves, supported—sometimes incited—ethnic cleansing of Indigenous people from lands to the west and north of those previously settled. And those Rangers, some well-disciplined troops and others renegades out for plunder, cleared those lands, often brutally, but ultimately effectively.[29]

If history is to remain alive as an intellectual discipline, it must adapt in the face of new facts and viewpoints. No single historical interpretation can remain current forever, no matter how reassuring or self-congratulatory. In the end Gary Clayton Anderson provided a fresh and thought-provoking perspective from which to analyze both the history of Texas and the Texas Rangers that includes full agency for Native Americans. As a part of that process, however, he required readers to abandon some familiar tropes for new understandings, to adopt a broad perspective beyond the narrow, parochial triumphalism of so many traditional interpretations of Texas history. The familiar "white civilizers versus red savages" stereotype must make way for a more inclusive view, one considering more people with complex cultures and motives as actors, rather than simply as bloodthirsty foes. The mythical, heroic Texas Ranger must now stand alongside his less virtuous colleagues, those who fought for plunder and out of racial hatred, and the "Noble Savage" must undergo analysis understanding whole cultures, not merely a propensity for violence. The new understanding Anderson offered loomed even larger than Texas itself, for ethnic cleansing remained a world phenomenon and required a larger scope of analysis. Therefore, the actions of the once-iconic Texan frontiersmen were no longer exceptional but comparable to other actors in other times and places, often in quite unflattering ways. This may be too much for proud Texans—far more deeply devoted to the preservation of their forbears' reputations and their own distinctive identities than to evolving methods of historical analysis and interpretation—to accept. But if readers of *The Conquest of Texas* allow the traditional icons to step off their pedestals and accept their full, less-than-glorious humanity, they may find a deeper understanding of their own.

Notes

1. Gary Clayton Anderson, *The Conquest of Texas: Ethnic Cleansing in the Promised Land, 1820–1875* (Norman: University of Oklahoma Press, 2005), back jacket, inside front flap.

2. "Gary Clayton Anderson," *Dodge Family College of Arts and Sciences, Department of History, University of Oklahoma*, accessed April 22, 2024, http://www.ou.edu/cas/history/people/faculty/gary-clayton-anderson; Gary Clayton Anderson, *Kinsmen of Another Kind: Dakota-White Relations in the Upper Mississippi River Valley, 1650–1862* (Lincoln: University of Nebraska Press, 1984); Anderson, *Conquest of Texas*; for more examples, see Anderson, *Little Crow: Spokesman for the Sioux* (St. Paul: Minnesota Historical Society Press, 1986); Anderson and Alan R. Woolworth, eds., *Through Dakota Eyes: Narrative Accounts of the Minnesota Indian War of 1862* (St. Paul: Minnesota Historical Society Press, 1988); Anderson, *Sitting Bull and the Paradox of Lakota Nationhood* (New York: Longman, 1997); Anderson, *The Indian Southwest, 1580–1830: Ethnogenesis and Reinvention* (Norman: University of Oklahoma Press, 1999).

3. Anderson, *Indian Southwest*, 3–4, 7, 8.

4. Anderson, *Indian Southwest*, 251, 255–57.

5. For a basic understanding of the traditionalist and revisionist schools of Texas history, see the introduction and William Clay Yancey's chapter on Ranger biographies in this volume; for representative examples of "genocidal" interpretations of Native American history, see David Stannard, *American Holocaust: Columbus and the Conquest of the New World* (New York: Oxford University Press, 1992); and Russell Thornton, *American Indian Holocaust and Survival: A Population History Since 1492* (Norman: University of Oklahoma Press, 1987); Anderson, *Conquest of Texas*, 379.

6. John W. Wilbarger, *Indian Depredations in Texas* [. . .] (1889; repr., Austin: Eakin Press and Statehouse Books, 1985), 386, 289; Christopher Long, "Wilbarger, John Wesley," *Handbook of Texas Online*, accessed January 1, 2022, https://www.tshaonline.org/handbook/entries/wilbarger-john-wesley. For other examples of "Pioneer historiography," see John Henry Brown, *History of Texas, from 1685 to 1892*, 2 vols. (St. Louis: L. E. Daniell, 1892–93), and *Indian Wars and Pioneers of Texas* (Austin: L. E. Daniell, 1896); John C. Duval, *The Adventures of Big-Foot Wallace, The Texas Ranger and Hunter*, ed.

Mabel Major and Rebecca W. Smith (1871; repr. Lincoln: University of Nebraska Press, 1966); Andrew Jackson Sowell, *Rangers and Pioneers of Texas* [. . .] (1884; repr., n.p.: Create Space Independent Publishing Platform, 2016), *Early Settlers and Indian Fighters of Southwest Texas* (1900; repr., Austin: State House Press, 1986), and *Life of "Big Foot" Wallace*: *The Great Ranger Captain* (1899; repr. Austin: State House Press, 1989).

7. The literature on captivity narratives is nearly its own distinct discipline and too voluminous to examine in depth here. For a few notable Texas accounts, see Benjamin Dolbeare, *A Narrative of the Captivity and Suffering of Dolly Webster Among the Camanche Indians in Texas* (1843; repr., New Haven: Yale University Library, 1986); Rachel Parker Plummer, *Narrative of the Capture and Subsequent Sufferings of Mrs. Rachel Plummer* (1838; repr., n.p.: Independently published, 2021); and Carl Coke Rister, *Comanche Bondage*: *Beale's Settlement and Sarah Ann Horn's Narrative*, introduction by Don Worcester (1839; repr., Lincoln: University of Nebraska Press, 1989).

8. Walter L. Buenger, "Three Truths in Texas," in *Beyond Texas through Time: Breaking Away from Past Interpretations*, ed. Walter L. Buenger and Arnoldo De Léon (College Station: Texas A&M University Press, 2011), 1–4; Walter L. Buenger and Robert A. Calvert, "The Shelf Life of Truth in Texas History," in *Texas through Time: Evolving Interpretations*, ed. Walter L. Buenger and Robert L. Calvert, (College Station: Texas A&M University Press, 1991), ix–xxiv; Margaret C. Berry, "Garrison, George Pierce," *Handbook of Texas* Online, accessed December 15, 2021, https://www.tshaonline.org/handbook/entries/garrison-george-pierce. Published by the Texas Historical Association; William C. Pool, "Barker, Eugene Campbell," *Handbook of Texas Online*, accessed December 15, 2021, https://www.tshaonline.org/handbook/entries/barker-eugene-campbell.

9. Rupert Norval Richardson, *The Comanche Barrier to South Plains Settlement*, ed. Kenneth R. Jacobs, introduction by A. C. Greene (1933; repr. Austin: Eakin Press, 1996), 32, 119–20, 127, 130–31. For a comparable treatment, although written four decades later, see T. R. Fehrenbach, *Comanches: The Destruction of a People* (New York: Knopf, 1974).

10. Walter Prescott Webb, *The Texas Rangers: A Century of Frontier Defense*, foreword by Lyndon B. Johnson (1935; repr., Austin: University of Texas Press, 1965), xv, 11–12; Anderson, *Conquest of Texas*, 11.

11. Américo Paredes, *"With His Pistol in His Hand": A Border Ballad and Its Hero* (Austin: University of Texas Press, 1958); Julian Samora, Joe Bernal, and Albert Peña, *Gunpowder Justice: A Reassessment of the Texas Rangers* (Notre Dame: University of Notre Dame Press, 1979); Robert M. Utley, *Lone Star Justice: The First Century of the Texas Rangers* (New York: Oxford University Press, 2002), ix–xiv, 287–302. For the revisionist school of Texas Ranger history, see the introduction and William Clay Yancey's chapter on Ranger biographies in this volume; for additional representative examples, refer to chapters on Mike Cox, Stephen Moore, Chuck Parsons, and Ben Procter in this volume.

12. Ernest Wallace and E. Adamson Hoebel, *The Comanches: Lords of the South Plains* (Norman: University of Oklahoma Press, 1952), 36, 265, 294, 301, 328; Morris W. Foster, *Being Comanche: A Social History of an American Indian Community* (Tucson: University of Arizona Press, 1991), xxi–xxiv.

13. Mildred P. Mayhall, *The Kiowas* (Norman: University of Oklahoma Press, 1962), 14, 72, 81; Marian T. Place, *Comanches & Other Indians of Texas* (New York: Harcourt, Brace & World, 1970), 4.

14. Dianna Everett, *The Texas Cherokees: A People between Two Fires, 1819–1840* (Norman: University of Oklahoma Press, 1990), 102; Foster, *Being Comanche*, vii, 47; Kevin Mulroy, *Freedom on the Border: The Seminole Maroons in Florida, the Indian Territory, Coahuila, and Texas* (Lubbock: Texas Tech University Press, 1993), 79; Thomas Kavanagh, *Comanche Political History: An Ethnohistorical Perspective, 1706–1875* (Lincoln: University of Nebraska Press, 1995).

15. Kelly F. Kimmel, *The Conquest of the Karankawas and the Tonkawas, 1821–1859* (College Station: Texas A&M University Press, 1999), x, 83; see Webb, *Century of Frontier Defense*, 79, for the "leadership" parallel; Anderson, *Indian Southwest*, 267n4; Gerald Betty, *Comanche Society: Before the Reservation* (College Station: Texas A&M University Press, 2002), 8, 118, 137.

16. For an introduction to genocide studies, see George J. Andreopoulos, ed., *Genocide: Conceptual and Historical Dimensions* (Philadelphia: University of Pennsylvania Press, 1994); Benedict Kiernan, *Blood and Soil: A World History of Genocide and Extermination from Sparta to Darfur* (New Haven: Yale University Press, 2007). Applications of genocide studies to Native American history includes: Stannard, *American Holocaust*; Thornton, *American Indian Holocaust*

and Survival; Robert H. Jackson and Edward H. Castillo, *Indians, Franciscans, and Spanish Colonization: The Impact of the Mission System on California Indians* (Albuquerque: University of New Mexico Press, 1995); Ward Churchill, *Struggle for the Land: Indigenous Resistance to Genocide, Ecocide, and Expropriation in Contemporary North America* (San Francisco: City Lights, 2002), and *Kill the Indian, Save the Man: The Genocidal Impact of American Indian Schools* (San Francisco: City Lights, 2004); and Barbara Alice Mann, *George Washington's War on Native America* (Lincoln: University of Nebraska Press, 2008).

17. Anderson, *Conquest of Texas*, 5, 7–8; Norman Naimark, *Fires of Hatred: Ethnic Cleansing in Twentieth-Century Europe* (Cambridge, MA: Harvard University Press, 2001), 3, 5–6.

18. Anderson, *Conquest of Texas*, 5, 7.

19. Anderson, *Conquest of Texas*, 7–9.

20. Anderson, *Conquest of Texas*, 7–9.

21. Anderson, *Conquest of Texas*, 53–54; 57.

22. Anderson, *Conquest of Texas*, 102, 124.

23. Anderson, *Conquest of Texas*, 212, 127, 128–30, 180.

24. Anderson, *Conquest of Texas*, 223; 228–29; 233–36; 259–26; 330–44; 357, 360.

25. Anderson, *Conquest of Texas*, inside front flap; 183.

26. Anderson, *Conquest of Texas*, 128, 136–37, 354, for example.

27. David Hackett Fischer, *Historian' Fallacies: Toward a Logic of Historical Thought* (New York: Harper & Row, 1970), 135–40; Anderson, *Conquest of Texas*, 180; Ranke quoted in Mark T. Gilderhus, *History and Historians: A Historiographical Introduction*, 7th ed. (Upper Saddle River, NJ: Prentice Hall, 2010), 45–46.

28. Anderson, *Conquest of Texas*, 14–15.

29. Gary Clayton Anderson, "American Indians and the Texas Revolution," (paper presented at the Battle of San Jacinto Symposium, Houston, TX, April 14, 2007), video, 49:16, https//:www.youtube.com/watch?v=dOA9ZVpwtOE; Naimark, *Fires of Hatred*, 3.

Chapter 15

When Truth Is No Longer a Casualty of Myth

Américo Paredes and the Texas Rangers

Manuel F. Medrano

J ames McPherson, former president of the American Historical Association, wrote, "Revision is the lifeblood of historical scholarship. . . . Interpretations of the past are subject to change in response to new evidence, new questions asked of the evidence, new perspectives gained by the passage of time. . . . Revisionism is what makes history vital and meaningful."[1] Historical equality exists only when victors and vanquished can both tell their stories, although many years may pass before equitable documentation occurs. Such was the case with the Texas Rangers and South Texas Tejanos.

For years their interaction was seen primarily through the eyes of Anglo landowners, historians, and the Rangers themselves, with writers such as Walter Prescott Webb and J. Frank Dobie at the forefront. Webb wrote this about the Ranger: "Of this far-famed corps—so much feared and hated by the Mexicans—I can add nothing to what has already been written . . . chivalrous, bold and impetuous in action, yet he is wary and calculating, always impatient of restraint, and sometimes unscrupulous and unmerciful."[2] Webb admitted that "many innocent Mexicans were made to suffer and that "many members of the force have been heartily ashamed of their part in the orgy of bloodshed, yet this orgy of bloodshed was what was necessary to make the region safe and secure for newcomer families."[3] In an apology of necessity, Webb argued that Tejano suffering was a reasonable price for Anglo success and security. Dobie wrote, "They were picked men who knew how to ride, shoot and tell the truth . . . on the Mexican border and on the Indian territory, a few rangers time and time again proved themselves more effective than a battalion of soldiers."[4] Rangers were also faithful guardians of their own tales, including the exploits of Captain Leander McNelly. In the mid-1870s his brigade butchered numerous criminals and Mexicans. McNelly "is an appealing composite of warlord and Christ figure . . . courageous and gentlemanly, utterly devoted to his men and his mission, a remorseless killer. . . . From McNelly flows the rich blood of Ranger lore. McNelly, however, was never a Ranger. He was a captain of the Washington Volunteer Militia."[5] Although many Tejanos disagreed, these descriptions enhanced the Rangers' reputation of perceived infallibility. Into the twentieth century, their storytellers were primarily those holding the legal and academic guns.

To many Tejanos, however, the Rangers were a law above the law that maneuvered the legal system from arrest to execution. Their victims and families knew what traditional academics and the Anglo public did not want to know or believe. The Rangers had a dark side, an underside, that was virtually undocumented. Some that was revealed, however, came from Rangers themselves. J. B. "Red" Dunn remembers being recruited into a unit near Corpus Christi. He described it as "the worst mixed lot of men that ever came together in one organization . . . some of the most dilapidated, diseased, moth-eaten specimens of humanity that I have ever seen."[6] Albert J. Myer, former military man, described them as "a lazy ruffianly scoundrel in a country where little is known of, less cared for, the laws of God or man and you have the material for a Texas Mounted Ranger . . . a brute."[7] He did say there were exceptions and his words were not meant for all. This was an obvious contrast to most of their mainstream depictions.

The Tejano perspective of the Rangers gained attention in the mid-twentieth century when folklorist/professor Américo Paredes revealed a story known but rarely told for many years. It did not glorify or condone their deeds. It condemned them by using Tejano accounts of the bloody Ranger violence in the borderlands, some told under breath for many years. What he wrote was unpopular and controversial, but it was the truth. Américo knew it, and he could prove it. Paredes was neither the first nor the last to question the Ranger myth, yet his writing resonated with many, including those who knew a different truth but had never seen it in print.

Those who came before Américo were also aware of this invisible history. Labor organizer/activist Emma Tenayuca stated that the land speculators cooperated with the Texas Rangers to kill unarmed Mexicans and seize lands, and follow that with "the formality of signing bills of sale—at the point of a gun."[8] Nearly five decades later, in his award-winning book, *Anglos and Mexicans in the Making of Texas, 1836-1986*, David Montejano wrote that the Rangers were more than lawmen with pistols. In addition to suppressing seditious Mexican bandits, "they played a critical part in paving the way for newcomer farmers."[9] King Ranch purchases in Kleberg County during the second half of the nineteenth century document minimal Tejano compensation for land they were sometimes threatened to sell. Miguel Elisondo received $1,800 for over fifty-three thousand acres and Flores Garcia was paid "sufficient" for over fifty-three thousand acres. By contrast Anglos were usually paid more. H. E. Woodhouse was paid $7,000 for over twenty-six thousand acres, and Charles Stillman received $20,000 in compensation for over ninety-five thousand acres.[10] King Ranch holdings eventually ballooned to approximately a million acres for pennies an acre.

A Paredes contemporary, who also lived in Brownsville, was José Tomás (J. T.) Canales. Canales was a landowner, distinguished attorney, judge, author, and legislator. A member of the Texas House of Representatives and a civil rights activist, he called "for an end to sanctioned state racial violence by the Texas Rangers of the

Mexican-descent population of the Lower Rio Grande Valley."
He was threatened by Congressman William H. Bledsoe and Ranger
Frank Hamer. His criticism resulted in a review of their conduct and
minimal changes in their organization and numbers.[11] On this issue
Canales stood firmly defiant against his own party, the establishment,
and the Rangers. Because of a hostile and powerful opposition,
little was done for many years. Eventually, before his death in 1976,
Canales witnessed some of changes he had championed over half a
century before.

In 1951 he addressed the Lower Rio Grande Historical Society
in San Benito, Texas. There, two and a half decades earlier, the Ku
Klux Klan, in full regalia, had marched downtown promoting its
nativist/racist agenda. The photograph of that march is, to say the
least, sobering. Canales began with a Spanish proverb: "La mentira
dura mientras la verdad llega" (A lie lasts until the truth arrives).
He proceeded by saying that shortly after the US-Mexico War,
adventurers "prompted by a desire to get rich quick, flocked into the
Rio Grande Valley to make their fortune at the expense of newly created
Americans of Mexican descent, who owned lands and property in this
section of Texas."[12] He named Charles Stillman, Richard King, and
Mifflin Kennedy among the culprits, and they all were supported by
the Texas Rangers. As a speaker Canales was forceful and confident;
as a proponent of Tejano rights, he was relentless.

In 1915 a child was born to Justo and Cleotilde Manzano Paredes.
His name was Américo, and he would eventually challenge the Ranger
institution and the men who helped create it, utilizing his family and
life history, extensive research, and *voluntad* (will).

His life began on the US-Mexico border during the Mexican Revolution and the Border Wars. It was a place where cultures, customs, and
languages merged and clashed and where he would learn the history
and culture that shaped his life. Don Américo remembered, "I'm a
Brownsville boy born September 3, 1915, during the height of the
border troubles when there was an ethnic cleansing, to use the current

term, along the border when Texas Rangers and others murdered a number of Mexicans and forced many others to leave the country."[13] These words initiated a series of interviews I conducted during the last years of his life and let me know immediately what was important to him.

Paredes's ancestors were elite ranching families rooted with José de Carbajal as Sephardic Jews in 1580 and José Escandón in 1749. Over the years, with little hope for justice, the families of these colonists were forced to forfeit their lands and political privileges. As a folklorist and historian, Paredes commented about this subjugation, blaming the opportunism and avarice of numerous North American adventurers.[14] Américo's father was born in Matamoros, Tamaulipas, in 1868, the oldest of seven children. Paredes remembered, "My father was always a rebel. He joined Catarino Garza's revolt [an attempted uprising against Porfirio Díaz in 1891]. He was wounded. Of course, his father [Américo's grandfather] had fought against the French."[15] Paredes's literary insurrectionism was a continuation of earlier family activism. Throughout most of his life, don Américo protested the mistreatment of Mexicanos by the Rangers and others through his writings.

Before the Great Depression, his father and uncle ran a dry goods store in downtown Brownsville. Shortly after the crash, the bank closed and left the family with no money. During these years Paredes became interested in folk ballads and folktales. When he was thirteen, Américo and his brothers spent their summers near Matamoros on his tío (uncle) Vicente's rancho. Américo reminisced about those times, recalling, "We would stay there living like Mexicans, listening to the old people tell their stories. My father would come down sometimes also, and at the end of August, they would drive us back to Brownsville and there I was living in another world."[16] Américo's niece, Blanca, remembered how much Américo enjoyed talking about those times on the rancho. Neither realized that those experiences would become the foundation for his life's work.[17]

Paredes later dedicated *Texas Mexican Cancionero: Folksongs of the Lower Rio Grande* to those individuals and times. He began collecting them as a youth. In the introduction he wrote,

> The songs collected here are a people's heritage—their unselfconscious record of themselves alien for the most part to documents and books. There are few enough writings about the Border people, who happen to be my people. The Anglos who came down to us as conquerors saw us as abysmal savages—benighted by papistry (priest-ridden as the great Texas liberal, J. Frank Dobie, used to say) and debased by miscegenation (with ditchwater instead of blood in our veins), as another great Texas liberal and scholar, Walter Prescott Webb, once put it). . . . The whole of a people's past is reflected in these songs, from the days when they journeyed out into Chichimecaland, mid-eighteenth-century pioneers, traveling north until they reached the Rio Grande, drank of its waters, and travelled no more.[18]

This was the European genesis of the Valley.

One cancionero ballad, "Los Tequileros" (The Tequila Runners), is about three *tequileros* killed by the Rangers when they crossed the Rio Grande. The following verse sarcastically describes the culprits: "The *rinches* are very brave, there is no doubt of that; / the only way they can kill us is by hunting us like deer."[19] In a second ballad, "Jacinto Treviño," Treviño, a wanted man, challenges the Rangers to capture him. He boldly mocks their parentage by telling them, "Come on, you cowardly *rinches*, you're not playing games with a child. / You wanted to meet your father? I am Jacinto Treviño!"[20] This verse exudes defiance and disdain.

To don Américo cultural conflict was at the core of the border ballad. Corridos often told stories about South Texas violence that involved Anglos and the Texas Rangers, or Rinches, as they were called by many, including Américo. During our interviews Américo used the term pejoratively. Alan, his youngest son, remembers that the violence "affected our family personally. [My father] told me about an uncle on his own horse, on his own land, who was murdered by a

Ranger."[21] Many Tejanos viewed them as untrustworthy, usually for more than one reason.

Paredes lived in Brownsville until near the end of World War II, working as journalist for the *Brownsville Herald* and as an employee of Pan American Airways. He entered the army in 1944, was stationed in the Far East, and was the political editor for the Pacific *Stars and Stripes*, a Tokyo-based daily newspaper for the armed forces.[22] The veteran returned with a new bride, Amelia Sidzu Nagamine, and a goal of achieving a doctorate in folklore, English, and Spanish at the University of Texas.

América completed his degree in 1956 and later explained, "I was very much aware . . . I was not the only one who believed that what we were taught in school at the time and what we knew in our hearts and what our parents taught us was different; that our heritage was not being the respect that it deserved . . . most of what our people knew were in corridos, in legends, and in oral history. And I wanted to bring these things to the majority."[23] His book *"With His Pistol in His Hand": A Border Ballad and Its Hero* would eventually do that. It is about a Tejano folk hero, Gregorio Cortéz, who managed a valiant escape from the Texas Rangers. In the last verse of the corrido, Cortéz mocks the Rangers: "Ah, so many mounted Rangers just to take one Mexican."[24] Paredes first heard the corrido when his mother sang it and later from the old men on the ranchos along the river.[25] His research was rigorous and meticulous, utilizing court records, newspapers, interviews, and correspondence, including those from Valeriano, the son, and Louis, the grandson, of Gregorio Cortéz.

One popular anecdote in the book is about the border Mexican. América wrote, "The Texas Ranger carries a rusty old gun in his saddlebags. This for use when he kills an unarmed Mexican. He drops the old gun beside the body and then claims he killed the Mexican in self-defense and after a furious battle."[26] A second one had Texas Rangers looking for a Mexican horse thief, encountering a half-dozen Mexican workers, and killing them. The Rangers report back to Austin that although outnumbered, they killed twelve of the bandits. The rest fled to the border. Austin is satisfied with the report, and the Rangers embellish their reputation. The real horse thief, however, fears he may encounter Rangers one day on some isolated road and they mistake him for a Mexican worker. Published in 1958 by UT Press, the book was not without controversy. Its condemning comments about Webb, Dobie, and the Texas Rangers concerned press director Frank Wardlaw. Webb, then serving on the UT press editorial board, informed Wardlaw that he enthusiastically supported the publication and regretted that he "was unable to give the Mexican attitude toward the Rangers, and their side of the border conflict, with any thoroughness."[27] Paredes made some modifications, but "the brutal criticisms of Webb" remained.[28] For example, Webb wrote that "the Mexicans suffered in their persons but in also their property."[29] Paredes countered that with what Webb neglected to convey, "this lawless law was enforced primarily by the Texas Rangers. It was the Rangers who could and did furnish the fortune-making adventurers with services not rendered by the United States army or local sheriffs."[30]

Unlike ceremonies for previous publications, no book signing was held at the University of Texas or at the University Co-op for Paredes. One person, a former Ranger, did, however, visit the UT Press offices looking for Paredes. Américo remembered, "Nada, nothing was done for my book." Less than a decade later, however, Chicanos in California, led by writer Tomas Rivera, said its message was important to the Movimiento. The book was popular there and, later, in Texas.[31] As a result Américo became "an underground celebrity."[32] The book is described as prophetic in its connection to the ongoing cultural conflict on the US-Mexico border. It is a weave of folklore, literature, memoir, and anthropology.[33] Throughout the book, Rangers reinforce Anglo beliefs that Mexicans are cruel, treacherous, cowardly, and degenerate. The book is now in its nineteenth printing.

George Washington Gomez: A Mexicotexan Novel, was nearly completed in 1940 but was not published for another fifty years. Its setting is Jonesville-on-the-Grande, and Gualinto, named after George Washington, is the main character. Throughout the book Texas

Rangers harass and threaten the Mexicano-Tejano population and murder among others, Gumercindo, Gualinto's father.[34] The Rangers believed he and Gualinto's uncle, Lupe Garcia, were members of Anacleto de la Pena's seditionist movement. It was sometimes convenient for Rangers to use guilt-by-association methods to justify their actions. The novel was written when the Rio Grande Valley was transitioning into the twentieth century. Commercial agriculture, the extension of the railroad, and the effects of the Mexican Revolution were but three of the dramatic developments of that era. One episode of guerrilla warfare occurred at Olmito, where a train was attacked and derailed. For the Anglo community, the event resulted in increased anti-Mexican sentiment and continued tolerance for violent Ranger activity, including forced sales of land. Gualinto and the Rangers in the book are modeled after people in Brownsville who Américo probably knew.[35]

After his retirement in 1984, Américo wrote *Uncle Remus con Chile*, a collection of "verbal lore that reflected the attitudes of Mexicans and Texas-Mexicans along the Lower Border toward Anglo-Americans, especially jokes and other narratives."[36] The first of its 217 texts is about the excesses of the Rangers—assassinations and threats to rancho owners to force them off their lands. One of Paredes's interviewees witnessed a Ranger murder a man in Brownsville. He followed the victim, who had his hands raised, into the post office and shot him in the back of the head. The Ranger alleged that the man was carrying a knife that the witness never saw.

Américo Paredes died on Cinco de Mayo in 1999 and a memorial was held on June 2 at the University of Texas. Former students, colleagues, musicians, and friends from throughout the country mourned and celebrated the man who for much of his life had raised, carried, and defended their cultural flag. Américo was more than a folklorist or author; he was an authority on the border corrido, an academic activist who challenged the traditional Texas Ranger story and those responsible for writing it. Most agree that his research was impeccable. It had to be, because the stakes were just too high. What

Texas children had been reading about the Rangers for nearly a century was filtered and incomplete. Américo used the power of his pen to remove some of the filter and complete part of the story. This was his regalo (gift) to those who followed.

Some scorned his audacity. Some applauded his courage, some the sheer power of his words. José Ángel Gutiérrez, Chicano activist, author, and Américo's former student, recalls,

> During the spring of 1963 is when I also began to have my first brushes of violence with the Rangers. . . . He [Captain A. Y. Allee] told us to stop registering voters and going to these rallies, and he advised us of the dangers of walking across town (Crystal City) at night. . . . He also ordered me to stop making inflammatory speeches because he said I was most effective at 'making these Meskins act crazy.' Again I denied doing anything like that; he got very upset and slapped me. As I flinched and turned away, he kicked me.

On one occasion he was thrown into the back of a squad car and told he would be killed, although he was eventually released. Gutierrez later received his PhD from the University of Texas and credits Paredes with impacting his life as a mentor and scholar.[37]

And there were others. José Limón, Notre Dame professor and former pupil and colleague, writes that "the corrido of border conflict is embedded in a history of social conflict, and therefore, as a text, it continually signifies and refers to the confrontation of larger social forces defined by ethnicity and class."[38] Paredes's life and book "exert a compelling influence on a new generation."[39] Anne Dingus contends that *"With His Pistol in His Hand"* "ushered in an era of revisionism by refuting mainstream, Anglo-dominated histories of Texas. Paredes's exhaustive research proved Cortéz's innocence and also debunked the 'pseudo-folklore'—long expounded by academics such as Walter Prescott Webb—that depicted Mexicans as cowardly and cruel, while exalting Texans, especially Texas Rangers, as a righteous and superior breed."[40] Their deeds and faults were now integrands of a public history.

The discussion about the real Texas Ranger history continues. General agreement exists about their purpose and charge. Tactics and autonomy, however, have been questioned since their inception, but rarely publicly. This, however, has changed during the last half century. Historians Benjamin Heber Johnson, William D. Carrigan, and Monica Muñoz Martinez, among numerous others, document the underside of the Rangers—forcing Mexicanos and Mexicano Americanos off their properties, threatening ranchers and farmers, and murdering and lynching townspeople with virtually no accountability. In a 2020 interview, journalist/historian Doug Swanson, author of *Cult of Glory: The Bold and Brutal History of the Texas Rangers*, spoke about the maintenance and celebration of the Ranger image, their perfection of police brutality on the border, and their skill as executioners for the powerful white community. Hundreds, if not thousands, of Mexicanos and Mexicano Americanos were executed, having committed no crime—except for having brown skin.[41] At an earlier time, these comments would have elicited mostly disdain and probably would not have been published. Today, they are part of the reexamination of Ranger history.

Américo Paredes provided a literary/historical voice for Tejanos, who for many years had been silenced. They knew what they knew, and he proved it. There is something to be said about an individual who champions the truth, and who does it so convincingly that both friends and enemies, many who dislike him, respect him. Even late into his life, his knowledge of and search for historical truth was unyielding. When I first interviewed him, Américo looked like Don Quixote in a grey guayabera. His persona, however, was powerful and disarming. As I entered his Austin home, I thought, "Damn. I'm going to interview and have pan dulce [sweet bread] with the man, Américo Paredes. How good is that?" It was better than I ever imagined. Sometimes in our lives we hear about a person who, without knowing us, has done something to make our lives better, and when we actually meet that person, we understand why. The more I knew Américo, the more I understood why.

Notes

1. James McPherson, "Revisionist Historians," *Perspectives on History* 41, No. 6 (September 2003), www.historians.org/publications-and-directories/perspectives-on-history/september-2003/revisionist-historians.
2. Walter Prescott Webb, *The Texas Rangers: A Century of Frontier Defense* (Boston: Houghton Mifflin, 1935; repr., Austin: University of Texas Press, 1965), 1.
3. Webb, *Century of Frontier Defense*, 127.
4. J. Frank Dobie, *Guide to Life and Literature of the Southwest* (Dallas: Southern Methodist University Press, 1952), 11.
5. Robert Draper, "The Twilight of the Texas Rangers," *Texas Monthly*, February 1994, 80–81.
6. J. B. "Red" Dunn, quoted in Webb, *Century of Frontier Defense*, 227.
7. Albert J. Myer, "'I Am Already Quite a Texan': Albert J. Myer's Letters from Texas, 1854–1856," ed. David A Clary, *Southwestern Historical Quarterly* 82, no. 1 (July 1978): 82.
8. Emma Tenayuca and Homer Brooks, "The Mexican Question in the Southwest," *Political Affairs*, March 1939, 259.
9. David Montejano, *Anglos and Mexicans in the Making of Texas, 1836–1986* (Austin: University of Texas Press, 1987), 65–66.
10. Montejano, *Anglos and Mexicans in the Making of Texas*, 126–27.
11. Evan Anders, revised by Cynthia Orozco, "Canales, José Tomás (J. T.)," *Handbook of Texas Online*, updated January 11, 2023, https://www.tshaonline.org/handbook/entries/canales-jose-tomas.
12. J. T. Canales, "Juan Cortina: Bandit or Patriot?" (address before the Lower Rio Grande Valley Historical Society, San Benito, TX, October 25, 1951), 1.
13. Américo Paredes, interview with author, Austin, TX, September 22, 1994.
14. Ramon Saldivar and Donald E. Pease, *The Borderlands of Culture and the Transnational Imaginary* (Durham, NC: Duke University Press, 2006), 31.
15. Paredes, interview with author, September 22, 1994.
16. Paredes, interview with author, Austin, TX, March 25, 1995.
17. Blanca Paredes, interview with author, Brownsville, TX, 2003.
18. Américo Paredes, *A Texas-Mexican Cancionero: Folksongs of the Lower Rio Grande* (Urbana: University of Illinois Press, 1976), xvii.

19. Paredes, *Texas-Mexican Cancionero*, 101.

20. Paredes, *Texas-Mexican Cancionero*, 70.

21. Alan Paredes, interview with author, Austin, TX, March 25, 1995.

22. Paredes, interview with author, March 25, 1995.

23. Paredes, interview with author, September 22, 1994.

24. Américo Paredes, *"With His Pistol in His Hand": A Border Ballad and Its Hero* (Austin: University of Texas Press, 1958), 5.

25. Paredes, interview with author, September 22, 1994.

26. Paredes, *"With His Pistol in His Hand,"* 5.

27. Frank H. Wardlaw, letter to Américo Paredes, January 14, 1956, Américo Paredes Papers, Nettie Benson Latin American Collection, General Library, University of Texas at Austin.

28. John Philip Santos, "Américo Paredes vs. J. Frank Dobie," *Texas Monthly*, October 2019, https://www.texasmonthly.com/being-texan/americo-paredes-j-frank-dobie/.

29. Webb, *Century of Frontier Defense*, 175–76.

30. Paredes, *"With His Pistol in His Hand,"* 31–32.

31. Paredes, interview with the author, March 25, 1995.

32. Anne Dingus, "Américo Paredes," *Texas Monthly*, June 1999, https://www.texasmonthly.com/articles/americo-paredes/.

33. Santos, "Américo Paredes vs. J. Frank Dobie."

34. Américo Paredes, *George Washington Gomez: A Mexicotexan Novel* (Houston: Arte Publico Press, 1990), 263.

35. Américo Paredes, *Uncle Remus con Chile* (Houston: Arte Publico Press, 1993), 12.

36. Paredes, *Uncle Remus con Chile*, 19.

37. Jose Angel Gutierrez, *The Making of a Chicano Militant: Lessons from Cristal* (Madison: University of Wisconsin Press, 1998), 43–44.

38. José Limón, "The Return of the Mexican Ballad: Américo Paredes and His Anthropological Text as Persuasive Political Performances," chap. 8 in *Creativity/Anthropology*, ed. Smadar Lavie, Kirin Nayarin, and Renato Rosaldo (Ithaca, NY: Cornell University Press, 1993), 194.

39. Limón, "Return of the Mexican Ballad," 184.

40. Dingus, "Américo Paredes."

41. Dave Davies, "'Cult of Glory' Reveals the Dark History of the Texas Rangers," *Fresh Air*, June 8, 2020, https://www.npr.org/2020/06/08/871929844/cult-of-glory-reveals-the-dark-history-of-the-texas-rangers.

Chapter 16

Reckoning with Ranger Terror

Monica Muñoz Martinez, State Violence, and Vernacular History

Andrew J. Hazelton

T he Texas Rangers have a reputation both storied and sordid. Popular writers and professional historians alike have studied the law enforcement agency and the people and captains who constituted it. Popular and public memories of the Texas Rangers hew close to the famed "one riot, one Ranger," which the Texas Ranger Hall of Fame and Museum roughly attributes to Captain Bill McDonald.[1] For many years scholarly and more popular treatments worshipped at this gilded altar. Historians writing from the perspectives of military history or the history of the US West have tended to emphasize the allegedly tough and intrepid character of the law enforcement agents they laud for pacifying restive frontiers or for restoring law and order to the people of the Lone Star State during times of crisis.

Alongside this narrative, a vital and honest counterhistory has endured. Victims of Ranger and other state violence along the Mexico-Texas border have created and sustained alternative readings of law enforcement and Anglo power. The most recent addition to this corrective tradition comes from Monica Muñoz Martinez in her book, *The Injustice Never Leaves You: Anti-Mexican Violence in*

Texas. The University of Texas public historian and 2021 MacArthur Fellow challenges traditional views of the Rangers and centers what she calls "alternative vernacular cultures," or "vernacular history-making." Martinez argues that communities victimized by racist law enforcement practices have nurtured hidden histories of state-supported violence against ethnic Mexican communities.[2] This chapter explores Martinez's work in light of the historic divide between both the public memory-traditionalist approaches and the lived reality of Ranger violence against people of Mexican descent in Texas. It begins by discussing some relevant historiography on which Martinez's work builds before it turns to the critical interventions of *The Injustice Never Leaves You* and the associated public history initiatives she and others have undertaken.

No foundational text in the historiography represents the reductivist and myopic tendencies in Ranger scholarship more than Walter Prescott Webb's *The Texas Rangers: A Century of Frontier Defense*, first published in 1935.[3] In search of a theme to tie his wide-ranging narrative together, Webb structured the book around prominent Ranger captains, their units, and key moments in the growth and development of the law enforcement agency. A nationally renowned historian at the University of Texas, Webb represented the racist perspective of early twentieth-century Texans in this and other works, only beginning to reassess some characterizations later in life as the Civil Rights Movement and some of his colleagues prodded him to reckon with his own views and words.[4] Of Mexican people Webb once wrote, "Without disparagement, it may be said that there is a cruel streak in the Mexican nature, or so the history of Texas would lead one to believe. . . . For making promises—and for breaking them—he had no peer."[5]

While Webb blended Anglo racial contempt into well-researched academic foundations as he studied the Rangers, he downplayed or ignored the extralegal violence that Rangers frequently dispensed from their legendary Colts. Horsemanship, backcountry skills, marksmanship, and vigor all characterized Webb's Rangers.[6]

These depictions matched popular notions of the Rangers as tough lawmen pacifying restless frontiers full of Indigenous and Mexican peoples. Webb borrowed from former Rangers' self-appraisals, recalling traditions established by John S. "Rip" Ford, whose reminiscences, writings, and memoirs formed the basis of many subsequent popular and academic histories.[7] In 1859 Ford had responded to Juan Cortina's rebellion against Anglo domination in South Texas by asking, "Shall we accept the challenge of the nation whose sons committed the massacres of the Alamo and of Goliad?"[8]

The traditionalist school of Ranger historiography follows in Webb's and Ford's footsteps. Authors offer occasional interpretive concessions here and there as partial remedy to blind spots but still dodge the weightier questions raised by more critical scholarship. For example, Robert Utley's two-volume history of the Rangers, published in 2002 and 2007 and intended "to replace Webb," criticized Webb's willingness to accept Ranger sources at face value. But Utley also chided revisionist scholars for their alleged presentism and encouraged historians to judge the Rangers and their chroniclers by the standards of their day. In an interview with *Texas Monthly*, Utley reminded readers, "Don't trash our forebears for not behaving as we wish they had. . . . We can describe how Rangers unlawfully killed several hundred Mexicans in 1915–16. We do not have to inform the reader that this was a very bad thing by today's values."[9]

This line of reasoning ignores the "values" of those killed; it negates their lives' value with as much finality as the Ranger bullets that took them. Surely these victims did not judge these events by the standards of the overall society in which they lived, which was dominated by Anglos and decidedly white supremacist. Despite the persistence of simplistic views and warnings to revisionist scholars to respect the context, ethnic Mexicans[10] in Texas and the historians who study them have cultivated meaningful, essential counterhistories. Monica Muñoz Martinez champions these narratives and forces a historical reckoning with injustice and racial terror. She builds on folk and academic traditions that offer radically different interpretations of the Rangers than those offered by traditionalists and popular culture. Ethnic Mexicans in the early twentieth century lionized folk hero Gregorio Cortéz, for instance. Cortéz shot and killed a Texas sheriff in 1901 after the latter shot Cortéz's brother over false allegations about stolen horses. He then evaded a Ranger manhunt for almost two weeks. Subsequent corridos in South Texas and along the US-Mexico border transformed Cortéz from historical actor into a legend of resistance against Anglos.

Later, folklorist and Brownsville native Américo Paredes collected the various versions of the Cortéz legend and analyzed it in his dissertation, which formed the basis for his 1958 book, *"With His Pistol in His Hand."* The work helped him earn a faculty position at the University of Texas.[11] There, Paredes repeatedly criticized his colleague Webb for erasing Ranger violence against ethnic Mexicans and Native Americans. In his book Paredes noted that Professor Webb had claimed his negative remarks about Mexicans were made "without disparagement," but went on to wonder how Webb might describe Mexicans "when he was in a less scholarly mood."[12] Yet Paredes is no hero for Martinez. In *The Injustice Never Leaves You*, she notes that while Paredes brought important folkways and alternative traditions of knowledge into academic circles, both Webb's and his narratives were "equally patriarchal and celebratory of armed masculinity."[13] Webb continued to inform most of the public memory and mainstream academic interpretations for decades, but Paredes mentored other ethnic Mexican students who challenged traditional views of the Rangers and Mexican Americans generally, joining colleague George I. Sánchez in combatting the dominant views and their coworkers' preconceived notions of Mexican aptitudes and character.[14]

Martinez's book, published in 2018, is a landmark piece of scholarship that joins other recent work dismantling the popular and scholarly myths surrounding the Texas Rangers. Historian Benjamin Johnson, for example, describes Ranger practices in South Texas during the Border War of 1915–1916 as approaching ethnic cleansing.[15] William D. Carrigan offers general contexts for understanding anti-Mexican violence in Texas in his books on lynching culture in Central Texas and mob violence against ethnic Mexicans in the United States more broadly.[16] Brian Behnken offers similar context in his book on ethnic Mexicans and law enforcement in the Southwest.[17] In his comparative study of the Texas Rangers and Canadian Mounties, Andrew Graybill points out that mounted constabularies served to dispossess and proletarianize South Texas Mexicans and the Metís peoples of the US-Canada border. In Texas, Rangers pushed ethnic Mexicans off their land, which forced them to accept wage work just as the railroads began incorporating South Texas into the urban-industrial economy of the eastern United States. Rancheros became ranch hands before farm work finally supplanted the ranching economy of the Lower Rio Grande Valley.[18]

Timothy Bowman, John Weber, and Cristina Salinas each have documented pieces of this process as it played out in the consolidation of South Texas agriculture in the first half of the twentieth century, highlighting the border and law enforcement as convenient tools for labor market management. They all follow lines of inquiry first traced by David Montejano in his *Anglos and Mexicans in the Making of Texas, 1836–1986*.[19] All who work on the border in the early twentieth century stress the importance of the Border War that erupted in response to the discovery of the Plan de San Diego, a plan for revolution and the restoration of a homeland in the borderlands for ethnic Mexicans and other peoples of color. Some versions of the document called for the execution of all white males over age sixteen. As simmering border unrest and cross-border raids during the Mexican Revolution raised the imagined stakes, Anglo society and Texas authorities mounted a vicious campaign aimed at demoralizing and terrorizing ethnic Mexicans. The Texas Rangers expanded their ranks and participated in extrajudicial vigilante and state-sanctioned violence that killed hundreds of ethnic Mexicans in 1915–1916. This campaign destroyed the capacity for future agitation against Anglo rule. In the 1910s, then, Anglos consolidated their newly imposed racial order and capitalist agriculture in the Lower Rio Grande Valley. Ranger violence helped subdue the last vestiges of armed resistance that had flared repeatedly since the Texas Revolution.[20]

The Border War and more broadly La Matanza—the wave of anti-Mexican killings that raged from 1910–1920 in Texas—figure prominently in *The Injustice Never Leaves You*. Martinez speaks plainly about her work and its importance in an introductory video created for the MacArthur Foundation. The book "recovers a brutal period of anti-Mexican violence in the early twentieth century. This was a period of state-sanctioned racial terror that included acts of lynchings, massacres, racially motivated homicides, and police violence and police murder," she says. "In some cases, these histories have been hidden," she continues, "but at worst, these histories have been celebrated." Martinez's book goes beyond the archival primary sources generated by law enforcement agencies or state investigatory boards because those sources contain sanitized versions of events that justify state actors in their use of racial terror. "I was really inspired to ask the bigger questions about which histories are written, how community members preserve histories for themselves, and how they pass them to the next generations," she notes.[21]

Martinez divides *The Injustice Never Leaves You* into six chapters covering two major themes. The first half of the book focuses on incidents of state-sanctioned violence against ethnic Mexicans in Texas. Others have written on these events at length; the point is not to document them again. Instead, Martinez deploys each of these moments to demonstrate linkages between "state racial terror and vigilantism" that has "long-standing consequences for people living near the border."[22] She also uses them as evidence for how the victims of this violence nurtured intergenerational historical memory as "a strategy of resistance against historical inaccuracies and social amnesias."[23] Archivists and professional historians "underestimated residents who had their own claim" to this history and who engaged in "valiant acts of preservation and remembrance" in a world defined and shaped by these violent episodes. These individuals "refused to be consumed by it."[24] Their "vernacular history-making" through websites, personal research, private archive building, and oral traditions figures prominently throughout the book.

The first chapter reinterprets the 1910 lynching of Antonio Rodríguez in Rocksprings, Texas. Here, Martinez recounts the notorious public murder of Rodríguez. A white mob hauled him out of the local jail, tied him to a mesquite tree, and burned him alive over accusations that he had killed the spouse of a local white rancher. While both English- and Spanish-language newspapers in Texas denounced Rodríguez's extrajudicial murder, ethnic Mexican newspapers like Laredo's *La Crónica*, edited by Jovita Idar, went further in their condemnations of lynchings in South Texas.[25] Martinez argues that the Rodríguez lynching helped inspire civil rights agitation and "lit a fuse that mobilized civil rights efforts."[26] Turning to the importance of vernacular history making, Martinez notes that she arrived at her study of the Rocksprings lynching by interviewing her uncle Rogelio Muñoz, who emigrated from Mexico in 1953. Muñoz worked as a field hand and sheep shearer in the Hill Country around Rocksprings, where he learned about the 43-year-old lynching from coworkers who told it as a campfire story after the day's work. In Martinez's interpretation of her uncle's case, the oral traditions of plain folk conveyed important warnings about the racial order in which Muñoz labored. In the version Rogelio Muñoz heard, Rodríguez was lynched for romantic involvement with an Anglo woman. The campfire story, then, helped ethnic Mexican workers navigate a midcentury Texas society that could pose real physical threats to a racialized labor force living and working in close proximity to whites. Muñoz later attended the University of Texas, where he and another student worked under the guidance of Américo Paredes to document some of the oral traditions that developed about the Rocksprings murder.[27]

The second chapter covers the more well-known murders of Jesus Bazán and Antonio Longoria by the Texas Rangers in 1915, and the third details the 1918 El Porvenir Massacre, in which a different Ranger company indiscriminately killed fifteen ethnic Mexican men and boys in West Texas. While contemporary observers and even some Rangers themselves recognized the extraordinary brutality of these events, public opinion, law enforcement agencies, and state officials sanctioned the violence as the necessary means to pacify the border and defang any potential threats to Anglo interests. Here, the argument again turns on the efforts of regular people to preserve memories and transmit narratives of the past that challenge official, popular, even scholarly views.

As US troops flocked to the border to saber rattle against the southern neighbor during the Mexican Revolution, the Texas Rangers expanded and augmented their forces in South Texas by hiring poorly trained, trigger-happy men eager to exact revenge on alleged bandits raiding Anglo property in the lower Rio Grande Valley.[28] Martinez argues that this moment in fact revealed "which residents had rights and which ones could be murdered."[29] Historian Mike Cox joins other scholars who argue that large numbers of ill-trained "irregular" Rangers contributed to excessive violence. Both cite the anxious climate created by the proximity of Pancho Villa's forces, who had attacked US territory during the 1916 Columbus, New Mexico, raid. Cox states that many of the irregulars functioned "as vigilantes incensed by raids from Mexico" in a statement casting blame on Ranger "bad apples" while half excusing those that spoiled.[30]

Martinez argues that drawing such distinctions ignores the basic truth that the Texas Rangers conducted a brutal campaign of repression and condoned or justified after the fact the actions of all who perpetrated the violence. Victims' bodies were left to rot in the open. Rangers warned family members not to bury them. Whether carried out by regular or irregular Rangers, such inhumanity was justified by official reports and the chain of command as appropriate (if sometimes unfortunate). Estimates vary, but at least three hundred ethnic Mexicans were killed as part of the 1910–1920 Matanza in Texas, with some estimates ranging into the thousands.

Martinez examines the efforts of survivors and descendants to interpret their own histories and cope with "mixed emotions of loss and indignation that cross generations."[31] She profiles Kirby Warnock and Norma Longoria Rodriguez, both of whom built archives and interpreted this history in public ways. Warnock interviewed his grandfather about the killings, making a documentary about the events, while Rodriguez compiled accounts, interviewed survivors, published on the subject, and worked on historical marker applications to commemorate the murders and La Matanza more broadly.[32] Martinez also examines the 1918 massacre of fifteen unarmed Mexican men and boys at El Porvenir. Rangers rounded them up in an early morning raid and executed them. Widows and children later used their Mexican citizenship to press claims for official recognition and restitution through the General Claims Commission of 1923, which the US and Mexican governments created to arbitrate disputes between residents of the two countries.[33] She also turns to the intergenerational weight of these events by highlighting how survivors and descendants created private archives about the event and transmitted memoirs to the next generation. Sometimes, inheritors have struggled with "frequent nightmares and flashbacks of past traumas," demonstrating the staying power of these historic injustices.[34]

The book's second half explores how Texas culture and society produced these violent episodes and how members of affected communities pressed their claims either historically or as part of reckoning with Texas history today. Martinez examines the 1919 José Tomás Canales investigation into police violence in Texas, as well as its supposed relationship to anti-Black lynching culture. Here, she asserts that anti-Black and anti-Mexican violence "mutually informed one another," stressing the Canales investigation as a moment when state violence against Mexicans was held to account, but only partially.[35] The 1919 hearings documented Ranger excesses during the Border War and convinced state authorities to reduce the Ranger force and move it toward professionalization. However, authorities failed to prosecute Rangers for extrajudicial murder; virtually all of those investigated continued working in law enforcement. Moreover, the culture of policing continued along lines of excessive force and racial violence.[36]

Martinez then explores how Texans have celebrated this culture of lawless lawmen, examining diverse expressions. Examples include commemorative postcards celebrating Ranger lynchings of ethnic Mexicans, including the infamous mounted Rangers lassoing dead Mexicans after the raid on Las Norias ranch, a photographic print in a Dairy Queen depicting a lynched "bandit," Walter Prescott Webb's scholarship, historical reenactors, Texas antique and memorabilia dealers, and the Texas Ranger Hall of Fame and Museum. Some of these examples are less effective than others, such as when Martinez explores the trauma she and others suffer at a Dairy Queen where staff offer culturally appropriative tacos near a print of a lynching scene that Martinez later reveals to be a still from a Western. The author shows how Texans casually celebrate lynching through such interior decorating, but is the photo so much more than a tasteless decoration by a rube franchisee casualizing murder next to frozen treats? There is something in the anecdote worth exploring, but it's a weaker example in a book with weightier evidence elsewhere. Martinez's treatment of the Ranger Hall of Fame and Museum is devastating, however. She indicts that institution for continuing "to mimic outdated narratives" while willfully ignoring serious critical academic work, both "new and old."[37]

The final chapter of *The Injustice Never Leaves You* engages with the work of descendants and scholars who bring these hidden histories to the fore as they reinterpret Texas. This effort joins Martinez's public history work in the Refusing to Forget and Mapping Violence projects. The centerpiece was an exhibit at the Bullock Texas State History Museum titled "Life and Death on the Border, 1910–1920." Curated by Jenny Cobb of the museum, it represented an unprecedented collaborative effort between museum staff and working academics, with advising from Martinez, literary scholar John Morán González, and historian Sonia Hernández. Martinez and collaborators acted as intermediaries between the official world of Texas public history and the "vernacular history makers" whose "private archives became invaluable for ensuring that the exhibit made room to display

personal artifacts that gestured to the gravity of human loss."[38] Images
of violence were contextualized to present the past to skeptics who
might be inclined to question revisionists' motives. Exhibit designers
worked to avoid sensationalizing the violence and reproducing
problematic imagery that has been used to celebrate a fictitious
past, such as the Las Norias ranch reprisal photo. The exhibit also
connected these events to the antiracist and civil rights efforts they
helped engender—such as Jovita Idar's protests in *La Crónica* and her
organizing efforts—and portrayed the long legacies of violence and
efforts of descendants to convey and redefine historic traumas.

The Refusing to Forget and Mapping Violence public history
projects continue to highlight the history of state-sanctioned violence
against people of color in Texas. Refusing to Forget is an educational
nonprofit founded by Martinez, Sonia Hernández, Trinidad Gonzalez,
John Morán González, and Benjamin Johnson. It helped develop
the exhibit at the Bullock Texas State History Museum, organized a
centennial conference on the Canales investigation, and worked with
the Texas Historical Commission to erect a set of historical markers
along the border.[39] The markers commemorate La Matanza, the Bazán
and Longoria murders, the El Porvenir Massacre, and journalist-activist
Jovita Idar. Meanwhile, the Mapping Violence digital humanities
project seeks to compile and map cases of racist violence in Texas
between 1900 and 1930. This effort joins with similar public history
initiatives such as the Racial Violence Archive and the Civil Rights
and Restorative Justice Project.[40]

The body of Martinez's work joins the revisionist tradition that has
always accompanied the dominant public memory and traditionalist
scholarship of the Texas Rangers. She knowingly nods toward
Américo Paredes in *The Injustice Never Leaves You*, partly as homage
and partly because her time and efforts with regular people engaging
in "vernacular history" recall some of the folklorist's methods.
There is often more dignity and honesty in the plain people than those
in power, both remind us. They keep alive important narratives that
challenge received wisdom and subvert myths that have been used to

justify violence against exploited peoples in Texas. This is necessary and important work, and it helps bridge divides between academia, popular culture, and the engaged public.

Martinez's work and the scholarship of like-minded historians, scholars, and activists have seriously challenged the public view and traditionalist interpretations of the Texas Rangers. Historians like Mike Cox and Robert Utley have tried to stake out a middle ground in the historiography. They regard revisionist interpretations as too judgmental of the past and too focused on present political concerns. Meanwhile, traditionalist scholars will tend to dismiss Martinez's insights completely and retreat to celebratory narratives, battle- and bullet-counting, and sketch biographies. The divide between older views of the Rangers and the most recent high-caliber scholarship reaches all the way to the Texas State Historical Association, an organization that has struggled to reconcile diverse viewpoints among its academic, popular writer, and local history and genealogy constituencies. A plenary panel at the 2022 convention seemed to capture the conundrum posed by this divide between the Rangers' critics and their defenders. The panel was titled "Forgetting and Remembering: Why Does Searching for an Accurate Past Provoke Backlash?"[41] The association recently became mired in disputes as members challenged the executive board's composition. The executive director, J. P. Bryan—a descendant of Stephen Austin—has denounced recent scholarship as too political and sued his own organization's board.[42]

One of the most important insights to glean from Martinez's work may be in highlighting the schism in Ranger interpretation and the resistance of scholars and the public alike when it comes to challenging sanctified narratives. Martinez brings to the surface the insights and impressive work of vernacular history makers after generations of pain and suppression. The intensely emotional nature of this work has served as a useful point of departure for conversations about restorative history practices that have the power to heal old wounds while drafting fuller, more truthful histories. Yet even the restorative work of placing Texas Historical Commission markers for its undertold history program recreated the racial divides that the El Porvenir Massacre enforced and embedded. Presidio County elites whose ancestors benefited from the massacre protested and disputed promotional events and press by survivors' descendants and scholars. The disagreements eventually delayed the marker's unveiling and installation, moving an event to El Paso. Even today suppression can halt or channel this glacial pace of progress in the state's public history and commemorative efforts.[43]

Despite the best work of generations of scholars challenging the typical understanding of the Texas Rangers, the popular and scholarly myths endure. The Rangers are enshrined not just in memory and as today's elite detective agency for the state of Texas, but even as a Major League Baseball team. Loving the Rangers is just another part of being a Texan, it would seem. Surely the state's underfunded public education system and the culture war politics at the Texas Education Agency will not counter these narratives without the pressure of activists, scholars, and the vernacular history makers that Martinez profiles. As the recent manufactured conflict over critical race theory in schools has demonstrated, however, such efforts will be met with white backlash in a bid to silence marginalized communities again. Traditionalist scholars will claim these myths and half-truths endure because the Rangers deserve admiration and a legendary reputation. Scholars who look for a middle ground will acknowledge Ranger atrocities but generally will excuse these as excesses, explained as part of the general standards of the day. Both will be cheered on by the Texas suburban history buff who stubbornly refuses to transcend simplistic narratives and biographies promoting a masculine, violent past tougher and more vital than his pampered, pickup truck present.

The divide between revisionist scholarship and the rest will no doubt endure, readers left to choose between parallel interpretive traditions. One of these has been state-sanctioned from the start; it has engaged in willful misrepresentations of the past. The other expresses a counterhistory that offers a more expansive view. Revisionists bring more context to bear. Monica Muñoz Martinez joins decades of high-quality, award-winning scholarship reaching back to Américo Paredes and beyond him to the witnesses, survivors, and descendants of these injustices. This historiography shows that Rangers wielded state violence to consolidate control over a region where ethnic Mexicans outnumbered Anglos, and as capitalist market transformations arrived with full force predicated on exploited labor. The Rangers in the early twentieth century functioned to dominate ethnic Mexicans and annihilate their capacities to resist. The Rangers continued to police race and class lines long after the events Martinez describes. They infamously deployed to Starr County as late as 1966 at growers' behest to disrupt labor organizing by the United Farm Workers, continuing a legacy of domination.[44]

Unfortunately, the historical amnesia about the Texas Rangers is likely to persist. However, Monica Muñoz Martinez's vital academic and public history work has highlighted the long reach of Ranger terror in ethnic Mexican communities and demonstrated the heroic efforts of regular people to chronicle and reckon with these painful pasts. Would that more Texans could accept these insights for the richer, more nuanced, and frankly more interesting history that they make.

Notes

1. Mike Cox traces the "One riot, one Ranger" origin to Albert Bigelow Paine's reconstruction of a story about Captain McDonald. In Paine's telling, when McDonald was dispatched to El Paso to stop a scheduled prizefight around which some unrest had developed, the mayor frantically asked the captain where the rest of the Rangers were. McDonald replied, "Hell, ain't I enough? There's only one prize-fight." Mike Cox, "A Brief History of the Texas Rangers," *Texas Ranger Hall of Fame and Museum*, accessed 2018, https://www.texasranger.org/texas-ranger-museum/history/brief-history/; McDonald as quoted by Albert Bigelow Paine, *Captain Bill McDonald, Texas Ranger: A Story of Frontier Reform* (J. J. Little and Ives, 1909), 220.

2. Monica Muñoz Martinez, *The Injustice Never Leaves You: Anti-Mexican Violence in Texas* (Cambridge, MA: Harvard University Press, 2018), 24; 27.

3. Walter Prescott Webb, *The Texas Rangers: A Century of Frontier Defense* (Boston: Houghton Mifflin, 1935; rep., Austin: University of Texas Press, 1965).

4. Webb's framing of conflict between Native Americans and Anglo society, for instance, positioned a "civilizing" white frontier moving westward and pacifying and confining Indigenous peoples. Webb adopted a similar dynamic with respect to Rangers' conflicts with ethnic Mexicans. Walter Prescott Webb, *The Great Plains* (Boston: Ginn, 1931; reprint, Lincoln: University of Nebraska Press, 1986).

5. Webb, *Century of Frontier Defense*, 14.

6. Webb, *A Century of Frontier Defense*, ch. 1, passim.

7. Ford's work was later published as an edited volume in John Salmon Ford, *Rip Ford's Texas: Personal Narratives of the West*, ed. Stephen B. Oates (Austin: University of Texas Press, 1963).

8. Bruce A. Glasrud and Harold J. Weiss Jr., *Tracking the Texas Rangers: The Nineteenth Century* (Denton: University of North Texas Press, 2012), 172.

9. Robert Utley, *Lone Star Justice: The First Century of the Texas Rangers* (New York: Oxford University Press, 2002); Utley, *Long Star Lawmen: The Second Century of the Texas Rangers* (New York: Oxford University Press, 2007); Stacy Hollister, "A Q&A with Robert Utley," *Texas Monthly*, November 2002, https://www.texasmonthly.com/articles/a-qa-with-robert-utley/.

10. I use this term to encompass both Mexican Americans and Mexican immigrants.

11. Américo Paredes, *"With His Pistol in His Hand": A Border Ballad and Its Hero* (Austin: University of Texas Press, 1958).

12. Paredes, *"With His Pistol in His Hand,"* 17.

13. Martinez, *Injustice*, 24.

14. Martinez, *Injustice*, 52.

15. Benjamin H. Johnson, *Revolution in Texas: How a Forgotten Rebellion and Its Bloody Suppression Turned Mexicans into Americans* (New Haven: Yale University Press, 2005), ch. 5, passim.

16. William D. Carrigan, *The Making of a Lynching Culture: Violence and Vigilantism in Central Texas, 1836–1916* (Urbana-Champaign: University of Illinois Press, 2004); Carrigan and Clive Webb, *Forgotten*

Dead: Mob Violence against Mexicans in the United States, 1848–1928 (New York: Oxford University Press, 2013).

17. Brian D. Behnken, *Borders of Violence and Justice: Mexicans, Mexican Americans, and Law Enforcement in the Southwest, 1835–1935* (Chapel Hill: University of North Carolina Press, 2022).

18. Andrew R. Graybill, *Policing the Great Plains: Rangers, Mounties, and the North American Frontier, 1875–1910* (Lincoln: University of Nebraska Press, 2007), 66.

19. Timothy Paul Bowman, *Blood Oranges: Colonialism and Agriculture in the South Texas Borderlands* (College Station: Texas A&M University Press, 2016), 24–26, 67; David Montejano, *Anglos and Mexicans in the Making of Texas, 1836–1986* (1987, repr., Austin: University of Texas Press, 2006), 125–27; Cristina Salinas, *Managed Migrations: Growers, Farmworkers, and Border Enforcement in the Twentieth Century* (Austin: University of Texas Press, 2018), 22, 31; John Weber, *From South Texas to the Nation: The Exploitation of Mexican Labor in the Twentieth Century* (Chapel Hill: University of North Carolina Press, 2015), 29–39.

20. For examples of such unrest, see Jerry D. Thompson, *Cortina: Defending the Mexican Name in Texas* (College Station: Texas A&M University Press, 2007). According to Thompson, Cortina engaged in social banditry to protest Anglo land appropriation in the Lower Rio Grande Valley. Similarly, Elliot Young explored the Catarino Garza revolt—directed against Porfirio Díaz, and which mobilized many disaffected people on both sides of the border—as an example of protest against ever-increasing consolidation of power by elites along the border. Elliot Young, *Catarino Garza's Revolution on the Texas-Mexico Border* (Durham, NC: Duke University Press, 2004).

21. "Monica Muñoz Martinez, Public Historian-2021 MacArthur Fellow (Extended)," YouTube video, 4:13, posted by "macfound," December 7, 2021, https://www.youtube.com/watch?v=ZiPL1QFSnn0.

22. Martinez, *Injustice*, 7.

23. Martinez, *Injustice*, 126.

24. Martinez, *Injustice*, 8–9.

25. Martinez, *Injustice*, 47–48.

26. Martinez, *Injustice*, 50.

27. Martinez, *Injustice*, 51–54.

28. Martinez, *Injustice*, 84–90.

29. Martinez, *Injustice*, 96.

30. Cox, "Brief History of the Texas Rangers."

31. Martinez, *Injustice*, 117.

32. Martinez, *Injustice*, 104–17.

33. Martinez, *Injustice*, 147–54.

34. Martinez, *Injustice*, 165.

35. Martinez, *Injustice*, 174.

36. Martinez, *Injustice*, 223.

37. Martinez, *Injustice*, 263.

38. Martinez *Injustice*, 280.

39. Refusing to Forget, "Exhibits," "Historical Markers," and "1919 Canales Investigation Conference, Refusing to Forget," accessed March 22, 2022, https://refusingtoforget.org.

40. Mapping Violence, "Overview," *Mapping Violence*, accessed April 4, 2022, https://mappingviolence.com/project/overview/.

41. Texas State Historical Association, "2022 Fellows Presentation Part II: Forgetting and Remembering: Why Does Searching for an Accurate Past Provoke Backlash," accessed April 8, 2022, https://am.tsha.events/2022-fellows-presentation-part-2/.

42. Sneha Dey, "A Battle over Who Gets to Tell Texas History Is Brewing into a War over the State Historical Association's Future," *Texas Tribune* (Austin), June 22, 2023, https://www.texastribune.org/2023/06/22/texas-state-historical-association-lawsuit/.

43. Daniel Blue Tyx, "Who Writes History? The Fight to Commemorate a Massacre by the Texas Rangers," *Texas Observer*, November 27, 2018, https://www.texasobserver.org/who-writes-history-the-fight-to-commemorate-a-massacre-by-the-texas-rangers/.

44. Bowman, *Blood Oranges*, 178.

PART 4

Other Notable Authors and Topics

Chapter 17

Historical Writings from A to Z
Other Ranger Historians

Darren L. Ivey

E lsewhere in this book, one may read of authors who have been prolific in their works concerning the Texas Rangers, the state of Texas, and the Southwest. Yet there exist those who have not, or at least not yet, delivered the output of the fine authors and historians profiled in earlier chapters. Still, they have contributed to the historiography of the Ranger service. The following A to Z discussion is by no means exhaustive, and the absence of specific authors does not equate to a dismissal of their influence.

Henry W. Barton (1912–1998) was a speech and drama instructor at Midwestern State University (formerly Hardin Junior College). He also served for twenty-seven years as an artillery officer with the 49th Armored Division, Texas Army National Guard. From 1959 to 1962, he wrote four articles for the *Southwestern Historical Quarterly* that dealt with the early history of Texas, up to and including the US-Mexican War. Barton followed up this work in 1970 with *Texas Volunteers in the Mexican War*, a review of the Texas fighting men who served during the conflict in Mexico. A reviewer for the *Corpus Christi Caller-Times* noted the book was "an invaluable contribution to historical archives and a book whose narrative is often fascinating to the non-academic reader who is merely curious about a little-written-about segment of the Texas past."[1]

John Boessenecker (b. 1953) graduated from San Francisco State University in 1975 with a bachelor of science degree in history. After serving eight years as a police officer, he attended the University of California Hastings School of the Law, obtained a juris doctorate degree, and was admitted to the California bar in 1985. He currently works as an attorney in San Francisco, California, specializing in trust and estate law. In addition to his legal career, he has authored numerous articles for historical quarterlies and magazines, as well as nine nonfiction books. Among other awards, *True West* named him the Best Nonfiction Writer in 2011, 2013, and 2019. While he has generally focused on California and Arizona history, Boessenecker wrote a biography of Frank Hamer in 2016, which has since replaced John Holmes Jenkins and H. Gordon Frost's work as the definitive account of that famous Texas Ranger. In reviewing the book, Richard Selcer noted that "Boessenecker has the rare ability to turn a mass of historical fact into a good story without compromising scholarship. . . . *Texas Ranger* is a rewarding read for anyone interested in true crime, Texas social history, or the bad, old days of law enforcement. Plus we have to thank Boessenecker for dusting off poor ol' Frank Hamer and saving him from being relegated to a Hollywood stock character."[2]

Donaly E. Brice (b. 1942) attended Southwest Texas State College (present Texas State University–San Marcos) and received a bachelor of science degree in education. Graduating from Sam Houston State University in 1968 with a master of arts degree in history, his thesis was "The Great Comanche Raid of 1840: Its Causes and Results." He taught American and world history, world geography, and civics at Mathis High School before enlisting in the US Navy in 1969. While assigned to the Pentagon, he volunteered at the Smithsonian Institution before being discharged in 1973. He went to work for the Texas State Library and Archives Commission in

1977 as a processing archivist, a research assistant, and a reference archivist. Brice retired in 2003, then returned to the part-time position of senior research assistant. In his capacity as an archivist, and even after his final retirement in 2014, he has assisted many Texana authors with their research, and his name likely appears on more acknowledgments pages in that genre than any other person. In addition to his involvement with the work of others, Brice's most significant contribution to Texas Ranger literature was to revise his master's thesis into *The Great Comanche Raid: The Boldest Attack of the Texas Republic*, which remains the only full-length treatment of that Comanche foray. Brice has written several journal articles, lectured, and presented papers at numerous symposiums, and collaborated on five more books.[3]

Jimmy L. Bryan Jr. (b. 1974) graduated with bachelor of arts and master of arts degrees from the University of Texas at Arlington in 1996 and 1999, respectively, and a PhD from Southern Methodist University in 2006. He is currently an associate professor of American history at Lamar University. In 2008 Bryan edited a reprint of *The Adventures and Recollection of General Walter P. Lane*, the memoirs of Walter Paye Lane, Texas Ranger during the Mexican War and a Confederate general. He followed up this project with *More Zeal Than Discretion: The Westward Adventures of Walter P. Lane*, the first full-length biography of Lane. Reviewing Bryan's work, Ed Bradley wrote that the professor was successful in "providing a thorough, well-researched, and smoothly written account of an overlooked figure in Texas history." Bryan has developed a personal thesis concerning Manifest Destiny, romantic adventurism, and the need for military renown to accomplish one's personal aspirations in antebellum America. His premise has been advanced in contributions to *Texans and War: New Interpretations of the State's Military History*, in which his chapter portrayed Lane and Samuel Hamilton Walker as soldiers of fortune, and *The Martial Imagination: Cultural Aspects of American Warfare*, where he discussed the role of Texas Rangers in American expansionism.[4]

Paul H. Carlson (b. 1940) received a bachelor of arts degree from Dakota Wesleyan University in 1962, a master of science degree from Minnesota State University at Mankato in 1967, and a PhD from Texas Tech University in 1973. He taught at Texas Lutheran University before becoming the chair of the History Department from 1983 to 1985. Carlson then returned to Texas Tech as an associate professor of history. He was editor of the *West Texas Historical Association Yearbook* and Double Mountain Books from 1996 to 2003. He served as associate chair of the History Department at Texas Tech University from 1998 to 2003, and as director of the Texas Tech University Center for the Southwest. He received the title of professor emeritus from Texas Tech in 2009. Carlson has authored, coauthored, or edited twenty-five books and 309 articles, essays, and reviews. In collaboration with Judge Tom Crum, Carlson spent years refining an argument that resulted in the book *Myth, Memory, and Massacre: The Pease River Capture of Cynthia Ann Parker*. In their multiple works, the two authors examine the fight at Pease River (or, more accurately, Mule Creek) and expose errors, fabrications, and ambiguities that have led to a distorted perception of the episode.[5]

Thomas W. Cutrer (b. 1947) graduated from Louisiana State University with a bachelor of arts degree in history in 1969. He served in the US Air Force as an intelligence officer and deployed to Southeast Asia in 1970, where he flew more than fifty combat missions over North Vietnam, Laos, and Cambodia. Leaving the service in 1972 and returning to LSU, Cutrer earned a master of arts degree in English literature in 1974. He attended the University of Texas at Austin and received a PhD in American civilization in 1980. He was appointed a humanities research associate / curator of history at the University of Texas Institute of Texan Cultures in San Antonio. Two year later he became associate director of the University of Texas Center for Studies in Texas History, associate director of the Texas State Historical Association, and managing editor of the *Handbook of Texas*. Since 1990 he has been a professor of history and American studies at Arizona

State University West. Cutrer has authored or edited eleven books, thirty-seven articles and introductions, and eight anthology chapters. His work *Ben McCulloch and the Frontier Military Tradition* examines the life of the Texas Ranger and Confederate general. Joseph G. Dawson III remarked, "Thomas W. Cutrer revitalizes the career of a flamboyant and once well-known southerner. . . . Cutrer's smooth writing benefits from the exemplary research in primary sources. The book is a pleasure to read. Cutrer recreates the atmosphere of life in frontier Texas and nineteenth-century America."[6]

James M. Day (1932–2005) received an associate of science degree at Tarleton State College in 1952, and a bachelor of arts degree in English from the University of Texas at Austin two years later. After US Army service, he returned to UT-Austin and earned a master's degree in history in 1958. From 1958 to 1959, he worked for the Texas State Library in Austin in the Archives and Legislative Reference Divisions. Day taught history and government at Howard County Junior College, then was director of the State Archives from 1960 to 1967. After obtaining a PhD in history from Baylor University, he became an associate professor of English at the University of Texas at El Paso in 1967. He served on the editorial boards of the West Texas Historical Association and the Texas Western Press. Day was recognized as a professor emeritus in 1991, then became executive administrator of the Mary L. Peyton Foundation. He authored numerous books and articles on Texas history, including *Captain Clint Peoples, Texas Ranger* and *The Indian Papers of Texas and the Southwest.*[7]

Jody Edward Ginn (b. 1969) served in the US Army as a Stinger missile operator and, as an army reservist, with Joint Task Force-6 in 1992. He graduated from Texas State University with a bachelor of science degree in criminal justice in 2001, a master of arts degree in public / applied history in 2008, and a PhD in American history from the University of North Texas in 2014. Beginning in 2001 he worked as a criminal investigator, a research historian, and a contract historical consultant before becoming an adjunct associate professor at Austin Community College in 2017. Two years later he became the executive director of the Texas Rangers Heritage Center in Fredericksburg, Texas. In 2022 Ginn became the director of development at the Texas Ranger Hall of Fame and Museum in Waco. In his role as professional historian, he has written one journal article, two anthology chapters, and a coauthored book. Ginn's earlier writings touching on the Texas Ranger have discussed the service's changing mythos from their earliest years as one of stalwart fighters for American democracy and Manifest Destiny to the equally stereotypical revisionist view of them as racist brutes. He has joined the ranks of contemporary Texas Rangers scholars who pursue a more nuanced and balanced approach that relies less on romanticism or racial divisions. His first solo work, *East Texas Troubles: The Allred Rangers' Cleanup of San Augustine*, was published in 2019. Exploring a completely untouched episode in Ranger history, Ginn presents the account of Rangers allying with a marginalized Black community to combat a brutish gang of white criminals. He not only reviews the reformation of the Texas Rangers under the Department of Public Safety but also refutes the conventional wisdom's certainty of the organization's racial attitudes during Jim Crow.[8]

Bruce A. Glasrud (b. 1940) received a bachelor's degree from Luther College in 1962, a master's degree from Eastern New Mexico University in 1963, and a PhD in history from Texas Tech University in 1968. He taught history at California State University at East Bay from 1968 to 1995 before being named professor emeritus. He then served as the dean of the School of Arts and Science at Sul Ross State University and retired in 2003. Throughout his career Glasrud has specialized in the history of African Americans in Texas and the West and has written, coauthored, or edited more than thirty books and approximately sixty scholarly articles. In 2012 he began work with Dr. Harold J. Weiss Jr. on the *Tracking the Texas Rangers* anthology series, which has resulted in three volumes covering the nineteenth and twentieth centuries and the authors who delve into the organization's history. In the first two offerings, the editors have provided comprehensive contextual material in the introduction, an informative bibliographical essay, and diverse viewpoints from leading Ranger scholars. Writing for the first volume's dust jacket, Robert M. Utley commented that the book "was a fair and balanced chronicle, both in narrative and interpretation."[9]

James Kimmins Greer (1896–1998) received a bachelor's degree in 1918, a master of arts degree in 1922, and a PhD in 1927, all from the University of Texas at Austin. He taught at Texas Women's University, Howard University, and Hardin-Simmons University before retiring in 1959. In addition to teaching, he edited or wrote four articles and six books, including *A Texas Ranger and Frontiersman: The Days of Buck Barry in Texas, 1845–1906*, the reminiscences of James Buckner "Buck" Barry, and *Colonel Jack Hays: Texas Frontier Leader and California Builder*, the biography of Jack Hays that has remained the only full-length work on this legendary Texas Ranger. A condensed version covering only Hays's Texas years was published in 1993. In the review he wrote for the *Southern Historical Quarterly*, Professor Walter Prescott Webb noted Greer discovered the Barry manuscript and persuaded Kossuth Barry to donate it to the University of Texas Library. Webb concluded his review with the observation: "As a record of the activities of the Texas Rangers, the book should rank with Samuel C. Reid's and Captain J. B. Gillett's accounts."[10]

J. Evetts Haley (1901–1995) graduated from West Texas Normal College (present-day West Texas A&M University) in 1925 with a bachelor of science degree in history. He subsequently worked for the Panhandle-Plains Historical Society as a field collector. In 1926 Haley obtained a master of arts degree at the University of Texas at Austin and later taught history there for seven years. Involved thereafter in ranching, he endowed the private Nita Stewart Haley Memorial Library and J. Evetts Haley History Center in Midland in 1976. Drawn to the stories of "men of fiber," he wrote fifteen books and dozens of articles and essays in the course of his career as a researcher and historian. None of his books focused exclusively on the Texas Rangers, but specific episodes in Ranger history may be gleaned from those pages. His first monograph, *The XIT Ranch of Texas and the Early Days of the Llano Estacado*, discussed the time Ira Aten spent as a division superintendent on the famous cattle spread. *Colonel Charles Goodnight: Cowman and Plainsman* touched on Lawrence Sullivan "Sul" Ross and the fight at Pease River. *Jeff Milton: A Good Man with a Gun* offered a firsthand account of the 1881 "Soldier's Riot" at Fort Concho and the activities of Captain Bryan Marsh and Company B, Frontier Battalion. *Fort Concho and the Texas Frontier* furthered examined the unrest. Haley's career stretched over six decades, and, as Mike Cox noted in the *Austin American-Statesman*, "He was a weathered bridge to the past, a man who had known buffalo hunters, pioneer ranchers, Indian-fighting Texas Rangers and old-time cowboys."[11]

Stephen L. Hardin (b. 1953) attended Southwest Texas State University and received bachelor of arts and master of arts degrees in history. Hardin then obtained a PhD from Texas Christian University. He taught at Victoria College before becoming a professor of history at McMurry University. In addition to his teaching career, he has become a historical commentator and advisor in Texas social and military history, including for the 2004 film *The Alamo*. Hardin has penned or edited six books, two journal articles, and a number of anthology chapters and book reviews. Written for the respected Osprey publishing house, his book, *The Texas Rangers*, is an easily accessible and richly illustrated capsule history of the service from its origins to 1991.[12]

William J. Hughes (1915–1986) obtained a bachelor of arts degree from the University of Colorado, a master of science degree in education from Western Illinois University, and a PhD in history from Texas Technological College in 1958. He taught at Dakota Wesleyan University before becoming a professor of history at Mankato State University in 1962. He retired as professor emeritus in 1977. His only book was *Rebellious Ranger: Rip Ford and the Old*

Southwest. One of two John Salmon Ford biographies published at about the same time, Hughes based his narrative on Ford's seven-volume memoirs. In reviewing the book, C. L. Sonnichsen commented, "Dr. Hughes' biography is thoroughly researched—so thoroughly, in fact, that Old Rip's voice is sometimes drowned out by the documentation." However, he concluded, "The book is a fitting tribute to the foremost among a group of pioneers of whom it was once said, 'Texas was their monument.'"[13]

Darren L. Ivey (b. 1970). In contrast to other writers mentioned here, he followed a different path to authorship by first working in a variety of blue-collar occupations, including retail, construction, and professional firefighting. Desiring to make a midlife career change, Ivey attended Kansas State University in 2014 and graduated four years later with a bachelor of science degree in history. He received a master of library science degree from Emporia State University in 2020, with a concentration in archives studies. In 2021 he became director of Library & College Archives at Barton Community College, as well as collections manager of the Cohen Center of Kansas History. Ivey has published four books and three book reviews. His three-volume *Ranger Ideal* series explores the lives of the men enshrined in the Texas Ranger Hall of Fame in Waco and examines their contributions to the service.

Nathan A. Jennings (b. 1980) graduated from Northwestern State University with a bachelor of arts degree in history in 2005. He is presently a lieutenant colonel in the United States Army and has served in cavalry and armor assignments with the 2nd Armored Cavalry Regiment, the 1st Infantry Division, and the 1st Cavalry Division. As a platoon leader and troop commander, he deployed twice to Baghdad and Kirkuk for Operation Iraqi Freedom. Jennings earned a master of arts degree from the University of Texas at Austin in 2013, then served as an associate professor of history at the US Military Academy. He attended the School of Advanced Studies at Fort Leavenworth, Kansas, and graduated with a master of military art and science degree in 2017. Following this training he became a NATO strategic planner in Afghanistan before returning to Fort Leavenworth as a doctrine author for the Combined Arms Doctrine Directorate. Jennings's current assignment is an associate professorship at the Command and General Staff College at Fort Leavenworth. He has written over thirty-one articles for assorted military and civilian publications, one anthology chapter, and his own book, *Riding for the Lone Star: Frontier Cavalry and the Texas Way of War, 1822–1865*. In the latter work, Jennings examined the amalgamation of the Spanish, Plains Indian, and Anglo-European horse cultures that resulted in a uniquely Texan approach to fighting. Reviewer Adam J. Pratt declared, "Jennings has written a thoughtfully organized and detailed account of warfare in Texas . . . by 1840 a distinct style of warfare had matured in Texas, and central to that maturation process was the reliance on the famed Texas Rangers."[14]

Dan E. Kilgore (1921–1995) worked as a certified public accountant in Corpus Christi. He was also an avid historian and collector of Texas and local history and served as president of the Nueces County Historical Society and the South Texas Historical Association. Additionally, he was vice president of the Texas State Historical Association. Following his passion Kilgore wrote a number of books and reviews and contributed articles to a variety of historical journals and newspapers. One of his most controversial monographs was *How Did Davy Die?* (1978), which theorized that legendary frontiersman Davy Crockett did not die fighting at the Alamo. The resulting uproar left Kilgore for a time "America's most hated man." However, the furor eventually subsided, and he remains best known for his earlier work, *A Ranger Legacy: 150 Years of Service in Texas* (1973). In this latter book, Kilgore brought together the research of Eugene Barker and Walter Webb with details derived from the Trespalacios Papers in the Bexar Archives to argue Moses Morrison's company was the first Texas Rangers unit. He also chronicled the Tumlinson family and their long service to Texas.[15]

Richard B. McCaslin (b. 1961) received a bachelor of arts degree in history / political science from Delta State University in 1982, a master of arts degree in history from Louisiana State University in 1983, and a PhD in history from the University of Texas at Austin in 1988. After teaching at LSU, UT-Austin, the University of Tennessee at Knoxville, Corpus Christi State University, Roane State Community College, High Point University, and Hawaii Pacific University, he became an associate professor of history at the University of North Texas, specializing in Texas and Civil War history. McCaslin received a Pulitzer Prize nomination for his 2001 book, *Lee in the Shadow of Washington*. After serving as a TSHA Endowed Professor of Texas History at UNT, he became director of publications at TSHA in September 2023. McCaslin has written, coauthored, edited, or compiled twenty-one books, twelve articles, and fourteen anthology chapters. His volume *Fighting Stock: John S. "Rip" Ford of Texas*, was the first biography of the renowned Texas Ranger in nearly fifty years. In 2021 he published *Texas Ranger Captain William L. Wright*, the first full-length biography of that well-respected lawman. In his review Professor Donald S. Frazier noted, "McCaslin is a stalwart in his field. An honest historian who follows the sources—all the sources—and reveals what he finds, he brings this prodigious skill and his keen expertise to this biography of Texas Ranger William L. Wright. The book reads well, and McCaslin tells a straightforward story of a straightforward Ranger."[16]

Douglas V. Meed (1927–2005). At the age of 17, he volunteered for the US Army during World War II. Meed served as an infantryman and later as a cryptanalyst in the Army Security Agency in Europe. After his discharge he attended the University of Texas at Austin and graduated with a bachelor's degree in journalism. He subsequently obtained a master of arts degree in history from the University of Texas at El Paso. Meed worked as a reporter and editor for an assortment of newspapers, including the *Houston Chronicle* and the *San Antonio Light*. He served in the US Information Agency as a foreign service

officer in Europe and Asia. Leaving government service, he worked
in public relations for the petroleum industry in the United States,
Europe, and the Middle East. Meed wrote and published numerous
magazine articles and eight books, including the first (and, at the time
of this writing, only) full-length biography of Texas Ranger Captain
John J. Klevenhagen.[17]

Richard J. "Rick" Miller (b. 1941). Following military duty with
the 82nd Airborne Division, he served as a Dallas police officer for
twelve years. During the course of his career, he obtained a bachelor
of arts degree in government from the University of Texas at Arlington
and a master's degree in public administration from Southern Methodist University. He was chief of police in Killeen from July 1976 to
August 1979 and a field training consultant for the Texas Commission on Law Enforcement, then assumed the leadership of the Denton
Police Department from December 1979 to August 1980. He attended
the Baylor University School of Law and received his juris doctorate.
Elected Bell County attorney in November 1992, he served in that
capacity until his retirement in November 2012. That same year
Miller penned *Texas Ranger John B. Jones and the Frontier Battalion,
1874–1881*, the first full-length biography of this original Frontier
Battalion commander and adjutant general. Debbie Liles noted, "For
the historian of Ranger history, this volume provides a thoroughly
detailed examination of events in chronological order. It will serve
as a resource for previously overlooked activities as well as a springboard for events that need further research."[18]

John Miller Morris Jr. (1952–2017) held a bachelor's degree,
a master's degree in community and regional planning, another in Slavic
literature and language, and a PhD in geography and planning from the
University of Texas at Austin. In addition to involvement in the family
farm, he taught at the University of Texas at San Antonio. He wrote
and edited numerous books, including an annotated narrative drawn
from three diaries belonging to Abner Theophilus "A. T." Miller, his
great-great-grandfather. In this work Morris presented his ancestor's

firsthand account of life serving under Captains William J. McDonald and Samuel McMurry in Company B of the Frontier Battalion. Ty Cashion commented that Morris had "a knack for breathing life into often-moribund passages dealing with mundane observations and comments about the weather and surroundings. Morris's ability to bring out of obscurity people and events familiar to the diarists, but otherwise lost to history, evinces the kind of research that only the most diligent, experienced scholar can produce."[19]

Stephen B. Oates (1936–2021) received bachelor of arts and master of arts degrees in 1958 and 1960, respectively, and a PhD in 1968, all from the University of Texas at Austin. After teaching at his alma mater, the University of Texas at Arlington, Texas Christian University, and the University of Houston, he became a professor of history at the University of Massachusetts at Amherst in 1968. In 1980, in addition to his regular history courses, Oates served as a Paul Murray Kendall Professor of Biography, a stint that lasted eighteen years. He was a historical consultant and on-screen commentator in Ken Burns's award-winning Civil War documentary in 1990. Oates was awarded the title of professor emeritus at Amherst in 1998; he then taught as an adjunct professor of English for seventeen years before finally retiring. Over the course of his career, he wrote or edited sixteen books, mostly biographies, focusing on nineteenth- and twentieth-century American history, as well as journal articles and essays. Among his Texas-based works was *Rip Ford's Texas*, which was drawn from John Salmon Ford's thirteen-hundred-page memoirs. Oates edited and reordered the original manuscript that was arranged by topic rather than chronology, combined overlapping subjects, verified quotes against primary sources, and removed sections of redundant or inconsequential material. The result was a polished, readable memoir that stayed true to Ford's original voice.[20]

Charles M. Robinson III (1949–2012) published his first book, *The Coins of Guatemala*, while a 14-year-old student. After time spent traveling the world as a seaman, he worked as an editor for the *San*

Benito News and a reporter for the *Valley Morning Star*. Robinson received a bachelor of arts degree in history from St. Edwards University and a master of arts degree in history from the University of Texas–Pan American. He was a history instructor at South Texas College in McAllen. He authored twenty-three books that focused on the Ame ican West, the Civil War, and the Spanish conquest of Mexico. One of them, *The Men Who Wear the Star*, was a single-volume history of the Ranger service from 1823 to 2000.[21]

David Paul Smith (b. 1949). After receiving bachelor of science and master of education degrees from Baylor University, he took a master of arts degree in history from Stephen F. Austin State University in 1975. He then worked for the Highland Park Independent School District as a history teacher before retiring in 2002. In 1987 he received a PhD in history from North Texas State University (present-day University of North Texas). Over the years Smith wrote several journal articles concerning the Civil War and the Texas frontier. In 1994 he published *Frontier Defense in the Civil War: Texas Rangers and Rebels*, a much overdue work that examined the activities of the state's frontier forces during the war.[22]

Paul N. Spellman (b. 1948) received a bachelor of arts degree from Southwestern University, a master of arts degree from the University of Texas at Austin, a master of education degree from Texas A&M University at Corpus Christi, and a PhD from the University of Houston. In 1997 he was employed at Wharton County Community College as a professor of US and Texas history. Spellman has written ten books, two anthology chapters, and numerous journal articles. The biographies, *Captain John H. Rogers, Texas Ranger* and *Captain J. A. Brooks, Texas Ranger*, offer the first full-length examination of the careers of these two Great Captains. Writing of the Rogers book, Dan K. Utley commented, "Texas historians have long held that when it comes to the Rangers, truth is often more than an even match for legend, especially with regard to individuals . . . those interested in Texas law enforcement history will find more than enough detail and substance on one of the Rangers' most influential and truly legendary early leaders."[23]

Charles D. Spurlin (1932–2013) attended Texas Tech University for one year, then enlisted in the US Army in 1951. He fought on the Korean peninsula, where he earned the Combat Infantryman Badge and the Purple Heart. After his discharge in 1954, he returned to Texas Tech and received a bachelor of arts degree two years later. He went to work for Gulf Oil before attending Sam Houston State Teachers College; he obtained a master's degree in history in 1961. He was employed by Victoria College that same year and taught history there until 2003. Later in his career, Spurlin served as chairman of the Social Sciences Department and director of the Local History Collection at the Victoria College / University of Houston–Victoria Library. He authored or edited nine books on the Mexican War, the Civil War in Texas, and the history of Victoria. Drawn from National Archives records, his *Texas Veterans in the Mexican War* was a personnel register of every Texas company, battalion, or regiment that entered federal service during the conflict. The later book *Texas Volunteers in the Mexican War* (which shares the same title as Barton's earlier work) examined the role Texans played in Mexico and on the frontier. Writing in 2000 Harold J. Weiss Jr. commented, "Some general histories [on the Mexican War] have given little coverage to the role of the troops from South Texas. Spurlin's volume fills this void. Historians need to consider the judicious assessment by the author that Texan volunteers listed in the appendices 'were essential to the American army's triumphs in Mexico, indispensable in the anti-guerrilla campaigns, and their frontier service allowed regular troops to perform duties in the war zone.'"[24]

Robert W. Stephens (b. 1930) graduated from Southern Methodist University, then served in the US Navy during the Korean War. Before becoming a writer and historian in 1970, he was employed by a life insurance company in Dallas. Stephens penned a short sketch of the Ranger service as promotional material for the Daisy

Manufacturing Company. He has authored biographies of notable
Rangers such as J. Walter Durbin, Manual T. Gonzaullas, George
H. Schmitt, and Daniel Webster Roberts. His *Texas Ranger Indian
War Pensions* examined the careers of sixty-three known and obscure
Rangers through the pension files in the National Archives. *Bullets
and Buckshot in Texas* was a collection of concise biographies on
thirty Lone Star lawmen and gunfighters, which included Rang-
ers Baz Outlaw, Scott Cooley, Charles H. Fusselman, and William
J. "Bill" McDonald. Stephens moved to Atlanta, Georgia, in 2011,
where he is completing two additional manuscripts.[25]

Harold J. Weiss Jr. (b. 1932) received his bachelor of science
degree from the University of Scranton in 1954 and a master of arts
degree from Pennsylvania State University in 1958, both in history.
He became a social studies teacher at Carson Long Institute in 1956
and an instructor of history and political science at Jamestown
Community College in 1959. Promoted to assistant professor in 1960,
Weiss was later chairman of the History Department. He was named
a full professor of history, government, and criminal justice and the
chair of the college's Division of Social Science and Business in 1970.
He was awarded a PhD from Indiana University at Bloomington in
1980; his dissertation examined the life and career of Captain William
J. McDonald. Weiss retired and was recognized as a professor emeritus.
A recognized authority on frontier law enforcement, Weiss has
written numerous journal articles and read papers during conferences
of the Western History Association and the Texas State Historical
Association. He authored *Yours to Command: The Life and Legend of
Texas Ranger Captain Bill McDonald*, which replaced Albert Bigelow
Paine's earlier work as the definitive biography of the illustrious Ranger
captain and US marshal. Jody Edward Ginn remarked, "Dr. Weiss . . .
expands the factual record of McDonald's Ranger career, he presents
it within the broader context of Texas history and the early development of professional law enforcement organizations throughout North
America. With the benefit of this contextual understanding, Weiss

interprets the actions of McDonald and his contemporaries, clarifying their historical significance." In addition, in collaboration with Bruce Glasrud, Weiss has coedited the two-volume *Tracking the Texas Rangers* series mentioned earlier.[26]

Notes

1. *Wichita Falls Times-Record-News*, September 16, 1998; *Corpus Christi Caller-Times*, September 6, 1970.
2. *San Francisco Chronicle*, November 18, 1999; Richard Selcer, review of *Texas Ranger: The Epic Life of Frank Hamer, the Man Who Killed Bonnie and Clyde*, by John Boessenecker, *Southwestern Historical Quarterly* 120, no. 2 (October 2016): 269.
3. Donaly Brice, email to the author, October 30, 2019.
4. Jimmy L. Bryan, curriculum vitae, copy in the possession of the author; Ed Bradley, review of *More Zeal Than Discretion: The Westward Adventures of Walter P. Lane*, Elma Dill Russell Spencer Series in the West and Southwest, no. 31, by Jimmy L. Bryan, *Journal of Southern History* 76, no. 1 (February 2010): 148.
5. Paul H. Carlson, email to the author, October 25, 2019.
6. Thomas William Cutrer, curriculum vitae, copy in the possession of the author; Joseph G. Dawson III, review of *Ben McCulloch and the Frontier Military Tradition*, by Thomas W. Cutrer, *Arkansas Historical Quarterly* 53, no. 2 (Summer 1994): 244–46.
7. *Austin American*, September 11, 1960; *El Paso Times*, April 19, 1960, May 4, 2005.
8. Jody Edward Ginn, email to the author, October 25, 2019; "Jody Edward Ginn, Ph.D.," *LinkedIn*, accessed August 2, 2023, https://www.linkedin.com/in/jodyedwardginn.
9. "Bruce Glasrud," *Black Past*, accessed October 18, 2019, https://www.blackpast.org/author/glasrudbruce/; "Bruce Glasrud," *LinkedIn*, accessed October 18, 2019, https://www.linkedin.com/in/bruce-glasrud-8b33547a; Bruce A. Glasrud and Harold J. Weiss Jr., *Tracking the Texas Rangers: The Nineteenth Century* (Denton: University of North Texas, 2012).
10. *Austin Statesman*, June 11, 1918, June 13, 1922, June 4, 1927; *Waco Tribune-Herald*, October 26, 1998; W. P. Webb, review of *A Texas Ranger and Frontiersman: The Days of Buck Barry in Texas, 1845–1906*,

by James K. Greer, *Southwestern Historical Quarterly* 36, no. 3 (January 1933): 233.

11. *Austin American-Statesman*, October 11, 22 (quotation), 1995; B. Byron Price, "J. Evetts Haley," in *Writing the Story of Texas*, ed. Patrick L. Cox and Kenneth E. Hendrickson Jr. (Austin: University of Texas Press, 2013), 115–17, 120–21.

12. "Vitae," *Stephen L. Hardin, Ph.D.: The Texan's Historian*, accessed October 17, 2019, https://stephenlhardin.com/vitae/.

13. *Peoria Journal Star*, August 29, 1986; C. L. Sonnichsen, review of *Rebellious Ranger: Rip Ford and the Old Southwest*, by W. J. Hughes, *Montana: The Magazine of Western History* 14, no. 4 (Autumn 1964): 70.

14. "Nathan Jennings," *LinkedIn*, accessed August 2, 2023, https://www.linkedin.com/in/nathan-jennings-262a4ba9; Adam J. Pratt, review of *Riding for the Lone Star: Frontier Cavalry and the Texas Way of War, 1822–1865*, by Nathan A. Jennings, *Journal of Southern History* 83, no. 2 (May 2017): 418–19.

15. *Corpus-Christi Caller-Times*, December 24, 1995.

16. "Richard B. McCaslin," curriculum vita, copy in the possession of the author; Donald S. Frazier, review of *Texas Ranger Captain William L. Wright*, by Richard McCaslin, *Journal of Southern History* 89, no. 1 (February 2023): 168.

17. *Austin American-Statesman*, February 20, 2005.

18. Gerald D. Skidmore Sr., *Historic Killeen: An Illustrated History* (San Antonio, TX: Historical Publishing, 2010), 62–63; *Waco Tribune-Herald*, May 23, 1976; *Fort Worth Star-Telegram*, December 22, 1979; *Dallas Morning News*, August 14, 1980; Debbie Liles, review of *Texas Ranger John B. Jones and the Frontier Battalion, 1874–1881*, by Rick Miller, *Southwestern Historical Quarterly* 117, no. 2 (October 2013): 219.

19. *Austin American-Statesman*, March 5, 2017; Ty Cashion, review of *A Private in the Texas Rangers: A. T. Miller of Company B, Frontier Battalion*, by John Miller Morris, *Southwestern Historical Quarterly* 106, no. 3 (January 2003): 488.

20. Eloise Lane, "Stephen B. Oates Made History Come Alive for His Students," *White Deer Land Museum*, accessed October 24, 2019, https://www.pampamuseum.org/-stephen-b-oates.html; Marquis Who's Who Moderator, "Stephen B. Oates," *Marquis Who's Who Top Educators*, accessed by October 24, 2019, https://topeducators.marquiswhoswho.com/2018/04/03/stephen-oates/; W. Turrentine Jackson, review of *Rebellious Ranger: Rip Ford and the Old Southwest*, by W. J. Hughes;

Rip Ford's Texas, by John Salmon Ford, Stephen B. Oates, *Journal of American History* 51, no. 2 (September 1964): 317–18.

21. "Charles Moore Robinson III 'Buzz,'" *San Benito News*, accessed October 24, 2019, https://www.sbnewspaper.com/2012/09/21/charles-moore-robinson-iii-buzz/;*Valley Morning Star*, June 22, 26, 2016.

22. David Paul Smith, email to the author, October 15, 2019.

23. Paul N. Spellman, email to the author, October 28, 2019; Dan K. Utley, review of *Captain John H. Rogers, Texas Ranger*, by Paul N. Spellman, *Southwestern Historical Quarterly* 107, no. 3 (January 2004): 484.

24. Sarah Massey, "Interview with Charles D. Spurlin, October 23, 1999, Goliad, Texas," Institute of Texan Cultures Oral History Office; *Victoria Advocate*, August 16, 2013; Harold J. Weiss Jr., review of *Texas Volunteers in the Mexican War*, by Charles D. Spurlin, *Southwestern Historical Quarterly* 104, no. 1 (July 2000): 124.

25. Robert W. Stephens, email to the author, October 28, 2019.

26. *Scranton Times*, December 19, 1960, December 14, 18, 1975, May 6, 1980; *Scranton Tribune*, September 2, 1959, December 20, 1960, May 6, 1980; Jody Edward Ginn, review of *Yours to Command: The Life and Legend of Texas Ranger Captain Bill McDonald*, by Harold Weiss Jr., *Southwestern Historical Quarterly* 114, no. 1 (July 2010): 89.

Contributors

Editors

Bruce A. Glasrud is professor emeritus of history, California State University–East Bay; retired dean, School of Arts and Sciences, Sul Ross State University, and a fellow of the Texas State Historical Association as well as the East, West, and Central Texas Historical Associations. Glasrud earned a PhD in history from Texas Tech University; he has published more than three dozen books, including *The African American West: A Century of Short Stories*, *Buffalo Soldiers in the West*, *Brothers to the Buffalo* Soldiers, and *Black Cowboys in the American West*, as well as the two-volume (with Harold J. Weiss) *Tracking the Texas Rangers* (UNT Press). He resides in San Antonio, Texas.

Harold J. Weiss Jr. is professor emeritus of history, government, and criminal justice at Jamestown Community College. He received his doctorate in history from Indiana University at Bloomington and is author of *Yours to Command: The Life and Legend of Texas Ranger Captain Bill McDonald* (UNT Press) as well as the two-volume (with Bruce A. Glasrud) *Tracking the Texas Rangers* (UNT Press). He lives in Leander, Texas.

Authors

Matthew M. Babcock teaches at the University of North Texas at Dallas. He earned his PhD in history at Southern Methodist University. Babcock's research interests focus on North American frontiers and borderlands, particularly the colonial southwest. Among his publications are *Apache Adaptation to Hispanic Rule* and a number of articles, including a historiographical essay on "Native Americans" in *Discovering Texas History*.

Timothy P. Bowman is a professor of history and department head at West Texas A&M University. He earned his PhD in history at Southern Methodist University. Currently he serves as book review editor for the *West Texas Historical Association* and is the author of *Blood Oranges: Colonialism and Agriculture in the South Texas Borderlands* and *You Will Never Be One of Us: A Teacher, a Court Case, and the Rural Roots of Radical Conservatism*.

Donaly E. Brice is the well-known, albeit retired, archivist from the Texas State Archives and a fellow of the Texas State Historical Association. Among his numerous publications are *The Great Comanche Raid, Texas Ranger N. O. Reynolds* (with Chuck Parsons), and *Texas Rangers: Lives, Legend, and Legacy* (with Bob Alexander).

Michael L. Collins, now retired and formerly Regents Professor of History at Midwestern State University, is author of *That Damned Cowboy: Theodore Roosevelt and the American West, Texas Devils: Rangers and Regulators on the Lower Rio Grande, 1846–1861*, and *A Crooked River: Rustlers, Rangers, and Regulars on the Lower Rio Grande, 1861–1877*. He also edited *A Texan's Story: The Autobiography of Walter Prescott Webb*.

Light Townsend Cummins has enjoyed a remarkable career, including appointment as the Guy M. Bryan Jr. Professor of History at Austin College (now emeritus), service as the official State Historian of Texas, a fellow of the Texas State Historical Association, and a Minnie Stevens Piper Professor. He is also the author of numerous award-winning books on Texas and southwestern history, including a book on Dallas sculptor Allie V. Tennant and *Discovering Texas History* (with Bruce A. Glasrud and Cary D. Wintz).

Andrew J. Hazelton is an associate professor of history at Texas A&M International University at Laredo. He earned his doctorate at Georgetown University and is the author of *Labor's Outcasts: Migrant Farmworkers and Unions in North America, 1934–1966*.

Kenneth W. Howell is a professor and head of the History Department at Blinn College. Among his numerous publications are *The Seventh Star of the Confederacy* and *Still the Arena of the Civil War: Violence and Turmoil in Reconstruction Texas*. He also published *Texas Confederate, Reconstruction Governor: James Webb Throckmorton*.

Darren L. Ivey is director of Library and College Archives at Barton Community College in Great Bend, Kansas. His interests involve the history of the military and the American West. He is the author of *The Texas Rangers: A Registry and History* as well as three volumes of *The Ranger Ideal: Texas Rangers in the Hall of Fame*.

Richard B. McCaslin, TSHA Professor of Texas History (retired) at the University of North Texas, is the author or editor of nearly twenty books, including *Tainted Breeze: The Great Hanging at Gainesville, Texas, October 1862*; *Lee in the Shadow of Washington*; *At the Heart of Texas: One Hundred Years of the Texas State Historical Association, 1897–1997*; *Fighting Stock: John S. "Rip" Ford of Texas*; and *Texas Ranger Captain William L. Wright*.

Manuel F. Medrano is professor emeritus at the University of Texas RGV. In addition to producing the Los del Valle Oral History Series, he has authored two biographies about nationally recognized Rio Grande Valley individuals: *Américo Paredes: In His Own Words, an Authorized Biography* and *The Life and Times of Sergeant Jose M. Lopez: Mexican by Birth, American by Valor*.

Mitchel P. Roth, professor of criminal justice and criminology at Sam Houston State University in Huntsville, Texas. He is the author of numerous books, including *Fire in the Big House: The Worst Prison Disaster in American History*; *A History of Crime and the American Criminal Justice System*; and *Convict Cowboys: The Untold History of the Texas Prison Rodeo*. His lengthy chapter on the Rangers in the sixtieth anniversary publication of the DPS is a first-rate introduction to the field.

Paul N. Spellman holds a doctorate from the University of Houston and is retired as a professor of history at Wharton Junior College. Among his many publications are biographies of two Texas Ranger captains: *Captain John H. Rogers, Texas Ranger*, and *Captain J. A. Brooks, Texas Ranger*.

Roger Tuller retired as a professor of history at Texas A&M University–Kingsville; he earned his PhD at Texas Christian University and continues his interest in the history of the American West. Among his publications is a study, *Let No Guilty Man Escape: A Judicial Biography of Isaac C. Parker*.

Leland K. Turner received his PhD in history at Texas Tech University. Currently an associate professor of history at Midwestern State University in Wichita Falls, Turner has published a number of articles on West Texas, including one on "The West Texas Plains" for *West Texas: A History of the Giant Side of the State*. He is nearing completion of a work that compares the cattle empires of the United States and Australia.

Rusty Williams writes about history through the stories of the people who lived it. He is the author of six books about Texas and the Southwest, including *Texas Loud, Proud, and Brash: How Ten Mavericks Created the Twentieth-Century Lone Star State*; *The Red River Bridge War: A Texas-Oklahoma Border Battle*; *Deadly Dallas: A History of Unfortunate Incidents and Grisly Fatalities*; and *My Old Confederate Home: A Respectable Place for Civil War Veterans*. Williams speaks regularly to organizations and groups about historical topics. He resides in Dallas.

William Clay Yancey is lecturer of history at the University of Texas–Rio Grande Valley. He earned his doctorate at the University of North Texas. Yancey is interested in the borderlands and nineteenth-century Texas.

Roy Young is an avid researcher and writer of the American West. He served as editor of the *Wild West History Journal* for thirteen years. Young is related to a large number of Texas Ranger families and is coauthor of *Chasing Billy the Kid: Frank Stewart and the Untold Story of the Manhunt for William H. Bonney* and coeditor of *A Wyatt Earp Anthology: Long May His Story Be Told.*

Bibliography

Archival Collections

Américo Paredes Papers. Nettie Benson Latin American Collection, General Library, University of Texas at Austin.

Frederick Wilkins Papers. UTSA Libraries, Special Collections, University of Texas at San Antonio.

Robert G. McCubbin Collection. Wild West History Association, Safford, AZ.

Walter Prescott Webb Papers, 1857–1966. Dolph Briscoe Center for American History, University of Texas at Austin.

Other Sources

Acuña, Rodolfo F. *Occupied America: A History of Chicanos.* 8th ed. London: Pearson, 2014.

Adams, Ramon. *Six-Guns and Saddle Leather: A Bibliography of Books and Pamphlets on Western Outlaws and Gunmen.* Norman: University of Oklahoma Press, 1954. Reprint, Cleveland: John T. Zubal, 1982.

Albers, E. G., Jr. *The Life and Reflections of a Texas Ranger.* Waco: Texian Press, 1998.

Alexander, Bob. *Bad Company and Burnt Powder: Justice in the Old Southwest.* Denton: University of North Texas Press, 2014.

Alexander, Bob. "The Best Texas Rangers Photos Ever." *True West,* April 2012, 34–41.

Alexander, Bob. "The Best of the Texas Rangers in Photos." *True West,* January 2019, 24–31.

Alexander, Bob. *Dangerous Dan Tucker: New Mexico's Deadly Lawman.* Silver City, NM: High-Lonesome Books, 2001.

Alexander, Bob. "Death on the Line." *True West,* May 2013, 24–31.

Alexander, Bob. *Fearless Dave Allison: Border Lawman.* Silver City, NM: High-Lonesome Books, 2004.

Alexander, Bob. "Guns, Girls & Gamblers: Silver City's Wilder Side." *Western Outlaw-Lawman History Association Journal* 14, no. 4 (Winter 2005): 12–20.

Alexander, Bob. "Hellfire & Hot Tamales." *True West,* September 2010, 61–63.

Alexander, Bob. *John H. Behan: Sacrificed Sheriff.* Silver City, NM: High-Lonesome Books, 2002.

Alexander, Bob. *Lawmen, Outlaws, and S.O.Bs: Gunfighters of the Old Southwest.* 2 vols. Introductions by Chuck Parsons. Silver City, NM: High-Lonesome Books, 2004–2007.

Alexander, Bob. *Old Riot, New Ranger: Captain Jack Dean, Texas Ranger and US Marshal.* Denton: University of North Texas Press, 2018.

Alexander, Bob. "An Outlaw Tripped Up by Love." *Quarterly of the National Association for Outlaw and Lawman History* 26, no. 3 (July–September 2002): 1, 7–16.

Alexander, Bob. *Rawhide Ranger, Ira Aten: Enforcing Law on the Texas Frontier.* Denton: University of North Texas Press, 2011.

Alexander, Bob. *Riding Lucifer's Line: Ranger Deaths along the Texas-Mexico Border.* Denton: University of North Texas Press, 2013.

Alexander, Bob. *Sheriff Harvey Whitehill: Silver City Stalwart.* Introduction by Robert K. DeArment. Silver City, NM: High-Lonesome Books, 2005.

Alexander, Bob. *Six-Shooters and Shifting Sands: The Wild West Life of Texas Ranger Captain Frank Jones.* Denton: University of North Texas Press, 2015.

Alexander, Bob. "Square Deals and Real McCoys." *Wild West Historical Association Journal* 4, no. 3 (June 2011): 32–52.

Alexander, Bob. *Whiskey River Ranger: The Old West Life of Baz Outlaw.* Denton: University of North Texas Press, 2016.

Alexander, Bob. *Winchester Warriors: Texas Rangers of Company D, 1874–1901.* Denton: University of North Texas Press, 2009.

Alexander, Bob, and Donaly E. Brice. *Texas Rangers: Lives, Legend, and Legacy.* Denton: University of North Texas Press, 2017.

Alexander, Bob, and Jan Devereaux. "Trumpeting Elephants & Kicking Asses: Republicans and Democrats, New Mexico Style." *True West,* January/February 2010, 27–31.

Anders, Evan, revised by Cynthia Orozco. "Canales, José Tomás (J. T.)." *Handbook of Texas Online,* updated January 11, 2023. https://www.tshaonline.org/handbook/entries/canales-jose-tomas.

Anderson, Gary Clayton. "American Indians and the Texas Revolution." Paper presented at the Battle of San Jacinto Symposium, Houston, TX, April 14, 2007. https//:www.youtube.com/watch?v=dOA9ZVpwtOE.

Anderson, Gary Clayton. *The Conquest of Texas: Ethnic Cleansing in the Promised Land, 1820–1875.* Norman: University of Oklahoma Press, 2005.

Anderson, Gary Clayton. *Ethnic Cleansing and the Indian: The Crime That Should Haunt America*. Norman: University of Oklahoma Press, 2014.

Anderson, Gary Clayton. *The Indian Southwest, 1580–1830: Ethnogenesis and Reinvention*. Norman: University of Oklahoma Press, 1999.

Anderson, Gary Clayton. *Kinsmen of Another Kind: Dakota-White Relations in the Upper Mississippi River Valley, 1650–1862*. Lincoln: University of Nebraska Press, 1984.

Anderson, Gary Clayton. *Little Crow: Spokesman for the Sioux*. St Paul: Minnesota Historical Society Press, 1986.

Anderson, Gary Clayton. *Sitting Bull and the Paradox of Lakota Nationhood*. New York: Longman, 1997.

Anderson, Gary Clayton, and Alan R. Woolworth, eds. *Through Dakota Eyes: Narrative Accounts of the Minnesota Indian War of 1862*. St. Paul: Minnesota Historical Society Press, 1988.

Andreopoulos, George J., ed. *Genocide: Conceptual and Historical Dimensions*. Philadelphia: University of Pennsylvania Press, 1994.

Angel, William D., Jr. "Controlling the Workers: The Galveston Dock Workers' Strike of 1920 and Its Impact on Labor Relations in Texas." *East Texas Historical Journal* 23, no. 2 (October 1985): 14–27.

Arquilla, John. *Insurgents, Raiders, and Bandits: How Masters of Irregular Warfare Have Shaped Our World*. Chicago: Ivan R. Dee, 2011.

Ashton, Dorothy C. "Sowell, Andrew Jackson." *Handbook of Texas Online*, updated March 23, 2019. http://www.tshaonline.org/handbook/online/articles/fso07.

Aten, Ira. *Six-and-One Half Years in the Texas Ranger Service: The Memoirs of Ira Aten*. Bandera, TX: Frontier Times, 1945.

Baker, Erma. "Brown, John Henry." In Tyler, *New Handbook of Texas*, vol. 1.

Bancroft, Hubert Howe. *History of the North Mexican States and Texas*. Vol. 2. San Francisco: History Company, 1889.

Banta, William. *Twenty-Seven Years on the Texas Frontier*. Austin: Ben C. Jones, 1893.

Barker, Eugene C. "The Government of Austin's Colony, 1821–1831." *Southwestern Historical Quarterly* 21, no. 3 (January 1918): 223–52.

Barker, Eugene C. "Journal of the Permanent Council (October 11–27, 1835)." *Quarterly of the Texas State Historical Association* 7, no. 4 (April 1904): 249–78.

Barker, Eugene C. *The Life of Stephen F. Austin: Founder of Texas, 1793–1836*. 1925. Reprint, New York: Da Capo Press, 1968.

Bartholomew, Ed. *Jesse Evans: A Texas Hide Burner*. Houston: Frontier Press of Texas, 1955.

Bartholomew, Ed. *Kill or Be Killed; a record of violence in the early Southwest: Charles Webb, John Wesley Hardin, John Selman, George Scarborough, Will Carver, Elijah Briant, Black Jack, and others*. Houston: Frontier Press of Texas, 1953.

Bartholomew, Ed. *Wild Bill Longley: A Texas Hard-Case*. Houston: Frontier Press of Texas, 1953.

Barton, Henry W. "The United States Cavalry and the Texas Rangers." *Southwestern Historical Quarterly* 63, no. 4 (April 1960): 495–510.

"The Battle of Antelope Hills." *Frontier Times* 1, no. 5 (February 1924): 11–14.

Bechtel, H. Kenneth. *State Police in the United States: A Socio-Historical Analysis*. Westport, CT: Greenwood Press, 1995.

Behnken, Brian D. *Borders of Violence and Justice: Mexicans, Mexican Americans, and Law Enforcement in the Southwest, 1835–1935*. Chapel Hill: University of North Carolina Press, 2022.

Bell-Fialkoff, Andrew. *Ethnic Cleansing*. New York: St. Martin's Press, 1996.

Bennett, Rebecca L. "Reviving History through Storytelling." *Hill Country View*, May 1, 2017.

Berg, Jeff. *New Mexico Film Making*. Charleston, SC: History Press, 2015.

Berry, Margaret C. "Garrison, George Pierce." *Handbook of Texas Online*, accessed December 15, 2021. https://www.tshaonline.org/handbook/entries/garrison-george-pierce.

Betty, Gerald. *Comanche Society: Before the Reservation*. College Station: Texas A&M University Press, 2002.

Bicknell, Thomas C., and Chuck Parsons. *Ben Thompson: Portrait of a Gunfighter*. Denton: University of North Texas Press, 2018.

Binkley, William C. Review of *The Texas Rangers: A Century of Frontier Defense*, by Walter Prescott Webb. *Journal of Southern History* 2, no. 3 (August 1936): 419–21.

Boessenecker, John. *Texas Ranger: The Epic Life of Frank Hamer, the Man Who Killed Bonnie and Clyde*. New York: Thomas Dunne Books, 2016.

Bowman, Timothy Paul. *Blood Oranges: Colonialism and Agriculture in the South Texas Borderlands*. College Station: Texas A&M University Press, 2016.

Bradley, Ed. Review of *More Zeal Than Discretion: The Westward Adventures of Walter P. Lane*, Elma Dill Russell Spencer Series in the West and Southwest, no. 31, by Jimmy L. Bryan. *Journal of Southern History* 76, no. 1 (February 2010): 147–48

Bratcher, James T. "The Texas Rangers: From Blood on Their Boots to Branch Davidian Onlookers." *Journal of the West* 46 (Summer 2007): 75.

Brazos [pseud.]. *Life of Robert Hall, Indian Fighter and Veteran of Three Great Wars*. 1898. Reprinted with an introduction by Stephen Hardin. Austin: State House Press, 1992

Brice, Donaly E. "The Great Comanche Raid of 1840." In Glasrud and Weiss, *Tracking: Nineteenth Century*, 62–86.

Brice, Donaly E. *The Great Comanche Raid: Boldest Indian Attack of the Texas Republic*. Austin: Eakin Press, 1987.

Brice, Donaly E., and Chuck Parsons. *Texas Ranger N. O. Reynolds, the Intrepid*. Denton: University of North Texas Press, 2014.

Britten, Thomas A. *The Lipan Apaches: People of Wind and Lightning*. Albuquerque: University of New Mexico Press, 2009.

Brown, John Henry. *History of Texas, from 1685 to 1892*. 2 vols. St. Louis: L. E. Daniell, 1892–93.

Brown, John Henry. *Indian Wars and Pioneers of Texas*. Austin: L. E. Daniell, 1896.

Brown, Richard Maxwell. *No Duty to Retreat: Violence and Values in American History and Society*. New York: Oxford University Press, 1991.

Bryan, Jimmy L., Jr. "Agents of Destiny: Texas Rangers and the Dilemma of the Conquest Narrative." In *The Martial Imagination: Cultural Aspects of American Warfare*, edited by Jimmy L. Bryan Jr., 53–69. College Station: Texas A&M University Press, 2013.

Bryan, Jimmy L., Jr. *The American Elsewhere: Adventure and Manliness in the Age of Expansion*. Lawrence: University Press of Kansas, 2017.

Bryan, Jimmy L., Jr. *More Zeal Than Discretion: The Westward Adventures of Walter P. Long*. College Station: Texas A&M University Press, 2008.

Bryan, Jimmy L., Jr. "The Patriot-Warrior Mystique: John S. Brooks, Walter P. Long, Samuel H. Walker, and the Adventurous Quest for Renown." In *Texans and War: New Interpretations of the State's Military History*, edited by Alexander Mendoza and Charles Grear, Centennial Series of the Association of Former Students 116, 113–32. College Station: Texas A&M University Press, 2012.

Buenger, Walter L. "Three Truths in Texas." In *Beyond Texas through Time: Breaking Away from Past Interpretations*, edited by Walter L. Buenger and Arnoldo De Léon, 1–4. College Station: Texas A&M University Press, 2011.

Buenger, Walter L., and Robert A. Calvert. "The Shelf Life of Truth in Texas History." In *Texas through Time: Evolving Interpretations*, edited by

Walter L. Buenger and Robert L. Calvert, ix–xxiv. College Station: Texas A&M University Press, 1991.

Burnam, Sada. "Reminiscences of Capt. Jesse Burnam." *Quarterly of the Texas State Historical Association* 5, no. 1 (July 1901): 12–18.

Callan, Austin. "Battle of Dove Creek." *Frontier Times* 24, no. 12 (September 1947): 542–44.

Callicott, William. *Bill Callicott Reminiscences.* Transcribed and annotated by Chuck Parsons. Waco: Texas Ranger Hall of Fame, 2006.

Campbell, Randolph B. *Gone to Texas: A History of the Lone Star State.* New York: Oxford University Press, 2003.

Canales, J. T. "Juan Cortina: Bandit or Patriot?" Address before the Lower Rio Grande Valley Historical Society, San Benito, TX, October 25, 1951.

"Captain June Peak, Texas Ranger." *Frontier Times* 4, no. 12 (September 1927): 5–6.

"Captain Shapley P. Ross." *Frontier Times* 5, no. 11 (August 1928): 437–38.

Carlson, Paul H., and Tom Crum. *Myth, Memory and Massacre: The Pease River Capture of Cynthia Ann Parker.* Lubbock: Texas Tech University Press, 2010.

Carnal, Ed. "Reminiscences of a Texas Ranger." *Frontier Times* 1, no. 3 (December 1923): 20–23.

Carrigan, William D. *The Making of a Lynching Culture: Violence and Vigilantism in Central Texas, 1836–1916.* Urbana-Champaign: University of Illinois Press, 2004.

Carrigan, William D., and Clive Webb. *Forgotten Dead: Mob Violence against Mexicans in the United States, 1848–1928.* Oxford: Oxford University Press, 2003.

Carrigan, William D., and Clive Webb. "The Lynching of Persons of Mexican Origin or Descent in the United States, 1848 to 1928." *Journal of Social History* 37, no. 2 (Winter 2003): 411–38.

Carriker, Robert C. Review of *Trails and Trials of a Texas Ranger*, by William Warren Sterling. *Montana: The Magazine of Western History* 20, no. 2 (Spring 1970): 82.

Cartwright, Gary. "Death of a Ranger." *Texas Monthly*, August 1978. https://www.texasmonthly.com/articles/death-of-a-ranger.

Casey Clifford B., and Lewis H. Saxton. *The Life of Everett Ewing Townsend.* Alpine: West Texas Historical and Scientific Society, 1958.

Cashion, Ty. *Lone Star Mind: Reimagining Texas History.* Norman: University of Oklahoma Press, 2018.

Cashion, Ty. Review of *A Private in the Texas Rangers: A. T. Miller of Company B, Frontier Battalion*, by John Miller Morris. *Southwestern Historical Quarterly* 106, no. 3 (January 2003): 488.

Churchill, Ward. *Kill the Indian, Save the Man: The Genocidal Impact of American Indian Schools*. San Francisco: City Lights, 2004.

Churchill, Ward. *Struggle for the Land: Indigenous Resistance to Genocide, Ecocide, and Expropriation in Contemporary North America*. San Francisco: City Lights, 2002.

Coffee, James L., Russell M. Drake, and John T. Barnett. *Graham Barnett: A Dangerous Man*. Denton: University of North Texas Press, 2017.

Collins, Michael L. *A Crooked River: Rustlers, Rangers, and Regulars on the Lower Rio Grande, 1861–1877*. Norman: University of Oklahoma Press, 2018.

Collins, Michael L., ed. *A Texan's Story: The Autobiography of Walter Prescott Webb*. Norman: University of Oklahoma Press, 2020.

Collins, Michael L. *Texas Devils: Rangers and Regulars on the Lower Rio Grande, 1846–1861*. Norman: University of Oklahoma Press, 2008.

Collins, Michael L. "Walter Prescott Webb." In Cox and Hendrickson, *Writing the Story of Texas*, 43–66

Conger, Roger N., ed. *Rangers of Texas*. Waco: Texian Press, 1969.

Cool, Paul. *Salt Warriors: Insurgency on the Rio Grande*. College Station: Texas A&M University Press, 2008.

Cox, Mike. "Battle of the Painted Rocks: Scraping off the Layers." *West Texas Historical Association Year Book* 78 (October 2002): 151–69.

Cox, Mike. *Historic Photos of Texas Lawmen*. Nashville, TN: Turner Publishing, 2008.

Cox, Mike. *Texas Ranger Tales: Hard-Riding Stories from the Lone Star State*. Guilford, CT: Lone Star Books, 2016.

Cox, Mike. *Texas Ranger Tales: Stories That Need Telling*. Plano: Republic of Texas Press, 1997.

Cox, Mike. *Texas Ranger Tales II*. Plano: Republic of Texas Press, 1999.

Cox, Mike. *The Texas Rangers: Men of Action and Valor*. Austin: Eakin Press, 1991.

Cox, Mike. *The Texas Rangers: Wearing the Cinco Peso, 1821–1900*. New York: Forge Books, 2008.

Cox, Mike. *Time of the Rangers: Texas Rangers, from 1900 to the Present*. New York: Forge Books, 2009.

Cox, Patrick. "Eugene C. Barker." In Cox and Hendrickson, *Writing the Story of Texas*, 23–42.

Cox, Patrick L., and Kenneth E. Hendrickson Jr., eds. *Writing the Story of Texas*. Austin: University of Texas Press, 2013.

Craig, David. *The Ethics of the Story: Using Narrative Techniques Responsibly in Journalism*. Lanham, MD: Rowman & Littlefield, 2006

Crouch, Barry A., and Donaly E. Brice. *The Governor's Hounds: The Texas State Police, 1870–1873*. Austin: University of Texas Press, 2011.

Cummins, Light T. "From the Midway to the Hall of State at Fair Park: Two Competing Views of Women at the Dallas Celebration of 1936." *Southwestern Historical Quarterly* 114, no. 3 (January 2011): 225–51.

Cummins, Light T. "History, Memory, and Rebranding Texas as Western for the Texas Centennial of 1936." In *This Corner of Canaan: Essays on Texas in Honor of Randolph B. Campbell*, ed. Richard B. McCaslin, Donald E. Chipman, and Andrew J. Torget, 37–58. Denton: University of North Texas Press, 2013.

Cummins, Light T. Review of *The Law Comes to Texas: the Texas Rangers, 1870–1901*, by Frederick Wilkins. *Choice Review* 36, no. 11 (July 1999).

Cummins, Light Townsend, and Mary L. Scheer, eds. *Texan Identities: Moving beyond Myth, Memory, and Fallacy in Texas History*. Denton: University of North Texas Press, 2016.

Curtis, Gregory. "West Is West." *Texas Monthly*, July 1999. https://www.texasmonthly.com/articles/west-is-west/.

Cutrer, Thomas W. *Ben McCulloch and the Frontier Military Tradition*. Chapel Hill: University of North Carolina Press, 1993.

Davidge, Sarah Ellen. "Texas Rangers Were Rough and Ready Fighters." *Frontier Times* 13, no. 2 (November 1935): 125–29 (originally published in the *Galveston Tribune*).

Davies, Dave. "'Cult of Glory' Reveals the Dark History of the Texas Rangers." *Fresh Air*, June 8, 2020. https://www.npr.org/2020/06/08/871929844/cult-of-glory-reveals-the-dark-history-of-the-texas-rangers.

Davis, John L. *The Texas Rangers: Images and Incidents*. San Antonio: Institute of Texas Cultures, 1991.

Dawson, Joseph G., III. Review of *Ben McCulloch and the Frontier Military Tradition*, by Thomas W. Cutrer. *Arkansas Historical Quarterly* 53, no. 2 (Summer 1994): 244–46.

Day, James M. *Captain Clint Peoples, Texas Ranger: Fifty Years a Lawman*. Waco: Texian Press, 1999.

Day, James M. "Rangers of the Last Frontier of Texas." *Password* 45 (Winter 2000): 159–74.

Day, James M. *Rangers of Texas*. Waco: Texian Press, 1969.

DeArment, Robert K., ed. *The Best of NOLA: Outlaws and Lawmen of the Old West*. Laramie, WY: NOLA and University of Wyoming, 2001.

DeLeon, Arnoldo. *They Called Them Greasers: Anglo Attitudes toward Mexicans in Texas, 1821–1900*. Austin: University of Texas Press, 1983.

DeMattos, Jack, and Chuck Parsons. *The Notorious Luke Short: Sporting Man of the Wild West*. Denton: University of North Texas Press, 2015.

DeMattos, Jack, and Chuck Parsons. *They Called Him Buckskin Frank: The Life and Times of Nashville Franklyn Leslie*. Denton: University of North Texas Press, 2018.

Denman, Clarence P. "The Office of Adjutant General in Texas, 1835–1881." *Southwestern Historical Quarterly* 28, no. 4 (April 1925): 302–22.

DeShields, James T. *Border Wars of Texas*. Austin: State House Press, 1993.

Devereaux, Jan. *Pistols, Petticoats, & Poker: The Real Lottie Deno: No Lies or Alibis*. Introduction by Robert G. McCubbin. Silver City, NM: High-Lonesome Books, 2009.

Diaz, George T. *Border Contraband: A History of Smuggling across the Rio Grande*. Austin: University of Texas Press, 2015.

Dingus, Anne. "Américo Paredes." *Texas Monthly*, June 1999.

Dixon, Kemp. *Chasing Thugs, Nazis, and Reds: Texas Ranger Norman K. Dixon*. College Station: Texas A&M University Press, 2015.

Dixon, Kemp. "The Diary of a Ranger's Wife, 1938–1939." *East Texas Historical Journal* 54, no. 1 (2016): 7–17.

Dixon, Kemp. Review of *Texas Rangers: Lives, Legend, and Legacy*, by Bob Alexander and Donaly Brice. *Southwestern Historical Quarterly* 122, no. 1 (June 2018): 121–22.

Dobie, J. Frank. "Duval, John Crittenden." *Handbook of Texas Online*, updated October 16, 2020. http://www.tshaonline.org/handbook/online/articles/fdu33.

Dobie, J. Frank. *Guide to Life and Literature of the Southwest*. Dallas: Southern Methodist University Press, 1952.

Dolbeare, Benjamin. *A Narrative of the Captivity and Suffering of Dolly Webster Among the Camanche Indians in Texas*. 1843. Reprint, New Haven: Yale University Library, 1986.

Draper, Robert. "The Twilight of the Texas Rangers." *Texas Monthly*, February 1994. https://texasmonthly.com/articles/the-twilight-of-the-texas-rangers.

Dukes, Doug. *Firearms of the Texas Rangers: From the Frontier Era to the Modern Age*. Denton: University of North Texas Press, 2020.

Dunn, John B. "Red." *Perilous Trails of Texas*. Edited by Lilith Lorraine. Dallas: Southwest Press, 1932.

Durgnat, Raymond, and Scott Simmon. *King Vidor: American*. Berkeley: University of California Press, 1988.

Durham, George, as told to Clyde Wantland. *Taming the Nueces Strip: The Story of McNelly's Rangers*. Austin: University of Texas Press, 1962.

Duval, John C. *The Adventures of Big-Foot Wallace., The Texas Ranger and Hunter*. Philadelphia: Claxton, Remsen, and Haffelfinger, 1871. Reprinted and edited by Mabel Major and Rebecca W. Smith. Lincoln: University of Nebraska Press, 1966

Elliott, Glenn. *Glenn Elliott: A Ranger's Ranger*. With Robert Nieman. Waco: Texian Press, 1999.

Ely, Glen Sample. *Where the West Begins: Debating Texas Identity*. Lubbock: Texas Tech University Press, 2011.

Esley, Jo Ella Powell. *Frontier Blood: The Saga of the Parker Family*. College Station: Texas A&M University Press, 2001.

Everett, Dianna. *The Texas Cherokees: A People between Two Fires, 1819–1840*. Norman: University of Oklahoma Press, 1990.

Favor, Bob. *My Rangering Days*. Abilene, TX: H. V. Chapman & Sons, 2006.

Fehrenbach, T. R. *Comanches: The Destruction of a People*. New York: Knopf, 1974.

Fischer, David Hackett. *Historians' Fallacies: Toward a Logic of Historical Thought*. New York: Harper & Row, 1970.

Fleischer, Mary Beth, ed. "Dudley G. Wooten's Comment on Texas Histories and Historians of the Nineteenth Century." *Southwestern Historical Quarterly* 73, no. 2 (October 1969): 235–42.

Foos, Paul. *A Short, Offhand, Killing Affair: Soldiers and Social Conflict during the Mexican-American War*. Chapel Hill: University of North Carolina Press, 2002.

Ford, John S. *Rip Ford's Texas: Personal Narratives of the West*. Edited by Stephen B. Oates. Austin: University of Texas Press, 1963.

Foster, Morris W. *Being Comanche: A Social History of an American Indian Community*. Tucson: University of Arizona Press, 1991.

Frantz, Joe B. "Remembering Walter Prescott Webb." *Southwestern Historical Quarterly* 92, no. 1 (1988): 16–30.

Frazier, Donald S. Review of *Texas Ranger Captain William L. Wright*, by Richard McCaslin. *Journal of Southern History* 89, no. 1 (February 2023): 168–69.

Friend, Llerena. "W. P. Webb's Texas Rangers." *Southwestern Historical Quarterly* 74, no. 3 (January 1971): 293–323.

Furman, Necah Stewart. *Walter Prescott Webb: His Life and Impact.* Albuquerque: University of New Mexico Press, 1976.

Furman, Necah Stewart. "Webb, Walter Prescott." *Handbook of Texas Online,* updated October 18, 2016. http://www.tshaonline.org/handbook/online/articles/fwe06.

Gammel, H. P. N., comp. *The Laws of Texas: 1822–1897.* Vol. 8. Austin: Gammel Book Company, 1898.

Gard, Wayne. *Frontier Justice.* Norman: University of Oklahoma Press, 1949.

Gard, Wayne. *Sam Bass.* New York: Houghton Mifflin, 1936.

Garrison, George P. *Texas: A Contest of Civilizations.* Boston: Houghton Mifflin, 1903.

Gilderhus, Mark T. *History and Historians: A Historiographical Introduction.* 7th ed. Upper Saddle River, NJ: Prentice Hall, 2010.

Gillett, James B. *Fugitives from Justice: The Notebook of Texas Ranger Sergeant James B. Gillett.* Austin: State House Press, 1997.

Gillett, James B. *Six Years with the Texas Rangers, 1873 to 1881.* Austin: n. p., 1921. New edition, edited by M. M. Quaife. New Haven: Yale University Press, 1925.

Gilliland, Maude T. *Horsebackers of the Brush Country: A Story of the Texas Rangers and Mexican Liquor Smugglers.* N.p.: Springman-King, 1968.

Gilliland, Maude T. *Rincon (Remote Dwelling Place).* N.p.: Springman-King, 1964.

Gilliland, Maude T. *Wilson County Texas Rangers, 1837-1977.* N.p.: Springman-King, 1977.

Ginn, Jody E. *East Texas Troubles: The Allred Rangers' Cleanup of San Augustine.* Norman: University of Oklahoma Press, 2019.

Ginn, Jody E. Review of *Yours to Command: The Life and Legend of Texas Ranger Captain Bill McDonald,* by Harold Weiss Jr. *Southwestern Historical Quarterly* 114, no. 1 (July 2010): 89–91.

Ginn, Jody E. "The Texas Rangers in Myth and Memory." In Cummins and Scheer, *Texan Identities,* 87–120.

Glasrud, Bruce A., and Harold J. Weiss Jr. "Crystallization of a Tradition: Texas Rangers and the Republic of Texas." Chap. 6 in *Single Star of the West: The Republic of Texas, 1836-1845,* edited by Kenneth W. Howell and Charles Swanlund. Denton: University of North Texas Press, 2017.

Glasrud, Bruce A., and Harold J. Weiss Jr., eds. *Tracking the Texas Rangers: The Nineteenth Century.* Denton: University of North Texas Press, 2012.

Glasrud, Bruce A., and Harold J. Weiss Jr., eds. *Tracking the Texas Rangers: The Twentieth Century.* Denton: University of North Texas Press, 2013.

Gooding, Ed, and Robert Nieman. *Ed Gooding: Soldier, Texas Ranger*. Longview, TX: Ranger Publishing, 2001.

Graber, Henry. *A Terry Texas Ranger: The Life Record of H. W. Graber*. Austin: State House Press, 1987.

Graham, Don. "Fallen Heroes." *Texas Monthly*, February 2005. https://www.texasmonthly.com/articles/fallen-heroes/.

Graham, Don. *Texas: A Literary Portrait*. San Antonio: Corona Publishing Company, 1985.

Graybill, Andrew R. *Policing the Great Plains: Rangers, Mounties, and the North American Frontier, 1875–1910*. Lincoln: University of Nebraska Press, 2007.

Graybill, Andrew. "Rural Police and the Defense of the Cattleman's Empire in Texas and Alberta, 1875–1900." *Agricultural History* 79, no. 3 (Summer 2005): 253–80.

Graybill, Andrew R. "Texas Rangers, Canadian Mounties, and the Policing of the Transnational Frontier, 1885–1910." *Western Historical Quarterly* 35, no. 2 (Summer 2004), 167–91.

Greene, A. C. *The 50+ Best Books on Texas*. Denton: University of North Texas Press, 1998.

Greer, James K. *Colonel Jack Hays: Texas Frontier Leader and California Builder*. New York: E. P. Dutton, 1952.

Greer, James K. *A Texas Ranger and Frontiersman: The Days of Buck Barry in Texas*. Dallas: Southwest Press, 1932.

Gutierrez, Jose Angel. *The Making of a Chicano Militant: Lessons from Cristal*. Madison: University of Wisconsin Press, 1998.

Haley, J. Evetts. *Jeff Milton: A Good Man with a Gun*. Norman: University of Oklahoma Press, 1949.

Hardin, Stephen L. *The Texas Rangers*. London: Osprey, 1991.

Hardin, Stephen L. *Texian Iliad: A Military History of the Texas Revolution, 1835–1836*. Austin: University of Texas Press, 1994.

Hardin, Stephen L. "'Valor, Wisdom, and Experience': Early Texas Rangers and the Nature of Frontier Leadership." In Glasrud and Weiss, *Tracking: Nineteenth Century*, 50–61.

Harris, Charles H., III, Frances E. Harris, and Louis R. Sadler. *Texas Ranger Biographies: Those Who Served, 1910–1921*. Albuquerque: University of New Mexico Press, 2009.

Harris, Charles H., III, and Louis R. Sadler. *The Archeologist Was a Spy: Sylvanus G. Morley and the Office of Naval Intelligence*. Albuquerque: University of New Mexico Press, 2009.

Harris, Charles H., III, and Louis R. Sadler. *The Border and the Revolution: Clandestine Activities of the Mexican Revolution, 1910–1920.* Silver City: High Lonesome Books, 1988.

Harris, Charles H., III, and Louis R. Sadler. *The Great Call-Up: The Guard, the Border, and the Mexican Revolution.* Norman: University of Oklahoma Press, 2015.

Harris, Charles H., III, and Louis R. Sadler. "Pancho Villa and the Columbus Raid: The Missing Documents." *New Mexico Historical Review* 50, no. 4 (Oct. 1975): 335–46.

Harris, Charles H., III, and Louis R. Sadler. "The Plan of San Diego and the Mexican-United States Crisis of 1916: A Reexamination." *Hispanic-American Historical Review* 58, no. 3 (August 1978): 381–408.

Harris, Charles H., III, and Louis R. Sadler. *The Plan de San Diego: Tejano Rebellion, Mexican Intrigue.* Lincoln: University of Nebraska Press, 2013.

Harris, Charles H., III, and Louis R. Sadler. *The Secret War in El Paso: Mexican Revolutionary Intrigue, 1906–1920.* Albuquerque: University of New Mexico Press, 2009.

Harris, Charles H., III, and Louis R. Sadler. *The Texas Rangers and the Mexican Revolution: The Bloodiest Decade, 1910–1920.* Albuquerque: University of New Mexico Press, 2004.

Harris, Charles H., III, and Louis R. Sadler. *The Texas Rangers in Transition: From Gunfighters to Criminal Investigators, 1921–1935.* Norman: University of Oklahoma Press, 2019.

Harris, Charles H., III, and Louis R. Sadler. "United States Government Archives and the Mexican Revolution." *New World: A Journal of Latin American Studies* 1 (1986): 108–16.

Harvard Law Review Association. "Law, Race, and the Border: The El Paso Salt War of 1877." *Harvard Law Review* 117, no. 3 (January 2004): 941–63.

Hatley, Allen G. *Bringing the Law to Texas: Crime and Violence in Nineteenth Century Texas.* La Grange: Centex Press, 2002.

Hatley, Allen G. *The Indian Wars in Stephen F. Austin's Colony, 1822–1835.* Austin: Eakin Press, 2001.

Holdridge, Doyle. *Working the Border: A Texas Ranger's Story.* Dallas: Atriad Press, 2009.

Hollister, Stacy. "A Q&A with Robert Utley." *Texas Monthly*, November 2002. https://www.texasmonthly.com/articles/a-qa-with-robert-utley/.

418   Bibliography

Hubbs, Barney, and Chuck Parsons. *Shadows along the Pecos: The Saga of Clay Allison, "Gentleman Gun Fighter."* Pecos, TX: West of the Pecos Museum, 1977.

Hughes, W. J. *Rebellious Ranger: Rip Ford and the Old Southwest.* Norman: University of Oklahoma Press, 1964.

Hunter, J. Marvin. "Captain Arrington's Expedition." *Frontier Times* 6, no. 3 (December 1928): 97–102.

Hunter, J. Marvin. "Texas Rangers Are Still Active." *Frontier Times* 22, no. 10 (July 1945): 294.

Hunter, J. Marvin, and Noah Rose. *The Album of Gunfighters.* n.p.: Hunter and Rose, 1951.

Hutson, Richard. "Ecce Cowboy: E. C. Abbott's *We Pointed Them North.*" In *Western Subjects: Autobiographical Writing in the North American West*, edited by Kathleen A. Boardman and Gioia Woods, 127–54. Salt Lake City: University of Utah Press, 2004.

Irving, Washington. *A Tour of the Prairies.* London: John Murray, 1835.

Ivey, Darren L. *The Ranger Ideal: Texas Rangers in the Hall of Fame.* 3 vols. Denton: University of North Texas Press, 2017–21.

Ivey, Darren L. *The Texas Rangers: A Registry and History.* Jefferson, NC: McFarland, 2010.

Jackson, H. Joaquin, and James L. Haley. *One Ranger Returns.* Austin: University of Texas Press, 2008.

Jackson, H. Joaquin, and David Marion Wilkinson. *One Ranger: A Memoir.* Austin: University of Texas Press, 2005.

Jackson, Robert H., and Edward H. Castillo. *Indians, Franciscans, and Spanish Colonization: The Impact of the Mission System on California Indians.* Albuquerque: University of New Mexico Press, 1995.

Jackson, W. Turrentine. Review of *Rebellious Ranger: Rip Ford and the Old Southwest*, by W. J. Hughes; *Rip Ford's Texas*, by John Salmon Ford, Stephen B. Oates. *Journal of American History* 51, no. 2 (September 1964): 317–18.

Jenkins, John H. *Basic Texas Books: An Annotated Bibliography of Selected Works for a Research Library.* 1983. Rev. ed., Austin: Texas State Historical Association, 1988.

Jenkins, John H., and H. Gordon Frost. *"I'm Frank Hamer": The Life of a Texas Peace Officer.* Austin: Pemberton Press, 1968.

Jenkins, John H., and Kenneth Kesselus. *Edward Burleson: Texas Frontier Leader.* Austin: Jenkins, 1990.

Jennings, Nathan A. "Ranging the Tejas Frontier: A Reinterpretation of the Tactical Origins of the Texas Rangers." *Journal of South Texas* 27, no. 2 (Fall 2014): 72–91.

Jennings, Nathan A. "Riding into Controversy: A Study in Contrasting Views of the Texas Rangers." *Journal of the West* 52, no. 2 (Spring 2013): 42–52.

Jennings, Nathan A. *Riding for the Lone Star: Frontier Cavalry and the Texas Way of War, 1822–1865.* Denton: University of North Texas Press, 2016.

Jennings, Napoleon A. *A Texas Ranger.* New York: Charles Scribner's Sons, 1899.

Jennings, Napoleon A. *A Texas Ranger.* Edited by Ben Procter. Reprint, Chicago: Lakeside Press, 1992.

Jennings, Napoleon A. *A Texas Ranger.* Reprinted with a foreword by J. Frank Dobie and introduction by Stephen L. Hardin. Norman: University of Oklahoma Press, 1997.

Johannsen, Robert. *To the Halls of the Montezumas: The Mexican War in the American Imagination.* New York: Oxford University Press, 1985.

Johnson, Benjamin H. *Revolution in Texas: How a Forgotten Rebellion and Its Bloody Suppression Turned Mexicans into Americans.* New Haven: Yale University Press, 2003.

Johnson, David. *The Mason County "Hoo Doo" War, 1874–1902.* Denton: University of North Texas Press, 2006.

Jones, Brian Jay. *Washington Irving: An American Original.* New York: Arcade, 2008.

Jones, Daryl. *The Dime Novel Western.* Bowling Green, OH: Bowling Green University Popular Press, 1978.

Kavanagh, Thomas. *Comanche Political History: An Ethnohistorical Perspective, 1706–1875.* Lincoln: University of Nebraska Press, 1995.

Kendall, George. *Dispatches from the Mexican War.* Edited by Lawrence Cress. Norman: University of Oklahoma Press, 1999.

Kiernan, Benedict. *Blood and Soil: A World History of Genocide and Extermination from Sparta to Darfur.* New Haven: Yale University Press, 2007.

Kilgore, Dan E. *A Ranger Legacy: 150 Years of Service to Texas.* Austin: Madrona Press, 1973.

"The Killing of Captain Frank Jones." *Frontier Times* 6, no. 4 (January 1929): 145–49.

Kimmel, Kelly F. *The Conquest of the Karankawas and the Tonkawas, 1821–1859.* College Station: Texas A&M University Press, 1999.

King, Wilburn H. "The Texas Ranger Service and History of the Rangers, with Observations on Their Value as a Police Protection." In Wooten, *Comprehensive History of Texas*, 2:329–67.

Knowles, Thomas W. *They Rode for the Lone Star: The Saga of the Texas Rangers*. Vol. 1, *The Birth of Texas–The Civil War*. Dallas: Taylor Publishing, 1999.

Koch, Lena Clara. "The Federal Indian Policy in Texas, 1845–1860: Chapter III. The Rangers and Frontier Protection." *Southwestern Historical Quarterly* 29, no. 1 (July 1925): 19–35.

Kuykendall, J. H. "Reminiscences of Early Texas: A Collection from the Austin Papers." *Quarterly of the Texas State Historical Association* 6, no. 3 (January 1903): 236–53; 6, no. 4 (April 1903): 311–30; 7, no. 1 (July 1903): 29–64.

Lackey, B. Roberts. *Stories of the Texas Rangers*. San Antonio: Naylor, 1955.

Lane, Walter P. *The Adventures and Recollections of Walter P. Lane*. Marshall, TX: New Messenger, 1923.

Lee, Nelson. *Three Years among the Camanches: The Narrative of Nelson Lee, the Texas Ranger, containing a Detailed Account of his Captivity Among the Indians, His Singular Escape Thorough the Instrumentality of his Watch, and Fully Illustrating Indian Life as it is On the War Path and In Camp*. Albany, NY: Baker and Taylor, 1859.

Levario, Miguel A. "Cowboys and Bandidos: Authority and Race in West Texas." *West Texas Historical Association Year Book* 85 (2009): 7–27.

Levario, Miguel A. *Militarizing the Border: When Mexicans Became the Enemy*. College Station: Texas A&M University Press, 2012.

Lewis, Archibald R., and Thomas F. McGann, eds. *The New World Looks at Its History*. Austin: University of Texas Press, 1963.

Liles, Debbie. Review of *Texas Ranger John B. Jones and the Frontier Battalion, 1874–1881*, by Rick Miller. *Southwestern Historical Quarterly* 117, no. 2 (October 2013): 218–19.

Limón, José. "The Return of the Mexican Ballad: Américo Paredes and His Anthropological Text as Persuasive Political Performances." Chap. 8 in *Creativity/Anthropology*, edited by Smadar Lavie, Kirin Nayarin, and Renato Rosaldo. Ithaca, NY: Cornell University Press, 1993.

Long, Christopher. "Wilbarger, John Wesley." *Handbook of Texas Online*, accessed January 1, 2022. https://www.tshaonline.org/handbook/entries/wilbarger-john-wesley.

Lyles, Ian B. "Mixed Blessing: The Role of the Texas Rangers in the Mexican War, 1846–1848." Thesis, Military Command and General Staff College, Fort Leavenworth, KS, 2003.

Malsch, Brownson. *Captain M. T. Lone Wolf Gonzaullas: The Only Texas Ranger Captain of Spanish Descent*. Austin: Shoal Creek, 1980.

Malsch, Brownson. *"Lone Wolf" Gonzaullas, Texas Ranger*. Introduction by Harold J. Weiss Jr. 1980. Reprint, Norman: University of Oklahoma Press, 1998.

Maltby, William J. *Captain Jeff, or Frontier Life in Texas with the Texas Rangers*. Colorado, TX: Whipkey Printing, 1906. Facsimile reprint with introduction by Rupert Richardson and Publisher's Notice by N. C. Bawcom. Waco: Texian Press, 1967.

Mann, Barbara Alice. *George Washington's War on Native America*. Lincoln: University of Nebraska Press, 2008.

Mann, William L. "James O. Rice: Hero of the Battle on the San Gabriels." *Southwestern Historical Quarterly* 55, no. 1 (July 1951): 30–42.

Marsden, Michael T. "Popular Images of the Canadian Mounted Police and the Texas Rangers." *Studies in Popular Culture* 16, no. 1 (October 1993): 1–14.

Martin, Jack. *Border Boss: Captain John R. Hughes, Texas Ranger*. San Antonio: Naylor, 1942.

Martinez, Monica Muñoz. *The Injustice Never Leaves You: Anti-Mexican Violence in Texas*. Cambridge, MA: Harvard University Press, 2018.

Martinez, Ramiro. *Creating the Professional Texas Lawman: Meeting the Challenge, 1900–2000*. New Braunfels, TX: Rio Bravo, 2009.

Martinez, Ramiro. *They Call Me Ranger Ray: From the UT Tower Sniper to Corruption in South Texas*. New Braunfels, TX: Rio Bravo, 2005.

Martz, Richard J. "'No One Can Arrest Me': The Story of Gregorio Cortez." *Journal of South Texas* 1 (1974): 1–17.

Mauldin, Steve. "Search for 'Brazos': The Mystery Writer of *Life of Robert Hall*." *Southwestern Historical Quarterly* 116, no. 4 (April 2013): 386–91.

Mayhall, Mildred P. *The Kiowas*. Norman: University of Oklahoma Press, 1962.

McCaslin, Richard B. *At the Heart of Texas: 100 Years of the Texas State Historical Association, 1897–1997*. Austin: Texas State Historical Association, 2007.

McCaslin, Richard B. *Fighting Stock: John S. "Rip" Ford of Texas*. Fort Worth: TCU Press, 2011.

McCaslin, Richard B. *Texas Ranger Captain William L. Wright*. Denton: University of North Texas Press, 2021.

McClung, John B. "Texas Rangers along the Rio Grande, 1910–1919." PhD Dissertation, Texas Christian University, 1981.

McDonald, Thomas O. *Texas Rangers, Ranchers, and Realtors: James Hughes Callahan and the Day Family in the Guadalupe River Basin*. Norman: University of Oklahoma Press, 2021.

McLemore, Laura L. *Inventing Texas: Early Historians of the Lone Star State*. College Station: Texas A&M University Press, 2004.

McPherson, James. "Revisionist Historians." *Perspectives on History* 41, No. 6 (September 2003). www.historians.org/publications-and-directories/perspectives-on- history/september-2003/revisionist-historians.

Meed, Douglas V. *Texas Ranger Johnny Klevenhagen*. Plano: Republic of Texas Press, 2000.

Mendoza, Alexander. "'For Our Own Best Interests': Nineteenth-Century Laredo Tejanos, Military Service, and the Development of American Nationalism." *Southwestern Historical Quarterly* 115, no. 2 (October 2011): 125–52.

Metz, Leon. *John Wesley Hardin: Dark Angel of Texas*. El Paso: Mangan Books, 1996.

"The Mexican and Indian Raid of '78." Quarterly of the Texas State Historical Association 5, no. 3 (January 1902): 248.

Meyer, Michael C. "Introduction." In Harris and Sadler, *Border and the Revolution*, 1–3.

Michel, Eddie. *A Breed Apart: The History of the Texas Rangers*. Denver: Outskirts Press, 2012.

Miletich, Leo N. *Dan Stuart's Fistic Carnival*. College Station: Texas A&M University Press, 1994.

Miller, Rick. *Sam Bass and Gang*. Austin: State House Press, 1999.

Miller, Rick. *Texas Ranger John B. Jones and the Frontier Battalion, 1874–1881*. Denton: University of North Texas Press, 2012.

Montejano, David. *Anglos and Mexicans in the Making of Texas, 1836–1986*. 1987. Reprint, Austin: University of Texas Press, 2006.

Moore, Stephen L. *Eighteen Minutes: The Battle of San Jacinto and the Texas Independence Campaign*. Dallas: Republic of Texas Press, 2004.

Moore, Stephen L. *Last Stand of the Texas Cherokees: Chief Bowles and the 1839 Cherokee War in Texas*. Garland, TX: RAM Books, 2009.

Moore, Stephen L. *Savage Frontier: Rangers, Riflemen, and Indian Wars in Texas*. 4 vols. Denton: University of North Texas Press, 2002–2010.

Moore, Stephen L. *Taming Texas: Captain William T. Sadler's Lone Star Service*. Austin: State House Press, 2000.

Moore, Stephen L. *Texas Rising: The Epic True Story of the Lone Star Republic and the Rise of the Texas Rangers, 1836–1846*. New York: William Morrow, 2015.

Morris, John Miller. *A Private in the Texas Rangers: A. T. Miller of Company B, Frontier Battalion*. College Station: Texas A&M University Press, 2001.

Moulton, Candy. "A Ranger War & Billy the Kid." *True West*, July 2007, 74–75.

Mulroy, Kevin. *Freedom on the Border: The Seminole Maroons in Florida, the Indian Territory, Coahuila, and Texas*. Lubbock: Texas Tech University Press, 1993.

Myer, Albert J. "'I Am Already Quite a Texan': Albert J. Myer's Letters from Texas, 1854–1856." Edited by David A Clary. *Southwestern Historical Quarterly* 82, no. 1 (July 1978): 25–76.

Nackman, Mark E. "The Making of the Citizen Soldier, 1835–1860." *Southwestern Historical Quarterly* 78, no. 3 (January 1975): 231–53.

Naimark, Norman M. *Fires of Hatred: Ethnic Cleansing in Twentieth-Century Europe*. Cambridge, MA: Harvard University Press, 2001.

Neighbours, Kenneth F. "The Expedition of Major Robert S. Neighbors to El Paso in 1849." *Southwestern Historical Quarterly* 58, no. 1 (July 1954): 36–59.

Nichols, Roy F. Review of *The Hero in America: A Chronical of Hero Worship*, by Dixon Wecter. *American Historical Review* 47, no. 2 (January 1942): 341.

Nielsen, George R. "Mathew Caldwell." *Southwestern Historical Quarterly* 64, no. 4 (April 1961): 478–502.

Oates, Stephen B. "Los Diablos Tejanos." *American West* 2 (Summer 1965): 41–50.

Oates, Stephen B. *Visions of Glory: Texans on the Southwestern Frontier*. Norman: University of Oklahoma Press, 1970.

Olmsted, Frederick L. *A Journey through Texas; Or, a Saddle-Trip on the Southwestern Frontier*. 1857. Reprint, Austin: University of Texas Press, 1978.

O'Neal, Bill. *The Bloody Legacy of Pink Higgins*. Austin: Eakin Press, 1999.

O'Neal, Bill. *The Johnson-Sims Feud: Romeo and Juliet, West Texas Style*. Denton: University of North Texas Press, 2010.

O'Neal, Bill. *Reel Rangers: Texas Rangers in Movies, TV, Radio, and Other Forms of Popular Culture*. Waco: Eakin Press, 2008.

O'Neal, Bill. *War in East Texas: Regulators and Moderators*. Lufkin: Best of East Texas Publishers, 2006.

Paine, Albert Bigelow. *Captain Bill McDonald, Texas Ranger: A Story of Frontier Reform*. New York: J. J. Little & Ives, 1909.

Paredes, Américo. *George Washington Gomez: A Mexicotexan Novel*. Houston: Arte Publico Press, 1990.

Paredes, Américo. *A Texas-Mexican Cancionero: Folksongs of the Lower Rio Grande*. Urbana: University of Illinois Press, 1976.

Paredes, Américo. *Uncle Remus con Chile*. Houston: Arte Publico Press, 1993.

Paredes, Américo. *"With His Pistol in His Hand": A Border Ballad and Its Hero*. Austin: University of Texas Press, 1958.

Parsons, Chuck. *Captain Jack Helm: Victim of Texas Reconstruction Violence*. Denton: University of North Texas Press, 2018.

Parsons, Chuck. *Captain John R. Hughes, Lone Star Ranger*. Denton: University of North Texas Press, 2011.

Parsons, Chuck. "George Culver Tennille." *Frontier Times*, December–January 1977.

Parsons, Chuck. "The Jesse Evans Gang and the Death of Texas Ranger George R. Bingham." *Journal of Big Bend History* 20 (2008): 75–87.

Parsons, Chuck. *John B. Armstrong: Texas Ranger and Pioneer Ranchman*. College Station: Texas A&M University Press, 2007.

Parsons, Chuck, ed. "Life of C. W. Polk." *Plum Creek Almanac* 29, no. 2 (Fall 2011): 7–74.

Parsons, Chuck. *"Pidge," Texas Ranger*. College Station: Texas A&M University Press, 2013.

Parsons, Chuck. *"Pidge": A Texas Ranger from Virginia*. Wolfe City, TX: self-published, 1985.

Parsons, Chuck. *The Sutton-Taylor Feud: The Bloodiest Blood Feud in Texas*. Denton: University of North Texas, 2009.

Parsons, Chuck. *Texas Ranger Lee Hall: From the Red River to the Rio Grande*. Denton: University of North Texas Press, 2020.

Parsons, Chuck. *The Texas Rangers*. Charleston, SC: Arcadia, 2011.

Parsons, Chuck, and Donaly E. Brice. *Texas Ranger N. O. Reynolds, the Intrepid*, Denton: University of North Texas Press, 2014.

Parsons, Chuck, and Norman Wayne Brown. *A Lawless Breed: John Wesley Hardin, Texas Reconstruction, and Violence in the Wild West*. Denton: University of North Texas Press, 2013.

Parsons, Chuck, and Marjorie Lee Burnett. *Bowen and Hardin*. College Station, TX: Early West, 1991.

Parsons, Chuck, and Marianne E. Hall Little. *Captain L. H. McNelly, Texas Ranger: The Life and Times of a Fighting Man*. Austin: State House Press, 2001.

Patterson, James, and Andrew Bourelle. *Texas Ranger*. New York: Little, Brown, 2018.

Pearson, Jim B. Review of *Trails and Trials of a Texas Ranger*, by William Warren Sterling. *Arizona and the Southwest* 12, no. 4 (Winter 1970): 395–96.

Peyton, Green. *For God and Texas: The Life of P. B. Hill*. New York: McGraw-Hill Book, 1947.

Phillips, Edward H. "The Sherman Courthouse Riot of 1930." *East Texas Historical Journal* 25, no. 2 (October 1987): 12–19.

Pierce, Jason E. *Making the White Man's West: Whiteness and the Creation of the American West*. Boulder: University Press of Colorado, 2016.

Pike, James. *The Scout and Ranger: Being the Personal Adventures of Corporal Pike, of the Fourth Ohio Cavalry, as Texas Ranger, in the Indian Wars*. Cincinnati and New York: J. R. Hawley, 1865.

Place, Marian T. *Comanches & Other Indians of Texas*. New York: Harcourt, Brace & World, 1970.

Plummer, Rachel Parker. *Narrative of the Capture and Subsequent Sufferings of Mrs. Rachel Plummer*. 1838. Reprint, n.p.: Independently published, 2021.

Pool, William C. "Barker, Eugene Campbell." *Handbook of Texas Online*, accessed December 15, 2021. https://www.tshaonline.org/handbook/entries/barker-eugene-campbell.

Pool, William C. *Eugene C. Barker: Historian*. Austin: Texas State Historical Association, 1971.

Prassel, Frank R. *The Great American Outlaw: A Legacy of Fact and Fiction*. Norman: University of Oklahoma Press, 1993.

Prassel, Frank R. *The Western Peace Officer: A Legacy of Law and Order*. Norman: University of Oklahoma Press, 1972.

Pratt, Adam J. Review of *Riding for the Lone Star: Frontier Cavalry and the Texas Way of War, 1822–1865*, by Nathan A. Jennings. *Journal of Southern History* 83, no. 2 (May 2017): 418–19.

Preece, Harold. *Lone Star Man: Ira Aten, Last of the Old Texas Rangers*. New York: Hastings House, 1960.

Price, B. Byron. "J. Evetts Haley." In Cox and Hendrickson, *Writing the Story of Texas*, 115–34.

Procter, Ben H. *Just One Riot: Episodes of Texas Rangers in the 20th Century*. Austin: Eakin Press, 1991.

Procter, Ben H. "The Modern Texas Rangers: A Law-Enforcement Dilemma in the Rio Grande Valley." In *Reflections of Western Historians*, edited by John A. Carroll, 215–31. Tucson: University of Arizona Press, 1969.

Procter, Ben H. "Texas Rangers." In Tyler, *New Handbook of Texas*, vol. 6.

Procter, Ben H. "The Texas Rangers: An Overview." In *The Texas Heritage*, edited by Ben Procter and Archie P. McDonald, 119–31. St. Louis, MO: Forum Press, 1980.

Procter, Ben H. "The Texas Rangers: An Overview." Chap. 9 in *The Texas Heritage*, edited by Ben H. Procter and Archie P. McDonald, 4th ed. Wheeling, IL: Harlan Davidson, 2003.

Ragsdale, Kenneth Baxter. *The Year America Discovered Texas: Centennial '36*. College Station: Texas A&M University Press, 1987.

Rasenberger, Jim. *Revolver: Sam Colt and the Six-Shooter That Changed America*. New York: Scribner, 2020.

Raymond, Dora N. *Captain Lee Hall of Texas*. Norman: University of Oklahoma Press, 1940.

Reid, Samuel C., Jr. *The Scouting Expeditions of McCulloch's Texas Rangers; Or, The Summer and Fall Campaign of the Army of the United States in Mexico—1846; Including Skirmishes with the Mexicans, and an Accurate Detail of the Storming of Monterrey; Also, the Daring Scouts at Buena Vista; Together with Anecdotes, Incidents, Description of Country, and Sketches of the Lives of the Celebrated Partisan Chiefs, Hays, McCulloch, and Walker*. Philadelphia: G. B. Zieber, 1847.

Reilly, Tom. *War with Mexico! America's Reporters Cover the Battlefront*. Edited by Manley Witten. Lawrence: University Press of Kansas, 2010.

Ribb, Richard H. "José Tomás Canales and the Texas Rangers: Myth, Identity, and Power in South Texas, 1900–1920." PhD diss., University of Texas at Austin, 2001.

Ribb, Richard H. "*La Rinchada*: Revolution, Revenge, and the Rangers, 1910–1920." In *War along the Border: The Mexican Revolution and Tejano Communities*, edited by Arnoldo De León, 56–106. College Station: Texas A&M University Press, 2012.

Richardson, Rupert Norval. *The Comanche Barrier to South Plains Settlement*. Edited by Kenneth R. Jacobs. Introduction by A. C. Greene. 1933. Reprint, Austin: Eakin Press, 1996.

Richardson, Rupert N. Review of *The Texas Rangers: A Century of Frontier Defense*, by Walter Prescott Webb. *Southwestern Historical Quarterly* 39, no. 4 (April 1936): 333–35.

Rigler, Lewis C., and Judyth W. Rigler. *In the Line of Duty: Reflections of a Texas Ranger Private*. Houston: Larksdale, 1984.

Rippy, J. Fred. "Border Troubles along the Rio Grande, 1848–1860." *Southwestern Historical Quarterly* 23, no. 2 (October 1919): 91–111.

Rister, Carl Coke. *Comanche Bondage: Beale's Settlement and Sarah Ann Horn's Narrative*. Introduction by Don Worcester. 1839. Reprint, Lincoln: University of Nebraska Press, 1989.

Roberts, Daniel W. *Rangers and Sovereignty*. San Antonio: Wood Printing and Engraving, 1914. Facsimile edition, combined with Mrs. D. W. Roberts, *A Woman's Reminiscences of Six Years in Camp with the Texas Rangers*, with an introduction by Robert Wooster. Austin: State House Press, 1987.

Robinson, Charles M., III. *The Men Who Wear the Star: The Story of the Texas Rangers*. New York: Random House, 2000.

Robinson, James Harvey. *The New History: Essays Illustrating the Modern Historical Outlook*. New York: Macmillan, 1912.

Robinson, Sherry L. *I Fought a Good Fight: A History of the Lipan Apaches*. Denton: University of North Texas Press, 2013.

Rodale, J. I., ed. *The Synonym Finder*. Emmaus, PA: Rodale Books, 1961.

Ross, Peter R. *The Reckoning: The Triumph of Order on the Texas Outlaw Frontier*. Lubbock: Texas Tech University Press, 2012.

Roth, Mitchel. "Bonnie and Clyde in Texas: The End of the Texas Outlaw Tradition." *East Texas Historical Journal* 35, no. 2 (October 1997): 30–38.

Roth, Mitchel. "Courtesy, Service, Protection." In *Courtesy, Service, Protection: The Texas Department of Public Safety's Sixtieth Anniversary*, edited by Mike Cox. Dallas: Taylor Publishing, 1995.

Roth, Mitchel. "Journalism and the US-Mexican War." In *Dueling Eagles: Reinterpreting the US-Mexican War, 1846–1848*, edited by Richard Fancaviglia and Douglas Richmond, 103–26. Fort Worth: TCU Press, 2000.

Rundell, Walter, Jr. "Walter Prescott Webb: Product of Environment." *Arizona and the West* 5, no. 1 (1963): 4–28.

Saldivar, Ramon, and Donald E. Pease. *The Borderlands of Culture and the Transnational Imaginary*. Durham, NC: Duke University Press, 2006.

Salinas, Cristina. *Managed Migrations: Growers, Farmworkers, and Border Enforcement in the Twentieth Century*. Austin: University of Texas Press, 2018.

Samora, Julian, Joe Bernal, and Albert Peña. *Gunpowder Justice: A Reassessment of the Texas Rangers*. Notre Dame: University of Notre Dame Press, 1979.

Sanders, Mark A. "Theorizing the Collaborative Self: The Dynamics of Contour and Content in the Dictated Autobiography." *New Literary History* 25, no. 2 (Spring 1994): 445–58.

Sandos, James A. *Rebellion in the Borderlands: Anarchism and the Plan of San Diego, 1904–1923*. Norman: University of Oklahoma Press, 1992.

Santos, John Philip. "Américo Paredes vs. J. Frank Dobie." *Texas Monthly*, October 2019.

Santos, John Philip. "The Secret History of the Texas Rangers: 'Cult of Glory' Upends Decades of Mythmaking." *Texas Monthly*, June 2020. https://www.texasmonthly.com/arts-entertainment/secret-history-texas-rangers/.

Screws, David E. "Hispanic Texas Rangers Contribute to Peace on the Texas Frontier, 1838–1880." *Journal of Big Bend Studies* 13 (2001): 27–36.

Selcer, Richard, ed. *Legendary Watering Holes: The Saloons That Made Texas Famous*. College Station: Texas A&M University Press, 2004.

Selcer, Richard. Review of *Texas Ranger: The Epic Life of Frank Hamer, the Man Who Killed Bonnie and Clyde*, by John Boessenecker. *Southwestern Historical Quarterly* 120, no. 2 (October 2016): 268–69.

"Served as a Texas Ranger." *Frontier Times* 5, no. 11 (August 1928): 438–39, and 447.

Shearer, Ernest C. "The Callahan Expedition, 1855." *Southwestern Historical Quarterly* 54, no. 4 (April 1951): 430–51.

Sinise, Jerry. *George Washington Arrington: Civil War Spy, Texas Ranger, Sheriff and Rancher: A Biography*. Burnet, TX: Eakin Press, 1979.

Skidmore, Gerald D., Sr. *Historic Killeen: An Illustrated History*. San Antonio, TX: Historical Publishing, 2010.

Smallwood, James M. *The Feud That Wasn't: The Taylor Ring, Bill Sutton, John Wesley Hardin, and Violence in Texas*. College Station: Texas A&M University Press, 2008.

Smith, David P. *Frontier Defense in the Civil War: Texas' Rangers and Rebels*. College Station: Texas A&M University Press, 1992.

Smith, Michael M. "General Rafael Benavides and the Texas-Mexico Border Crisis of 1877." *Southwestern Historical Quarterly* 112, no. 3 (January 2009): 235–60.

Smithwick, Noah. *The Evolution of a State; Or, Recollections of Old Texas Days*. 1900. Reprint, Austin: University of Texas Press, 1983.

Sonnichsen, C. L. *I'll Die Before I'll Run: The Story of the Great Feuds of Texas*. New York: Harper & Brothers, 1951.

Sonnichsen, C. L. Review of *Rebellious Ranger: Rip Ford and the Old Southwest*, by W. J. Hughes. *Montana: The Magazine of Western History* 14, no. 4 (Autumn 1964): 70.

Sowell, Andrew J. *Early Settlers and Indian Fighters of Southwest Texas*. 1900. Reprint, Austin: State House Press, 1986.

Sowell, Andrew J. *Life of "Big Foot" Wallace: The Great Ranger Captain*. 1899. Reprint, Austin: State House Press, 1989.

Sowell, Andrew J. *Rangers and Pioneers of Texas, with a concise account of the early settlements, hardships, massacres, battles, and wars, by which Texas was rescued from the rule of the savage and consecrated to the empire of civilization.* San Antonio: Shepard Brothers, 1884. Reprint, n.p.: Create Space Independent Publishing Platform, 2016.

Spellman, Paul N. *Captain J. A. Brooks, Texas Ranger.* Denton: University of North Texas Press, 2007.

Spellman, Paul N. *Captain John H. Rogers, Texas Ranger.* Denton: University of North Texas Press, 2008.

Spellman, Paul N. "Dark Days of the Texas Rangers, 1915–1918." *South Texas Studies* 12 (2001): 79–97.

Spinks, S. E. *Law on the Last Frontier: Texas Ranger Arthur Hill.* Lubbock: Texas Tech University Press, 2007.

Spring, Agnes Wright, ed. *The Arrow: Official Publication of the Pi Beta Phi Fraternity* 38, no. 4 (Spring 1922).

Spurlin, Charles D. *Texas Volunteers in the Mexican War.* Austin: Eakin Press, 1998.

Stannard, David. *American Holocaust: Columbus and the Conquest of the New World.* New York: Oxford University Press, 1992.

Stephens, Robert W. *Captain George H. Schmitt, Texas Ranger.* Dallas: Robert W. Stephens, 2006.

Stephens, Robert W. *Texas Ranger Sketches.* Dallas: Privately published, 1972.

Sterling, William W. *Trails and Trials of a Texas Ranger.* Norman: University of Oklahoma Press, 1959.

Sublett, Jesse. "Lone on the Range: Texas Lawmen." *Texas Monthly*, December 21, 1969, accessed December 5, 2019. https://www.texas-monthly.com/articles/lone-on-the-range-texas-lawmen.

Sullivan, W. J. L. *Twelve Years in the Saddle: For Law and Order on the Frontiers of Texas.* Austin: Von-Boeckmann-Jones, 1909. Facsimile edition, New York: Buffalo-Head Press, 1966.

Swanson, Doug J. *Cult of Glory: The Bold and Brutal History of the Texas Rangers.* New York: Viking, 2020.

Tenayuca, Emma, and Homer Brooks. "The Mexican Question in the Southwest." *Political Affairs*, March 1939, p. 259.

"Texas' Once Famous Ranger Band Found to Have Degenerated." *Frontier Times* 12, no. 8 (May 1935): 363.

"The Texas Rangers Brought Law and Order." *Frontier Times* 12, no. 10 (July 1935): 425.

"Texas Rangers and Their Great Leaders." *Frontier Times*15, no. 11 (August 1938): 471–76.

Thompson, Jerry. *Cortina: Defending the Mexican Name in Texas*. College Station: Texas A&M University Press, 2007.

Thornton, Russell. *American Indian Holocaust and Survival: A Population History since 1492*. Norman: University of Oklahoma Press, 1987.

Tinkle, Lon. *An American Original: The Life of J. Frank Dobie*. Boston: Little, Brown, 1978.

Tobin, Gregory M. *The Making of a History: Walter Prescott Webb and the Great Plains*. Austin: University of Texas Press, 1976.

Traylor, Maude Wallis. "Captain Samuel Highsmith, Ranger." *Frontier Times* 17, no. 7 (April 1940): 291–302.

Trujillo, Larry. Review of *Gunpowder Justice: A Reassessment of the Texas Rangers*, by Julian Samora, Joe Bernal, and Albert Pefia. *Crime and Social Justice*, no. 13 (Summer 1980): 61–64.

Tyler, Ron, ed. *The New Handbook of Texas*. 6 vols. Austin: Texas State Historical Association, 1996.

Utley, Dan K. Review of *Captain John H. Rogers, Texas Ranger*, by Paul N. Spellman. *Southwestern Historical Quarterly* 107, no. 3 (January 2004): 483–84.

Utley, Robert M. *Billy the Kid: A Short and Violent Life*. Lincoln: University of Nebraska Press, 1989.

Utley, Robert M. *Cavalier in Buckskin: George Armstrong Custer and the Western Military Frontier*. Norman: University of Oklahoma Press, 1988.

Utley, Robert M. *The Commanders: Civil War Generals Who Shaped the American West*. Norman: University of Oklahoma Press, 2018.

Utley, Robert M. *Custer and Me: A Historian's Memoir*. Norman: University of Oklahoma Press, 2004.

Utley, Robert M. *Four Fighters of Lincoln County*. Albuquerque: University of New Mexico Press, 1986.

Utley, Robert M. *Frontier Regulars: The United States Army and the Indian, 1866–1891*. New York: Macmillan, 1973.

Utley, Robert M. *Frontiersmen in Blue: The United States Army and the Indian, 1848–1865*. New York: Macmillan, 1967.

Utley, Robert M. *Geronimo*. New Haven: Yale University Press, 2012.

Utley, Robert M. *High Noon in Lincoln: Violence on the Western Frontier*. Albuquerque: University of New Mexico Press, 1987.

Utley, Robert M. "Images of the Texas Rangers." Chap. 24 in *The Way West: True Stories of the American Frontier*, edited by James A. Crutchfield. New York: Forge, 2005.

Utley, Robert M. *The Indian Frontier of the American West, 1846–1890*. Albuquerque: University of New Mexico Press, 1984.

Utley, Robert M. *The Lance and the Shield: The Life and Times of Sitting Bull*. New York: Henry Holt, 1993.

Utley, Robert M. *The Last Days of the Sioux Nation*. New Haven: Yale University Press, 1963.

Utley, Robert M. *The Last Sovereigns: Sitting Bull and the Resistance of the Free Lakotas*. Lincoln: University of Nebraska Press, 2020.

Utley, Robert M. *Lone Star Justice: The First Century of the Texas Rangers*. New York: Oxford University Press, 2002.

Utley, Robert M. *Lone Star Lawmen: The Second Century of the Texas Rangers*. New York: Oxford University Press, 2007.

Utley, Robert M. "Tales of the Texas Rangers." *American Heritage* 53, no. 3 (June/July 2002): 40–47.

Utley, Robert M. "The Texas Ranger Tradition Established: Jack Hays and Walker Creek." *Montana: The Magazine of Western History* 52, no. 1 (Spring 2002): 2–11.

Utley, Robert M. *Wanted: The Outlaw Lives of Billy the Kid and Ned Kelly*. New Haven: Yale University Press, 2015.

Van Oden, Alonzo. *Texas Ranger's Diary and Scrapbook*. Edited by Ann Jensen. Dallas: Kaleidograph Press, 1936.

"Vernon Wilson Was a Texas Ranger." *Frontier Times* 6, no. 7 (April 1929): 257–58.

Villanueva, Nicholas, Jr. *The Lynchings of Mexicans in the Texas Borderlands*. Albuquerque: University of New Mexico Press, 2017.

Wallace, Ernest, and E. Adamson Hoebel. *The Comanches: Lords of the South Plains*. Norman: University of Oklahoma Press, 1952.

Ward, James R. "Establishing Law and Order in the Oil Fields: The 1924 Ranger Raid in Navarro County, Texas." *Texana* 8, no. 1 (1970): 38–46.

Ward, James R. "The Texas Rangers, 1919–1935: A Study in Law Enforcement." PhD diss., Texas Christian University, 1972.

Weaver, John D. *The Brownsville Raid*. New York: W. W. Horton, 1970.

Webb, Walter Prescott. "The American Revolver and the West." *Scribner's Magazine* 81 (January–June 1927): 171–78.

Webb, Walter Prescott. "The Art of Historical Writing." In *History as High Adventure*, edited by E. C. Barksdale, 131–42. Austin: Pemberton Press, 1969.

Webb, Walter Prescott. "Bank Robbers Slain: Texas Ranger Captain Takes No Chances on Escape of Two Desperadoes Taken in Crime." *State Trooper* 8 (November 1926): 7–8.

Webb, Walter Prescott. "Fight against Texas Rangers: A Discussion of the Motives Involved in the Suit to Enjoin Continuance of the Force." *State Trooper* 6 (July 1925): 11.

Webb, Walter Prescott. *The Great Frontier*. Boston: Houghton Mifflin, 1952.

Webb, Walter Prescott. *The Great Plains*. Boston: Ginn, 1931. Reprint, Lincoln: University of Nebraska Press, 1986.

Webb, Walter Prescott. "History as High Adventure." *American Historical Review* 64, no. 2 (Jan. 1959): 265–80.

Webb, Walter Prescott. "Larger Texas Force: New Governor Expected to Increase Ranger's Strength to Combat Conditions of Lawlessness." *State Trooper* 8 (February 1927): 17–18.

Webb, Walter Prescott. "Lawless Town Gets Ranger Justice: Cleanup of Law Breakers in San Antonio Is Object Lesson of Need of Strong State Force." *State Trooper* 5 (April 1924): 13–14.

Webb, Walter Prescott. "Lone Ranger Gets Bandits: Texas Officer Secures Surrender of Gang which Robbed Banks and Shot Up One Town." *State Trooper* 7 (March 1926): 9–10.

Webb, Walter Prescott. "May Increase Rangers: Texas Legislature Considering Measure Which Would Increase Force and Raise Rangers' Pay." *State Trooper* 8 (June 1927): 13–14.

Webb, Walter Prescott. "Oil Town Cleaned Up: Texas Rangers Summoned to Restore Order When Local Officials Could Not Enforce Law." *State Trooper* 8 (December 1926): 11–12.

Webb, Walter Prescott. "Rangers Arrest Lawmakers: Texas Representatives Taken in Custody When One Accepts $1000 from Opponent of Measure." *State Trooper* 8 (April 1927): 11–12.

Webb, Walter Prescott. "Rangers Called in to Clean Up Austin: Texans Have Closed Forty San Antonio Gambling Dens." *State Trooper* 6 (November 1924): 21–22.

Webb, Walter Prescott. "Rangers Reorganized: Governor of Texas Appoints Captains to Replace Men Appointed in Ferguson Regime." *State Trooper* 8 (July 1927): 13–14.

Webb, Walter Prescott. Review of *A Texas Ranger and Frontiersman: The Days of Buck Barry in Texas, 1845–1906*, by James K. Greer. *Southwestern Historical Quarterly* 36, no. 3 (January 1933): 233.

Webb, Walter Prescott. *The Story of the Texas Rangers*. Austin: Encino Press, 1957.

Webb, Walter Prescott. "Texas Ranger Case Important: Statement of Law Involved in Use of Force to Preserve State's Authority Is Comprehensive." *State Trooper* 6 (August 1925): 13–14, 20.

Webb, Walter Prescott. *The Texas Rangers: A Century of Frontier Defense*. Boston: Houghton Mifflin, 1935. Edited and reprinted from the original edition, with a foreword by Lyndon B. Johnson. Austin: University of Texas Press, 1965.

Webb, Walter Prescott. "Texas Rangers in Eclipse: Present State Administration Has Discredited Force by Policy of Interference with Its Duties." *State Trooper* 7 (January 1926): 13–14.

Webb, Walter Prescott. "The Texas Rangers in the Mexican War." MA thesis, University of Texas, 1920.

Webb, Walter Prescott. *The Texas Rangers in the Mexican War*. Austin: Jenkins Garrett Press, 1975.

Webb, Walter Prescott. "Texas Rangers of Today: A Description of the Present Status of the Oldest Police Force in America." *State Trooper* 5 (March 1924): 5–6.

Webber, Charles W. *Old Hicks the Guide*. 1848. Reprint, Upper Saddle River, NJ: Literature House/Gregg Press, 1970.

Webber, Charles W. *Tales of the Southern Border*. Philadelphia: Lippincott, 1856.

Weber, John. *From South Texas to the Nation: The Exploitation of Mexican Labor in the Twentieth Century*. Chapel Hill: University of North Carolina Press, 2015.

Wecter, Dixon. *The Hero in America: A Chronical of Hero Worship*. New York: Charles Scribner's Sons, 1941.

Weiss, Harold J., Jr. "Alternative Scenarios: Three Late 19th Century Texas Ranger 'What-ifs.'" *Wild West Historical Association Journal* 9 (December 2016), 18–26.

Weiss, Harold J., Jr. "Organized Constabularies: The Texas Rangers and the Early State Police Movement in the American Southwest." *Journal of the West* 34 (Jan. 1995): 27–33.

Weiss, Harold J., Jr. Review of *Texas Volunteers in the Mexican War*, by Charles D. Spurlin. *Southwestern Historical Quarterly* 104, no. 1 (July 2000): 123–24.

Weiss, Harold J., Jr. "The Texas Rangers Revisited: Old Themes and New Viewpoints." *Southwestern Historical Quarterly* 97, no. 4 (April 1994): 621–40.

Weiss, Harold J., Jr. *Yours to Command: The Life and Legend of Texas Ranger Captain Bill McDonald.* Denton: University of North Texas Press, 2009.

Weiss Harold J., Jr., and Rie Jarratt. "McDonald, William Jesse." *Handbook of Texas Online,* updated October 8, 2023. http://www.tshaonline.org/handbook/online/articles/fmc43.

Welsh, Michael. *Landscape of Ghosts, River of Dreams: An Administrative History of Big Bend National Park.* Washington, DC: Department of the Interior, National Park Service, 2002.

Wilbarger, John W. *Indian Depredations in Texas, reliable accounts of battles, wars, adventures, forays, murders, massacres, etc., etc., together with biographical sketches of many of the most noted Indian fighters and frontiersmen of Texas.* 1889. Reprint, Austin: Eakin Press and Statehouse Books, 1985.

Wilkins, Frederick. *Defending the Borders: The Texas Rangers, 1848–1861.* Austin: State House Press, 2001.

Wilkins, Frederick. *The Highly Irregular Irregulars: Texas Rangers in the Mexican War.* Austin: Eakin Press, 1990.

Wilkins, Frederick. *The Law Comes to Texas: The Texas Rangers, 1870–1901.* Austin: State House Press, 1999.

Wilkins, Frederick. *The Legend Begins: The Texas Rangers, 1823–1845.* Austin: State House Press, 1996.

Wooster, Ralph A. *Lone Star Generals in Gray.* Austin: Eakin Press, 2000.

Wooten, Dudley G. ed. *A Comprehensive History of Texas, 1685–1897.* 2 vols. Dallas: William G. Scarff, 1898.

Yoakum, Henderson K. *History of Texas: From Its First Settlement in 1685 to Its Annexation to the United States in 1846.* 2 vols. 1855. Reprint, Austin: Steck, 1935.

Young, Elliot. *Catarino Garza's Revolution on the Texas-Mexico Border.* Durham, NC: Duke University Press, 2004.

Young, Lee, and Nita Thurman. *Lee Young: Memoirs of a Black Seminole Texas Ranger.* McKinney, TX: Lee Young and Associates, 2013.

Index

A

West Texas Collection (Angelo State University, San Angelo, TX), 62
West Texas Historical Association, 199, 383
West Texas Historical Association Yearbook, 382
Wharton County Junior College (TX), 131, 392
White, Richard, 297, 325
Whitehill, Harvey, 225, 228, 244
Whitman, Charles, 184
Whitman, Gayne, 85
Wichita campaign of 1870–1871, 22, 173
Wichita Falls, TX, 289
Wichita Indians, 327
Wilbarger, John W., 21–22
Wilbarger, John Wesley, 328
Wild West Historical Association, 235
Wild West History Association Journal, 321
Wilke, L. A., 309, 321
Wilkins, Frances Lutcher (Semaan), 295
Wilkins, Frederick John, Jr., 295, 306
   analysis of Texas Rangers works of, 107, 297–307
   background of, 294–95
   contributions Texas Rangers history by, 104–5, 268, 295–97, 301–2
   narrative writing style of, 296–97
   sources used by, 50–54
William Morrow / Harper Collins Publishers, 211
Williams, Mike, 201
Williamson, Robert M. "Three-Legged-Willie," 7, 215, 258
Williamson County, TX, 152, 204
Wilson, Vernon, 149
Winchester repeating rifles, 102, 259

Winchester Warriors, by Bob Alexander, 231, 234, 238, 240, 242
   sources used in, 50, 61–62
   use of photographs in, 233–34
Winther, Oscar Osborne, 253
Wisconsin, 129, 193, 196, 198
Wisconsin Historical Society, 124
"With His Pistol in His Hand," by Américo Paredes, 127, 331, 353–54, 356
Woll, Adrian, 17–18, 299
Wood, George T., 49
Wood, John H., 243
Woodhouse, H. E., 349
Wooten, Dudley G., 19–20, 124, 138–40
World War I, 12, 256, 259, 275–76, 282
World War II, 12, 183, 256, 259, 295, 389
Worster, Donald, 297
Wright, E. A. "Dogie," 63
Wright, William L. "Will," 12, 147, 260, 389

Y

Yellow Wolf, Chief (Comanche Indian), 217
Yena, Donald M., 205
Yoakum, Henderson K., 16–19
Young, Lee Roy, 13, 184
Yours to Command, by Harold J. Weiss Jr., 48–50, 60, 394
Ysleta, TX, 240

Z

Zukor, Adolph, 76
Zuni Indians, 82